Honor in Command

NEW PERSPECTIVES ON THE HISTORY OF THE SOUTH

UNIVERSITY PRESS OF FLORIDA

Florida A&M University, Tallahassee
Florida Atlantic University, Boca Raton
Florida Gulf Coast University, Ft. Myers
Florida International University, Miami
Florida State University, Tallahassee
University of Central Florida, Orlando
University of Florida, Gainesville
University of North Florida, Jacksonville
University of South Florida, Tampa
University of West Florida, Pensacola

New Perspectives on the History of the South
Edited by John David Smith

"In the Country of the Enemy": The Civil War Reports of a Massachusetts Corporal, edited by William C. Harris (1999)
The Wild East: A Biography of the Great Smoky Mountains, by Margaret L. Brown (2000; first paperback edition, 2001)
Crime, Sexual Violence, and Clemency: Florida's Pardon Board and Penal System in the Progressive Era, by Vivien M. L. Miller (2000)
The New South's New Frontier: A Social History of Economic Development in Southwestern North Carolina, by Stephen Wallace Taylor (2001)
Redefining the Color Line: Black Activism in Little Rock, Arkansas, 1940–1970, by John A. Kirk (2002)
The Southern Dream of a Caribbean Empire, 1854–1861, by Robert E. May (2002)
Forging a Common Bond: Labor and Environmental Activism during the BASF Lockout, by Timothy J. Minchin (2003)
Dixie's Daughters: The United Daughters of the Confederacy and the Preservation of Confederate Culture, by Karen L. Cox (2003)
The Other War of 1812: The Patriot War and the American Invasion of Spanish East Florida, by James G. Cusick (2003)
"Lives Full of Struggle and Triumph": Southern Women, Their Institutions and Their Communities, edited by Bruce L. Clayton and John A. Salmond (2003)
German-Speaking Officers in the United States Colored Troops, 1863–1867, by Martin W. Öfele (2004)
Southern Struggles: The Southern Labor Movement and the Civil Rights Struggle, by John A. Salmond (2004)
Radio and the Struggle for Civil Rights in the South, by Brian Ward (2004)
Luther P. Jackson and a Life for Civil Rights, by Michael Dennis (2004)
Southern Ladies, New Women: Race, Region, and Clubwomen in South Carolina, 1890–1930, by Joan Marie Johnson (2004)
Fighting Against the Odds: A Concise History of Southern Labor Since World War II, by Timothy J. Minchin (2004)
"Don't Sleep with Stevens!": The J. P. Stevens Campaign and the Struggle to Organize the South, 1963–80, by Timothy J. Minchin (2005)
*"The Ticket to Freedom": The NAACP and the Struggle for Black Political Integratio*n, by Manfred Berg (2005)
"War Governor of the South": North Carolina's Zeb Vance in the Confederacy, by Joe A. Mobley (2005)
Planters' Progress: Modernizing Confederate Georgia, by Chad Morgan (2005)
The Officers of the CSS Shenandoah, by Angus Curry (2006)
The Rosenwald Schools of the American South, by Mary S. Hoffschwelle (2006)
Honor in Command: Lt. Freeman S. Bowley's Civil War Service in the 30th United States Colored Infantry, edited by Keith P. Wilson (2006)

Lt. Freeman Sparks Bowley, 30th U.S. Colored Infantry. Civil War Library and Museum, Military Order of the Loyal Legion of the United States, Philadelphia.

Honor in Command

Lt. Freeman S. Bowley's Civil War Service in the 30th United States Colored Infantry

Edited by Keith Wilson

Foreword by John David Smith

University Press of Florida
Gainesville/Tallahassee/Tampa/Boca Raton
Pensacola/Orlando/Miami/Jacksonville/Ft. Myers

Printed in the United States of America on recycled, acid-free paper

11 10 09 08 07 06 6 5 4 3 2 1

A record of cataloging-in-publication data is available from the Library of Congress.
ISBN 0-8130-2998-8

The University Press of Florida is the scholarly publishing agency for the State University System of Florida, comprising Florida A&M University, Florida Atlantic University, Florida Gulf Coast University, Florida International University, Florida State University, University of Central Florida, University of Florida, University of North Florida, University of South Florida, and University of West Florida.

University Press of Florida
15 Northwest 15th Street
Gainesville, FL 32611-2079
http://www.upf.com

For Isobel

Contents

Figures

Maps

Foreword

Historians and writers from Ulrich Bonnell Phillips, C. Vann Woodward, and Howard Zinn to Wilbur J. Cash, William Faulkner, and Lee Smith have underscored the South's distinctiveness. For many persons the South signifies more than a region. For them it represents an idea, an abstraction, even an ideology. For some the South has become an obsession. Since the colonial period, the South has been both connected to and distanced from the rest of North America. Its settlement pattern, its crops, and, most significantly, its commitment to racial slavery earmarked the Old South as different from the rest of the nation. As Woodward noted in 1960, the South has many "burdens." Its defeat in the Civil War and its experiences during and after Reconstruction left an indelible blot on the fabric of southern history. Yet in the twenty-first century, the South seems very much "American"—more like the rest of the country, not some mythic land apart.

Dating back to the 1880s, historians and critics have defined and redefined southern history in innumerable ways. The "Nationalist" historians, the "Dunning School," the "Agrarians," the "Revisionists," the "Post-Revisionists," the Marxists, and, today, all manner of postmodernists have tried to squeeze some contemporary meaning from southern history. Historians and others regularly interpret the region's history and culture in such varied journals and magazines as the *Journal of Southern History*, *Southern Review*, *Southern Humanities Review*, *Southern Living*, *Southern Exposure*, and *Southern Cultures*. In 1979 the *Encyclopedia of Southern History* appeared, followed ten years later by the *Encyclopedia of Southern Culture*. Both within and beyond the region, there seems to be an insatiable appetite for information on the South and its people.

In fact, no region in America, including New England and the West, has received as much in-depth analysis and reflection as has the American South. Insiders (native southerners) and outsiders (non-southerners, including an unusually large number of northern and European specialists on the South) agree that the Southland has a particular *Weltanschauung*, one loaded with irony, pathos, paradox, and racial and class conflict. In some universities southern history long has reigned as a major research specialty. They confer doctorates in the field. Many academic publishers consider "southern studies" a strong part of their list. Books about the South sell on both sides of the Mason-Dixon line and overseas. Associations and institutions sponsor regular symposia and conferences regionally, nationally, and internationally on the South's past.

In the last century, when the South ranked as "the nation's economic problem No. 1," sociologists dissected the region's pathologies, especially its historic race problem and poverty. Today, social scientists and economists marvel at the "Sun Belt"—its thriving and alluring prosperity built atop long-standing anti-union sentiment, its daunting skyscrapers, its rapid transit systems, its social and racial progress. Atlanta, the region's bourgeois Mecca, has numerous lesser rivals throughout the former Confederacy—Dallas, New Orleans, Miami, Nashville, Charlotte, Raleigh, and Richmond. Cable television, chain restaurants, New York department stores, "malls" and their accompanying outlet shops—even the *New York Times*' "national edition" (printed in several southern cities and delivered to the doorsteps of thousands of southerners)—dot the southern landscape like the proverbial cotton plants of old.

An appreciation of the South's distinctiveness and its diversity lies at the heart of the University Press of Florida's *New Perspectives on the History of the South* series. This broadly based series publishes the highest quality new scholarship on the history of the American South. The books cover all aspects and periods of the southern past, with special emphasis on the region's cultural, economic, intellectual, and social history.

Keith P. Wilson's *Honor in Command*, the latest volume in the series, is an important edited memoir of a young white officer who served as a lieutenant in a U. S. Colored Troops (USCT) regiment during the Civil War. Freeman Sparks Bowley (1846–1903) grew up in Maine, studied at Highland Military Academy, Worcester, Massachusetts, and, after passing a competitive examination in April 1864, received his commission in the 30th United States Colored Infantry (USCI).

Joining his regiment at Manassas Junction, Virginia, Bowley and his men, like many USCT units, served largely in support roles, though these assignments were far from hazard free. The regiment largely guarded wagon trains, escorted prisoners, constructed forts, and performed fatigue duty. In July 1864, however, Bowley and his men engaged the Confederates at the Battle of the Crater, where Bowley was captured. He spent much of the remainder of the war in prison camps in Virginia and in North and South Carolina. Following Appommattox, Bowley rejoined the 30th USCI and participated in police and peace-keeping duties throughout eastern North Carolina. The army mustered him out of service in December 1865. In his later years Bowley worked as a journalist in Massachusetts and as a fireman for the Southern Pacific Railroad

Company in San Francisco. Active in the Grand Army of the Republic (GAR) in California, in 1899 he published his memoir, "A Boy Lieutenant in a Black Regiment," in a series of articles in the GAR weekly newspaper the *National Tribune*.

These articles serve as Wilson's core text and, in addition to an excellent introduction, he provides emendations and annotations (including the verification of proper names and places in the regimental records of the 30th USCI and other sources at the National Archives). In his edition Wilson wisely retained Bowley's use of stereotypical black "dialect"—an indicator of the Jim Crow context when the Civil War veteran penned his memoir. But, as Wilson makes clear, by celebrating the Civil War service of the 30th USCI, Bowley's narrative challenged late nineteenth century national myths of reconciliation and reunion.

Wilson has carefully and painstakingly edited Bowley's chronicle of duty, honor, and manhood. Bowley valued both his close bonds with other northern white officers and with his black enlisted men from Maryland. His vivid recollections of his service in the Civil War and Reconstruction thus provide insights into the evolution of today's decidedly distinctive and diverse South.

John David Smith
Series Editor

Preface and Acknowledgments

In the course of my research for this book I have been assisted by many people and institutions. Without the valuable support and expertise of librarians and archivists working in the numerous archives, libraries, and research centers, my research project would not have been possible.

At the National Archives in Washington, D.C., I received important assistance from Mike Musick, DeAnne Blanton, and other archivists. I am also indebted to the archivists and librarians working in the newspaper library of the Library of Congress and the United States Army History Institute at Carlisle Barracks, Pennsylvania. Archivists and librarians working in the Massachusetts Historical Society, the Boston Public Library, the American Antiquarian Society, and the Connecticut Valley Historical Museum provided me with much valuable information on Freeman S. Bowley's time in his home state of Massachusetts. I am indebted to the archivists and librarians at the California Historical Society and the San Francisco Public Library for helping me to research Bowley's activities in California, the state where he spent most of his working life. The librarians at the South Carolinian Library, University of South Carolina, provided me with valuable assistance while I was researching Bowley's prisoner of war experiences in Columbia, South Carolina. Chris Calkins, historian at the Petersburg National Park Battlefield, provided some excellent insights and research leads on the Battle of the Crater. The librarians of Monash University have given me extensive assistance. I am also indebted to the staff of the La Trobe University library for allowing me to access their collection of Civil War memoirs.

I would like to thank associate professor Harry Ballis, head of the School of Humanities, Communications and Social Sciences, Monash University, for supporting this project. I would also like to thank the School of Humanities, Communications and Social Sciences' Research Committee for the grants I received to assist with the editing of Freeman Bowley's memoir. Monash University's Outside Study Program enabled me to make two research trips to the United States. Without this support it would not have been possible for me to write this book. Over the years I have been working on my research project I have valued the support given by friends and colleagues. I am particularly indebted to John, Karen, and Sarah Wires, who generously opened their home to me when I visited the United States. I owe an important debt to Tom Dunning and Warren Ellem, my doctoral supervisors at La Trobe University, for developing my interest in Civil War history. I would also like to thank the members of the American Civil War Round Table of Australia for all the support they have shown in my Civil War research.

A number of people have played a critical role in the production of my book. I am particularly indebted to Pauline Reeve for her excellent assistance with the editing process, to Michele Fielding for transcribing the newspaper text, to Anne Lorraine for assistance with map production, and to Gavin Hansford and Russell Stewart for their technical assistance and expertise in photography and image reproduction. I appreciated and benefited from Susan Corrado's copyediting of the manuscript, Sue Pohl Baldwin's careful proofreading of the text and Roberta Engleman's indexing skills.

I owe a special debt of appreciation to John David Smith, the general editor of this series, for his support and guidance. The editorial staff at the University Press of Florida, particularly Meredith Morris-Babb, Jacqueline Kinghorn Brown, and Derek Krissoff, all provided excellent advice during the revision and editing process.

Finally, I would like to thank my wife, Anne, for her perceptive advice and constant encouragement. Without her support this project would not have been possible.

Editorial Method

While editing Freeman Sparks Bowley's Civil War memoir I have followed carefully the first complete published edition of his narrative, which appeared in the principal Grand Army of the Republic weekly newspaper, the *National Tribune*, between April 20, 1899, and September 7, 1899. Published under the title "A Boy Lieutenant in a Black Regiment, by Capt. Freeman S. Bowley, Late First Lieutenant, 30th U.S.C.T.," Bowley's story took pride of place on the first page of each weekly edition of the newspaper. Described by the editor, in an advertising blurb in the April 13, 1899, edition of the *National Tribune*, as being "historically true and vivid in its interest," Bowley's narrative reflects the author's careful attention to historical detail and his strong interest in personal relationships. As part of the editorial process I have had to make only minor changes to historical record. Likewise, I have had to make only minor changes to personal names and those private, incidental records of events that touched upon the details of army life. Bowley's accuracy in this regard reflects the close personal relationship he had with many of his fellow officers. It also points to the strong bonds of comradeship that he shared with many of the enlisted men who served in his company. Bowley's historical accuracy may also be a product of the writing process. My job as editor was made easier because during his life Freeman Bowley wrote constantly about his Civil War experiences. In his effort to continually retell his war adventure he struggled to maintain historical accuracy, for he believed it was the "truth" embodied in his narrative that made it nationally significant.

I have reproduced the text of Bowley's memoir in its entirety. In addition I have included in an appendix an extract from an article he had published in the *Overland Monthly* in 1870. This short narrative, describing Bowley's first-hand encounter with slavey, is an earlier version of an incident described in his memoir. As such it illuminates the text by providing a valuable commentary on Bowley's racial beliefs, and the influence of contemporary social values on his writing.

Some editorial changes have been made. I have removed the subheadings that appeared in the newspaper edition because I believe they interrupted Bowley's literary style and the clarity of his prose. In addition, I have standardized the indentations, spacing of lines, and the print. Although I have noted the correct spelling of proper names, I have not attempted to modernize the spelling. Nor have I attempted to "translate" Bowley's use of African American "dialect." This course of action would rob the memoir of much of its cultural integrity and hide from the reader many of Bowley's subtle racial beliefs. In those rare cases when individuals have been incorrectly named I have provided a correction in square brackets. I have provided annotated information on individuals, military units, events, literary allusions, and anachronistic references to food, places, and folk beliefs. In a few cases I have been unable to identify individual soldiers or verify the accuracy of other newspaper extracts quoted by Bowley in the *National Tribune*.

The National Archives, Washington, D.C., contains valuable information on Bowley's regiment, the 30th USCI. These records are found in Record Group 94, Adjutant General's Office, Regimental Books and Papers USCT and U. S. Volunteer Organizations and include regimental and company descriptive books, general orders and special orders books, guard reports, and morning reports. I used these military records to check the 30th USCI's service record and the description of the men in his regiment. In addition, I cross-checked these regimental and company records with the soldiers' own compiled military service records found in the Carded Records, Volunteer Organizations: Civil War, series 519, Record Group 94, together with the pension files found in Record Group 15.

Although I was unable to find a collection of Freeman S. Bowley's private papers, I did discover that there are extensive records of his military service deposited in Letters Received, series 360, Colored Troops Division, Record Group 94, National Archives. These records, together with Bowley's pension file and his compiled service record, enabled me to make relatively minor corrections to the historical accuracy of his Civil War narrative.

Chronology

1846 April 10: Freeman Sparks Bowley is born in Orlando, Maine, the only child of Jesse D. and Juliet Bowley.

1862 September: Jesse Bowley enlists in the 46th Massachusetts Volunteers for nine months' service. He is discharged early because of ill health.

1863 July: Freeman Bowley is enrolled at the Highland Military Academy in Worcester, Massachusetts.

1864 February 1: As a member of the Highland Military Academy cadet unit, Bowley attends a mayoral reception held at Worcester to welcome home the soldiers of the 21st Massachusetts Volunteers. Inspired by the patriotic fervor exhibited at this reception he decides to seek a commission in the United States Colored Troops.

1864 March 14: Freeman Bowley writes to Secretary of War Edwin Stanton seeking a commission in a black regiment.

1864 April 1–April 4: Bowley visits Washington, D.C., meets President Lincoln, and passes Maj. Gen. Silas Casey's Officer Examination Board examination, gaining the rank of 1st lieutenant, first class.

1864 April 5–April 30: At home in Worcester, Bowley equips himself for military service.

1864 May 1–May 4: Bowley journeys to his regiment, arriving at the camp of the 30th USCI at Manassas Junction, Virginia, on May 4.

1864 May 4–May 20: Bowley's regiment crosses the Rapidan River at Germanna Ford, takes up a supporting position on the Wilderness battlefield, and then guards crossroads and wagon trains in the vicinity of the Chancellorsville battlefield. It then moves through Salem Church, swinging south of Fredericksburg to pass through Bowling Green and Polecat station. Finally, on May 20 it reaches the Pamunkey River.

1864 May 20–June 18: The 30th USCI rests on the banks of Pamunkey River for a few days, then proceeds to Cold Harbor, collects 1,200 rebel prisoners of war, and then escorts them to the Union supply base at White House Landing. The regiment then moves south, reaching the Petersburg battlefield, via Old Church, on June 18.

1864 June 18–July 29: The 30th USCI does occasional service on the Petersburg front line, but spends most of its time building forts in the vicinity of Prince George Courthouse and doing fatigue duty at Gen. Burnside's headquarters.

1864 July 30–July 31: Bowley is captured at the Battle of the Crater; along with other prisoners of war he is paraded in the streets of Petersburg.

1864 August 1–August 4: Bowley and other soldiers captured at the Crater are sent to the Danville Prison, Virginia. They stay there several days before proceeding further south to Columbia, South Carolina.

1864 August 5: Bowley arrives at Columbia, South Carolina, and along with his fellow officers, is confined in the Richland Jail. He remains there until December 11.

1864 December 12–February 15, 1865: Along with other prisoners Bowley is moved from the Richland Jail to Camp Asylum, Columbia. He remains there until the encroachment of Sherman's army forces Confederate authorities to evacuate the prisoners to North Carolina on February 15, 1865.

1865 February 15–February 26: Bowley and other prisoners are transported north by train, traveling via Charlotte and Greensboro to Camp Holmes in the vicinity of Raleigh, North Carolina. During the course of the journey Bowley makes several unsuccessful escape attempts. After spending a few days at Camp Holmes Bowley is moved to Goldsboro, North Carolina; he arrives there on February 26. One day later, he signs for parole.

1865 March 1: Bowley is part of a prisoner of war exchange that takes place at Northeast River, 10 miles from Wilmington, North Carolina.

1865 March 2–March 6: Bowley is reunited with his regiment and then travels by steamer to Annapolis, Maryland. At Annapolis he secures 30 days' leave and then on March 6 proceeds to his hometown of Worcester, Massachusetts.

1865 March 6–April 11: Bowley is on leave in Worcester.

1865 April 12: Bowley reports to Camp Parole, Maryland, to serve his time on parole.

1865 April 14: Assassination of President Lincoln.

1865 April 19: Bowley serves on escort duty in Washington, D.C., during Lincoln's funeral.

1865 May 1–December 14: Early in May Bowley rejoins his regiment in North Carolina. For most of the year Bowley's regiment carries out policing and peace-keeping duties at Goldsboro, Morehead City, and Beaufort City, North Carolina. In October Bowley's company is sent on detachment duty to the village of Edenton at the head of the Albemarle Sound. Early in December his company rejoins the 30th USCI on Roanoke Island. In mid-December the 30th USCI leaves Roanoke Island for Baltimore, Maryland.

1865 December 22: At Fort Federal Hill, Baltimore, the 30th USCI is mustered out of service.

1866 November 1866–November 1867: Bowley unsuccessfully seeks a commission in the regular army. He lives in Springfield, Massachusetts, works as a reporter for the *Springfield Republican* newspaper, and serves as a captain in the Springfield City Guard.

1867 November 1867–November 1868: Bowley leaves Springfield to work in San Francisco as a fireman for the Southern Pacific Railroad Company.

1868 December 31: Bowley marries Flora Pepper in Springfield.

1869–1903: Freeman Bowley returns to San Francisco with his wife. There he raises four sons, Bennet H. Bowley, Delevan B. Bowley, Albert J. Bowley, and Freeman W. Bowley, and a daughter who married and became Mrs. J. C. Hoffman. Two sons pursue careers in the U. S. Army; Freeman rises to the rank of lieutenant colonel and Albert becomes a major general. Bowley continues to work as a fireman for the Southern Pacific Railroad Company and becomes an active member of the Lincoln Post of the Grand Army of the Republic of California. Throughout his life he continues to publish accounts of his Civil War service.

1903 January 24: Freeman Sparks Bowley dies in San Francisco.

Abbreviations

Adjt.; Adj't	Adjutant
Art.	Artillery
Brig.	Brigadier
Cav.	Cavalry
Cld.	Colored
Co.	Company
Col.	Colonel
CTD	Colored Troops Division
Gen.	General
Hvy. Art.	Heavy Artillery
Lt.	Lieutenant
Maj.	Major
NA	National Archives
Pvt.	Private
RG	Record Group
ser.	series
Sgt.; Serg't	Sergeant
USCI	United States Colored Infantry
USCT	United States Colored Troops
Vols.	Volunteers

Introduction

Honor in Command

The defining moment in Freeman Sparks Bowley's life occurred on February 1, 1864, at Worcester, Massachusetts, while he was attending the reception being held in the city's Mechanics Hall to welcome home the soldiers in the 21st and 25th Massachusetts Volunteers. As a member of the Highland Military Academy cadet company, Bowley was part of the official escort for the veteran regiments. During the course of the reception he saw a sight that "thrilled" him "through and through." When Mayor D. Waldo Lincoln addressed the soldiers of the 21st and informed them that he was going to present their "old colors," their "old Color-Sergeant, who stained them with his blood," Thomas Plunkett, advanced. As he slowly made his way to the official platform Sergeant Plunkett struggled to hold, in his artificial arms, the national flag he had so courageously fought to defend on the Fredericksburg battlefield. This demonstration of personal courage so moved Freeman Bowley that he resolved "then and there" that his name should be "borne on the roll of the country's defenders."[1]

Shortly after witnessing these moving scenes Bowley wrote to the secretary of war, Edwin M. Stanton, seeking to gain a commission in a black regiment. Thus began Bowley's commitment to the Union Army and its cause. This burst of idealism and boyhood enthusiasm would lead him into the 30th USCI (United States Colored Infantry), a regiment composed of former slaves and free blacks from Maryland, and then on to the battlefields at the Wilderness and the Crater, and then into the prisoner of war camps at Danville, Virginia, Columbia and Florence in South Carolina, and finally into the army of occupation in the coastal regions of North Carolina.

Freeman Sparks Bowley (1846–1903), the only child of Jesse Bowley, a printer by trade, and his wife, Juliet, never wavered in his commitment to the Union Army or his enthusiasm for military service. After the war ended he unsuccessfully tried to gain a commission in the regular army. Not discouraged by his failure Bowley managed to secure an appointment in the local militia unit, as captain of the Springfield, Massachusetts, City Guard. He held this position while working as a reporter for the *Springfield Republican* newspaper. Late in 1868, Bowley married his childhood sweetheart, Flora Pepper, and moved to San Francisco, California, where he took up employment as a fireman and engineer for the Southern Pacific Railroad Company for the remainder of his working life. It was while living in San Francisco that he became an active member of the Lincoln Post of the Grand Army of the Republic. He wrote extensively about his war service in a veterans' newspaper and in a popular journal. The war never left Freeman Bowley, for even during the last years of his life he was busy narrating his war experiences and pleading his case for a Medal of Honor for his brave exploits during the Battle of the Crater. Just as the Civil War shaped the destiny of the United States and brought it a new understanding of freedom and a new concept of nationhood, so it also gave meaning to Bowley's life. The war had shaped his concept of patriotism, civic pride, national duty, and, above all, his concept of self and his commitment to honorable service. Bowley's war service was essentially an honorable journey in the service of the nation, his family, and comrades, and the memoir he wrote in the 1890s was a testament to his concept of honor. Yet it was more than this, for it also makes a powerful claim for the black soldiers to be included on the nation's honor roll.[2]

Civil War historians have long recognized the importance of honor as a powerful motivating factor in the Civil War. James McPherson argues that these concepts of honor were inextricably linked to a sense of duty. Victorian Americans were bound by moral obligations involving a sense of reciprocity. The soldier had a duty to defend the Union and protect his home and community from the invading foe because the nation, community, and home were the crucible of his being. Randall Jimerson links this concept of honor with soldiers doing "masculine duty," a theme that Reid Mitchell develops in *The Vacant Chair*. Mitchell reminds us that the Civil War was about young men negotiating their way to honorable manhood; this coming-of-age experience was a commitment to publicly acclaimed codes of honor. In his study of honor and secession Bertram Wyatt-Brown has pointed out that honor involved claims of self-worth being validated by community acclaim. Although Wyatt-Brown claims that Northern honor was different from Southern honor in that it gave national honor and the civic order primacy over community and family honor and individual liberty, he admits that the Northern and Southern codes of honor were inextricably linked to notions of personal character and reputation. The young men who joined the Union and Confederate armies saw their war service in terms of a test of character. Certainly Lt. Bowley believed that by enlisting in a black regiment he was putting his reputation on the line. Bowley believed he was acting honorably because he was protecting his family and community from a rebel foe, doing his patriotic duty by defending the Union and proclaiming his manhood. Yet Bowley's service had another dimension. Throughout his memoir he constantly reminded the reader that his service in a black regiment directly challenged Southern codes of honor.

Bowley's concept of honor was inextricably tied to his concept of sacrifice. As he wrote his memoir, the burdens of sacrifice weighed heavily upon him. Weakened by a debilitating illness he had acquired while living as a prisoner of war in the rat holes of Camp Asylum, Columbia, South Carolina, he painfully wrote his memoir only a few years before he died. Because his body had been sacrificed for the nation he accepted pain and discomfort as a mark of honor. But what he could not accept was his loss of standing and reputation. He was acutely aware that officers and men of the United States Colored Troops had lost their place in the nation's history. Their voices were not heard at the celebratory reunion banquets or at the solemn monument dedications that occurred in the last decade of the nineteenth century. As a veteran of the prison camp and a witness to the Crater battlefield massacre, Bowley believed he had a sacred duty in his memoir to publicly validate his personal courage and to defend the honor of the officers and men who had served with him. Conscious that he was prevailing against the spirit of his age, he wanted to resurrect the ideological meaning of the war. Like other contemporary memorialists he too eulogized the veteran, but Bowley's praise never served to displace the deeper meaning of the war. The war was, for him, a revolutionary conflict that had given rise to new concepts of freedom and citizenship. These were the very values that gave meaning to his sacrificial service in the USCT (United States Colored Troops), and when these values faded from the nation's memory he felt an acute loss of self-worth and believed his honor had been tarnished. A small minority of other soldiers also shared Bowley's grievances. Donald R. Shaffer's research has shown that black veterans and some of their officers continued to fight valiantly to affirm their place in the nation's historical memory. Certainly Bowley never saw his loss of reputation exclusively in personal or individual terms. His memoir was a testament to the heroism and patriotism of the officers and men who had served with him, particularly those who had paid the supreme sacrifice. Such sacrifices directly challenged the South's role in the war and its notions of valor. He accused rebel Southerners of denigrating and exploiting the black race in order to bestow honor on another. In his eyes it was the Southern planter who dishonored the nation's flag by clinging to slavery, proclaiming secession, and waging a bloody war on the nation.[3]

When 17-year-old Freeman Bowley took the first tentative steps to claiming his manhood by seeking a commission in a black regiment, he was, in a symbolic sense, continuing his father's war. Only months before the civic reception, his father, Jesse, had returned to Worcester, Massachusetts, his "health broken down by the Gettysburg campaign." Invalided out of the service, his father's poor health had placed the family in a precarious situation. Freeman, an only child, recognized the sacrifices his parents had made for his education at the academy, and he knew that his father's poor health would mean he would have to "leave school and go to work." Mindful of his duty to contribute to the family's income, Freeman refused to consider enlisting as a private because "the $400 bounty which volunteers then received would not go far in those high-priced times." In these circumstances the establishment of United States Colored Troops regiments provided an alternative pathway to achieving his goal.[4]

Bowley's decision to enlist in the Union Army caused considerable domestic strife, but he resolved to remain true to his patriotic calling and put national duty ahead of family harmony. When he sought to gain his father's blessing for his efforts to gain a commission in a black regiment he was rebuffed. Jesse Bowley "flatly declared" that his son "should not go." Citing his own poor health Jesse declared that one casualty "in the service of his country" was "enough from a family as small as ours." He also objected to his son "entering a black regiment," fearing that should he fall "into the hands of the Confederates, nothing more would ever be heard." In addition, he doubted whether his son "could pass for second lieutenant." Since he failed to get his father to change his mind Freeman finally framed his appeal in a national patriotic context. He told his father "the story of Serg't Plunket [Plunkett] and the flag" and "the intense desire" it had aroused in him to serve his country. After listening "with flush face and shining eyes," his father admitted that while he could not "bear to let" him go, if he was determined "to try for a commission," he would help him.[5]

Once Bowley received his commission the responsibilities of military service began to weigh heavily upon his family. Although his invalid father was proud of his son's achievement, "he well knew how" his son's "youth and inexperience would weigh against" him. In order to prepare Freeman for war his father made "a list of the articles necessary" for war. Going to war became a family affair. While his mother, Juliet, busied herself providing enough supplies for "a baggage-wagon," his father "cut everything down to the service basis" and showed his son how to pack his knapsack. He also gave his son some valuable advice, advice that even in his darkest hour Freeman clung to. Jesse reminded his son that all men experienced fear. The challenge was to preserve his manhood by controlling his fear. "You will be scared when you go under-fire—every one is," remarked his father, "but stay with the line, and you will get your head again." If fighting for the Union was a man's responsibility it was also a son's honorable duty.[6]

There was nothing unique about Freeman's motivation. Countless soldiers writing about their military experiences linked the desire to volunteer and serve in the Union Army with their determination to claim their manhood by defending their family's honor. Defense of the home was inextricably linked to masculine virtue. For Freeman Bowley and many other young men, coming of age meant volunteering and so becoming an adult by adopting the masculine role. The characteristics of youth and boyhood—innocence, dependency, youthful enthusiasm, spontaneity, and self-indulgence—were left behind as the young man asserted his independence by leaving the comfort of his parents' home for the army tent and the company of his comrades. For Freeman Bowley the war had special meaning as a coming-of-age experience. He titled his memoir *A Boy Lieutenant in a Black Regiment*. This title pointed to military life as an adventure, a time of testing and manly maturation. Many soldiers commonly used the term "boys" extensively to refer to their comrades, which in part reflected the soldiers' attempt to place the military experience in the context of their life's experience. The war was another adventure. Adolescent soldiers such as Bowley were very mindful of their youth and lack of experience. The term was also used to highlight the spirit of camaraderie and the strong bonds of comradeship that existed among the men. However, "boys," essentially a term of endearment, was also used to emphasize the manly challenge inherent in military service. In this sense the language of the men was juxtaposed to their deeds. Only a few days after joining his regiment, Bowley was placed in the line of battle, ready for action. The brigade commander rode along the line and "in ringing tones" shouted, "Now boys, for the honor of the Black Brigade! Show the Sixth Corps you are men!"[7]

Bowley's narrative clearly indicates that he was acutely aware of the salient features of honorable manhood. He relished the tender contact he made with the "sweet girls" he met; he was proud of the way he lived a disciplined life and hardened himself against the horrors of war. He was also proud of the way he became a leader of his men and chivalrously protected weak and defenseless women and children. Above all else, Freeman Bowley was proud of the way he upheld family honor and committed himself loyally to his comrades by showing bravery when in combat. These attributes that Bowley so much admired and wrote about in his narrative stood in marked contrast to the military vices that marked another popular image of manhood, namely the "man's man." Gambling, drinking, brawling, and whoring held little appeal for him because they violated his notions of self-restraint, self-respect, and, above all else, family honor. A dutiful son, the barroom and whorehouse did not feature on his military landscape.[8]

The physical and moral contests that Freeman Bowley describes in his memoir are played out in four distinctly different arenas. His manhood and his honor code are tested on the march, on the battlefield, in prison, and in the army of occupation in North Carolina. Each of these contested landscapes contained its own particular set of challenges. Whereas his time on the march and in the army camp tested his leadership qualities and his ability to train and discipline his men, his experience on the battlefields of the Wilderness and the Crater tested his personal courage and deep commitment to his comrades and the Union. In the Richland Jail and Camp Asylum prison Bowley had to struggle to remain loyal to the Union and hold on to the values of civilized society. Finally, in North Carolina, he had to cast aside all notions of blind vengeance and justly impose the rule of U.S. law on a conquered people.

The first test of Freeman Bowley's maturing manhood occurred not on the battlefield nor in the army camp, but at the Worcester railway station. He so feared that the emotional intensity of bidding farewell to his parents would reduce him to an "officer blubbering and crying" that he vainly tried to discourage his mother from attending. Fortunately, when the time of departure arrived, he managed to control his emotions, even though he had a "lump" in his throat when he made his final farewells. Gradually, when the clouds of despondency lifted he considered himself "the most fortunate and happy boy in the world."[9]

Bowley arrived at the camp of the 30th USCI in the vicinity of Manassas Junction, Virginia, on May 4, 1864. At that time the 30th was part of the 1st Brigade, 4th Division of Maj. Gen. Ambrose E. Burnside's Ninth Army Corps, and as such it was mainly involved in supporting Grant's 1864 Overland Campaign by doing sentinel duty and guarding wagon trains and prisoners.[10]

Although Bowley received a warm reception from his fellow officers, he detected in their greetings subtle signs of disappointment. In his company commander Capt. Arthur Smith's eyes he "detected a look of disappointment similar to that which the Colonel's face had worn." Freeman was convinced they considered him "too young and boyish." The situation got no better when he met the enlisted men. The "quizzical expression" evident on their faces revealed that they were "disappointed too." Bewildered by this mixed reception, Bowley was also confronted by the foreign "blackness" of the men. Like a traveler in a foreign land he felt ill at ease in his new military environment. It all was a "little too much" for him.[11]

Like many officers embarking on their military careers, Bowley felt the burdens of command weighing heavily upon him. In the interest of maintaining military order and discipline, the Union Army deliberately created distance between the officers and enlisted men. Traditionally the officers came from a higher social class; they were wealthier and better educated than their men. These class differences were magnified by differentials of service. The officers received much higher pay and significantly better food, clothing, and armaments, and they were given the legal sanction of authority. Yet even though all of these factors could legitimize authority, they could not win respect and acclaim. Since respect was the seal of honorable service it had to be earned in the camp and on the field of battle.

In order to win their spurs and gain the respect of their fellow soldiers, many officers started their military careers by adopting the model of authority that they were most familiar with, that of the family. By adopting a paternal role, officers placed themselves in the place of a de facto parent, who gave guidance and governance to "the boys" serving under them. Such a model had strong appeal because army life was seen as a test of character and rite of passage to manhood. Good leadership was all about officers setting an honorable example and instilling in the men all those values that would make them patriotic veterans. The fact that many officers were community leaders who had recruited the men or been elected by the men themselves meant that they could call upon a reservoir of goodwill. Freeman Bowley lacked these advantages. A stranger in this regiment of Maryland blacks, he had no social network to call upon. Moreover, a racial hierarchy prevented him from identifying too closely with the men. Even an appeal to manly service appeared problematic. Conscious of his youthful innocence, Bowley had the distinct impression that his fellow officers and the enlisted men believed he was a callow youth facing a man's challenge.[12]

Although Bowley was influenced by the racism of his day, believing that blacks were "simple, timid," and "superstitious," he also believed that once they were subject to military training by competent officers they would become brave and patriotic soldiers. Yet his faith in the army as a vehicle to elevate blacks was not matched by a forthright statement of the training process. His memoir is bereft of any specific statements about appropriate models of leadership, and he does not inform the reader of the specific strategies he used to train his men. Instead, he describes his adjustment to army life and the duties of command by drawing upon a series of vignettes that describe the routine features of army life. Embedded within these vignettes are personal comments that reveal his growing sense of inclusion, comradeship, military stature, leadership, and respect. A capable young officer, Bowley set out to win respect by exercising kind but firm leadership, performing his military duties competently, showing courage in the face of battle, and, above all, demonstrating a patriotic commitment to the Union and emancipation.

Immediately upon joining his unit, he made deliberate efforts to understand the social dynamics of the company he was commanding. Intrigued by the "peculiar negro dialect" of the men, Bowley discovered there were "some very original characters in the company." This strategy of seeing the men as individuals, rather than just "soldiers," meant that he was able to work out ways of relating to his men in a manner that nullified opposition and elicited support.[13]

On the second day with the regiment, his men "did not seem so black, nor so much alike as they did at first." Bowley studied his men and observed that one non-commissioned officer, Sgt. John Offer, a "big," "burly," "jet-black negro" preacher from the Eastern Shore of Maryland, looked at him "with a feeling akin to contempt." Bowley "mentally resolved" to "keep him in his place and teach him a lesson at the very first opportunity." Rather than seek a direct confrontation, he decided to seize upon a simple incident to change the relationship between him and his men. He observed that Sgt. Offer was laboring from wearing a poorly packed knapsack. When the march halted he repacked Offer's knapsack and had the satisfaction of hearing him say it was "a heaper-sight easier." At the next stop he "showed several others how they could make their burdens easier." The men appreciated this practical advice, and Capt. Smith gave him "an approving word." Later during the march, when Thomas Festus, "the oldest man in the company, showed signs of giving out," Bowley carried his musket. The "looks of approval among the men amply repaid" him. These simple acts of kindness created feelings of mutual affection.[14]

By themselves acts of empathy and kindness could not win for the officers the respect of their men. Not wanting to be led by well-meaning fools, the men wanted leaders who could combine compassion with military competency. Freeman Bowley was aware of this and made great efforts to proficiently train his men. His devotion to duty was clearly revealed when, only one week after joining the regiment, he was ordered to drill his men in "the manual of arms."

For an hour Bowley drilled them on this one lesson and they improved "wonderfully," so much so that he was praised by the colonel. This praise "excited" the men's pride so that Bowley's word became the "authority to settle all disputed questions among them." With pride Bowley narrated that "Company H began to have the reputation of being the best-drilled company in the manual of arms of any in the regiment." A competent teacher, Bowley could no longer be dismissed as a mere boy. "Reckon de little Lieutenant knows a heap mor'n whut he looks," remarked one veteran soldier.[15]

After approximately a month in the service Bowley could confidently state that "a great change had come over" him. "From the timid, bashful, irresolute boy," he had "come to have confidence" in himself. He now believed he could do his "duty as well as anyone." Thoughts of "homesickness never occurred," and the "prospect of death or wounds never troubled" him. Yet these bold assertions masked fears about the unpredictable and horrific nature of war that continued to haunt him as he marched south with Burnside's army.[16]

Although death and suffering surrounded and disturbed Bowley in his march into the heart of the Confederacy, it never unmanned him. As he passed through the Wilderness battlefield the bush fires were so hot "that the men had to run." Even though the "sickening stench of burning flesh" disturbed him, he moved resolutely forward.[17]

Freeman Bowley became hardened to the gruesome features of war, but he never became completely inured to suffering or death. On one occasion tears came to his eyes as he buried some friends from the 37th Massachusetts Volunteers. On another occasion, moved by compassion, he had to act quickly to save a crippled Union veteran who was bleeding to death.[18]

Bowley uses these incidents to remind the reader that even in the face of death and suffering there was a place for grief and compassion, especially when it came to meeting the needs of comrades and friends. Tears and mournfulness did not necessarily imply a loss of manhood. On the contrary, they were powerful indicators that the soldiers had not been brutalized by war or made totally immune to pain and suffering. What really counted and distinguished the men from the boys was persistent fortitude. The crippled soldier shouted his message, "Stay with 'em boys," loudly, and Bowley clearly heard it. While he knew that expressions of grief and compassion were acceptable and at times even expected, he also knew that he could not allow himself to be consumed by them. Therefore, he concluded his description of this incident by saying that "an hour for breakfast, and back we went over the same road." The war continued.[19]

Although kindness, military competence, and courage were vital qualities that all enlisted men looked for in their officers, black soldiers searched for one important additional quality. Because they believed they were fighting a war of liberation, they expected their officers to be ideologically and personally committed to the notions of black freedom and citizenship. Freeman Bowley had this kind of commitment. In his narrative his commitment to black freedom is portrayed not in ideological speeches, but in the subtle personal relationships he had with specific black soldiers. His personal admiration for individual soldiers serving with him is contrasted with his more general contempt for Southern slavery and the barbarism displayed by rebel soldiers. For the black men serving under him this was a powerful statement of abolitionist principles. After all, relationships built on trust and human dignity meant far more to these men than lofty sounding words of antislavery rhetoric.[20]

Freeman Bowley's determination to treat his men justly sealed his commitment to black freedom. A spirit of comradeship and admiration developed from simple acts of kindness. In camp he assisted Sgt. Bob Bowen to write sensitive love letters to his sweetheart, Miss Tilley. On the battlefield, Bowen supported Bowley's leadership by rescuing the regimental colors and leading pursuing Confederate troops away from a vulnerable Union position. In his memoir he acknowledged that Bowen's action "was our salvation, for every Confederate rushed to the breastwork and fired at Bob, while we ran for the Crater." Conscious of his own developing manly stature, Bowley looked for signs of maturing manhood in the men he commanded. He found it in the acts of valor committed by men such as Sgts. Bowen and Offer on the battlefield. The praise he gave to his soldiers was genuine, even though at times his assessments were laced with notions of racism. By praising the valor of these soldiers he was not only trumpeting his own leadership, but was also endorsing their claims to freedom and citizenship. After all, it had been Bowen who had saved the nation's flag.[21]

Although the relationship with his men was largely harmonious, it was occasionally fraught with tension and difficulty. Most of the difficulties arose because slave culture did not fit easily within the boundaries of army life. Throughout his narrative Bowley employs a series of comic portraits to describe the naive, childlike character of the black soldiers. For the most part Bowley tolerated the peculiar ways of his men. Often he found their folkways amusing. For example, in his memoir he narrates a "noisy wrangle" between Joe Wright, "a big, jet-black man," and 1st Sgt. Scott, a free black brick maker from Baltimore, over the existence of "Ole Stonewall Jackson's ghos.'" Bowley told this story to "show how the old superstitions still clung to the negroes," and also to illustrate "the difficulties that their white officers had to contend with." Moreover, he acknowledges that when training black soldiers, officers must be cognizant of their slave traditions. In order to support this belief, he describes Maj. Leeke teaching Bowley's company how to form a skirmish line. "Just imagine you are hunting for coons, and keep your eyes open," shouted the major as he moved the line forward. Amusing though these tales of black folklore were, Bowley did admit that at times the former slaves' beliefs caused serious discipline problems. For example, on at least two occasions the soldiers in Co. H were scattered by imaginary ghosts who invaded their lines.[22]

In some ways Bowley's comments on slave folklore represent a negative view of the black soldier. His somewhat stereotypical representation of his enlisted men points to the pervasive influence of contemporary racial imagery. Such characterization suggests that Bowley's narrative technique is undermining the ideological themes of his work, which focus on black manhood and national honor. Yet this reading of Bowley's story ignores the impact of his military experience and his deft use of literary form. Another commentator on the black military experience, Col. Thomas Wentworth Higginson, also used racial stereotypes, dialects, and black folklore to characterize his soldiers. Like Higginson, Bowley was acutely aware of the way war eroded and changed social distinctions prevalent in American society. Bowley's military career, which, in less than one year, was marked by his elevation from schoolboy to company commander, was testament to this. Because he believed that military service was a time for personal growth and progress he also believed the Union Army could be a school for the black soldier. With this end in view, his narrative looks beyond the small picture of a military commander preparing his men for combat, to focus on a wider canvas of the officer as a military guide, or teacher, who is raising his students to manhood. Like an experienced schoolmaster, Bowley constantly refers to his soldiers' dialect and superstitions in ways that enable him to maintain his distance and authority while he pleads their cause. This writing technique makes his story all the more convincing because it reinforces differentials in military rank. It also affirms distinctive racial identities at a time when the nation's future was uncertain and it was undergoing profound social change. Moreover, it also enables him to uphold Northern cultural values as the national norm. Bowley informs the readers that these are the very values his black soldiers aspire to. Towards the end of his narrative he does this by answering a query by a recruit: "Wha' foh all de ossifers allers talk to Bob Bowen jes like he one ob de white men?" Bowley answers this question by explaining how Bowen's devotion to duty and courage under fire enabled him to hold the line and secure the national flag at the Battle of Hatcher's Run. By heroic action on the battlefield racial identity is made militarily and socially acceptable; patriotism becomes the pathway to citizenship.[23]

Although Bowley makes use of contemporary racial conventions, he is not rigidly bound by them. For example, many of Bowley's black soldiers are named. Joe Wright and 1st Sgt. Scott are individuals with rounded personalities. Another important difference is the placement of the folklore portraits. They are strategically located next to stories of black valor and devotion to duty. For example, immediately after Bowley describes the "coon hunt" skirmish line, he describes his troops firing and successfully holding the line against an enemy attack. After describing the soldiers in disarray fleeing from a wild steer, Bowley describes a rejuvenated military unit marching with disciplined alacrity through the town of Bowling Green. Rather than using his folklore portraits as evidence to denigrate the black soldier, Bowley uses them as yardsticks to demonstrate just how far the soldiers have traveled along the road to manhood. Bowley's stories have intriguing comical characters—Monkey Jackson, Joe Wright, and Hillary Herbert—but they also have many more model heroes such as Bob Bowen, John Offer, and John Dudley. Furthermore, even when Bowley uses slave dialect to narrate the soldiers' point of view he is not necessarily using it as an instrument of entertainment. Embedded within simple messages of former slaves like John Offer are profound statements of patriotism. The very nature of the slave language gives the soldiers' message a potency it would otherwise not have had.

Bowley was acutely aware that performance in combat was the ultimate test of manhood. Yet when he was called into combat at the Battle of the Wilderness he almost failed this test. He was so overcome by fear he had to shut his "teeth tight" to "prevent them from chattering." Yet frightened though he was, he regained his sense of composure by remembering his father's advice to "keep with the line."[24]

For the first two months of service Freeman Bowley's baptism by fire occurred in a routine, intermittent, almost incidental manner. The boy who had been mesmerized by the heroism of Sgt. Plunkett on the Fredericksburg battlefield now found himself facing an enemy that was far more elusive than he had imagined. As he became more like a hardened veteran and less like an enthusiastic boy, his understanding of his own masculinity deepened. He discovered that valor was a concept that had many complex layers of meaning. One could, for example, show bravery by charging enemy lines on the battlefield. Yet one could also display valor by digging trenches and building forts in the face of deadly enemy fire. Bowley learned to display this kind of courage while commanding fatigue parties during the siege of Petersburg. He soon realized that it "really required more nerve than to stand in line of battle." Gradually, over time, he became less fearful of combat, so much so that in late May 1864 he confidently reported that the "guard mount and picket detail no longer had any terrors," because he now "marched with the swing of a veteran."[25]

Almost three months after joining his regiment Bowley had his first experience of intense battlefield combat, when he took part in the Battle of the Crater, an ill-fated attempt to break the Petersburg siege by mining Confederate lines. This battle made an indelible impression on Bowley because it marked the high water mark of his military service. After the war he wrote four different accounts of the battle and made two unsuccessful applications for a Medal of Honor based on his exploits at the Crater. Although the details of these accounts differ in some particulars, the rationale for writing remained basically the same. Keen to have his honorable part in the conflict publicly recognized, he sought to correct the historical record by describing the gallantry of the Colored Division. By doing so he was endeavoring to restore their honor and expunge any notions that the black troops and their officers could be the scapegoats for Union defeat.[26]

During the charge on the enemy lines at the battle of the Crater, the courage of Bowley and his men was severely tested by the rapid enemy fire, which ripped through the advancing lines of Union soldiers. Such was the aggressive spirit in the black soldiers that when one rebel officer tried to rally his men with the cry "Drive them back! They are nothing but niggers," his challenge provoked a savage response from the black soldiers. "A very howl of rage like the roar of wild beasts went up from the blacks" and, led on by Sgt. Offer, whose "frenzied manner made him a grotesque and, at the same time, a most horrible-looking object," they threw themselves at their assailants, killing and overpowering them. This depiction of the black soldiers' raw, animal-like aggression pointed to the vital role Bowley believed the white officers played in controlling their emotionally charged soldiers in the heat of battle. Fortunately for him his men fought honorably and took prisoners of war.

As the tide of battle began to turn against the Union forces, Bowley's commitment to the fight began to weaken and he began to consider whether he should "run back to the Union breastworks or stay on the field and try and hold the ground already gained?" Finally, his dilemma was resolved when he considered his family's honor and recalled his father's advice to "stay with the line." With resolute determination, he gathered his men around and led them back to the Crater.[27]

Bowley describes the Crater as a hellhole seething with men, some of whom committed sublime acts of heroism, while others perpetrated despicable acts of savagery. Like a crucible, the intense heat of the battle separated those noble, manly soldiers who did their duty from the dross who thought only of their own personal safety or of inflicting barbaric revenge. Bowley describes the different types of the soldiers by drawing brief character sketches of the combat performance of certain individuals. For example, the cool, calculated leadership provided by war amputee Brig. Gen. William Bartlett is contrasted with the frenzied actions of an anonymous officer who had clearly lost self-control. "All the time he was yelling, he took good care to keep well down out of range."[28]

In his description of the battle Bowley links the inspirational leadership of courageous individuals to his concept of masculinity. His heroes are men who inspire others to do their honorable duty. When a sergeant of the 9th New Hampshire "sprang to the top of the works" waving a flag and called out, "Men of the 9th N. H., will you leave these old colors for the rebels? Rally, rally, rally on the old flag!" a "little band clustered around him, and fought as only veterans can." Black soldiers showed equal valor. When an attempt was made to "dig a covered way to the side towards the Union lines," white soldiers refused to work in it once the rebels "got the range." A black soldier then "took the pick" and, while "the bullets struck all around him," kept working until "one bullet shaved a tuft of wool from his head."[29]

Bowley describes conditions in the Crater as if describing a slaughter pen. Men staggered to their posts suffering from "well-nigh intolerable" thirst and blood "collected in small pools in every little cavity." The men were "nearly choked" by the "sickening stench." Against this background of hopeless despair, the fighting spirit of the black soldiers shone brightly. According to Bowley, a deep devotion to duty explained their manly resistance. While firing at the enemy he remarked to the lone surviving black soldier who had rallied with him, "Sergeant, things are looking very bad for us;" the sergeant replied, "Sah, we has to die right yere." Bowley noted that this remark had not been made in a "spirit of bravado" nor in "a tone of regret," but as "a matter of fact, our duty had called us to this place, and it was part of that duty: 'to die right yere.'"[30]

In this struggle for survival the American Indians fighting alongside the black soldiers also exhibited all the benefits of Union Army military training. Bowley reports that Indians from the 1st Michigan Sharp Shooters did "splendid work, crawling to the very top of the bank, and rising up," taking "quick and fatal aim" before dropping quickly down again. Although he noted that these soldiers chanted their "death song" when mortally wounded, he also observed that they fought like loyal, disciplined Union soldiers when facing the enemy.[31]

In the heat of battle the valor of the former slaves and former "savages," the black soldiers and American Indian troops, stands out in marked contrast to the heinous nature of the rebel attack. Upon reaching the Crater, Bowley looked back only to see "Confederates bayoneting the wounded men who had just been shot down."[32]

In order to focus the reader's attention on the brutality of the rebels, Bowley added two powerful eyewitness reports of rebel massacres. These postscript accounts serve to reinforce the accuracy of Bowley's own description and also to underline the magnitude of the massacre. According to Bowley, "nearly three times as many were butchered" at the Crater as at Fort Pillow. Yet while "the whole civilized world was appalled and shocked" at the massacre at Fort Pillow, the massacre at the Crater "seems to have escaped general notice." After describing the brutal slaying of a colored soldier who had surrendered and was pleading for his life, eyewitness George Bernard, a Confederate veteran from the 12th Virginia Volunteers, exclaimed, "It is shocking!" that this "horrible act" was "but a sample of many other bloody tragedies during the first 10 minutes after our men got into the trench." Apparently the soldiers "seemed infuriated at the idea of having to fight negroes." The second eyewitness, Capt. D. E. Proctor, 30th USCI, reported that he saw "bayonets plunged into colored men who had surrendered." Fiendish fighters, "the enemy even placed our colored wounded men upon their works and fired between their legs, well knowing that we would not return the fire without endangering the lives of our own men."[33]

Bowley's description of the heinous fighting tactics employed by the rebels serves two purposes. First, it serves to highlight the inherent dignity of Yankee manhood. Yet Bowley is careful not to paint a simplistic picture. Although most Yankee soldiers do their patriotic duty, some are infected by the cruelty of the conflict. Some lose their manhood; others give up in despair. The black soldiers show fortitude, but their passions need to be restrained by their officers. Second, Bowley's description of rebel atrocities serves to highlight his own honorable part in the conflict. Although not featuring prominently in the narrative of the battle, Bowley pictures himself providing calculated leadership and a courageous example to his troops. His exploits are such that after his surrender Gen. Bartlett "complimented" him on his "behavior during the fighting in the Crater." Yet here again the picture is not simple. When describing the desperate defense of the Crater, Bowley mentions that Gen. Bartlett ordered a breastwork be built across to a traverse to shield the defenders from enemy fire. The black soldiers who were detailed to build this barricade used lumps of clay and "dead men." Such was the desperation of the defenders that even some wounded were thrown in. The "cries of the wounded, many of them pressed down under the dead, were piteous in the extreme." What Bowley fails to tell the reader is that he was directly in charge of building the barricade. Therefore, by his own admission, Bowley was implicated in the same kind of savagery that besmirched Confederate manhood. All this points to the concept of manhood having meaning, on the battlefield, only when reference is made to "the other," in this case the Confederate soldiers. There was a fine line between the hardened soldier and the savage fighter. Bowley recognized this and also knew that in order to convincingly describe his honorable war service as a coming-of-age experience he had to vividly describe the bloody realities of war.[34]

Yet Bowley never believed that honor was exclusively a matter of personal courage. In his eyes the chivalrous victor could be just as noble as the courageous fighter. The very essence of honorable service required combatants to respect the integrity of each other. Therefore, according to the conventions of civilized warfare, the wounded enemy was to be given sustenance and offers of surrender were to be accepted. Flushed by the fury of battle, Bowley knew that the rebel soldiers were not bound by these honorable codes, and this knowledge tempted him to abandon his comrades.[35]

Shortly after his capture at the Crater, while being registered by rebel soldiers as a prisoner of war, Bowley contemplated escaping cruel punishment or even death by denying he was an officer in a black regiment. Yet he finally resolved to remain loyal to his regiment and defiantly proclaimed he was an officer in the "Thirtieth United States Colored Infantry!" Bowley remained loyal for two reasons. First, he could not deny "the black men who had rallied with" him at the Crater. Second, he told his fellow officers that he believed the "Government would protect us." Bowley put his faith in the government, and "the remembrance of that hearty, manly clasp of President Lincoln's hand" assisted him to make that decision. As an aspiring recruit, Bowley had met Lincoln in Washington, D.C., while waiting to come before Maj. Gen. Silas Casey's Examination Board. Now as a battle weary veteran, memories of that fateful visited flooded back to him. Faced with the prospect of imprisonment or death, the "manly" handshake made between two men became a bond of honor that sealed Bowley's duty to the Union.[36]

Only a few days after the Battle of the Crater concluded, Confederate authorities attempted to publicly humiliate and dishonor their captured prisoners by parading them before the citizens of Petersburg as trophies of war. To heighten the humiliation, Confederate authorities sat the "hero" of the battle, Gen. Bartlett, on a "sorry looking horse" without a saddle, and in an effort to depict their Yankee captives as no better than "negroes," they alternated columns of Union officers with black prisoners of war. Located in the "third file of officers," Bowley was subject to verbal abuse from the civilians "which exceeded anything of the kind" that he had "ever heard." "The women were particularly bitter." Bowley uses the plight of Gen. Bartlett and the suffering of the Union prisoners on the Petersburg streets to remind his readers of the North's moral superiority. The institution slavery had not only debauched the rebel soldiers, but it had corrupted the civilian population.[37]

For the next seven months, Bowley languished in prison in Columbia, South Carolina. Yet the war was not over for him; combat had simply taken a different form. The harsh realities of prison life shook his moral values to the core. Prison life challenged his basic notions of manhood and his loyalty to the Union. It tested his moral values, the very values that linked him to his home community and family.

Although he was far removed from hearth and home, Bowley's indebtedness to his family increased as prison conditions deteriorated. The letters he received from home and his "blue-eyed Massachusetts girl" nourished his soul and lifted his spirits in his darkest hours. Remittance money he had managed to secure from his father covered the cost of his "winter's board at Columbia," because it enabled him to buy extra rations. Bowley believed this money "probably" saved his life and the lives of his two comrades. In many ways distance and suffering only increased the obligation Bowley felt to honor his family. Above all else it was his love for his family that kept him loyal to the Union.[38]

Late in November 1864, while hovering between life and death in the Asylum Prison at Columbia, South Carolina, Bowley was invited to join the "Foreign Legion" that Confederate authorities were forming from prisoners of war. His description of this event is detailed and emotive, and in places it appears to bear some of the hallmarks of an aging veteran's memory rather than sounding the ring of historical truth. All the inducements to turn traitor are listed in precise detail and in a manner that seeks to convince the reader of their accumulative attractiveness. Bowley was to be given "a full uniform, sword belt and revolver," a servant, a captain's commission, and non-combat duties. Reports of flattery and threats of indefinite imprisonment appear to give the anecdote even more authenticity. Finally, Bowley reminds the reader that "this was an offer to a boy not 19 years of age" who was "proscribed by reason of his being an officer in a black regiment," who was "weak from hunger and disease" and with "little prospect of anything but death before him."

Before rejecting the offer, Bowley contemplated the way acceptance would violate his manhood. He believed it would betray his duty to the Union, first revealed to him by "the armless Sergeant waving the bloodstained flag in the hall in Worcester," the men who died by his "side in the Petersburg Crater," his "soldier father," his mother "whose only child" he was, and finally his "dear blue-eyed girl way up in Massachusetts." Firm in his duty to the Union, loyal to his comrades, and determined to uphold family honor, Bowley rejected the offer, saying that rather than be a "Galvanized Yank," he would see the "Foreign Legion and the whole Confederacy deeper in h______, than a pigeon could fly in a thousand years."[39]

Loyal though he was, Bowley knew that the hardship of prison life could strip away the trappings of civilization and reduce men to a form of slavery. This threat of moral degradation haunted Bowley throughout his time in prison. Indeed, it partly explains why he objected so strongly to the unsanitary conditions, the imprisonment of Capt. Harris in chains, and the savaging of Lt. Parker by dogs. Conditions that apparently placed the prisoners at the same level as slaves were anathema to him. Yet Bowley did not see the full depravity of prison life until shortly before he was paroled. In February 1865, while under guard at Raleigh, North Carolina, Bowley met over 3,000 prisoners from Andersonville. He was shocked by the prisoners' physical appearance. Many of the men were "so emaciated that the bones had worn through the skin at elbows and hips." Brutalized though these men were, Bowley praised them because they honored their commitment to the Union "and cheerfully accepted a horrible death than turn traitors to their country."[40]

On March 1, 1865, Bowley was exchanged at Northeast River, near Wilmington, North Carolina. Bowley's time on parole was a time of personal acclamation. His homeward journey was marked by the ringing endorsement of his honorable service. The men of his division and regiment warmly embraced him as a comrade and fellow veteran. This military endorsement was enhanced by the kindness of strangers, who during the course of his homeward journey recognized his patriotic sacrifices and comforted him. In Philadelphia, "a beautiful young lady" wearing a "Quaker bonnet" went to the "Soldiers Refreshment Rooms" to bring him "a bowl of steaming soup and a cup of tea." She considered it "a pleasure to do a little for a soldier who has sacrificed so much." At home in Worcester, Freeman was welcomed back as a dutiful son. A true veteran, Bowley's father respectfully listened to his son's heroic adventures with "flashing eyes." Proud of his accomplishments, Bowley greatly enjoyed visiting the home of his sweetheart, the "blue-eyed girl" who had faithfully written to him while he was in prison. Yet it was at the Highland Military Academy that Bowley's service was most publicly acclaimed. Attired in a new officer's uniform, he was welcomed back by his "cadet friends" "as one from the grave." They clearly envied his "practical army experience." Basking in personal glory, Bowley used his visit to his old school to settle old scores and teach some of his former instructors true military lessons. He adopted a "dignified" stance to those officers "who had formerly patronized" him and "managed to impress upon them the great difference between a real soldier and officer of the army and a school-boy cadet official." His transformation was now complete; roles had reversed. The former schoolboy now lectured his former teachers with all the authority of a veteran.[41]

Bowley returned to his regiment in May 1865 and soon realized that conditions had changed. The war was over, and patterns of leadership that were appropriate for a combat situation were not suitable for an army of occupation. New codes of behavior needed to be developed for peacetime soldiers occupying the land of their old masters.

When Bowley joined his regiment at Goldsboro, North Carolina, he knew that as a soldier in the army of occupation he had a duty to secure the nation's victory over the rebels by establishing a new order in the South. He linked these larger national goals to his personal performance of routine military duties in the coastal regions of North Carolina. In his memoir he makes the association between his personal duty and national policy simply by describing the military adventures of the black soldiers in his company. These stories describe Bowley training his men for their new national roles as peacekeepers, law enforcers, and citizen soldiers. This narrative technique enables him to portray the black soldier both as the vehicle and product of a new national order.

Throughout much of North Carolina, in the months immediately following the war, a state of unrest prevailed. In this explosive situation Bowley believed that he had to exercise firm control over his men. While he was stationed near Beaufort, North Carolina, "the restless spirit of the negro soldier manifested itself" in a powerful way. Frustrated by long hours of fatigue duty, many men braved severe punishments to raid and plunder neighboring plantations. Others simply deserted. In these trying circumstances Bowley worked hard to minimize racial tension. In this regard he taught his men how to exercise self-restraint and not to retaliate when they were provoked by the former rebels. They received one such lesson while they were engaged in fatigue duty at Goldsboro in the hot summer of 1865.[42]

On one occasion, in order to escape Goldsboro's burning sun, Bowley took his men into the garden attached to an "attractive-looking house." Initially the owner of the house and garden, Confederate veteran Colonel Poole, welcomed Bowley. However, this attitude abruptly changed when Bowley accused Poole of being one of the contemptible Confederate officers who had imprisoned him at Goldsboro in February 1865. In his defense Poole sought the protection of his parole status. "It's a good thing for you that you are, sir," Bowley replied, adding that but for this protection he would have challenged him to fight to "prove" whether he was a soldier or "only a contemptible coward who bullies unarmed men." The tension further increased when Col. Poole set his "big brute of a dog" to attack the soldiers. Immediately, Bowley shot the dog and his men seized Poole. Exercising considerable restraint Bowley reminded Poole that the "'nigger-driving' days are over" and that if he wanted "to be protected as a paroled prisoner" he had to conduct himself "like a gentleman." After Bowley had finished admonishing Poole for dishonorably violating his parole, he and his men departed. The whole incident was a lesson in self-restraint and military decorum. Bowley knew, however, that his men's passion for revenge could overwhelm the positive impact of his honorable behavior. Therefore, he moved his men "away to another locality," because he feared that they would do Poole "or his property some mischief."[43]

Whether or not the emotive incident in Col. Poole's garden took place in the precise manner that Bowley describes is open to question. For an aging veteran, writing at the twilight of his life for a national newspaper, the temptation to reconstruct this personal anecdote in a manner that incorporated national themes of retributive justice and social reconstruction must have been great. Yet regardless of the precise accuracy of the incident, the readers of the *National Tribune* would have agreed with Bowley that "the nigger-driving days are over," slavery and the Confederacy were dead, and the South was now part of an indivisible union.

The 30th USCI continued its peace-keeping duties until it left North Carolina in mid-December 1865. Before the regiment left for Baltimore a death occurred in Bowley's company that seemed to bring together all the conflicting strains of military service that he had experienced. The death of George Uncles placed him in a pensive and contemplative mood, which encouraged him to reflect upon the meaning of his own life. In some ways Bowley identified with Uncles. Small in stature, he was an "active, wiry little fellow always ready to do his duty." His devotion to duty was also exemplary; at the Battle of the Wilderness he had "thrown away his knapsack, that he might keep up with the column." On his deathbed Bowley tried to speak a few words of comfort to him, only to be cut short by Uncles's pleading that he inform his "mudder" that he was a faithful soldier. At the funeral of this "good, faithful soldier," Bowley placed over the grave a headboard he had carved with his "own hands." In addition to the normal information, including "name, company, regiment and date of death," Bowley added in capital letters the epitaph "HE ALWAYS STAYED WITH THE LINE." The death of Uncles had a resonance about it because it reminded him of his own mortality.[44]

It reminded him of his father's words delivered to him just before he departed for the war. These words—"stay with the line"—echoed in his mind during the Battle of the Wilderness and in all subsequent battles. In the face of mortal combat, they steeled his courage and placated his troubled heart. Now at the graveside of George Uncles they came back to him. Bowley felt the death of Uncles keenly, for he had "grown up" with this young soldier. Like Uncles he, too, had been on a journey to prove his manhood. During the course of this journey, in camp, on the march, and in combat, a sense of community had developed between the men in Co. H. They had lived together, marched together, and fought together. Now at the graveside of one of their comrades they mourned together. As a group the men had shared common values: a patriotic duty to the Union and to antislavery, a commitment to defend and honor their loved ones, and a loyalty to each other.

Even so, the community that developed in Co. H was not, and never could be, a community of equals. Freeman Bowley commanded his company, and while badges of rank and notions of racial superiority separated him from his men, they also gave him authority over them. Because he saw himself as a paternal figure he never exercised his authority in an arbitrary or tyrannical manner. Indeed, he believed his "boys" needed firm direction, governance, and guidance. While imposing military discipline on his men Bowley also nurtured kindness in the ranks. He punished the miscreant but also wrote letters home for illiterate soldiers. Almost his last official duty as an officer was mixed with elements of compassion. Only a few days before his regiment was discharged from service at Fort Federal Hill, Baltimore, Bowley kept his promise and consoled the mother and sister of George Uncles. On December 22, 1865, "the time of parting came." Every soldier "in Co. H came to" him and shook him "by the hand." They gave him "every kind wish" and received his "in return." These handshakes reaffirmed the bonds of comradeship that had been forged during the war. The war had changed Bowley and it had changed the men who had fought with him. When they marched out of Fort Federal Hill, "their ranks dissolved in the moving tide of civil life," the "glorious old 30th" became "only a memory." Yet Bowley never discarded these chords of memory. Throughout his life he told and retold the stories of how he commanded the soldiers in Co. H, 30th USCI, as they made their triumphant journey through the South.[45]

Becoming Soldiers

In the process of making his transition to military service, Freeman Bowley became aware of the fact that his soldiers were also adapting to the rhythms of army life. On his second day with the regiment he heard his soldiers continually complaining about the interrupted nature of the march. Sgt. Worrell replied to one "young feller" that "w'en you's ben in de army as long as I has" then you would know "dis yere am de way ob de millingtery." Like Bowley the young black soldiers had difficulty adjusting to army life. At one level this transition was a personal, individual matter. Every soldier had to make his own way in the army and gain acceptance as a soldier. Yet at another level, transition was about recognition on a wider scale. In varying degrees the black soldiers sought recognition and respect from their white officers, the wider body of white Union soldiers, and their home communities. In their struggle to gain acceptance as Union soldiers rather than armed former slaves, they had to find ways of dealing with the inherent racial prejudice of white soldiers.[46]

For black recruits the challenges of army life loomed particularly large because there was little in the antebellum experiences that had prepared them for it. Even notions of freedom and justice were novel experiences for soldiers who had formerly been slaves. Many of these soldiers learned their military lessons the hard way. Harsh disciplinary practices brought them into line. Black soldiers coped with the difficult and at times traumatic nature of army life by making adjustments to their personal routines and by reshaping their cultural activities. There was nothing unusual about this. Soldiers throughout the Union and Confederate armies composed songs, changed stories, and adapted religious practices in a way that enabled them to ease their transition to army life. For black soldiers the transition process was more difficult for two reasons. First, their antebellum social heritage was very different from that shared by Billy Yank and Johnny Reb. Second, black soldiers had to fight for recognition and acceptance. Racially prejudiced Northern soldiers were very reluctant to see them as comrades in arms. Most rebel soldiers considered the blacks in blue to be simply slaves in open rebellion.[47]

During his first day with the 30th USCI Freeman Bowley discovered that music played a vital role in helping the soldiers cope with the hardships of army life. Late in the afternoon, after supper, the regiment resumed its long march south singing "The Colored Volunteer" to the tune of "that old-time, well known song, 'That's What's the Matter, Boys.'" Composed to promote a spirit of defiance, the song ridiculed the Confederacy and scoffed at Jeff Davis' threat to hang black soldiers upon capture. Such songs not only helped the long hours pass quickly, but also helped to strengthen the esprit de corps of the regiment. Union Army anthems became liberation choruses as the soldiers moved deeper into the South. When Bowley's division passed through the village of Bowling Green, Virginia, at 9 o'clock in the evening one night in mid-May 1864, it appeared as if the apocalypse had descended on the village. For the frightened rebel civilians "peeping from the windows," the end of their world was nigh. As the 5,000-strong force of black soldiers passed down the village street, lit by the light of the burning courthouse, they triumphantly sang "John Brown's Body Lies Buried in the Ground." Each soldier was "singing and yelling at the top of his voice."[48]

Many black soldiers believed that they were fighting in God's Army. Their religious beliefs and practices sustained them because they gave divine meaning to the war. On one occasion, while on an evening walk, a somewhat despondent Freeman Bowley came across a prayer meeting of black soldiers. The exhortations of "one powerful black soldier" who declared he was "willin' to die for de flag" and beseeched the Lord to "comfort de lubbed ones at home" moved him to tears. Spirituals were sung lustily because they gave the war a religious meaning. The religious beliefs of the soldiers also galvanized them for battle. White officers could appeal to the soldiers' burgeoning sense of manhood. However, only the leaders from the ranks could set the impending conflict in a spiritual setting that steeled the soldiers for battle. Immediately before the men of the 30th USCI went into the fateful Battle of the Crater, Maj. Leeke turned to Sgt. Offer and remarked, "It's our turn now." This "preacher" from the "Eastern Shore of Maryland" assumed his "Sunday voice" and urged "ebery man" to "liff up his soul in pra'ar for a strong heart."[49]

The religious practices and religious activities of the men of the 30th USCI were sustained by a strong community life that flourished within the regiment. In his narrative Bowley reports that the men in his company were engaged in a great range of cultural activities including music making, worshiping, reading newspapers, writing letters, and telling stories. These pastime activities enabled the soldiers to employ their cultural traditions in a way that made them better soldiers. The leisure pursuits provided entertainment, allayed fears, and helped sustain bonds of comradeship. Above all else they helped the soldiers to sustain their own moral values and their own sense of military self-worth. Yet the communities that developed in black regiments were not culturally uniform, nor were they permanently stable and always aligned to the military purposes of the Union Army. Freeman Bowley discovered this when his parole ended and he returned to his company in May 1865.[50]

Bowley's first day back with his old company was a disturbing one. He soon discovered the company's sense of social cohesion and community spirit had dissipated. Discipline problems were rife and the men's morale was low. This deterioration had largely been brought about by the sudden influx into the company of large numbers of North Carolina former slaves. The presence of these raw recruits represented a dramatic cultural shift that radically changed the boundaries of the military life. This situation had been exacerbated by poor leadership. Normally a good company commander could use the appropriate training strategies to enforce discipline and military decorum. However, in the eyes of Bowley, Co. H had been poorly led by a "recently appointed" lieutenant who had "neither the tact nor the experience to command colored men." Faced with a crisis of considerable proportions Bowley set about changing the military profile of the company. By astute use of disciplinary strategies he struggled hard to remake the military community by replacing "slave habits" with the rule of military law and regulation. Yet in the midst of this challenge Bowley never acted entirely alone. Indeed, many veteran Maryland soldiers proved to be valuable allies.[51]

In order to improve the standard of drill in the company Bowley divided the recruits "into little squads" and, "selecting the best-drilled non-commissioned officers and men, set them at work on the squads." This action made the maintenance of drill standards an issue of collective concern. He further strengthened his hand by dealing severely with breaches of discipline by the recently recruited former slaves. On one occasion he "bucked and gagged" a recruit who answered him back "saucily on drill." Although this soldier was released once he was "well humbled," only a stern warning from Bowley saved him from additional punishment at the hands of the veteran soldiers. This desire to inflict additional punishment was not simply a reflection of the men's esteem for Bowley. Cultural differences played a part too. The Maryland soldiers believed that they were decidedly superior to the former slaves from North Carolina. "Is de dumbest niggers alive," remarked one "disgusted Corporal" to Bowley. Bowley shared many of the soldier's beliefs, describing the recruits as being "downright ugly" and "a very different class from our old Baltimore and Maryland men." Although he acknowledged that his Maryland soldiers had once been "raw and awkward," this admission did not nullify his low opinion of North Carolina men. Like most veterans who had won their laurels in combat, these Maryland soldiers probably did not want their reputations harmed or their way of life and military routines upset by ignorant recruits who were supposedly bound by slave ways. While there is no direct evidence that Bowley deliberately exacerbated the cultural conflict in his company in order to assert his authority, his memoir suggests that he used the cultural differences to his advantage.[52]

While the black soldiers' cultural activities, such as singing and praying, helped them to make personal adjustments to army life, they were less useful when it came to repelling the barbs of criticism thrown at them by the white soldiers. On the contrary, many of these leisure-time pursuits seemed to confirm notions of difference and inferiority. In order to win recognition as Union soldiers, blacks had to find new ways of challenging their critics. They successfully did this by reconfiguring the antebellum resistance strategies they learned to combat Northern racism and Southern slavery. These resistance strategies were linked to powerful demonstrations of patriotic loyalty and military capability.

Much of the criticism of the black soldier took the form of soldierly banter. While some of the language used was not violently racist, it did betray the underlying spirit of racism that pervaded the Union Army. Black soldiers were sensitive to these public displays of ridicule because they knew they seriously undermined their status as soldiers. To leave such attacks, however mildly delivered, unanswered was to reinforce notions of second-class status and racial exclusion. In order to blunt such attacks the black soldiers learned measured forms of response that did not provoke excessive antagonism. One such response was delivered to the men of the Fifth Corps in mid-May 1864. These soldiers had lined Orange Plank Road, near the Chancellorsville battlefield, especially to mock the black troops as they passed by. The black soldiers responded to the "chaffing" not by hurling abuse back at their critics, but by presenting "a creditable military appearance" and demonstrating their patriotism. Ranks were closed and rifles brought to the right shoulder. Then one "colored soldier with a clear, mellow voice," led the black soldiers in a rousing chorus.

The song "Will you, will you, Fight for de Union?" reverberated down the road and changed the atmosphere so much that "the Fifth Corps boys" "rewarded" the soldiers with a "generous round of applause." By deftly employing their musical skills and diverting the focus of attention away from themselves to the sacred cause for which they and the white soldiers were fighting, the black soldiers subtly changed what might otherwise have been an acrimonious situation into a patriotic celebration. The white soldiers admired the black soldiers' musical talents, but they had even more respect for the patriotic anthems they were singing.[53]

On another occasion Bowley's men passed by a large number of hospital tents as they escorted rebel prisoners to White House Landing. Keen to "put on style" and impress the "lady nurses," the men braced themselves and marched with military precision. This display provoked shouts of derision and mockery from groups of fresh troops, "young fellows, evidently college boys." "Come see the black cloud" was the call of these "hundred-days men." The ragged appearance of the black soldiers encouraged one to shout out, "why don't you hire out for a scarecrow in the cornfield?" Rather than engage in endless banter, the black soldiers simply replied by pointing to their prisoners, saying, "dese yere's de kind o' co'n I'se bin a shukin." In this case action did speak louder than words.[54]

Racist stereotyping, such as that experienced by Bowley's soldiers, was widespread in the ranks of the Union Army. Blacks were depicted as comical, passive, and fawning creatures. Embedded in the racist slurs of "scarecrow" and "black cloud" was a belief that black soldiers were lacking moral fiber, individuality, and humanity. Bowley's men aggressively challenged such stereotyping not by seeking to directly confront their accusers, but by linking their cultural skills to their military proficiency and patriotic spirit. The music of the black soldiers provided a positive point of initial contact because it appealed to the white Union soldiers' love of home and commitment to the Union. Songs such as "Will you, will you, Fight for de Union" and "The Girl I Left Behind Me" reminded black and white soldiers that by defending the Union they were protecting their loved ones. They had a shared commitment to a noble cause. The songs that Bowley's men sang had become marching songs, and the black soldiers marched as well as, if not better than, most white soldiers. Because white soldiers had such a negative image of the blacks' character, displays such as that performed by the 30th USCI appeared all the more remarkable. For some soldiers it was beyond belief. Commenting in his memoir on the stunned silence of the young "hundred-days men," Bowley wrote that "it had dawned on their minds that the splendid marching black regiment was their superiors as soldiers." Then, in a statement that would have resonance with the veteran soldiers reading the serialized version of his memoir in the *National Tribune*, Bowley added, "in the army effectiveness, not social qualities, was what counted."[55]

The integration of black soldiers into the Union Army was not just about rebutting the critics. The soldiers themselves had to feel confident about their performance and continually affirm their progress as soldiers. The encouragement and praise given by their officers played an important part in this affirming process. Bowley praised his men when they performed well at drill or carried out their picket duties with military proficiency, and this praise encouraged them to perfect their performance.

In the process of affirming themselves as Union soldiers, the men of Co. H constantly measured themselves against the white soldiers. Less than one week after Bowley had joined his regiment it became obvious that his veteran soldiers were far superior to the Union recruits that had recently joined the army. As they journeyed south Bowley's men witnessed thousands of "fresh troops" making their way out of Fredericksburg. Many of these men were heavy artillery men equipped as infantry. Unaccustomed to marching, these "fat" men labored under the hot sun. "Their faces were red and flushed, and the perspiration fairly rolled off of them." In desperation these fat soldiers lightened their burden by abandoning their equipment and clothing. As they traveled in their wake, the black veterans "exchanged their mud-soaked clothing for new, clean articles picked up by the roadside." The black soldiers' new uniforms thus became badges of their military superiority.[56]

On another occasion the men of the 30th USCI exploited inexperienced white troops. Shortly after the White House Landing incident, Bowley's men were camped next to an Ohio regiment composed of "the very best citizens of the Buckeye State." Not content to live off army rations, these pampered soldiers had their own provisions, which they shared with their black neighbors. Yet this act of generosity did not stop the black soldiers from mocking the Ohio men as they attempted to perform their drill maneuvers. In jest the black soldiers offered advice: "take de same pardner yo' had yisterday" and "Is yo' gwine toe dro'r yo' butler now, honey?" were among the remarks hurled at the Ohio men, who "flushed and shot angry glances at their black tormentors." The tormenting did not end at nightfall. In the darkness an Ohio soldier began singing a sentimental favorite, "Just before the battle, mother," with a "sweet tenor voice," only to be greeted by mock, "comical imitation" from the camp of the 30th USCI. The next day the hapless Ohio men discovered their black neighbors had stolen their "new Springfield rifles" and their "new rubber blankets." The ragged soldier whom they had ridiculed as being "Jim Crow" was now attired in a brand-new uniform, courtesy of his tormentors. "Reckon dem hundred-dazers won't want to see no mo 'black clouds' right away" was his remark as he "complacently surveyed his new suit."[57]

At one level the mockery and theft of the 30th USCI was no different from the friendly banter and indulgence that occurred extensively throughout the Union Army. Yet at another level, the banter of the black soldiers was significant because it marked a new extension of traditional ways of challenging white dominance. Blacks had long used humor and song to subtly ridicule white notions of superiority. Now the attack on white dominance was more open and more assertive. It was the very routine and commonplace nature of the black soldiers' behavior that made it significant. Now they had the confidence to act like other Union veterans and belittle and mock fresh recruits. The scourge of racism had not disappeared, but its potency had been severely reduced by the jocular confidence of the soldiers and the accolades they won for their patriotic performance of military duties.

Bowley affirms his black troops' military prowess by drawing upon two powerful witnesses to comment on their performance. Like a Greek chorus these witnesses are both commentators and participants in the conflict. The power of their testaments rests not so much on what they say but on where they are positioned in the conflict. Bowley's commentators fall into two groups, Union heroes and vanquished rebels.

Before he presents the testimony of the Union heroes Freeman Bowley sets their reports against the harsh background of the war. However, here the scene is not the battlefield, but the hospital tent and the burial ground. It is as if Bowley is calling upon the dead and the maimed to testify to the black soldiers' valor. Their testimony is weighty and cannot be easily dismissed because their lives and bodies have been sacrificed on the altar of the Union. They have paid a high price for their loyalty and patriotism.

On the morning of May 5, 1864, his regiment halted near the Sixth Corps hospital. With some time to spare, the young Bowley "visited the house, which had been taken by the Surgeons as an operating room." There he witnessed a "powerful soldier" with "his leg shattered by a shell" being taken to the operating table "screaming and resisting violently" and shouting, "Oh Doctor, don't take off my leg! I can't be a cripple all my life." After applying "chloroform" the "mangled limb was amputated." Nauseated by this bloody sight Bowley left the house and immediately came upon "a pit" approximately "10 feet long, five feet wide, and four feet deep." It was half-filled with "amputated members of the wounded."[58]

Two days later Bowley discovered a burial site where Union soldiers were being laid. Shocked at discovering among the dead acquaintances from the 37th Massachusetts Volunteers, Bowley and his men paid a ritual tribute to these fallen heroes. In an act of simple reverence he had his men "bring some pine boughs and place over them, that the wet mud might not strike their faces." "With moist eyes" and a heavy heart he turned to be greeted by a tragicomic figure, a veteran from the "old Vermont Brigade," "hopping all around" the cook-fire. Fearing for the soldier's safety Bowley warned him that he could instantly fall and bleed to death. This warning was greeted with the desperate retort of the hungry soldier: "Reckon I might as well bleed to death as starve to death." Immediately the black soldiers divided their meager rations with him, and after he had "ate heartily" they assisted him into an ambulance. As he departed he spoke words of encouragement and support to his black comrades: "Stay with 'em boys; stand by the old flag till the crows come home! I've been pegging at the Johnnies for three years, and I guess I've done 'em more damage than they have me."[59]

Less than one month later, Bowley's men were facing ridicule and mockery from the young "hundred-days men" at White House Landing. Yet this criticism was silenced in a crushing way when the wounded veterans rushed from their hospital tents and praised the black soldiers for their marching. Comments such as "You are marching fine, boys," "That's the style; keep it up," and "Thim black b'yes is marchin foine" echoed through the lines. Such positive endorsement from heroic veterans, in the face of the demeaning comments by raw recruits, made the black soldiers "fairly glow and swell with delight."[60]

Even the rebel prisoners found the sneering of the "hundred-days men" intolerable. They indirectly defended the black soldiers by attacking the credentials of their critics. "If ever you get to the front, young feller, you'll find out that paper collars don't make a soldier," shouted the prisoners to the young mockers. Bowley uses the testimony of rebel prisoners to powerfully endorse the fighting capabilities of the black soldiers. Sometimes this endorsement is mixed with the pain and suffering, as if the wounds themselves are badges of authority that enable the Union and Confederate soldiers to speak with conviction and certainty. This was particularly the case at the Battle of the Crater.[61]

As the black soldiers moved down the covered way towards the crater that had been blown in the rebel lines at Petersburg July 30, 1864, they encountered streams of injured soldiers retreating from the heat of battle. When Bowley's men came upon a group of wounded rebel prisoners, they allayed their fears that they would be massacred. Their compassionate act of giving "cool water" to the enemy evoked the warm messages from some of the prisoners. The black soldiers then met a badly wounded Union captain who was seated on a stretcher and wearing an unruffled countenance. He cheerfully greeted the black soldiers by saying, "Go in my bully black boys!" Even before they had entered the fire of battle, Bowley's men were recognized as noble opponents and honorable allies.[62]

Impressive though the Union captain's exhortation was, it may have been partly a product of Bowley's clouded memory rather than a true representation of the historical record. Like many aging veterans writing about their Civil War experiences, he may have been forgetful. Then again, he may have succumbed to the temptation to reconstruct his recollections in order to support the broader ideological themes of his narrative. If this was the case, then the image of wounded veterans at White House Landing rushing from their hospital tents to line the road and praise black soldiers may be more imaginary than real. The confusion and turmoil of battle may have also contributed to Bowley exaggerating the warm welcome given to black troops as they marched forward into the Crater. Finally, the sympathetic response of rebel prisoners to the black soldiers may have had more to do with their current predicament than with any notions of genuine respect. Yet while the precise accuracy of his narrative is debatable, there is no doubt that Bowley's story shares, along with other Civil War memoirs of his day, a strong focus on the glorious role of the veteran soldier. In fact, Bowley appropriates the myth of the veteran in order to enhance the military standing of the black soldiers, even if at times these same soldiers are characterized by racial stereotyping. It is the veteran soldiers, particularly those who have been wounded in battle, that become the black soldiers' strongest defenders. Their testimony discounts the derision of the raw recruits and short-term soldiers, the "hundred-days men." It is as if the experience of battle transcends racial lines and enables the blindfold of racial prejudice to be at least partially lifted.

In some ways Bowley's focus on the pain and suffering of war, on the pit of dismembered limbs and the screaming soldier on the operating table, stands in contrast to much of the reunionist mythology that imbued the Civil War writing in the last decades of the nineteenth century. Even so, there is no doubt that Bowley employs the literary conventions of pathos and sentimentality when describing the suffering of wounded soldiers. However, when he does so he places the black soldier at the center of the suffering, and this makes his description so markedly different from others. Bowley uses sentiment to emphasize the patriotism and moral fortitude of the black soldier. Yet his commentary extends beyond the ranks of the black soldiers to the meaning of the war itself. Bowley uses the black soldier to explore the deeper meaning of the war and reveal manhood being formed in combat. It is as if the fire of battle burns off the dross of civilization and reveals the true human spirit. By describing the actions of his soldiers in the hellholes of war, at the graveyard, and on the bloody Crater battlefield, he underlines the nobility of their cause. Led by young white officers, the men of the 30th USCI are representing the Republic. They are "Union" soldiers in every sense of the word. Through simple acts of kindness they helped to bind the nation together. They shared their scarce rations with the old, crippled Vermont soldier at the graveside and their precious water with wounded rebels in the covered way en route to the Crater. It takes a soldier to recognize another soldier, and these wounded veterans recognized the moral worth of the black troops. Such recognition was a strong impetus for the black soldier to move forward in defense of the Union.[63]

Early in December 1865, approximately eight months after the war had ended, the 30th USCI finished its tour of duty with the army of occupation in North Carolina. Bowley's men began the first part of their long, arduous journey to Baltimore traveling by open barge along the Dismal Swamp canal. "Cold" and "dirty," the men "huddled together" to keep warm. With thoughts of home and loved ones foremost in their minds they ached for peace and the joys of civilian life. Yet for these tired veterans there was one last battle to be won. As the barge slowly made its way into the port of Norfolk, Virginia, it passed by a large man-of-war in midstream. Upon seeing Bowley's men huddled in the open barge, the sailors on board the ship began to mock the soldiers "unmercifully." "An' is the rest of yez regiment down South a'pickin' cotton?" shouted one Irish sailor. "Quick as a flash," Sgt. Bob Bowen launched the attack. Taking the regiment's colors from their cases, he held them up. "The flags were tattered, torn, bullet riddled," and "stained with blood and powder." Then Sgt. Bowen shouted out, "Sixteen hundred men have followed dem colors, an' we'se alls dat's leff. Dem colors was at Fort Fisher, an' de line didn't break an' run back!" The last sentence struck home hard; it was a "center-shot" because during the second attack on Fort Fisher the "naval assaulting force had been broken and forced back to the beach." The sight of the battle-torn colors and Bowen's proud reply left the sailors stunned. For a moment they "gazed at the war-worn flags," and "then they cheered long and loud." This triumph was not recorded in the annals of war, yet Bowley and his men knew that they had won an important victory.[64]

The black soldiers of Co. H had adapted well to army life. They had used their cultural traditions, their humor, songs, and stories to help them learn the military routines and repel the barbs of the mockers. They had won the praise of their officers and the support of Union war heroes who carried with them the scars of battle. Even some of the rebel prisoners had recognized them as soldiers and worthy opponents. On the battlefields of the South they had demonstrated their love of freedom and their patriotic commitment to the Union. But for these veterans sailing into Norfolk harbor the conflict was not yet over; it had taken a different form. Slavery was dead, but racist stereotyping remained. In the years following the war they had to devise new ways to preserve their freedom and hold on to their national citizenship, which they had fought so hard to win during the bloody Civil War.

Remembering Slavery and the Civil War

The Civil War was a revolutionary conflict that liberated the slaves and gave a new birth of freedom. Yet by the last decades of the nineteenth century the revolutionary spirit of the Civil War had lost much of its fire. The faded memory of the meaning of the war was, at least in part, a product of the aging process. As veterans grew older, memories became more clouded and confused. However, prevailing cultural myths and conventions also played their part in distorting the memory of the war. David Thelen reminds us that "memory is constructed, not reproduced" and that this construction is "not made in isolation but in conversations with others" in a broad social context. Both David Donald and Gerald Linderman have argued that in an effort to alleviate their personal failings, pain, and guilt, the old men who formed the Civil War generation strenuously endeavored to reconfigure the social memory of the war in a way that unified the nation. In his seminal work on the memory of the Civil War, *Race and Reunion: The Civil War in American Memory*, David Blight argues that the dual impact of the persuasive power of the Lost Cause mythology and the universal celebration of the veteran clouded national perceptions of the meaning of the war by hiding the treachery of the Southern traitor and marginalizing the role of the slave and the black soldier in the war. In the great plethora of Civil War narratives that were written at the end of the century blacks were written out of their nation's history.[65]

Like all writers constructing their memoirs, Bowley used this literary form to help him order his personal experiences and manufacture personal truth.

The writing process validated his war experiences, sharpened his sense of self, and gave him a strong sense of moral superiority and clarity. He never wavered in the righteousness of his cause. Throughout his life he returned again and again to his memory of the war. Yet his writing, in common with other reflective narratives, was not exclusively personal. True to his craft, Bowley was writing to engage the reader in new ways. The reader became the subject as well as the object of his writing. He wanted the reader, invariably the Civil War veteran, to enter into the author's experience, to share his commitment to the nation, and, in a figurative way, fight his war. Therefore, as well as writing to inscribe his honorable service on the nation's historical record, he was also writing to reaffirm the Union victory and to celebrate the restoration of the nation on Northern terms. In this sense Bowley's memoir was celebrating what John R. Neff has called "the Cause Victorious." In many ways he also was writing to give voice to the keenly felt, but largely marginalized, grievances of black veterans and concerned USCT officers. This intent places him in the company of other, more eminent figures who continued to champion the war as a conflict that brought a new birth of freedom to the nation. Bowley may have lacked the literary merit of Albion W. Tourgee and the ideological fervor of Frederick Douglass, but his narrative was permeated with authority and influence. This was because it gave voice to two groups of indomitable but largely forgotten soldiers, the black troops and their officers, and the Union prisoners of war.

In the process of constructing his memoir Bowley resurrected the racial dimensions of the conflict. His recollections vividly describe the cruelty of slavery and condemn the treachery of Southern secessionists. Written in a spirit of reconciliation, Bowley's narrative offers a version of the war that retains the abolitionist spirit of the conflict. Yet, at the same time, he also challenges the authenticity and integrity of the nation's memory.[66]

Bowley's Civil War narratives provide an interesting commentary on historical memory and changing perceptions of the war. Written in the first person over a 30-year period, Bowley's writings use various literary forms for very different readerships. His work was first published in 1870 in the popular California magazine, the *Overland Monthly and Out West Magazine*. In an effort to correct the historical record and celebrate his patriotism, Bowley, a faithful member of the Lincoln Post of the California Commandery of the Grand Army of the Republic, presented papers at veteran reunions and had these papers published in the Military Order of the Loyal Legion of the United States publications. His story was extensively serialized in the veteran's weekly newspaper, the *National Tribune*, and even appeared in an abbreviated, sanitized version as a children's book, *A Boy Lieutenant*, published by the Henry Altemus Company in 1906. Along with these public versions, he also reproduced variations of his story in the petitions he made to the U.S. government for a Medal of Honor. Bowley's story, then, is reinterpreted over time for a variety of readers. At each stage of this rewriting process, some subtle changes are made to accommodate the demands of the particular readership and the nuances of the age. Like a mosaic built up over a long period, Bowley's war story reflects the meaning of the war at different points of time. The value of Bowley's story rests not only with its incremental construction, but also in the way it is told. A former reporter with the *Springfield Republican* newspaper in Massachusetts, Bowley tells his story with the intensity of the trained observer. Yet what makes his story unique is not the vivid description, but the way he encapsulates in his story the personal stories of the men serving under him. The soldiers that served under Lt. Freeman Bowley in Co. H emerge from the pages of his narrative as characters with individual traits and feelings. His men have names, family backgrounds, and personalities. Social equality was not an issue because Bowley always believed he was socially and culturally superior to his men. Even so, it was precisely because Bowley was able to transcend class and racial boundaries and share a spirit of camaraderie with his men that his black soldiers are an integral part of his story. Bowley's tale is not an isolated tale of a lone hero, but a shared story. The title of his memoir, "A Boy Lieutenant in a Black Regiment," suggests that he saw military service as a rite of passage to manhood. During the course of his education he learned lessons from the black soldiers and the Southern slaves. Indeed, Bowley's encounter with slavery left an indelible mark on his education.[67]

The Union soldiers who marched into the South had little understanding of slavery. Many saw the Southern landscape as an essentially alien and exotic place, inhabited at least in part by a strange race of inferior and submissive Negro slaves. Freeman S. Bowley's attitude towards slavery was in some ways similar to that of many other Union soldiers. Although he opposed slavery, he was no fervent abolitionist. He joined the USCT mainly because it was the best pathway to a commission. Yet unlike most other soldiers in the Union Army, Bowley's service with the USCT led him to understand slavery in a unique way. In camp Lt. Bowley saw the mark of slavery on the character of his men, while on the march he gained valuable assistance from slaves who served as spies and guides.[68]

Bowley's first and most immediate encounter with slavery was in the customs of the men. Intrigued by the folkways of his Maryland former slaves, Bowley found the legacy of slavery somewhat comical and amusing. The slave dialect amused him, and the so-called "quaint sayings of the men" were "all new and novel" to him. However, his benign interest in slavery changed when he discovered that his men would rather disobey orders than abandon long-held beliefs. On two separate occasions the men in Bowley's company abandoned their lines when they were attacked by Confederate ghosts.[69]

Bowley's first encounter with Virginia slavery occurred when he was lost behind enemy lines with a party of his soldiers. It was a desperate situation because he knew that "in case of capture," his "white skin would not save" him "from being hung to one of the live-oak trees which abounded in this country." Bowley and his men were saved from this fate by the actions of an old slave, who was drawn to the lost party by the actions of Pvt. John Jackson, nicknamed "Monkey." Monkey, a former slave from Frederick County, Maryland, drew the old slave towards Bowley by employing secret slave signal calls he had learned during his days of servitude. As the slave approached, Bowley and his men were horrified to discover that he had been hamstrung by having his tendons cut away just above the heel. "I runned away an' w'en dey kotched me dey ham-strung me," explained the old man. Joyfully proclaiming that he was "mighty glad to do sumfin foh de Linkum men," the old man drew a map to guide them safely back to Union lines.

This meeting with an old slave was significant because it brought home to Bowley in an immediate and personal manner the plight of the Southern slave and the cruel treachery of the rebels. Bowley's convictions about the corrupting power of slavery were confirmed in a most persuasive way in an incident that Bowley deleted from his memoir but included in his early published writings (see Appendix).

Shortly after his encounter with the old hamstrung slave, Bowley and his party set out on the route that had been prescribed for them. During the course of his journey he discovered "a log-and-splint house, situated in the middle of a corn-field." Located near the house were two USCT soldiers, stripped of their uniforms and "suspended from an oak tree, by their thumbs." A group of rebel soldiers was busy whipping their captives. Bowley and his men could hear the "whiz and crack" of the black snake-whip "as it struck and see the blood follow the stroke." Accompanied by "a dirty-looking female," some "tallow-faced children," and "large, ferocious, yellow dogs," the rebel soldiers relished their tasks. Launching a surprise attack, Bowley quickly overcame the rebels. Immediately, roles reversed, with Bowley allowing his men to tie up the offending rebels. Thirty-nine lashes were well laid on their backs. Bowley had to exercise all of his military authority to save the rebel captives from a lynching. The rebels were being punished for being the cruel instruments of slavery. Slavery seemed to debase the South and its people. Bowley could see the lines of slavery crudely cut into the face of the debauched woman who had shouted encouragement to the rebel soldiers as they went about their cruel task. "Clad in a dirty cotton dress, hair uncombed, face unwashed, feet bare, a snuff-stick in her mouth, and the snuff-juice running down her chin, she presented a picture for 'hirelings' to gaze upon." She captured Bowley's attention because she epitomized the impact of slavery on the womenfolk of the South. Just as it had brutalized the men, so it had also corrupted their womenfolk. Unlike the women of the North, this Southern woman was not the harbinger of civilization or domesticity.[70]

Captured at the Battle of the Crater, Bowley's next firsthand encounter with slavery occurred while he was a prisoner of war in Richland Jail in Columbia, South Carolina. From his jail cell he witnessed the sale of slaves on "the steps of the Courthouse, only a block away." Close by was the "negro calaboose" where runaway slaves were held and routinely whipped. The screams of the suffering slaves unnerved the prisoners. Bowley reported that "these sights never failed to arouse our greatest indignation, and the shrill screams of some poor negro woman crying, 'Oh-h-h, Lordy!' would start a fearful stream of maledictions from the profane ones of our number." Even in prison Bowley discovered that the themes of the suffering and loyalty were inextricably linked. Slaves were punished for their expressions of freedom and their loyalty to the Union. When Bowley informed a slave laborer working in the prison that he had formerly commanded a company of black soldiers, the slave replied that he would "like mighty well to be one ob dem." Ever faithful to the cause, this slave regularly smuggled newspapers into the prison for Bowley. Eventually he was caught and "given a 100 lashes on the bare back." He returned to his labor "stiff and sore" but not demoralized from his "terrible beating." Indeed, as he passed by Bowley he defiantly remarked, "Dey may kill dis nigger, but dey can't make him hate de Yankees."[71]

Bowley's description of the "faithful negro" who smuggled newspapers into the prison conforms to some of the conventions found in the great body of Civil War soldiers' memoirs and prisoner of war narratives published in the last decades of the nineteenth century. In these narratives Southern blacks are described as benign African folk who are trapped by docility, primitive superstitions, and customs. Ann Fabian reminds us that the Civil War "prisoner's stories can be read as artifacts of racism." The way the prisoners told their tales "helped to reconstruct racism for postwar white Americans." Incorporating imagery borrowed from the slave narratives, the prisoners recreated caricatures of Southern blacks that describe them as being exotic, comical, docile, anonymous, and generously devoted to the Union. Bowley's narrative is also laced by some of this racist imagery. Not even "100 lashes" could turn Bowley's "big, powerful black fellow" from the Union. Yet Bowley's depiction of black defiance is no simple projection of conventional literary form. It is far more complex than that.

When Bowley escaped from imprisonment in Raleigh, North Carolina, he headed straight for the "negro quarters" and entered the home of a black couple in order to "apply for assistance." Yet only little, reluctant assistance was forthcoming. Even when Bowley meets "friendly negroes" the relationships that develop are hardly conventional. The old guide who drew a map on the road to guide Bowley's lost platoon back to the safety of Union lines may have been an anonymous figure, but he is certainly not a comical, docile, or intellectually inferior stereotype. He has not passively accepted his enslaved state; his love of freedom is powerfully cut into his hamstrung body. Moreover, it is the former slave, Pvt. "Monkey" Jackson, who calls him forth, wins the old man's trust, and gains the valuable knowledge that ultimately leads the lost party to safety. In this incident Lt. Bowley is little more than a passive observer.

Bowley's depiction of Southern blacks is complex. While it contains some of the racial imagery found in other prisoner of war narratives, it is also distinctly different and less discriminatory. Perhaps this is because his service with black soldiers encouraged him to see them in a different and more positive light. After all, Monkey Jackson may have been a comical figure, but he was also a brave and patriotic Union soldier as well. Military service tempered Bowley's racism.[72]

The callous barbarism of war was seldom described in the great collections of Civil War memoirs that were being published towards the end of the century. In an era that celebrated the nobility of the manly veteran, stories of murder, massacre, and mayhem were seldom heard. The horrific tragedy of war is described in terms of personal suffering and injury, but the wanton cruelty of war, its vindictive, revengeful nature, was forgotten. Yet this aspect of the war remained fresh in Bowley's memory, and it filled the pages of his memoir.[73]

Freeman Bowley's combat experience was largely confined to one battle, the

Battle of the Crater. Although a Union defeat, this battle marked a defining point in his military service. What impressed him the most was not so much the heat of battle but the racial dimensions of the conflict. The Battle of the Crater stands infamously as the most extensive massacre of black troops during the war. Bowley was aware of these outrages and highlighted them in his memoir. Indeed, after he has described his own heroic role in the battle and his capture, he interrupts the flow of his personal narrative to devote a whole section to battle casualties and eyewitness accounts of rebel cruelty. Included in this chapter is a Confederate veteran's graphic description of the murder of a black soldier who was attempting to surrender.[74]

Bowley challenged the reunion myths of his day by selectively calling on figments of Confederate memory to validate his story and uncover past injustices. He is setting the record straight, rewriting history in a way that places the black soldiers and their officers at the center of the conflict. Of course, by embellishing the black soldiers' role he was drawing attention to his heroic leadership and placing himself in the heat of the battle. Bowley was unashamedly aware of this, and this formed the basis of his claims to be awarded a Medal of Honor. Yet Bowley's story was no simple exercise in self-aggrandizement. Joseph T. Glatthaar is correct to claim that combat forged bonds of comradeship between white officers and the black soldiers who served under them. In the case of Bowley, not even a humiliating defeat could break these bonds.[75]

Although Bowley's recollection of the Civil War challenged many of the prevailing perceptions of the war and its meaning, his memoir adopts some of the literary forms and themes of the mythology literature. In his writings he celebrates the honorable and manly exploits of the Civil War veterans to push forward the theme of sectional reconciliation. He does this particularly effectively when describing the Battle of the Crater. Bowley describes this battle differently from his other combat experiences. It has national symbolic significance as well as personal meaning. He describes the Crater as if it is the crucible of the nation; it is a place where honor codes are challenged and personal courage tested. Representatives of the nation poured into the Crater that had been blasted in the Confederate lines. The symbolic nature of the heroic conflict that occurred there is emphasized by the way Bowley describes, in graphic detail, the fighting qualities of all involved. This was not just a life-and-death struggle between white Northern and Southern troops. African American troops are there, and so too are American Indians. It as is if these minority groups, these despised races, are fighting for their place in the nation's history. Like many contemporary writers, Bowley celebrates the courage of the veteran in order to further sectional reconciliation. It is the experienced soldier, from the North and South, whose noble manhood has survived the test of battle, who can heal the wounds of the nation. Yet Bowley pushes the theme of reconciliation much further than any of his contemporaries by focusing on the heroism of the black soldiers. This is set alongside that of Billy Yank and Johnny Reb in a way that recognizes their manhood and validates their claims for national inclusion. Bowley uses the small, inconsequential incidents in the battle to show that former masters and former slaves can be reconciled by their manly virtue. As Bowley's soldiers waited in the covered way ready to move into the Crater, lines of wounded soldiers passed by them. Following the wounded came 50 prisoners of war. Covered in dirt and showing "signs of having been dug out of the clay," these soldiers were thrown into "the greatest alarm" when they caught sight of the black troops. In desperation they pleaded with their guards, urging them to prevent the niggers bayoneting them. One badly wounded rebel cried out, "don't let the niggers kill me! I can't live long; let me die in peace." "Don't be skeered, we don't kill wounded men," replied a black corporal as he bent down and gave the wounded rebel water from his own canteen and dressed his wounds. The prisoners looked on in amazement. "Here, boy, take these," exclaimed a soldier as he thrust two long plugs of Virginia tobacco into the hand of the black corporal. "God, if I had a million dollars here, you should have it all. He's my young brother, and I never looked for any kindness from any of yo' uns," added the soldier. According to Bowley this "little act" of compassion seemed to restore the confidence of the rebel prisoners, and as they moved further down the Union line one of them shouted, "Good boy, Sam, I hope that you don't catch it to-day."[76]

After being captured at the Crater, Bowley, along with other prisoners of war, was being transported by train to Columbia, South Carolina, when the train was threatened by an unruly mob of civilians. USCT officers were singled out for special reprisals and eventual lynching. The lives of these officers were saved only when one of the Union officers challenged the guards. "Soldiers of Stonewall Jackson's Brigade," shouted the officer. "Shall it be said of you that you stood idly by and saw prisoners captured in battle, murdered by citizens and shealts, who stayed at home, and never heard the sound of cannon or smelt Yankee gunpowder? If you value your good name, save these men from the mob. If they are to die let them die like soldiers!" This appeal to the battle-hardened veterans' manhood and sense of honor had the desired effect, and the USCT officers were soon rescued. Yet even though Bowley was dismissive of the unruly mob, he believed that in the South there remained a core of citizens who retained their moral virtue. While he was being escorted north to Virginia to be placed on parole, Bowley praised the citizens of Raleigh, North Carolina, for supplying the wretched survivors of the Andersonville Prison with food and clothing.[77]

But were these individual acts of compassion also acts of reconciliation? Did they point to an end to the sectional conflict, a new age of harmony and peace? Certainly anecdotal stories of friendship and compassion shown by rebel and Yankee soldiers to each other fill the pages of that vast array of Civil War memoirs that began to appear in the bookshops in the last decade of the nineteenth century. Such stories helped to soften the memory of the war and promote a spirit of sectional reconciliation that was becoming more powerful every day. In one sense Bowley's story belongs to this tradition. Themes of reconciliation are writ large in his memoir. However, there is an important difference. Bowley's theme of reconciliation is racial as well as sectional. The former slaves share their provisions with the wounded rebel prisoners on the battlefield of the Crater, and by this act of generosity they validate their honorable fighting qualities. Recognition is the key element in any process of reconciliation. Before harmony can be restored, before agreement can be reached, each protagonist has to recognize the integrity of the other. Bowley knew this, but he also knew that the best way to tell his story was to wrap it in the conventions of the day that celebrated the noble manhood of the veteran. Throughout his narrative, battle-hardened veterans display manly virtue, while raw recruits and cadet guards exhibit foolish arrogance. There was nothing deceptive or contrived about his use of this literary convention. By celebrating the veteran he was acclaiming his own rise to manhood.

Bowley wrote his text over a 30-year period, and during the writing process he carefully shaped his story so it would enhance his military record and fit the readership of the day. For example, the incident of the black soldiers whipping captured rebel soldiers first appeared a few years after the war had ended, when Bowley was still a young man and the Northern desire for recrimination was strong. It did not appear in the 1899 newspaper version. By this time Bowley was in very poor health, and the spirit of the age was for harmony and reconciliation. Yet he does not completely hide the horrors of slavery. The hamstrung slave who guides Bowley's lost party home is first introduced in the 1899 story. Bowley vividly describes the courageous action of the old slave because it enables him to build on his theme of racial reconciliation. By his action the old man wins for himself a place in the new Union, a place that is implicitly more deserving than any given to his cruel master. The process of forgetting and remembering also occurs when Bowley describes combat on the battlefield. While he vividly describes the heinous horror of the Crater, he deftly avoids his responsibility for building a barricade of dead and dying soldiers. Any admission of his true role in the conflict would tarnish his reputation as a soldier. Significant gaps in his memory occur even when he recounts the more routine duties of military service. For example, he makes no reference to his important role as the regiment's adjutant. This is probably because his poor administration of the soldiers' pay damaged his standing and limited his promotion opportunities. Yet even though Bowley crafted his story over time, the pulse of the narrative remained the same. The black soldiers and their officers are at the center of his story, and their character and heroism are drawn in fine detail. In this respect Bowley's story is somewhat different from the memoirs of other USCT officers. No other line officer has written so extensively or in so much personal detail about his daily routine with black troops.[78]

In his opening address at the Library of Congress Civil War Symposium in November 2002 Gary Gallagher identified three interpretations of Civil War memory: the Lost Cause interpretation, which celebrated Southern antebellum society and Confederate valor, the Reconciliationists' interpretation, which drew upon notions of manly honor to heal sectional wounds, and finally the Unionist interpretation, which celebrated the antislavery impulse of war. Freeman Bowley wrote his memoir in order to bridge the Reconciliationist and Unionist traditions. He refused to believe that sectional reconciliation should be bought at the expense of racial exclusion. Therefore, he used his recollections of the past to challenge current perceptions of the war. By doing so he found himself at the confluence of memory and history. It is this turbulent convergence of personal memory and national history that makes his story so interesting and historically relevant. At one level Bowley's memoir is a simple adventure story, a product of a soldier's memory. But at another, higher level it is a bold attempt to claim for the officers and men of the USCT public acclaim and a place in the historical record of the nation.[79]

Honor in Command

1

A Commission in a Black Regiment

First Lieutenant! Did I hear aright? Yes, there it was on the sheet, written in a bold, round hand. First Lieutenant! I should have a bar on my shoulder-straps, and command the company in the absence of the Captain. The room swam around. I felt as if I was walking on air.

Dedication

At a critical time in the history of this country the boy officers of black regiments, believing it to be their duty, risked social ostracism, dared an ignominious death and cast their lot with a despised race. Under the training of his officer the negro developed the highest soldierly qualities and won imperishable renown. To these boy officers this story is affectionately dedicated by their comrade—The Author.[1]

Introduction

An apology seems necessary for a serial which contains only the simple narrative of an obscure individual, who took a most humble part in the great war of rebellion.

Of the making of war books there has been no end. The leaders have fought their battles over, wielding the pen as vigorously as ever they wielded the sword; the drummer-boy and the private have related their recollections; regimental histories without number have shown the heroic part taken by particular regiments, and how the day, the battle, the army, or perhaps the whole Nation were saved by the devotion and sacrifice of this regiment; many States have published histories of the part taken by their troops; the Confederate veterans have shown themselves to be good writers, and abundantly able to take care of the Southern side of the question; novelists have found in the civil war a never-failing source from which to supply their imaginations. Amid this great mass of history, story and romance, there is one portion that has generally escaped notice of the public, and one which the rising generation knows almost nothing; viz., The Colored Troops.

In the Winter of 1863–64, when the Federal Government was offering every inducement to volunteers to enlist in the Union armies, and when State officials were exercising all their efforts to fill their respective quotas, a new auxiliary appeared—the colored volunteer; 166 regiments, containing 178,975 colored men, were enlisted and mustered into the service of the United States.[2] Fully 90 per cent of these troops were enrolled during the last year of the war, and a greater portion of them after the massacre at Fort Pillow, April 12, 1864.[3] The number of deaths among these colored soldiers was 36,847, which, when the short time of service is taken into consideration, shows a much greater percentage death rate than that of the white troops.[4]

All of the colored regiments were officered by whites, young men, the greater part of whom had not even attained their majority. In addition to the perils of battle which hang over an officer commanding raw and inexperienced troops, these young officers were made the objects of a special act of the Confederate Congress which proclaimed "that every white person, being a commissioned officer, or acting as such, who shall command the negroes or mulattoes in arms against the Confederate States, or who shall arm, train, or organize them for service, shall be deemed as inciting servile insurrection, and shall, if captured, be put to death or otherwise punished, as a court-martial may direct."[5]

The experience of these young officers has never been related; the story of their training and transforming the simple, timid, superstitious negro to the brave and fearless soldier, whose charge was the wonder and admiration of the whole military world, whose steadiness and staying qualities were tested on many a bloody battlefield, and whose loyalty to the old flag could never be shaken—that story has never been told.

That the young people of the present day may learn something of the part taken by the boy officers of black regiments during those war-time days this true narrative has been written.

During the month of February, 1864, two regiments of Massachusetts volunteers, who had re-enlisted for another three years—"veteranized," it was called—came home of their furlough of 30 days. A fine reception was given them by the citizens of Worcester.[6]

At that time I was a cadet in the Highland Military Academy, and our cadet company formed part of the veteran's escort. With the rest, I marched into the hall where the formal proceedings were held, and there I saw a sight that thrilled me through and through.[7]

One of the regiments which was being received was the 21st Mass., whose former Color-Sergeant, Thomas Plunket [Plunkett], had lost both his arms and won an immortal name at the battle of Fredericksburg. It was told of him that, during the battle, a shell from the enemy burst directly in the National colors, the flag which he was carrying, smashing and nearly tearing off both his arms. The fragments of shell wounded one arm near the shoulder, and the other between the wrist and elbow. As he fell on the flag, drenching it with his blood, he called to his comrades to hold up the colors. The same shell killed the Corporal who was carrying the State flag. The flags were quickly taken up and carried with the advancing line. When his comrades lifted him upon a stretcher, he bade them put him down and save some of the wounded who were not so badly hurt.

"Leave me boys," he said; "I am done for; save the men who are not mortally wounded."

But his comrades carried him off, and, after long months of suffering, he had recovered sufficiently to be present at the reception.

The Mayor of Worcester, led him upon a platform, and addressing the regiment, said:

"Soldiers of the 21st, I present to you, again, your old colors, and your old Color-Sergeant, who stained them with his blood!"

As Plunket [Plunkett] advanced, supporting as best he could, with his helpless stumps, the very flag that he had carried at Fredericksburg, a wild cheer went up from the veterans, and tears ran freely down their bronzed faces. When I heard that great patriotic shout I resolved then and there that I too would have a part in the stirring scenes of the war, and that my name should be borne on the roll of the country's defenders.[8]

How I carried out this resolution I shall tell you in these pages, and what I am about to narrate is throughout the plain and true story of my own experiences.

Not long before this incident my father had returned to Worcester from the army, his health broken down by the Gettysburg campaign. I was an only child, and I knew that my parents had made a great sacrifice to keep me at the Academy. I knew, too, that if my father's health did not improve, I must soon leave school and go to work. If I enlisted as a private, the $400 bounty which volunteers then received would not go far in those high-priced times. I was almost 18 years old, and had been thoroughly trained in tactics at the Academy. In my enthusiasm for the military art, I had purchased military books and read and studied them carefully, often into the late hours of the night. I had noticed every move and motion of the veteran regiments, and had detected several inaccuracies in the officers' handling of their men. I was confident that if I could only get a commission, I could do as well as they did. But how could I get it? I knew no one who had influence at the Statehouse in Boston, and the new regiments forming were all fully officered.[9]

As I pondered over the matter, still under the influence of my enthusiasm, I came upon something which gave me a clew to success. Congress had passed a bill providing for the enlistment of colored men, to be organized into regiments and to be known as the United States Colored Troops. These regiments were to be officered by white men, the majority of whom were to be deserving soldiers recommended for promotion. Candidates for commissions in this corps were to be examined by a board of Army officers convening at Washington. Convinced that here was my opportunity, I wrote to the Secretary of War, asking permission to appear for examination for the position of Second Lieutenant in one of the new colored regiments.

I gave my age as 18, and my conscience smote me a little as I wrote this, for I still lacked two months of that age. There came to me, almost as soon as a reply could be received, a large official envelope, which I opened with a beating heart. It was an official blank of the War Department, giving permission to appear before the Examination Board at Washington, signed by order of Edwin M. Stanton, Secretary of War. My name was written in the blank space and underscored by a line of red ink.[10]

Full of delight and confidence, I showed the letter to my father. He flatly declared that I should not go. He had lost his health, he said, in the service of his country, and one was enough from a family so small as ours. He objected, too, to my entering a black regiment, for he feared that if I fell into the hands of the Confederates nothing more would be ever heard from me. Moreover, he did not believe that I could pass for Second Lieutenant.

Then I argued the case with him, telling him how much I could help with my pay as a commissioned officer, and how, if I remained at home, I might be drafted and forced to go to the front as a conscript. But these arguments failed to move him in the least. At last I told him the story of Serg't Plunket [Plunkett] and the flag at Mechanics Hall, and the intense desire with which it had filled me to serve my country.

My father listened with flushed face and shining eyes. At last he said: "Well, if I were well again I should go back with those boys. I can't bear to let you go, but if you are bound to do so, and want to try for a commission, I will help you."

Fig. 1.1. "The President was busily writing at his desk, and did not even look up when we entered." *National Tribune*, April 20, 1899.

Next morning I started for Washington. On the train were two fellow cadets who were going to visit their father, a member of Congress.[11] This gentleman met us at Washington and took us to see many things that interested me greatly. We went to the White House, where the card of my host obtained for us admission to President Lincoln's room. I shall never forget the smallest occurrence of that visit. The President was busily writing at his desk, and did not even look up when we entered. Seated on one side of the room were a lady and gentleman. After a few moments the President laid down his pen and turned to the lady. "Well, madam, what is it?" he said.

She stepped to the desk and said something in a low tone.

"Apply to Gen. Augur, commanding the District, madam," the President answered.[12]

"But he refused to give me the pass to Richmond," said the lady.

"Then I can't help you," said Mr. Lincoln. "I am sorry, but I never interfere with the Generals. That is all. Good-day."

At a movement of his hand a colored servant opened the door and bowed the lady out into the hall.

"Now, Mr. ______, what can I do for you?" said the President, addressing the gentleman, who was seated with his back to us. As the man rose, our host told us that he was a member of Congress. He turned, and we saw that his face was cut and battered, as if in a street fight.

"Why, what has happened to you?" inquired President Lincoln kindly.

"Mr. President," began the Congressman,—his voice pitched high, as if he was addressing the House of Representatives,—"I am here to ask of you the release of a young man whose family are personal friends of mine. This young man left his home in Baltimore and entered the Confederate army. Your troops have captured him; he is now at Point Lookout, a prisoner. This morning, going down to the wharf at Baltimore to see some friends off, I missed my footing and fell into the dock. My face was badly cut by the ice, as you see. I narrowly escaped with my life; but Mr. President, such was my anxiety for this young man, that, with my face bleeding, I have come to you for an order for his release."

The man held out his hand as if he expected the order for the release would be at once forthcoming.

"Nothing easier," said the President. "Just have your young man take the oath of allegiance, and he will be released. It does not require any order from me."

"But, Mr. President, his family does not wish him to take that oath."

"Then he will have to stay there like any other prisoner until he is exchanged," said Mr. Lincoln. "If he takes the oath he will be released at once, and we won't bother him as long as he behaves himself; if he takes the oath and goes into the Confederate lines, and we catch him again, he will certainly be shot."

"But Mr. President, I demand! I insist," said the Congressman, now greatly excited.

"Now, don't get agitated and forget yourself, sir," said the President severely; "for if you do I shall call the guard and have you put out."

The servant opened the door and bowed politely. The Congressman retired, crestfallen.

At last we were introduced to the President. He shook hands with us, and spoke a few kind words to each. I have no more treasured recollection than the memory of the strong, manly clasp of that big hand, and the kindly expression of the honest, rugged face.

The next morning I reported for my examination. Several applicants were there, and the clerk informed me that probably it would be two or three days before I would be examined. Most of those waiting were soldiers, and nearly all were young men. As soon as they were called into the adjoining room for examination, they turned pale to a man; and after a time they reappeared with flushed faces. Before long the clerk of the board came out and informed each of the decision in his case. If the applicant had been successful, he was sent to the Surgeon for medical examination; if he had been rejected, he retired, and we saw him no more.

Those who passed were divided into three classes, according to the merit which they appeared to show, and from those who had passed in the first class the first selections were made. It was better to pass as First Lieutenant in the first class, than as Captain in the third.

Every man was eagerly questioned when he returned from the examination room, by the waiting applicants. One young soldier, who it seemed to me would obtain at least a Captaincy, was rejected.

"What was the matter?" I asked him.

"I couldn't explain about muster-rolls and company papers," he said.

This statement struck terror to my heart. The tactics, for the "school of the soldier" to brigade evolutions, I had at my tongue's end, but of muster-rolls, reports of ordnance, camp and garrison equipage, final statements, descriptive lists and company accounts I knew next to nothing. I was already practically rejected, and pictured to myself the shame of returning home defeated. The fact that none but my parents knew the object of my visit to Washington, afforded me no consolation whatever.

But my name had not yet been called; there might be time to prepare myself.

I rushed out of the room, and found a book-store where military books were sold. Rummaging there for something which bore upon the subject which I wished to study, I presently found a little volume which was entitled "The Company Clerk: What to Do, and How to Do It." I bought the book and hastened back to my room at the hotel.[13]

It was 4 o'clock in the morning before I lay down the "Company Clerk," but by that time I had committed to memory most of its instructions, and had studied out and mastered its blank forms. The next day, in a corner of the examining office, I still studied and waited. On the afternoon of the third day my name was called. Entering the examining room, I saw Gen. Silas Casey, the President of the Board, seated at the end of a long table, on each side of which were two Colonels and two Captains. All eyed me sharply as I entered. Gen. Casey gruffly asked my name, age, birthplace, and what was the uniform I wore. His manner was so brusque that I was greatly frightened and trembled violently.

"Young man," he said, "if you should pass this examination and join your regiment, you would expect to go into battle, would you not?"

"Ye—yes, sir," I faltered.

"And do you think, sir, you will be as badly frightened as you are now, sir?"

It stung me, and I answered quickly: "I hope not; I don't think that I can ever be scared any worse."

"Proceed with the examination, Colonel," said the General.

A tall, dark man with eagles on his shoulder-straps, spoke kindly to me, telling me to be seated, and to take my time in answering his questions. Then the examination proceeded. My confidence returned, and my answers came promptly to his questions. I ignored the other examiners, and fixed my gaze in this Colonel's black eyes.

Whether I was right or wrong, he did not correct me. Questions in tactics, mathematics, history, geography, and military papers followed each other in bewildering rapidity. How I blessed that little "Company Clerk."

Gen. Casey interrupted the examination to ask who was the Military Instructor at the Highland Academy, and when I answered "Capt. James Wheeler, formerly of the 4th Inf.," I scored a point without knowing it, for the 4th Inf. was Gen. Casey's old regiment. I was asked to explain certain points in the skirmish drill. Did I know the bugle calls? I did. Could I sound them? No. Did I know what words went with the bugle calls? Some of them. And so on for an hour and a half. Then I was sent to the clerk. After I had waited 10 minutes, he said: "Go in there!" pointing to an adjoining room. If I had been less excited I would have known that I had passed, and was going to the Surgeon for medical examination; but I was too badly flustered to realize the significance of this order.

Entering the room, I found the Surgeon, a gray-haired, gentleman in spectacles, reading a newspaper.

He looked up. "Take off all your clothing," he said, and resumed his reading.

I obeyed, and stood waiting in a very uncomfortable way. When the doctor had finished reading his article, he gave me a searching physical examination. Then he said: "Put on your clothing, and report to the clerk."

I went to that official, feverish with anxiety to learn my fate. He was exasperatingly slow. He wrote out my full name and postoffice address. Then he said: "You have passed as First Lieutenant, first class. Go home and get ready. In about two weeks you will get your appointment."[14]

First Lieutenant! Did I hear aright? Yes, there it was on the sheet, written in a bold, round hand. First Lieutenant! I should have a bar on my shoulder-straps, and command the company in the absence of the Captain.

The room swam around. I felt as if I was walking on air. An hour later I was on the train bound for home. How slowly the train seemed to travel.

2

Joining the 30th United States Colored Infantry in the Field

I raised my cap in answer to the salute, and took my place in the line of file-closers, passing by the left of the company. How black the men were. I never imagined that men could be so black. No wonder that the Confederates called them "smoked Yankees."

When the train arrived in Worcester, I made all haste for my home, and bursting into the house exclaimed: "Well, mother, I am Uncle Sam's man now!"

She turned pale, but forcing a smile said: "I don't believe you have passed."

"Oh, but I have, though," I exclaimed eagerly, "and passed as First Lieutenant too!"

My father came in, and to him I repeated my statement. At first his face wore an incredulous look, but seeing from my manner that I was speaking the truth, he shut his lips tightly. To him, an old soldier, the responsibilities, trials and temptations of the position I was about to assume were all apparent, and while he was proud that his son had been deemed fitting for such a position, he well knew how my youth and inexperience would weigh against me. He asked me many questions regarding the examination, and then remarking that we must get my outfit ready at once, sat down and made out a list of the articles necessary for my equipment.

The following week was a busy one. The new uniform was ordered; a sword, belt, sash, revolver, haversack and canteen purchased. My mother would have fitted me out with supplies enough to have loaded a baggage-wagon, but my father's experience as a soldier cut everything down to the service basis.

"A towel, a piece of soap, and an extra pair of stockings are all you want to carry with you," my father insisted. "Your valise will go with the baggage-wagons, and the chances are you won't see it once in two months."

Getting out his old knapsack, he showed me how a knapsack should be packed, and how the straps should fit the man, so as to make the soldier's burden carry as easily as possible.

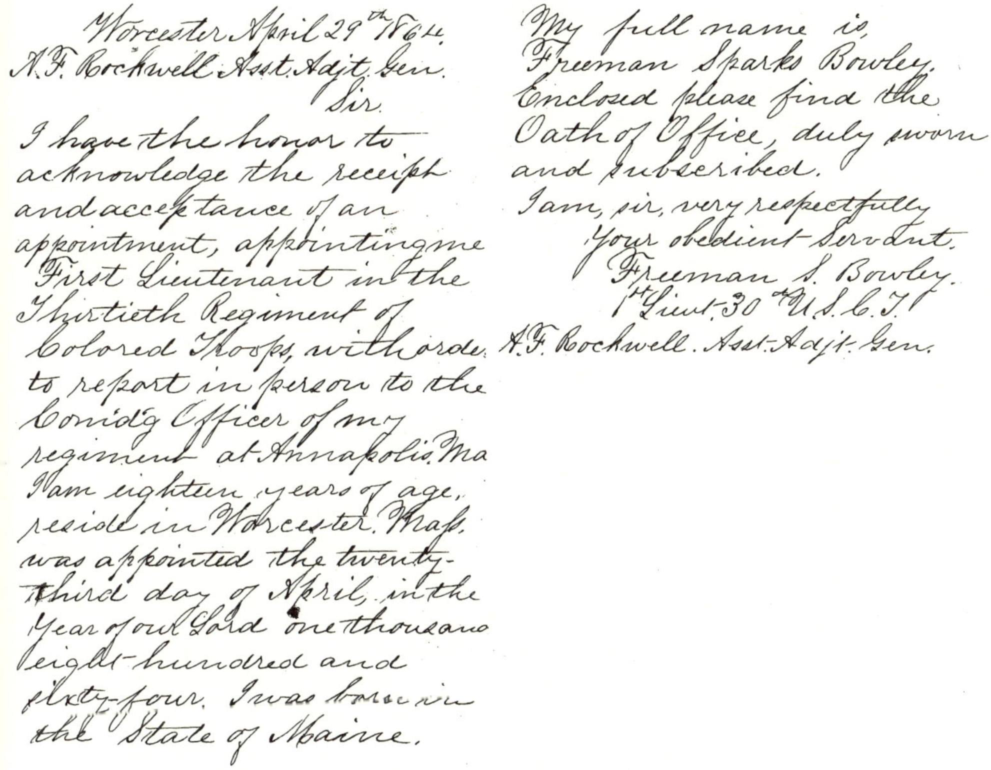

Worcester April 29th 1864.
A. F. Rockwell Asst. Adjt. Gen.
Sir.
I have the honor to acknowledge the receipt and acceptance of an appointment, appointing me First Lieutenant in the Thirtieth Regiment of Colored Troops, with order to report in person to the Comd'g Officer of my regiment at Annapolis, Md.
I am eighteen years of age, reside in Worcester, Mass. was appointed the twenty-third day of April, in the year of our Lord one thousand eight hundred and sixty-four. I was born in the State of Maine.
My full name is, Freeman Sparks Bowley.
Enclosed please find the Oath of Office, duly sworn and subscribed.
I am, sir, very respectfully
Your obedient Servant.
Freeman S. Bowley.
1st Lieut. 30th U.S.C.T.
A. F. Rockwell. Asst. Adjt. Gen.

Fig. 2.1. Freeman Bowley's letter confirming his acceptance of his commission. Letters Received, B-561 1864, ser. 360, Colored Troops Division, National Archives.

I paid some farewell visits, among them one to a rosy-cheeked lass named Flora, whose brother was a Sergeant in the 37th Mass., in the old Sixth Corps. Many messages were given me to deliver to soldiers in the Army of the Potomac, and I promised to see all the parties interested if possible. When the uniform came home, it was necessary, of course, to array the new Lieutenant in all his military toggery and have his photograph taken.[1]

During the third week my appointment came. With delight I read my name and the official information that the President of the United States, reposing special trust and confidence in my patriotism, valor, fidelity and ability, had appointed me a First Lieutenant in the 30th United States Regiment of Colored Troops. Accompanying the appointment was a formidable oath of allegiance,

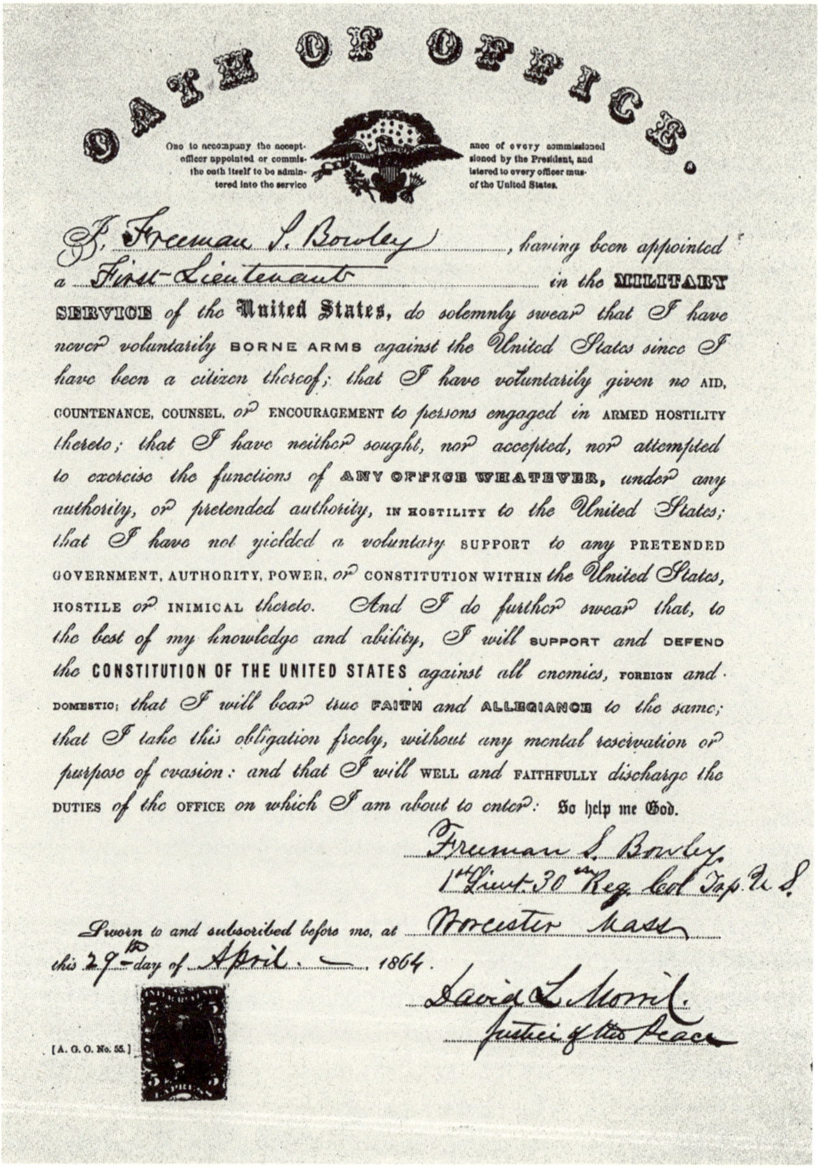

OATH OF OFFICE.

One to accompany the acceptance of every commissioned officer appointed or commissioned by the President, and the oath itself to be administered to every officer mustered into the service of the United States.

I, Freeman S. Bowley, having been appointed a First-Lieutenant in the MILITARY SERVICE of the United States, do solemnly swear that I have never voluntarily BORNE ARMS against the United States since I have been a citizen thereof; that I have voluntarily given no AID, COUNTENANCE, COUNSEL, or ENCOURAGEMENT to persons engaged in ARMED HOSTILITY thereto; that I have neither sought, nor accepted, nor attempted to exercise the functions of ANY OFFICE WHATEVER, under any authority, or pretended authority, IN HOSTILITY to the United States; that I have not yielded a voluntary SUPPORT to any PRETENDED GOVERNMENT, AUTHORITY, POWER, or CONSTITUTION WITHIN the United States, HOSTILE or INIMICAL thereto. And I do further swear that, to the best of my knowledge and ability, I will SUPPORT and DEFEND the CONSTITUTION OF THE UNITED STATES against all enemies, FOREIGN and DOMESTIC; that I will bear true FAITH and ALLEGIANCE to the same; that I take this obligation freely, without any mental reservation or purpose of evasion: and that I will WELL and FAITHFULLY discharge the DUTIES of the OFFICE on which I am about to enter: So help me God.

Freeman S. Bowley
1st Lieut. 30th Reg. Col. Trp. U. S.

Sworn to and subscribed before me, at Worcester Mass
this 29th day of April — 1864.

David L. Morril.
Justice of the Peace

[A. G. O. No. 55.]

Fig. 2.2. Freeman Bowley's Oath of Office. Letters Received, B-561 1864, ser. 360, Colored Troops Division, National Archives.

Fig. 2.3. "My father's soldierly advice was this: 'Your orders are to report at once.'" Freeman S. Bowley, *A Boy Lieutenant*.

which must be sworn to before a notary public, and orders to report at once to the commanding officer of the regiment at Annapolis, Md.[2]

With a desire to show my new uniform and shoulder-straps, I thought that I might take two or three days to myself, but my father's soldierly advice was this: "Your orders are to report at once. Get ready and leave to-night on the 8 o'clock train."

It would be much easier, he explained, to join the regiment before it left for the field. Gen. Grant has assumed command of the armies and an active campaign would surely begin.

Fig. 2.4. "The lump in my throat was almost choking me." Freeman S. Bowley, *A Boy Lieutenant*.

My father's further words of advice were few. "Don't drink too much water," he said; "be gentlemanly with your men, but never familiar. If a man answers you impertinently or refuses to obey, knock him down. You will be scared when you go under fire—every one is; but stay with the line, and you will get your head again after a little."

My parents accompanied me to the railroad station. I had objected to my mother going to see me off, fearing that she might cry and make a scene; but before the train arrived I was shaking with fear lest I would be the one who would make the scene, and present the strange spectacle of an army officer blubbering and crying.

The lump in my throat was almost choking me when I kissed my parents good-by. My mother waved her hand bravely and threw a kiss as the train moved off—and then went home and cried all night.

Now I was on my way to the war. There was no mistake this time. Somehow I did not feel so enthusiastic as I had expected to feel; but I thought the matter over many times during my journey to Annapolis, and deemed myself the most fortunate and happy boy in the world.

At Annapolis I found the Post Headquarters and reported. A young Lieutenant glanced at my orders, turned to a clerk and said: "Send this officer to Washington; his regiment left here last week." The clerk made the order, and the Lieutenant signed it and gave it to me without a word. I noticed the words "14th U.S. Inf.," after his name and title. Evidently he considered an officer of a "nigger regiment" beneath his notice. This was my first introduction to the "Regulars." Afterwards I met many of them and found them courteous, agreeable gentlemen.[3]

Arriving at Washington and reporting, another order was given to me to go to Alexandria. No boat went until the next day, and I was obliged to wait. Reporting at Alexandria, I was told that the colored division was somewhere near Manassas Junction. The train had left; there would not be another until the next day.

I spent the remainder of the day in seeing the sights of Alexandria. I saw the Marshall House, where Col. Elmer Ellsworth, of the New York Fire Zouaves, one of the first victims of the civil war, was killed, and the church where Washington attended. The town was full of soldiers. How swarthy and sunburnt they were.[4]

The sentinels on duty at various places saluted me gravely, but there was a look of amusement from those bronzed fighters which caused me to flush to the ears, for I knew that my new uniform and equipments, and my decidedly green and juvenile air were being criticized by the veterans.

Early the next morning, May 4, the train left Alexandria. It was filled with officers and soldiers returning to their regiments. A Captain of the Provost-Guard was conductor, and inspected every man's papers, for all were under orders or returning from furloughs.

Manassas Junction was reached at noon. Everything here was bustle and activity. Officers rode about on horseback, giving orders to crowds of soldiers and to the drivers of army wagons, which drawn by six mules each, swarmed about the station.

I was at a loss to know what to do. Seeing a colored soldier in the crowd, I observed him closely, and was delighted to see the figure "30" on his cap.

"Where is the camp of the 30th?" I asked.

"Right ober dat-a-way, Lieutenant," the black soldier answered, indicating the direction by a jerk of his chin.

I asked him if he would carry my valise, at the same time producing a bit of the ragged fractional currency which was our only small change at that period.

"Deed an' deed, ob co'se I will, Lieutenant. No truble fer to tote dat walise."

A walk of a mile brought us to the regiment. Here I was at last. Ten lines of shelter-tents marked the position of the 10 companies.

The regimental flags, covered with water-proof cases, and stuck in the ground before the "fly" of a wall-tent, indicated the Colonel's Headquarters.

An officer, no more than 25 years old, who wore a brown moustache, a slouched hat, and army trousers tucked in his boots, was seated on a hardtack-box by a campfire. He wore no shoulder-straps, but a silver eagle was on each shoulder. It was the Colonel.[5]

I saluted and produced my orders. He read them carefully and looked me over. I distinctly saw an expression of disappointment come upon his face.

"This is your first service, I presume?" he said.

"Yes, sir."

"Well," he went on, after a pause, "you won't have to wait long for your initiation."

"I'm glad of that," I answered.

He introduced me to some other officers near, and directed the Adjutant to assign me to Co. H. The order was made, and the Adjutant went with me to the company, and introduced me to Capt. Smith and Lieut. Edgerton.[6]

The Captain spoke pleasantly, but I detected a look of disappointment similar to that which the Colonel's face had worn. It was plain that they considered me too young and boyish. I felt hurt and crushed, but resolved that I would stay with them, and support them to the best of my ability, if I died in doing it.

The drums were beating for battalion drill, and the First Sergeants were forming the companies in front of their tents.

"Come down, and I will introduce you to the company," said the Captain.

As the Captain approached, the Sergeant saluted and reported: "All present or accounted for, sir."

The men stood in two ranks at "shoulder arms," or "carry arms," as it is now called.

Bringing me to the front of the company, the Captain gave the command, "Attention, company! Men, this is Lieut. Bowley. He has been assigned to this

Fig. 2.5. Lt. Delevan Bates, Company I, 121st New York Infantry. Delevan Bates was appointed colonel of the 30th U.S. Colored Infantry in March 1864. RG98S-CWP Collection, United States Army Military History Institute.

Fig. 2.6. Maj. Arthur J. Smith, 30th U.S. Colored Infantry. Capt. Arthur J. Smith was in command of Company H, Bowley's company, when Bowley took up military duties. Smith was promoted to the rank of major in October 1864. RG98S-CWP Collection, United States Army Military History Institute.

company. He will be obeyed and respected accordingly. Present h'arms! Shoulder h'arms! Lieutenant, take your post!"

I raised my cap in answer to the salute, and took my place in the line of file-closers, passing by the left of the company. How black the men were. I never imagined that men could be so black. No wonder that the Confederates called them "smoked Yankees." Perhaps the massing of colors produced this peculiarly intense effect. On the faces of some I detected a sort of quizzical expression. Evidently the men were disappointed, too. This seemed to me a little too much.

The company started for the line where the regiment was forming, but we were not to have the battalion drill that day. A mounted Orderly brought up the Colonel an order. "Pack up and be ready to move in 10 minutes," was the word.

Back to the company streets the men went at a double-quick. Down came the shelter tents, and they were rolled up in a surprisingly short time. An army wagon was at the Colonel's tent. "Better put your valise in there," said Capt. Smith. I did so and it was 10 months before I saw it again.

I retained my rubber blanket, and filled my haversack with hardtack. Other regiments of the division came marching by, and our regiment formed and joined in with them. All went marching down the Warrenton turnpike. We were going to the front.

All were marching with a long, swinging step. I had noticed and practiced the gait of the veteran regiments that I had seen, and easily fell into that long, swinging stride, that "reaching for the last inch," as it was happily called.

None of the officers had their swords drawn, but carried them in the scabbard or dragged them clattering along on the ground. Nearly every officer wore ordinary army shoes. I had on the light shoes of civilian life.

The men were smoking, chatting and laughing. Officers from the adjoining companies came up and scraped acquaintance. All were eager for news. I learned that the regiment was in the First Brigade, Fourth Division, Ninth Corps.[7]

Late in the afternoon a short halt was made, and the men ate their supper of hardtack and salt pork. I shared with my brother officers a nice lunch which I had in my haversack; but to me the hardtack tasted sweet and good, and I relished it.

The supper seemed to have brightened up the men, and when the march was resumed a song was started. It was what was known as "The Colored Volunteer," sung to the air of that old-time, well-known song, "That's What's the Matter, Boys."[8] The lines ran like this:

Jeff Davis says he'll hang us[9]
If we dars to meet him armed
Berry big t'ing, but be not t'ht all alarmod;
For fust he's got to gotch us—
Dat am berry cl'ar;
An dat's what's de matter
Wid de Colored Voluntar!
Dat's what's de matter, boys,
Dat's what's de matter;
Dat's what's de matter
Wid de Colored Voluntar.

We waded across Broad Run and two other streams. The water was more than knee deep, but no halt was made to take off shoes and stockings. After we had crossed the streams we marched straight on through the dust beyond. Ruefully I gazed at my new uniform trousers, first soaked in water and now covered with dirt.

Darkness came on, but we still pressed forward. And now stinging pains began to shoot upward from my feet. Every step increased the pain, until my suffering became intense. But still I kept on. The chattering and joking of the men had ceased. Nothing was heard but the steady shuffling sound of the marching column, and an occasional sharp command, "Close up!"

It was 11 o'clock at night when the regiment halted in a field near Warrenton. The arms were stacked and the men lay down behind them. Some of the soldiers built a fire and were gathered around it. I heard the Sergeant of the guard say to them sharply, "De Ossifer ob de Day say foh you men to g'way fum dis yore fiah and go to sleep mejitly."

"De Ossifer ob de Day mighty 'ticlar," growled one as he retired slowly.

"De Ossifer of de Day say he recken you alls'll need all de sleep yo'can git, befo yo gets to de end ob dis march," retorted the Sergeant.

In 10 minutes I was sound asleep, wrapped in my rubber blanket, lying by the side of Capt. Smith. It seemed as if I had hardly closed my eyes when I heard the bugles sounding. The Sergeant-Major was saying, "Have your men ready to march in half an hour."

It was a little past 3 o'clock, and I was so sleepy! Then I realized what the words of the bugle meant, when at reveille it said:

Oh, I can't get 'em up,
I can't get 'em up,
I can't get 'em up in the morning.

A cup of coffee was soon made by the Captain's servant, Ben, and by the time the day was breaking we were on the march again.

The first steps were agony to me, but I shut my teeth and kept going. The day was hot and the road dusty. Only short halts were made.

During the day I studied my men. Most of them were broad-shouldered, powerful fellows. They did not seem so black, nor so much alike as they did at first.

I took particular notice of the Sergeants of my company. At the head of the company was First Serg't Scott, a bright, intelligent looking mulatto, quiet and gentlemanly in his demeanor. Marching near me was Second Serg't Thomas Warrell [Worrell], over six feet high, black as the ace of spades, and greatly inclined to show his authority and crowd the men. The Third Sergeant was John Dudley, a middle-aged, tall, slim man, with a brown-colored face. He had been a sailor and had made several whaling voyages.

The Fourth Sergeant was a big, burly, jet-black negro with a woolly beard all over his face. His name was John Offer, and he had been a preacher on the Eastern Shore of Maryland. It did not take me long to find out that Serg't Offer looked upon me with a feeling akin to contempt, and I mentally resolved that I would keep him in his place, and teach him a lesson at the very first opportunity. He was carrying a large knapsack, loosely packed, with long ill-fitting straps, that let it fall away from his shoulders and made it burdensome to carry. I heard him complain that his shoulders were paining him, and when a halt was made I went to him and telling him that, "a knapsack packed in that manner would soon kill a man," repacked it in snug shape, and with my knife cut new holes in the straps and fitted it snugly upon his shoulders. I had the satisfaction of hearing him say that it was "a heaper sight easier." At the next halt I showed several others how they could make their burdens easier, and was rewarded by an approving word from Capt. Smith. The quaint sayings of the men amused me greatly, and their peculiar negro dialect was all new and novel to me. I found too, that there were some very original characters in the company, and that one of the stupid ones was the butt of all his comrades.

Toward noon the dull booming of cannon was heard. The men at the front had found the enemy.

One man, Thomas Festus by name, the oldest man in the company, showed signs of giving out, and I carried his musket for him. The looks of approval among the men amply repaid me.[10]

It was 10.30 o'clock when we halted that night near Rappahannock Station. With throbbing, blistered feet I lay down near stacks of muskets and was asleep at once.

At 2 o'clock in the morning I was roused again. The line was forming, and in five minutes we were on the march again.

At daylight we crossed the Rappahannock River on a pontoon bridge. The artillery was booming loudly at the front and the dropping sound of musketry could be heard. Staff officers were hurrying up the column. Gaps between the regiments were closed by double-quicking.

The Rapidan River was crossed at Germania [Germanna] Ford on another pontoon bridge at 7 o'clock. The crackling of musketry was growing sharper all the time.

Along a narrow road through a tangled forest we hurried on. A short halt was made near a house where the ambulances were bringing in wounded. A flag with a Greek cross indicated that it was the Sixth Corps hospital.[11] I visited the house, which had been taken by the Surgeons as an operating room. As I entered two attendants brought in a powerful soldier, his leg shattered by a shell. A handkerchief had been tied around the limb and twisted tightly with a bayonet. Even to my unpracticed eye it was plain that the leg was hopelessly mangled, and nothing but amputation would save the man's life. At the sight of the table and the Surgeons, who stood with rolled-up sleeves, the wounded man began to scream and resist violently. "Oh, Doctor, don't take off my leg!" he cried. "I can't be a cripple all my life!"

"That's all right, my boy," said the Surgeon soothingly; "but I must tie up these arteries or you will bleed to death. Better take a little chloroform to stop the pain."

The Surgeon glanced significantly at an attendant, who clapped a sponge to the nostrils of the wounded man. "Now take long breaths and count seven slowly," said the Doctor. Before seven was counted the man was insensible, and in a few seconds the mangled limb was amputated and the stewards were applying the bandages. I hurried outside. I was growing sick. Outside, under the trees and tents, were hundreds of wounded. There was a pit near the house, 10 feet long, five feet wide, and four feet deep, half-filled with amputated members of the wounded. Many of them had the army shoe and stocking still on them. Some of the hands, I noticed, were powder-stained and blackened, showing that their owner had been in the front line-of-battle, and had been doing his duty faithfully.[12]

But there was no time for sentimental musings. The order rang out sharply, "Fall in—Forward, March!" We were off again, still pushing for the front. The officers' swords were drawn and their pistol holsters were pulled well around on the right side.

The musketry was rolling wildly now. Wounded men, painfully making their way to the hospital, lined the road.

"Double-quick, men. Close up, boys; never mind the sore feet. Drop your knapsack if you can't carry it."

Every man was in his place. Suddenly we turned off the road in the tangled brush. A shrill, ear-piercing yell was heard.

"Dat am de Johnnies, suah 'nuff," said Serg't Worrell, who has been an army teamster for nearly three years. "You yere's dat music," he added, addressing the men in the ranks, as a terrific crash of musketry rose in answer to the charging yell. "How you likes it? It's to yere dat an' not git skeered by it, dat de Guv'ment feed you fer; dat's what dey gib you dese bu'ful guns fer; no skulking now; 'member, niggers is cheap dese days, an' doan' ye dare to flinch."

When we turned off into the brush I knew we were going into line-of-battle, and my heart seemed to sink into my boots. Only by shutting my teeth tight could I prevent them from chattering. I must have paled for I saw the men looking at me.

The "army ague" had attacked me, and I had it badly.[13] My father's words came to me, "Keep with the line," and I would have died sooner than stop then.

When we halted I took out a piece of hardtack and munched it. It might have been sweet or salt, for all I knew; but somehow it restored my confidence. Overhead I heard the droning sound of nearly-spent bullets.

Though we were near enough to hear the yells of the Confederates, the colored troops were not to fight nobly, or otherwise, that morning. We were soon hurried back to Germania [Germanna] Ford, over the road by which we had come. Here we were placed in a position to support a battery of artillery which was guarding the pontoon-bridge.

I took the opportunity to bathe in the Rapidan River, for my blistered feet had made my stockings stiff with blood. It seemed to me that I was sore from head to foot. Here I obtained a pair of Uncle Sam's army brogans. With these easy shoes upon my feet, my condition was greatly improved, and I experienced no further serious trouble on that score.[14]

The men made coffee and fried hardtack. They would have wasted their rations had not their officers sternly insisted on a limited allowance.

Towards 5 o'clock in the afternoon the musketry increased on the left, and we were soon called up. Over the same road we marched once more, until we reached the Fredericksburg plank road; and then turned to the left.

The Cavalry Corps were crossing in front of us, and we waited for them. They were moving out on a sharp trot.

Forward we went again; halted once more; started again and halted in the most tiresome and provoking way. The men couldn't understand it. "Won'ner what all dis yere hawin' an' geein' foh?" inquired one tired, disgusted private. "Young feller," said Serg't Worrell oracularly, "w'en you's ben in de army as long as I has, you'll know dat dis yere am de way ob de millingtery!" This was the solution always given by the white soldiers to anything they did not understand; "it's military" settled all questions.

Just before dark a terrible uproar broke out on the right. We were faced about and started in that direction. Soon we met a staff officer; his horse was covered with dust and foam.

"For God's sake hurry up, boys; they are flanking the Sixth Corps!"

The ranks closed up, the step was quickened. Then we went on at double-quick. Down the plank road from the right were coming ambulances; the drivers were lashing their horses to a run, and the wounded occupants screaming in agony as the vehicles jolted and crashed over the terribly-rough road. Intermingled with the ambulances were the reserve ammunition-wagons of the Sixth Corps.

The evening drew on, but to the right the sky was bright with the flashings of musketry. A battery of artillery was going with us to take a position on some crossroads. The drivers were lashing the excited horses and urging them ahead regardless of everything. The cannoneers were clinging to the limber chests; for a man to fall in that race meant death. "Clear the road and let the artillery pass!" was the cry. All around we heard screaming, shouting and bugle-calls. To the right those terrible crashings of musketry and the yells of the charging enemy were still kept up. Wounded men and stragglers were met, and all told stories of disaster.

The bullets began to hum overhead. We were breathless, nearly exhausted, and ready to drop. Our brigade commander rode along the line. In ringing tones he shouted, "Now, boys, for the honor of the Black Brigade! Show the Sixth Corps you are men! This is your chance!"[15]

Off went the knapsacks and blankets. Our double-quick increased to a run. From the ranks came responses: "We're comin' right along, Kunnel! Tell the Sixth Co' we'se reddy to stay right wid 'em!"

We were almost at the scene of fighting. The firing slackened, "Halt!" came the command. We were not needed.

The brave men of the old Sixth Corps had repulsed the enemy and re-established their lines. We retraced our steps towards the left again. No credit was ever given for that noble effort of exhausted, footsore men; not even a mention of it in the official reports.

There was no rest for us. All night we were on the move, passing through burning woods. In places the fire was so hot that the men had to run. There was a sickening stench of burning flesh, and we knew that it was human flesh. We witnessed the most dreadful scenes; more than 200 Union wounded had perished miserably in those flames.[16]

The morning found us sleepy, tired, dusty and cross. Officers and privates were all of the same color—all thickly covered with red dust.

Our route took us on the Orange plank road past the Fifth Corps Hospital, with its army of wounded. We were halted close up to the front line, where we were massed in columns of regiments.

"We are going in this time, sure," said Capt. Smith, who was an old soldier. The excitement had died away. How I ached and throbbed, and how sleepy I was! Soldiering was not all fun, even if one were an officer.

Gen. Grant and staff passed us here. The General-in-Chief wore the regulation army hat and a plain blouse, with three little stars on the shoulders. His army trousers, the same as worn by privates, were tucked in a very muddy pair of cavalry boots. He presented anything but a military appearance. He was smoking a cigar, and seemed to be taking no interest whatever in the proceedings about him. It is needless to say that the officers and men took enough interest in him to make up for his lack of attention. It is said that he ordered the Colored Division to guard the wagon-train. At any rate, we did not "go in," but moved to the left again, towards Chancellorsville.

In doing so we passed in the rear of the lines of the Fifth Corps, and the soldiers thronged to the road to see the Colored Division. Our men, aware that they were objects of criticism, closed up their ranks, brought their guns to the right shoulder, and presented a creditable military appearance.

The white soldiers were not disposed to let them pass without some "chaffing," to which the colored men were quite equal. One colored soldier with a clear, mellow voice, raised the song:

Will you, will you
Fight for de Union?[17]

Instantly the whole line took up the chorus:

Ah-ha! Ah-ha!
We'll fight for Uncle Sam!

The singer continued:

Oh!-o! Oh!-o!
She fights for de Union!

Chorus:
Ah-ha! Ah-ha!
She fights for Uncle Sam!

Solo:
Maryland! My Maryland!
She *stays* wid de Union!

Chorus:
Ah-ha! Ah-ha!
She *stays* wid Uncle Sam!

Grand chorus, given with rousing effect:

Den harness up de mules
Be keer'ful how you dribe!
Jeemses Ribbar! Joe Johnsing,[18]
An' de colored Gineral of the Black Brigade!

A generous round of applause from the Fifth Corps boys rewarded the singers.

All day we maneuvered in the tangled forest. Night found us in the line-of-battle in the slashed timber of the old Chancellorsville battleground. That night I slept as one dead.

When we were called in the morning the road in the rear of our line was thronged with thousands of wounded men, who were painfully making their way towards Fredericksburg. Thousands there were, literally, for the killed, wounded and missing at the battle of the Wilderness were more than 15,000.[19] Ambulances and army wagons were filled with the severely wounded. Many were shrieking, crazed with agony; others were calling for water; some were praying to die, and some begging to be shot or to be given a bayonet; but the most, by far the most, bore their agony in silence. The ghastly-blue, tightly compressed lips and pain-distorted faces showed their terrible sufferings, but hardly a moan escaped them. In one of the ambulances lay a powerful young Sergeant, apparently mortally wounded. On the seat with the driver was a Confederate soldier with an amputated arm. A black soldier, seeing the rebel, called out:

"Hi dar, you Johnny; you-alls uster tell we'uns dat de Yankees had ho'ns!" and clapping his hand on the bayonet at his side said, "Who's got de ho'ns now?"

The query struck the wounded Sergeant as so ludicrous that he laughed until the tears ran down his cheeks.[1][20]

The army was moving by the left flank; it was occupied in the most active warfare, and this awful procession must reach Fredericksburg as best it could. Here I saw war in its true colors. When the wounded had passed we moved to another position a mile south of the old Chancellorsville House. Here we built breastworks. As we were likely to remain a few hours, and as the men were raw and inexperienced, the Colonel ordered a drill in the manual of arms.

"Lieutenant, you may drill the company," the Captain said. I soon found that in the "loadings," the most important part of the manual, the men were awkward and clumsy. Some of them could hardly load their pieces in five minutes.

---

1 This is a true incident. The wounded Sergeant was A. J. Buckles, Color-Sergeant, 19th Ind., of the old Iron Brigade. He was thought to be mortally wounded, but insisted on being sent to Fredericksburg. He told me that he believed that this laugh saved his life. He recovered and is still alive, living in California. In 1890 he was elected Department Commander, Grand Army of the Republic, Department of California—F.S.B. [Abram J. Buckles, the "Color Bearer" of the 19th Ind. Infantry, was wounded on July 1, 1864, at the Wilderness. Service record of A. J. Buckles, 19th Indiana Infantry, Carded Records, Volunteer Organizations: Civil War. Wilson.]

Taking a musket from a Sergeant, I illustrated every motion, and explained every point. The cadets at our academy had always drilled with precision and celerity, and I did my best, making the men count aloud and keep the time. They were quick to imitate, and were not long in catching the trick. For an hour I drilled them on this one lesson, and they improved wonderfully. They had just finished an exercise, and the rammers had all been returned with a snap, almost as one man, when an officer stepped beside me. It was the Colonel. "Very well done; very well, indeed," he remarked, and passed on.

I was happy, and the men were delighted.

After the drill, I saw them still practicing at loading, and heard them say, "Reckon de little Lieutenant knows a heap mor'n whut he looks."

The day had been drizzly, and when the night came on, the rain fell in torrents. We crept under our rubber blankets, and we were congratulating ourselves that we should have some sleep that night, even if it did rain, when the Adjutant's voice was heard: "Pack up! Lively now! Get your men out as quick as you can!"

We crawled out, roused the men, and were soon on the road in the darkness, splashing through the mud and water. And such mud—soft, slippery, and sticky, letting the foot go down more than ankle deep, then holding on with a suction that made the next step a labor. Woe to him who lost a shoe; he must grope and feel for it in the mud, and comrades who followed behind would tumble over him and rail at him heartily. Nearly all night we trudged in the mire, not knowing in the least where we were going, and not caring very much.[21]

A cavalry fight had taken place on our line-of-march, and we fell over dead horses frequently. It must have been 3 o'clock in the morning when we halted, closed up the regiment and formed in line-of-battle. Soaked to the skin and tired out, I sat down on a little pine bush, with my rubber blanket over my head, and went to sleep in the pouring rain.

When I awoke, it was daylight, and I was so stiff and cramped that I thought I could never move again. The men were lying around, some of them half buried in the mud. All were splashed from head to foot with the red soil of Virginia. A fire was soon made, some coffee prepared, and with hot fried pork and fried hardtack we felt greatly invigorated.

The men rallied one another on the personal appearance, and appeared to take things as a matter of course. We learned by and by that an attempt of the enemy to capture some of our wagon-train had been the cause of our night's tramp.

Some ambulances had halted near us, and the drivers were digging a wide grave. Near-by lay three men, stark and stiff. I went over to them. Two of the faces wore a familiar look. On the breast of each was pinned a paper, and I read: "Capt. Pease, 37th Mass. Vols." "Harry Eddy, Co. A, 37th Mass. Vols." "—56th P.V."

During the month of August previous the 37th Mass. had been detached from the Army of the Potomac and ordered to New York City. I had visited them there and spent a week in camp with them at Fort Hamilton. I had formed the acquaintance of the two men who lay dead in front of me.[22] When the ambulance drivers placed them in their grave, all three side by side, I had some of my men bring some pine boughs and place over them, that the wet mud might not strike their faces. A poor tribute, but all that I could do.

I turned away with moist eyes, and I was surprised to see hopping all around our cook-fire a white soldier with one leg. The limb had been amputated near the hip, and the bandage was wet with blood.

"What are you doing?" I exclaimed. "Don't you know that you are liable to fall and bleed to death?"

"Reckon I might as well bleed to death as starve to death," retorted the veteran, who was from the old Vermont Brigade.[23]

The black soldiers instantly divided their coffee and hardtack with him, and he ate heartily. Then they assisted him into the ambulance, and he thanked them and said: "Stay with 'em, boys; stand by the old flag till the cows come home! I've been pegging at the Johnnies for three years, and I guess I've done 'em more damage than they have me."

An hour for breakfast, and back we went over the same road to our former camp at Chancellorsville.

Rations were running low, and the men were cautioned to save all they could, for the five days' supplies were likely to have to last seven days. Fresh beef was issued, and was soon sizzling in the frying pan.

"Lieutenant! Oh, Lieutenant!" The Adjutant was calling my name. "You are detailed for picket. Report with your detail to the Division Officer of the Day at Division Headquarters." It seemed "tough," but it was "all in the three years," and it would not do to growl the first time.

"All right, Adjutant! I'll be there. Here, Ben, give me a cup of coffee," I said "and I'll be off."[24]

Taking charge of the detail of about 50 men, I reported at Division Headquarters. Details were there from other regiments, making 200 men or more. We went out on the Orange turnpike, and under the direction of the Division Officer of the Day established a picket-line through the woods.

This was the part of the Chancellorsville battleground where the Eleventh Corps had been routed the year before. The dead of that fight had been but half buried. The rain had washed the soil away that had been thrown over the bodies, and from every side grinning skulls peeped out at you; skeleton hands stretched out on all sides. It was impossible to avoid stepping upon dead men's bones.[25] My part of the line was half a mile or more in length. At our left was the turnpike. Our cavalry videts were out on the road in front of us; beyond them were the enemy. The army had moved to the left and the guns were now thundering at Spotsylvania.[26] Our picket-line was the extreme right of the army. We were informed that the enemy's cavalry were scouting not far off, and would probably "feel for us" during the night. A breastwork of brush was built across the road.

Every man was instructed what to do if we were attacked. The pickets were posted in groups of three or four men at intervals of about 30 rods, in sight of each other. One man watched behind a tree or shelter and the others slept. When the picket had been on watch for two hours he waked one of his comrades to relieve him. There were no fires, no smoking, no talking; all was quiet, and all on duty watched intently.[27]

I was nervous from the excitement of the past few days, and from a sense of responsibility. The woods were full of strange sounds. Owls were hooting, and whippoorwills singing their mournful songs. Great, vicious, wolfish dogs, that had subsisted for months on the dead, were prowling through the woods.[28]

Four times that night I visited every picket-post on my line, and as the bones of men snapped under my tread, or my foot struck a skull, it required all my nerve to keep from breaking down. The men were alert and nervous; it was dangerous to approach them; they were likely to fire without challenging. I arranged a signal by clapping my hands, so that they would recognize me; but once I lost my bearings, and was suddenly stopped by the ominous clicking of a musket-lock. I quickly gave the signal, and was relieved to hear a low challenge; "Who cum dar?" I made myself known, and found that all of the men on the post were up and had me covered with their rifles. No attack was made that night, but towards the morning one of the pickets near the road challenged sharply, and then fired. The yelping of a dog followed. I went out to investigate.

The picket said that he saw something creeping up towards him, and when he challenged, it sprang towards him, and then he shot. Daylight revealed a huge dog, a most horrible-looking creature, lying dead, not 20 yards from the picket's post. I think that the man told the truth, and that the animal would have attacked the soldier, if it had not been shot.

The next afternoon we were called in, and followed the division, which had moved to Salem Church, eight miles away.

3

On the March

The guard mount and picket detail no longer had any terrors for me. My health was good, my face tanned to a nut-brown, my feet toughened to a leather-like toughness, and I marched with the swing of a veteran.

Thousands of fresh troops, coming by the way of Fredericksburg, were on their way to the front. Most of them were heavy artillerymen equipped as infantry, from the fortifications around Washington. The men were fat, and their faces were red and flushed, and the perspiration fairly rolled off of them. No wonder they sweated; every man had a knapsack as big as a hardtack box. It did not take them long to get rid of their superfluous baggage, and the roads were lined with woolen blankets, overcoats, extra clothing, books, playing cards, and all the knick-knacks that a soldier accumulates in camp.[1]

Many of our men exchanged their mud-soaked clothing for new, clean articles picked up by the roadside. The first death in the company occurred here. A stout young fellow, attacked by cramps, lay down crying, "Oh, Lordy, I'se got misery in my heart; I'se agwine ter die, I'se agwine ter die." The Surgeon did his best, but the next morning the man was dead.

We buried him in a shallow grave beside the road, with a piece of hardtack box for a headboard.

The men had received rations the day previous; and the Surgeon told me that, without doubt, the man had killed himself by eating all his ration of sugar at once, and then stuffing himself with fried fat salt pork.[2]

A prayer meeting in another regiment attracted me that evening. Grouped under the great pine trees, the scene lighted up by fires of pine knots, the men, all wearing their accouterments, gathered. Every black face was sober and reverent. The leader "lined off" the words of the hymn, and all sang the words together.[3] The voices rose sweet and mellow. Then came prayers and exhortations. The words were those of ignorant men, but there was in them a pathos which I have never heard equalled.

The cannon were roaring at Spottsylvania [Spotsylvania], and the dropping sound of musketry was heard all the time. One powerful black soldier prayed,

"Oh, Lord Jesus, you knows we's ready an' willin' to die for de flag; dat's what we'se-hyah foh; but, O, Lord, if we falls, comfort de lubbed ones at home."

A responsive "Amen" came from all the bearers; and I turned away with tears in my eyes, for I too was thinking of home, and the black soldier had spoken my unuttered prayer.

I had now been a soldier a week. My "initiation" was progressing rapidly.

Accompanying the Fourth Division of the Ninth Corps were two cavalry regiments, the 3d Ohio, a small veteran regiment, and the 3d N. J., better known as the "Butterflies," so-called on account of their fantastic uniforms. The jackets and caps of the privates were perfect bouquets of yellow braiding and knots, while a commissioned officer "Butterfly," seen in the sunlight, was a glittering, gorgeous spectacle of gold braid and trimmings. Nearly every Division Headquarters had one or more "Butterflies" attached to it as Orderlies. No doubt, at home, on their own soil, the Jersey men were great "swells," and produced a profound impression, but when they arrived at the front the old vets made their lives miserable. Whenever one of them appeared the cry arose: "Butterfly! Butterfly! Catch him and put him in a canteen!"[4]

The "Zoo-zoos," or as they were generally called, the "Redlegs," the soldiers name for Zouave regiments, were particularly acrimonious toward the "Butterflies."[5] Perhaps jealousy had something to do with it.

The Fourth Division was in the pine woods at the left of Spottsylvania [Spotsylvania], when, late one afternoon, the cavalry carbines began to crack at a furious rate. The 3d Ohio Cav. and the "Butterflies" had every man engaged. The enemy had developed in force, and there was a call for the infantry.

Our regiment went off on the double-quick. I was doing my first detail as Officer of the Guard. Gathering up my sentinels, I followed the regiment on the run. When we overtook the rest, Co. B, the left flank company, was deploying, as skirmishers. Maj. Leake [Leeke], who was directing the movement, promptly ordered my guard to deploy with the others, and they were soon strung out five or six paces apart.

"Now just imagine you are hunting for coons, and keep your eyes open. Skirmishers, forward, guide left—March!" shouted the Major.

"'Pears like 'twas de coons doin' de huntin' dis time, yah! yah!" laughed a black soldier, as the line moved forward with alacrity.

We passed through the woods to an open field. Across the field some 300 yards away were the Confederate cavalry skirmishers. A few bullets came whizzing our way.

Here was my chance. I would fire my first shot for the old flag and the Union. Taking a rifle, I aimed, with great deliberation, at a horseman, who appeared to be an officer, and fired. The rifle was an old Enfield. It kicked spitefully and gave me the impression that my shoulder had been almost dislocated. And the officer? He did not notice it at all, but rode down his line perfectly unconcerned.

Our firing was soon stopped, as it was not desired to show our force. The enemy fell back into the woods out of our sight. We remained in line all night, but when daylight came there was no enemy in our front.

Our division moved towards Port Royal, crossing the railroad south of the hills of Fredericksburg. Capt. Smith pointed out to me the place where he and a few comrades had been taken prisoners, after the battle of Fredericksburg. They were doing picket-duty, and when the Union army fell back across the river they were left behind. Daylight found them with Confederates on all sides. As Capt. Smith remarked: "Four men couldn't lick or stop the whole rebel army, so they scooped us in."

To our division was assigned the task of guarding the great wagon-trains that supplied the Army of the Potomac. Those who have never seen an army train, can form but a faint idea of its magnitude. These were the "fighting trains" carrying ammunition, rations, forage, and supplies only. Everything was reduced to the lowest basis. Three baggage wagons, only, were allowed to our brigade for four regiments. The brigade commander had a small "A" tent, carried on a pack-mule.[6] All the wagons were marked with the brigade, division, and corps to which they belonged, and the articles they were intended to carry. For instance, a wagon marked, "First Brig., Fourth Div., Ninth Corps. Ammunition. E. B. Cat. Cal. 58," would indicate that that particular wagon was loaded with elongated ball cartridges, caliber .58, for the use of the brigade named. Gen. Grant, in his Memoirs, states that this great train would have filled a road from the Rapidan River to Richmond.[7]

Each wagon was drawn by six mules, and they were driven by one driver, who rode the "high wheeler," and directed the movements of the team with a single rein or "jerk line." It is my honest belief that the "army mule" is a long-suffering, much abused and badly slandered animal. Certain it is that he filled a most important and responsible position in those war-time days, and if his heels were sometimes treacherous it was not to be wondered at, considering the abuse that he received.

To guard those great trains was a most arduous and thankless duty. We were kept almost constantly marching and maneuvering to protect the wagons from the dashing Confederate cavalry, who were always hovering around the flanks and rear ready to pounce upon an unprotected train. "Going into camp," was simply forming the regiment in line-of-battle in an advantageous position and stacking the guns. The men lay behind the stacks with their accouterments on and the officers slept in front of their companies. Such was the tension on the men's nerves that I have known the whole division to spring to their feet in the middle of the night and seize their guns. The alarm might be caused by a stack of arms falling down or a sleeper crying out in his sleep, but if once the alarm started it spread instantly and almost silently along the whole line.

As nearly as human endurance made it possible we must march all day and go on picket or build roads all night. If ever the weary men were comfortably resting in a shady spot the bugle, it seemed, would surely be heard calling:

> I know you are tired and don't want to go,
> But put on your knapsack and come along slow.

"Fall in!" was the order then, and away we went, plodding through the dust. "Dat ole bugle, he nebber git weary," said the men. Accompanying the army was a great herd of beef cattle, known among the soldiers, after their fashion of bestowing an odd name upon everything, as the "Bull Corps." One night, near the North Anna, we halted to allow a wagon-train and the Bull Corps to pass. The four regiments of the First Brigade went into the pine woods to the left of the road, stacked their arms and lay down to rest. The Second Brigade did the same on the opposite side of the road. All went well until the Bull Corps had nearly passed, when a steer broke from the herd and ran through a line of stacked muskets, overturning some and discharging one. A few men lying nearby woke in a panic, grasped their muskets and fired. Immediately a scattering fire broke out along the whole-line, and in another instant the Second Brigade, believing itself attacked, returned the fire.

Our regiment was the one nearest the road, and consequently we were directly between two fires, and also under the hoofs of the frightened cattle, which were now stampeding in all directions.

We were all lying flat, and yelling "Stop that firing! Lie down 30th!" when, by the misty moonlight, I saw a huge steer plunging directly towards me. Preferring the chances of being shot to the certainty of being trampled upon, I arose and ran behind a big pine. Spat came a bullet, striking the tree not a foot above my head. This roused my temper. Jumping in among a group of men where some of the firing was coming from, I laid about vigorously with the flat of my sword, at the same time yelling to them to cease firing. I soon quieted that

Fig. 3.1. "Reckon yo' writes a mighty fine letter, Lieutenant." *National Tribune*, May 11, 1899.

group. Meantime other officers were taking equally severe measures, and order was soon restored.

A few men had received bullet wounds in this foolish panic, but most of the casualties, it was found, came from the officers' swords.

When the army moved to North Anna there was for a time that the Second Corps was separated from the rest of the army, and was in a most critical position. The troops were rushed to close the gap, and about 9 o'clock one evening, our division passed through the village of Bowling Green. Someone had set fire to the Courthouse, and when we passed, the village street was lighted up by the burning building. Our men were in high spirits. A rumor prevailed that Gen. Lee with his Confederate army were in full retreat, and that Gen. Grant was racing him to Richmond.

The troops passed through, singing "John Brown's Body Lies Buried in the Ground," and the frightened women and children whom I saw peeping from the windows must have surely thought that "his soul was marching on," when nearly 5,000 negro soldiers passed, each one singing and yelling at the top of his voice.

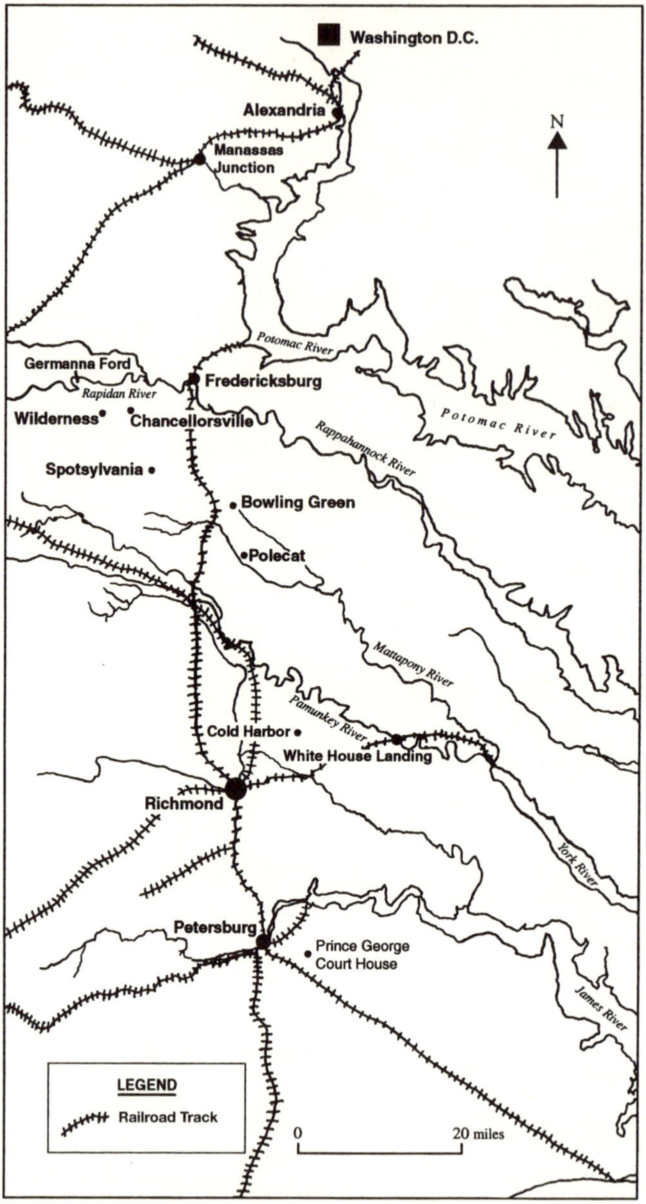

The journey south: Manassas Junction via Germanna Ford, Wilderness, Chancellorsville, Bowling Green, Polecat, Cold Harbor, White House Landing to the Petersburg battlefield.

Map 1. Movement of Freeman S. Bowley's Regiment, the 30th UCSI, to the Petersburg battlefield, May–June 1864. (Adapted from U.S. War Department, *Atlas to Accompany the Official Records*, Plates CXVII, CXXXVII, CXXXVIII.)

We camped about six miles south of Bowling Green at a station called "Polecat."

I had just finished writing a letter, using an empty hardtack-box as a desk, when big Bob Bowen stepped up near me, stood at "attention," and taking off his cap stood twisting it in his hands.

Bob was a powerful young fellow of 20, six feet high, splendidly built, with great ox-like eyes and a clear, wine-black complexion of the kind known among the men as "right-bright." "Well, what is it, Bob?" I asked.

"Reckon yo' writes a mighty fine letter, Lieutenant," said Bob interrogatively.

"What makes you think so?" I asked, somewhat amused.

"'Pears dat-a-way toe me, sah. 'Spects yo's bin writin' toe yoah young lady, sah?" replied Bob.

"Yes," I said, "I've been writing to a young lady," and desiring to help him out of his embarrassment, for the big beads of perspiration were rolling down his face, "I think you want me to write a letter for you to your young lady. Isn't that it?"

"Dat's it, 'zactly," said Bob. "All right Bob," I said, "I'll fix up that letter for you right now. Where is it going, and who is the young lady?"

"Young lady's named Tilley, sah; lib ober on a Eastern Sho,' sah; b'longs to ole Marse Bowen, sah, same ole Marse Bowen dat own me, sah. He own a heap ob people, and a right smart big place near Chestertown, sah," said Bob, fairly gasping for breath, as all this information rolled off at once.

"Well," I asked, "can Miss Tilley read and write? And what is her other name, Tilley—what?"

"Nebber had no oder name, dat I knows ob; just b'longs to ole Marse; don't reckon she knows 'zed' from 'crowsfut,' no mo'n I does," answered Bob, whose ideas of the alphabet were somewhat vague.

"But who will read her letter for her?" I inquired, wishing to know into who's hands the epistle would fall.

"Reckon she'll git Miss Julia, de young Missis, to read it, sah. Yo' see, sah, Tilley's house gal—Miss Julie's own sarbent; no field han' 'bout her. Mighty peart gal, dat Tilley," answered Bob proudly.

"All right, Bob, I think I understand; now, we'll date this letter—

'Polecat, May,'—

"Hol' on dar, Lieutenant, hol' on; foh de lau's sake, doan write da-a-way. Miss Julia nebber stop laughin' at Tilley; dat 'Polecat' spile de letter suah," interrupted Bob anxiously.

"How will we date it, then?" I asked. "We always put a date on a letter."

"Dog my cat if I knows," answered Bob despondently.

"Let's see; how will this do? Camp 30th U. S. Col. Inf., May,"—

"Dat a heap better," said Bob, much relieved.

Then I began the letter, and Bob dictated and I arranged his crude ideas. He told the girl how he thought of her day and night; how, when the regiment was in line-of-battle, its colors blew around, and touched his cheek; which was true, for Co. H was the sixth in line, and the colors and color-guard stood between the fifth and sixth companies. How he tried to do his duty, and if he died he would die by the side of the old flag. He told her, further more, that he had not made the acquaintance of any colored ladies since he had left home, and that he didn't want to hear of any of the young fellows from the other plantations calling around to see her. Altogether, love, patriotism, and admonition were pretty well mixed in Bob's letter. The epistle was finished, and I addressed a personal postscript, giving a good account of Bob's conduct. It was duly sealed, directed, and indorsed "Soldier's letter," for stamps were scarce.

While I was writing it the men gathered in groups a little way off, and I soon had another applicant, Perry Gibson [Gibbs]. Perry was a married man, and owned a little farm in Anne Arundel County, Md.[8]

"How many children have you, Perry?" I asked.

"Nine, sah; all as black as crows; no milk and 'lasses ones in dat fam'bly," was the proud response.

From this time forth I had plenty of letter writing to attend to. The men were a little afraid of the Captain, and the Second Lieutenant made fun of them, and the negroes were as sensitive to ridicule as most white persons are. When the answer came, the letters were brought to me to be read, and with a delicacy that I never expected from them, the men always remained out of earshot while a comrade's letter was being read to him. The answer to Bob's letter brought to me a very pleasant note from Miss Julia, and I remember that the answer to Perry's letter contained the information that the "old blue sow had nine pigs: the children is doin' well, and the sweet 'taters is doin' well."

Poor Perry! He was shot dead in the trenches of Petersburg a month later, and the wife and nine children, "all as black as crows," never saw the husband and father again. I found that I had gained the confidence and esteem of my men. The few words of appreciation from the Colonel, while they were drilling at Chancellorsville, as already narrated, had excited their pride, and they made every effort to improve. Every hint and lesson given was eagerly seized upon, and the quicker ones assisted the slower ones in perfecting themselves in the use of their arms. Company H began to have the reputation of being the best-drilled company in the manual of arms of any in the regiment.

"De little Lieutenant say 'Dis-a-way,'" or "De little Lieutenant do dat-a-way," was authority to settle all disputed questions among them.

Another man was taken sick with "misery in de heart," and died before we could send him to the hospital. When Capt. Smith learned that the man was dead, he ordered Serg't Scott to form the company.

I wondered what it was all about, for the Captain seemed decidedly angry. Marching the company off by themselves, he halted and formed them in close order, four ranks deep, and thus addressed them:

"This dying business has got to be stopped! Another man died last night, and I don't want any more of it! If, hereafter, any man says he's got misery in his heart and says he's a going to die, I'll tie him up by the thumbs, and if he don't stop dying I'll shoot him."

This astonishing speech would have been received with derision by white soldiers, but the black men were much impressed by it. They stood in great awe of their Captain, and took it all in sober earnest.

"If any man is sick," continued the Captain, "let me know and I'll send him to the doctor, and he will give him medicine, and if that man keeps a-going he will come out all right. If he lies down and thinks he is going to die, very likely he will die; but I propose to have this dying stopped!"

The Captain was right. He had solved the problem. It was the lack of will-power, the giving up, and inability to shake off indisposition that cost many a soldier his life. It is worthy of note that no more sudden deaths occurred in Co. H. All who died after that time made a good struggle for life, and it might be said that they died legitimately.[9]

I found that a great change had come over me. From the timid, bashful, irresolute boy, I had come to have confidence in myself and to consider that I could do my duty as well as anyone. I had commanded the company on battalion drill on several occasions, and acquitted myself creditably.

The guard mount and picket detail no longer had any terrors for me. My health was good, my face tanned to a nut-brown, my feet toughened to a leather-like toughness, and I marched with the swing of a veteran. I was hungry all the time and ate my full share of hardtack and pork. How good the coffee, made in an old black tin cup, used to taste. Never have I tasted any since that equalled it. I was never able to find the wagon that contained my valise. If ever it came to the regiment I was sure to be off on picket, and if I went to the wagon-train it had gone to some other place. The lack of change of underclothing troubled me but very little. I washed my clothes when an opportunity presented itself, and waited until they dried. Sometimes I had to put them on wet, as orders came for the regiment to move, and there was no time for drying. I had gained the knack of getting all the comfort there was to be had out of our daily life. Did the column halt, I was down in the shade and asleep in a moment. If there was a stray pig or chicken, and there were very few stray ones in that section of the country, some of my men always found them, and the "little Lieutenant" always had his share. Letters from home and friends cheered me up, and the thought of homesickness never occurred to me. The prospect of death or wounds never troubled me.

"Time 'nuff to shake han's wid ole Scratch w'en he stan' in de do'," said the black soldiers.

From Polecat we marched to Milford Station, and from there the division's route lay well east of the railroad. We had struck into a portion of the country that had never before been traversed by the army. Contrabands, as the runaway slaves were called, began to follow us, but none of the able-bodied men showed any inclination to enlist. The appearance of soldiers of their own color excited these simple people greatly. "Foh de lan's sake!" exclaimed one fat aunty, "whar yo'alls niggers cum frum? Nebber seed such a heap o' nigger men in all my bawn days!"

"Dis yere's nuffin," answered a black Sergeant. "Dis only de advance-geerd. De r'ar of de column ain't left Baltimo' yet."

We halted one day near a little log house, built after the universal style of the poor whites of Virginia, and most of the officers entered it.

A young woman of 20, dressed in homespun, but unmistakably pretty, with her year-old baby, were the only occupants. The house was neat, and various little feminine ornaments showed the taste of a housekeeper. The baby, a beautiful boy, with big, blue eyes and golden curls, was dressed in what had evidently been a white muslin dress of his mother's. His garment was cut low neck and short sleeves, and showed the chubby little fellow off to great advantage.

The baby sat up in an old-fashioned cradle on rockers, and the officers gathered around him admiringly. His mother was evidently frightened at the sight of black troops and so many Yankee officers with clanking swords. Her confidence was returning as she found that everyone treated her politely and admired the baby, when Capt. Woodward, six feet tall, heavily bearded, dark and swarthy with sword, dragging along the ground, entered. He strode straight for the cradle. "Where's that little rebel? Give him to me!" he exclaimed in his heavy, gruff voice.

Fig 3.2. Capt. George T. Woodward, Company E, 30th U.S. Colored Infantry. RG98S-CWP Collection, United States Army Military History Institute.

The mother started up deadly pale. "Oh, my baby! Oh, gentlemen, don't let him!" but her cry of alarm turned to a smile of pleasure, for the Captain had caught up the baby, tossed him high, and as he came down the bearded lips were kissing the baby's dimpled neck and shoulders. And the baby, with that intuition of babyhood which always recognizes a friend, was crowing with glee, and pulling the Captain's black whiskers. No need to reassure the mother; she knew that no harm would come to her darling while that big, brave man was near to protect him.

"You fellows don't know how to handle a baby," said the Captain to the other officers. "I suppose your husband's off in the rebel army," he added, addressing the woman. "Yes, sah; he's wid Gen. Stuart's cavalry," she replied.[10]

"You tell him the next time that you see him," said the Captain, "that he is a big fool to be fighting the Yanks, when he's got such a pretty wife and baby. He had better be at home taking care of them."

"I dun told him so, sah," she answered simply, and wondered why the officers smiled.

We left her with a generous supply of coffee, sugar, and hardtack. At least one woman in Virginia had a good opinion of "the Yanks" when we resumed our march. We encamped on the banks of Pamunkey River, and for two or three days we enjoyed a much-needed rest. Many troops passed us on their way to the front, among them the famous "Potomac Home Brigade," with "P. H. B." on their caps.[11]

"Dere's heaps ob disjointed calvary goin' to de front," said a black soldier to me one day. The negroes always said "calvary" for cavalry. "Disjointed cavalry" was the soldier's name for a cavalry regiment which was sent to the front as infantry, armed only with carbines. "Dismounted cavalry" were cavalrymen fighting on foot, but with one man out of four holding the horses not far away.

The "disjointed cavalry" to whom my man had referred were three full regiments of at least 1,200 men each, all armed with the new Henry 16-shooter, the first of that modern arm that we had seen.[12]

A few nights afterwards, during the first week in June, the army lay at Cold Harbor. The enemy charged the Union line, and ran squarely against this brigade of "disjointed cavalry." Then what a terrific crackling of muskets there was! The sky was lighted up, and the glare of the musketry made everything as bright as day. So deadly was the fire of these new weapons that but few of the assaulting line ever got back to their own side again. Most of them lay flat on their faces until the firing ceased and were then taken prisoners.

"Say, Yanks," they asked our men, "what kind of guns yo'uns got, that you kin load 'em Sunday and shoot all the week?"

Twelve hundred prisoners were captured in this encounter, and two days later the 30th U.S.C.T. was detailed to take half of the prisoners to White House Landing, the Union base of supplies.[13]

Our prisoners were mostly Georgians, fine-looking young fellows; but they were greatly chagrined by being guarded by colored troops.

"My father had more than a hundred niggers picking cotton on his plantation down in Georgia," said one; "I reckon he'd be a ra'rin', if he knew that a big nigger with a gun and bayonet was a-drivin' me off a prisoner." I told him it was the "fortune of war."

"Yes, misfortune for me, I reckon," he answered quickly.

A hot, dusty march of 15 miles brought us to the "White House." A Virginia mansion had given the place its name, but of this mansion only the chimney remained.

Fig 3.3. "Lady nurses were attending the wounded." Freeman S. Bowley, *A Boy Lieutenant*.

By the time we reached there our prisoners and the black soldiers were on the best of terms. The blacks were alert and watchful, but they allowed their prisoners every opportunity to obtain water and such like favors, and the Confederate veterans fully appreciated the excellent discipline and drill that the black soldiers showed.

All about was a great city of tents. Thousands of these covered the ground. Every department of the great army was represented. Thousands of wounded were there, being cared for by the Medical Department, assisted by the Sanitary and Christian Commissions. Lady nurses were attending the wounded. How sweet and homelike these ladies looked to us in their neat calico dresses! We almost envied the wounded under their tender care.

Our men were ragged, dirty, dusty and tired, but they now considered themselves veterans; and how they straightened up and put on style when they saw the nurses! Even the prisoners aligned their ranks and took the proper marching distance.

We were the first troops directly from the front bringing the first large lot of prisoners, and everyone turned out to see us. Among them were some young fellows, evidently college boys, belonging to one of the regiments of "hundred-days men" that were stationed there.[14]

They began making fun of our men, "Say, fellows, come see the black cloud," shouted one.

"Say, Jim Crow, why don't you hire out for a scarecrow in the cornfield?" This to a soldier with a very ragged uniform and a very bright gun.

"Dese yere's de kind o' co'n I'se bin a shukin,'" answered the black man, with a nod towards the prisoners.

Some of the Confederates shouted back, "If ever you get to the front, young feller, you'll find out that paper collars don't make a soldier!"

We marched our prisoners down near the river. Out in the stream gunboats were slowly moving back and forth. A force of "bluejackets" and hundred-days men took charge of the prisoners.[15]

The drummers were seen bracing up their drums, and word was passed along the line for the men to retain the fixed bayonets on their guns. We were to march back again through the main street.

The men dusted each other off as best they could, and brushed the dust off their guns and accouterments. With the fifes and drums playing "The Girl I Left Behind Me," we started back again, and it was wonderful to see how that music, poor enough, too, no doubt lightened the tired feet, and how the ranks stepped off in solid, swinging steps. Again the whole population turned out to see us.[16]

"Ebery man ke'p his eye on de coat collar ob de man in front ob him," said Serg't Worrell authoritatively.

"De man in front ain't got no collar on he coat!" giggled a voice in the ranks.

"Yo' Hillery Herbert [Wesley/Hilary Herbert], stop ye' triflin'; I'se gwine to settle wid ye d'rectly we gits inter camp!" said the Sergeant severely.

From the hospital tents came the wounded who were able to move around, and from them came words of praise and encouragement. "You are marching fine, boys." "That's the style; keep it up." "Buffy boys, you're all right!" greeted us on all sides. A grizzled Sergeant, with that peculiar, square-set build and air that always indicated the "Regular," remarked to his comrade: "Be jabers, an' thim black b'yes is marchin' foine. The ould Fourth herself couldn't bate thim!"

Surely, praise could go no higher than that, and the men heard it, and fairly glowed and swelled with delight. We were to go into camp near the camp of the hundred-days men. They were all out watching us; but there was no more chaffing or references to "black clouds."

Somehow, it had dawned on their minds that the splendid-marching black regiment was their superiors as soldiers, and that in the army effectiveness, not social qualities, was what counted.

Our march was parallel to the color-line of the camp of the white troops. The music ceased.

Our Colonel was heard commanding: "By the left flank!" The Captains all repeated, "By the left flank!" The file closers cautioned in a low tone of voice, "By the left flank—Halt!"[17]

The men faced to the left, stepped into two long lines, and stood fast. As they did so, they brought their guns from the "right shoulder shift" to a "shoulder" in regular time and cadence—one-two-three!

A murmur of admiration came from the hundred-days men.

The Major was on the right flank, ready to correct the alignment. A wave of his sword announced that even his critical eye was satisfied. The alignment was perfect!

"Order-r-r!—H'ms!! The 600 musket-butts struck the ground with a solid "chug!" A generous clapping of hands from the hundred-days men testified their appreciation.

"Stack-H'ms!" There was a clash of steel as the bayonets interlocked, and the long line of stacked muskets stood glittering in the sun.

"Break ranks-M'ch!" We were in camp. Our new neighbors were an Ohio regiment, composed of the very best citizens of the Buckeye State.[18] Clergymen, doctors and lawyers were well represented in its ranks. But they were fearfully homesick. The army ration was too coarse for them, and most of them, it was said, were buying their supplies from the sutlers at a cost of about five dollars per day to the man—more money than any 10 of our men possessed. They had an abundance of rations,—coffee, sugar, salt pork, beans and hardtack,—and they freely offered the black boys all that they wanted.

The 30th accepted the hospitality, and cooked and ate nearly all night.

It was the turn of the black soldiers to laugh when a detail was ordered from the white men, and their Adjutant attempted to form them on the color-line, and made a mess of it.

Such remarks as "Is yo' gwine toe dro'r yo' butler now, honey?" "Take de same pardner yo' had yisterday." "Change de step; you'll march easier," greeted them on all sides, and they flushed and shot angry glances at their black tormentors. Our men cast envious glances at the new Springfield rifles of the Ohioans, for our old Enfield muskets were second-hand, and not good ones at that.[19]

Darkness came on, and the "tattoo" roll-call was over, and it would soon be time for "taps."

From the camp of the Ohio soldiers came the sound of singing, a sweet tenor voice that vibrated with the sentiment of the song, and seemed to quiver with homesickness.

The words rang out sweetly in the night air:

Just before the battle, mother,[20]
I am thinking most of you,
While upon the field we're lying,
With the enemy in view.
Comrades brave around me lying,
Filled with thoughts of home and God,
For well they know that on the morrow,
Some will sleep beneath the sod.

Chorus:
Farewell, mother, you may never clasp me to your heart again,
But, oh, you'll not forget me, mother,
If I'm numbered with the slain.

The singer paused. From the camp of the 30th, in shrill falsetto voice and comical imitation of the singer rose this song:

Just behind the battle, mother,
I am thinking most of you,
While upon the field we're lying,
With no enemy in view.

Comrades brave around me lying,
Filled with hardtack and salt-pork,
For well they know that on the morrow,
They'll get some more hardtack and pork.

Chorus:
Farewell mother, you may never clasp me to your heart again,
But if I can jump another bounty,
I'll soon be home again!

And then those black tramps laughed until their yah! yahs! almost drowned out the sound of the taps.

There was no more singing that night.

We left very early next morning, before daybreak. When sunrise came it revealed the fact that nearly half of the regiment had new Springfield rifles. Many of their new rubber blankets, too were, I fear, never again seen by the hundred-days men at White House Landing. The ragged soldier whom the white soldiers had addressed as "Jim Crow" was attired in a brand-new uniform. The scamp had discovered the tents of his tormentors, stolen their clothes, and left his own ragged duds in exchange.

"Reckon dem hundred-dazers won't want to see no mo' 'black clouds' right away," was his remark, as he complacently surveyed his new suit. His prophecy was a true one. We met the 39th regiment of our brigade on their way to White House Landing, with the balance of the prisoners. They told us afterward that when they went into camp on the same ground that we had occupied that the white troops established a heavy camp guard and threatened to shoot any black soldier who attempted to cross the line.

We reached the front about noon and went into camp behind some breastworks, about two miles southwest of Old Church. We were all busily engaged in cooking dinner, for nearly everyone had obtained something extra for their bill of fare, when a firing broke out in the cavalry picket-line. It kept increasing all the time. Soon a cavalry-man came dashing in.

"The rebels are coming! The rebels are coming!" was his cry. Others followed him, and the firing was growing nearer all the time. Still, no one in our camp paid any attention to it; everybody was trying to hurry up his dinner!

Capt. Smith's Ben had the preparations for our dinner well advanced, and the Captain ordered it served at once, much to Ben's disgust, who was thereby deprived of a chance to give the dinner a finishing touch and a display of his culinary skill.

The cracking of carbines kept increasing, and the fleeing cavalrymen began to come in by groups. Many were leading horses with empty saddles, and many riderless horses came in with the others, with no one to care for them. Half a mile from us, in the rear, a full division of cavalry were encamped, and we could hear the bugles sounding "to horse." A sharp command, "Fall in," sent our men into line, and they left their little dinners cooking over the fires with rueful faces. An increased rattle of carbines and a few louder musket-shots told us that the enemy had reached our infantry videts, and that some of our cavalrymen were trying to make a stand there. Less than half a mile in front of us Co. A of the 30th had been stationed on the main road as a reserve for the infantry picket-line. The regiment was hastily faced by the flank, and started on the run to their assistance. Many of the men had snatched their boiling-hot coffee from the fire, hoping to obtain a chance to drink it, but we were ordered off so quickly that they all lost their coffee. The distance to the infantry reserve was soon covered, and we arrived there in time to see our cavalrymen driven in a disorderly crowd down the road, through the ranks of Co. A. We were obliged to get out of the road to allow them to pass. Co. A opened a sputtering musketry fire on the Confederate cavalry who were pursuing the Union cavalrymen, and caused a momentary checking. The regiment was rushed into line-of-battle across the road and halted. The confusion among the enemy's cavalry was only temporary.

"They are going to charge. Here they come! Now, men, steady!" were the cries heard all around. The voice of Col. Bates was heard above all the confusion. His command rang out clear and cool: "Fire by rank—Battalion, ready-rear rank-aim!"

The charging column was fearfully near—not more than 10 rods away. We could see their eyes and the ashy color of their faces as they saw the leveled musket-barrels pointed at them. But on they came. "Fire! Load. Front rank-aim-fire! Load!"

At the first command a splendid volley came from the rear rank, and a few seconds later the rammers were jingling as they rammed the cartridges. The first volley threw the enemy in confusion; the second one caused them to wheel and gallop back over the road which they had come. Some of their horses fell within 10 yards of our line; yet not one of our men had wavered or shown the least signs of flinching. I had fired my pistol with the others, and when the dust and smoke cleared away I expected to see the road filled with dead and dying, but to my amazement a dozen dead and wounded horses, three or four dead men, as many wounded, and a few hats and carbines were the only results of our volley. We saw some riders check their horses and pick up a comrade whose horse had been shot, and then ride off on an easy canter. Our cavalry had rallied behind us, and as the bugle sounded many riderless horses came up into line, and with head erect and flashing eyes they aligned themselves as correctly as if they had carried a trooper.

Our cavalry passed through our ranks, going at a smart trot in the direction of the foe. In a few minutes, the remainder of our division came up, and with the 30th at the head of the infantry column we started briskly after the enemy. When we reached the place where our cavalry had rallied with the infantry videts, we found the body of the Cavalry Captain[1] who had attempted to check the rebel charge.[21] The body had been stripped of everything but his undershirt. A bronzed bearded Sergeant was kneeling by the side of the dead man, crying as if his heart would break. He was chewing tobacco and swearing with all the fluency of the veteran trooper. It was a queer combination of genuine grief, tobacco and profanity.

A chase of three miles or more failed to give us another glimpse of the enemy, and we were turned about and retraced our steps. We met some newspaper correspondents from Army Headquarters, and to one of them, a tall, dark, slim man, I gave a description of the fight. He seemed much interested, and afterwards I learned that he was Whitelaw Reed [Reid], the *New York Tribune's* correspondent.[22] I anticipated a glowing account of our skirmish, and was not a little chagrined some days afterwards to read the following in an obscure corner of the paper:

"A reconnoitering party of the enemy's cavalry drove our cavalry videts in on Gen. Ferrero's Division, near Old Church, last Friday. Gen. Ferrero sent his colored braves out, and pushed the enemy back to his place again."

No mention of the regiment; nothing of the gallant men who fell in attempting to stay the enemy's charge, or the poor fellows who were swept off as prisoners. The loss of a hundred men was an item hardly worth a mention in those days.

I could not help but think that if that newspaper correspondent had been in the road when the enemy's cavalry came tearing along, his account of the skirmish would have been a little more vivid in its description.

1 Capt. Peter Backus [Joseph Backus], 1st Conn. Cav. A most gallant officer. Killed June 10, 1864, near Old Church, Virginia.—F.B.S.

4

Picket Duty at Petersburg, Virginia

It was easy to say, "Advance the posts!" but to go stumbling around through the woods in a pitchy darkness and hunt up each separate post, running the risk of an ambush from the enemy known to be near, or being shot by mistake by your own men, bitten by moccasins and rattlesnakes, getting lost, scratched with briars, and drenched with wet underbrush, or mired in the swamp, was difficult and dangerous, and disagreeable in the extreme.

Our little fight that day proved that the colored troops did possess fighting and "staying" qualities.

What follows will show how the old superstitions still clung to the negroes, and of the difficulties that their white officers had to contend with.

There was a noisy wrangle down among the company tents. Joe Wright, a big, jet-black man, was saying angrily:

"Some of dese yere yallar niggers walkin' round tinks demse'ves men, kase dey got two-free stripes on dere arms."

"And some of these black mokes don't know as much as Thompson's colt!" retorted First Serg't Scott, who was the "yaller nigger" referred to.

"What's the matter, Joe?" I asked.

"Sergeant say, sah, dere ain't no ghostes, but de culled ladies at de big plantation ober yander, dey says, sah, dat Ole Stonewall Jackson's ghos' do ride up an' down dese yere roads some nights, an' I b'leves he do. Dis here place is Ole Stonewall's ole stompin' groun'; dere's heaps ob men been killed 'bout yere; w'y shouldn't de ghostes ride out on de dark ob de moon?"

Argument was useless with one like Joe. It was, indeed, Stonewall Jackson's "ole stompin' groun,'" for in this very vicinity he had made his famous moves in the Summer of 1862. The officers found out that the story of "Ole Stonewall's ghos'" had spread through the whole division.[1]

On the night of June 12 we drew in our pickets and moved off down the White House Road as quietly as possible. We were the rear-guard of the whole army, and the army was 10 miles away; but, of course, we in the line did not know that. The brigade and division commanders were fully alive to our dangerous position, and kept the column moving at a lively rate.

The night was hot and the roads were dusty. It was nearly 2 o'clock, and we had not halted. The men were beginning to lag and show signs of distress. Everybody was sleepy and cross. The moon shone just enough to make everything appear weird and unreal.

Suddenly, a cry was raised, "Ghos'! Ghos'! Look out, dar!"

Something was coming with a terrible crashing sound. Every man around me vanished, the fugitives knocking me into the ditch as they left the road. Something white, leaving a trail of sparks behind it, went by with a terrible clatter. I pulled my pistol, but by the time it was drawn there was nothing to shoot at.

My first thought was that the Confederate cavalry had dashed through our line. I got out of the road and watched for the riders, but none came. For a moment everything was silent, then officers began calling and yelling to their men, but none responded.

Not a soldier was to be seen or heard. The whole Fourth Division, Ninth Corps, over 4,500 men, seemed to have vanished entirely, and it was over an hour before they could be got together again. The "ghost" had scattered the division into thin air. And what was the ghost? It turned out to be a pack-mule belonging to Division Headquarters.

The pack-saddle had turned under the mule, scaring him, and causing him to run away. A lot of mess-pans and kettles were attached to the saddle, and the animal's iron shoes, striking them, made the clatter and sparks. Some pieces of shelter tent attached to the pack, streaming and flapping, gave the appearance of white wings.

When the cry of "Ghos'!" was raised, and this terrible apparition came into view, it was all that was needed to rout the whole division.

The men were much ashamed when they learned the cause of their fright. With a view to prevent like occurrences in the future, strict orders were issued to the officers to shoot down the first man who left the line under such circumstances.

Several incipient panics occurred some weeks later, but they were promptly checked by the officers and by the resolute example of many of the men themselves.

A hard march brought us the next night to the banks of the James River. A long pontoon bridge stretched from bank to bank. Across it the great trains were crossing. Great ferry-boats filled with troops were flying back and forth. Below the pontoon bridge in the river, were a large fleet of schooners loaded with forage for the cavalry and army teams. On some of them the baled hay was piled at least 15 feet high above the deck.

There were hospital steamers for the sick and wounded, schooners loaded with powder and shell for the artillery, schooners with rations and Quartermaster supplies;—a great and valuable fleet. And that the enemy might not attack them, on the upper side of the pontoon bridge were lines of gunboats, "double-enders" as they were called, and still farther up the river were the ironclad monitors. Occasionally the monitors threw a shell from their big 15 inch guns, with a sullen heavy roar, in marked contrast to the sharp crack of the rifled fieldpieces that we were accustomed to hear; but what they were shooting at we could not ascertain. A few cavalrymen were left with us as videts and they reported that the enemy's cavalry were scouting around in close proximity. Our whole division was drawn up in line-of-battle, the covers taken off regimental flags, and a heavy skirmish-line advanced. Whether an attack was expected, or this was done to make a show of force to the enemy's scouts, no one knew. No enemy came to trouble us, and late in the afternoon the pontoon bridge was taken up. After dark the cavalry videts were drawn in, and with the Second Brigade were ferried to the south side of the river. About 10 o'clock the boats came back for us, and we were taken across with the others.

The next evening, June 17, 1864, we arrived on the Petersburg line. It was dark before we reached there, and we passed some hospital tents filled with colored wounded, and learned that Hink's Colored Division, of the Eighteenth Corps had been engaged, and that the men had acquitted themselves most gallantly.

The next morning we were placed in the second line-of-battle, where, for a while, we were exposed to a furious fire of shell. At the first shell that went shrieking over nearly the whole column bowed like tall grass before the wind. At the next one, some crouched, and others watched for it to explode. When the third and fourth ones came along, the jokers were ready with their nonsense:

"Wha' dat feller want?" "Whar he gwine?" "Yere him say 'Want yer, want yer?'" were some of the remarks. Soon they paid but little attention to them, probably because no one on our part of the line was hurt, most of the shells going over and bursting beyond us.

The Officer of the Provost Guard stopped an old negro soldier going to the rear. He had his knapsack, gun, and accouterments, and was making off the field, doubled up as if he had a colic. He was an ashen gray, as pale as a negro could be.

"Where are you going? What are you skulking for?" demanded the officer sharply.

For an answer the man straightened up, and lowered his hands. A shell had torn him, and he was literally carrying his bowels in his arms. A glance showed that the wound must be a mortal one. The officer took off his hat. "I beg your pardon for speaking so," he said; "I did not know that you were wounded." He sent some stretcher-bearers to assist the wounded man.

The first line-of-battle ahead of us had failed to carry the main line of works in front of them, but had captured an outer line, and quickly reversed the works and dug themselves into shelter. We were protected by a strip of woods and a little hill, and were soon marched off by a circuitous route and halted near what was known as the "Shane House." A few men were left to guard the muskets and knapsacks, and then nearly the whole division, with shovels and axes, were sent off on fatigue duty. The shovel-men were set at work under directions of the engineering officers, building a fort for a battery of siege artillery that was expected from City Point. Hand barrows were made for hardtack boxes, and a house was torn down and the lumber used to bank up the earthwork of the fort.

Part of the axmen were set to building a road through a forest of young pines to the Jerusalem Plank Road. They cut down the trees, which were about six inches in diameter, trimmed out the poles, and laid them side by side and covered them with dirt. This made a solid road for the wagon-train to pass over. It was nearly two miles in length and was finished before daylight the next morning.

My party of axmen was assigned the duty of getting out abatis—"abatee" the soldiers always pronounced it. We cut down small hard-wood trees, and trimmed and sharpened their branches. These were to be placed in front of the breastworks to prevent a solid rush by the enemy should they attempt a charge.[2]

The Confederate artillerymen noticed our detail working in the brush, and although the distance was fully two miles, they sent shells over there, and some of the working party were injured.

The sutler wagons, the first that we had seen, came up and pitched their tents, and were ready for business. On the side toward the enemy they built a breastwork of logs and earth to protect their tent, and sold cheese, ginger cakes and canned peaches, with the shells bursting within a hundred yards of them.

The night of June 22, 1864, was intensely dark. About midnight a terrible musketry-firing broke out on the left of the Ninth Corps, about three-fourths of a mile from where we lay.

The sky was lighted up, and we could hear the shrieks and yells of the men, but who was attacked, or who was defeated, we did not know. Our men were got into line, and waited for long hours, but no orders came to us.

Afterwards we learned that a gap had been left between the Ninth and Second Corps. The enemy found this out, and taking advantage of it, threw a heavy force around in the right and rear of the Second Corps. The men in the trenches, one-half on duty, the others asleep, were surprised by a terrific crashing volley from the rear and right flank that in some instances killed or wounded almost every man in the trench.

The wildest alarm and confusion prevailed, and the Confederates pressed their success to the utmost. They retired to their own lines almost as suddenly as they had appeared, taking with them 2,200 prisoners. The Second Corps lost nearly 3,000 men by this daring midnight attack.[3]

A few days before this, Gens. Wilson and Kautz, with their cavalry, had made a raid on the Weldon Railroad, but they had been so roughly handled by the enemy that the Sixth Corps had been detached and sent to their assistance.[4] It was the stretching out of the line to the left by the Second Corps that left open the gap that proved so disastrous to the Union side. The day after this attack there was a general readjustment of the lines, and our division was placed in some breastworks that had been occupied by the Sixth Corps. There was no firing in our front, and only the enemy's pickets were visible.

In a day or so the Sixth Corps returned and relieved us, and we went back to the Ninth Corps line, and were set at work at our old job, building a fort for a battery of siege artillery.

The siege-guns came up early in the morning, and our fatigue party, as the laborers were called, were placing some gabions in position, finishing up an embrasure, when the enemy's artillery opened on us.[5] The shells came so thick and fast, and burst so close to us, that the men were obliged to seek shelter.

Whether the Confederates did this to annoy the working party, or with an idea to make us show what kind of artillery we had there, we did not know. If they had any curiosity regarding those guns, it was destined to be satisfied at once. The guns were long, black, rifled 32-bounders, the largest that we had seen. The planks for their traverse bed had been laid behind the embrasures. Everybody took hold and pushed, and they were rolled into position.

"Those fellows over there are getting too familiar altogether," said the artillery officer in charge. "We will have to teach them a lesson." His orders rang out: "Attention! Cannoneers, to your posts! In battery! Load!"

The long swabs wiped the black throats of the guns, and a red flannel bag, the powder cartridge, was pushed home, followed by a conical percussion shell.

"Number three, ready. Serg't Halpin, you may try a shot at those fellows," directed the officer.

A sandy-haired, freckled-faced, cross-eyed Sergeant leaped upon the parapet, took a good look to estimate the distance, and then began to alight the gun.

"If dat Sergeant shoot de way he lookin', he gwine to hit de Sanitary tent, way ober yonder!" said a black Corporal, as the cross-eyed soldier squinted along the sides of the big rifle, apparently looking at right angles with the object aimed at.

The Sergeant waved his hand.

"Fire!"

A sharp, cracking report, which nearly raised us off our feet, and made our ears ring, followed. A cloud of dust rose, and the shell exploded in the rear of the Confederate line.

"Good line shot; a little too much elevation; try again," said the officer, who was watching through a field-glass.

Again the gun was loaded, and the cross-eyed Sergeant turned the elevating screw a very little, and waved his hand. Bang! A second's time, and we saw the enemy's yellow brass gun take a backward leap, and it was instantly enveloped in a cloud of smoke from our bursting shell. Serg't Halpin had sent a shell through the embrasure of the enemy's line knocking over and disabling the gun.

Instantly Serg't Halpin jumped upon the breech of his own gun, and throwing up his hat, flapped his arms and crowed like a rooster—"Cock-a-doodle-doo! Johnnies, how are you?"

"Good shot!" said the officer.

"What do you think about the 'Sanitary tent' now, Sambo?" asked one of the artillerymen, addressing the black Corporal.

"Yo' can't mos' allers ginerally sometimes tell by de looks ob a toad how far he gwine ter hop," answered the Corporal reflectively.

The Confederates took the hint, and there were no more shells from that battery that day.

When we returned to our camp at sundown, tired out with the hard, heavy work, we were ordered to pack up at once. We were to go on picket in the rear. A four-mile tramp through a stifling dust, and we halted; the regiment was divided into details, and sent off in various directions under charge of staff officers. Co. H was placed on one of the roads, and with about 20 men I was sent still farther out, near the edge of a piece of woods, with a clearing in my front. It was dark long before we arrived there, and I placed my men in little groups of threes, as best I could in the darkness, retaining a Sergeant and five men with me on the main road. I had just lain down on my rubber blanket, when the Sergeant came to me.

"Hear de dogs a-barkin' down de road, sah?" he asked. I listened. The dogs were barking and barking loudly, too.

"Reckons dey's barkin' at sumfin', sah," said the Sergeant. I laid my ear upon the ground. There was a faint fluttering sound. I knew that it must be the sound of hoofs, and that a large force of cavalry was approaching. Were they friends or enemies? I did not know that any Union forces were expected from that direction. Notice was quietly sent to the men on the side posts to watch out sharply, and if we on the road fired, then they were to open fire and fall back into the brush, and keep up their firing until they were forced back. Then they were to spread out and try and reach the main body of the regiment as best they could. Word was also sent to the Captain that a large force was approaching. By this time they were so near that there was no mistaking the approach of a large body of mounted men. I placed my men on each side of the road; if they were enemies and charged us, we could retreat into the brush. Then I thought seriously for a moment. If it was the enemy approaching, the videt who challenged would be answered with a shot, perhaps a volley. His chances for getting killed were first-class. If they were Union troopers, and one of my men challenged them his negro dialect and accent would almost certainly be mistaken for a Confederate challenge, and would be answered with a shot. I decided instantly that it was my duty to challenge them myself, and take the chances. The hoofs were near, and the jingling sound of the sabers, as they rattled against the stirrups, could be heard.

I whispered my final instructions to the Sergeant, and ran noiselessly toward them for 20 or 30 paces. With my heart in my mouth, I challenged loud and clear, "Who comes there?"

There was a checking of the horses, and I heard the clicking of carbines as the answer came back, "Advance-guard, 1st Conn. Cav. What regiment is that?"

"Halt, advance-guard. Dismount. Advance one, and be recognized," I ordered, not answering the question.

"What regiment is that. Answer, quick!" came back so sharply that I answered "30th United States," and repeated my order for one man to advance.

"Go up there, Sergeant," said someone who seemed to be in command, "and find out who those people are."

The Sergeant advanced, and I covered him with my pistol. When within 10 paces I halted him.

"Who are you?" I asked.

"1st Conn. Cav.," he answered.

"Who are you?"

There was no mistaking the accent and the Yankee style of his answer, and I replied:

"We are the troops that you rallied behind at Old Church the other day."

"Then you belong to the Colored Division, of the Ninth Corps," he said.

This satisfied me, and I stepped out and in a few words he explained the situation. They were part of a brigade and had been cut off from the others and were trying to get back to the Union lines by a circuitous route. He quickly notified his officer, and word was sent back to the main body that the Union pickets were found, and I notified my Captain that the approaching force was a friendly one.

"It was a lucky thing that you challenged yourself," said the cavalry officer. "Had one of the darkies halted us, the chances are that we would have shot him." I did not tell him how badly frightened I was, and how I had been tempted to place that duty on one of my men. It was a little incident, but it had great effect on my men.

"De little Lieutenant didn't ax nobody—jes' walk right out en de road hisse'f," the men said to their comrades when they returned to the regiment.

The next morning all the pickets were called in and the regiment went back to the Petersburg line. A little hill and belt of pine woods protected us from the enemy's artillerists. Though out of range of bullets, stray shells often came our way and caused a scattering of the men. We were encamped on the open plain, and the fierce, hot sun beat down on our unprotected heads, the little shelter tents seemingly affording no shade whatever.

The last week of June, 1864, will long be remembered on account of its extreme heat, by the soldiers who were near Petersburg, Va. A constant procession of wagon trains, filled with Quartermaster and Commissary stores and ammunition, also ambulances with wounded men, passed near us, keeping up a stifling dust.

For once we were glad to see the Sergeant-Major come around, and hear his order, "Pack up!"

An unusual amount of halting, waiting and changing of position took place.

The whole division was going; the men's haversacks were stuffed with rations. No one knew our destination and but few cared, in their anxiety to escape that terrible dust. A hot, dusty march of 10 miles brought us to "Second Swamp," one of those swampy, spreadout lakes of the Blackwater River located about six miles southeast of Prince George Courthouse.

A camping-ground for the division was selected in a strip of pine woods, with a large open field in front of us.

Breastworks of logs were ordered to be built immediately. The men were experts by this time, and soon a solid breastwork of earth and logs, with a "head log" on top was erected. One company from each regiment was detailed for picket, and each company sent off in a different direction.

For the first time in weeks no sound of musketry reached our ears, and it seemed a welcome relief. Artillery-firing at Petersburg could be heard, reminding us of the trenches. So quiet did everything seem that we almost wondered at the orders for building breastworks.

Blackberries were ripe and abundant. A number of milch cows were captured and our mess secured one of the best. That night we had the luxury of milk in our coffee, blackberries with our hardtack and a cool clean carpet of pine boughs to spread our rubber blankets on. How we did enjoy that fragrant, elastic bed.

Long and tiresome battalion drills, both forenoon and afternoon, occupied the following days. It was always the same evolution, that of deploying into line-of-battle from double column at half distance; first it was executed in quick time, then as the men became more familiar with the maneuver, on the double-quick, then on the run, always ending with a terrific bayonet charge at an imaginary enemy. Then the regiments were united and the same drill gone through with as brigade evolutions.

"Depend upon it, this division is going to be put in somewhere to make a desperate charge," said Capt. Smith; "all this drilling isn't for nothing; some morning just at daybreak we will make a charge on the rebel line."

On the morning of July 2 some Union cavalry, part of Gen. Wilson's expedition, passed our lines. They reported that they had been badly defeated near Ream's Station, on the Weldon Railroad. Most of the command, they said, were coming in by way of the Jerusalem Plank Road. They had been separated from the main body and obliged to take this route to avoid capture.

The next morning our Adjutant, who had been up to Division Headquarters, came galloping back with the information that Gen. Wilson's troops had reached the left and rear of the Union line at Petersburg, having been badly cut up and defeated near the Weldon Railroad, with the loss of 2,200 men and all their artillery and trains. A large force was said to be following them. The Signal Corps had reported that a great body of the enemy was moving around the left of our army at Petersburg.[6] Probably they were intending to attack the Sixth Corps, which had been sent to the assistance of the defeated cavalry. It might be that they were making a grand movement to crush our left; also, that the Cavalry Corps, an artillery brigade, and part of the Second Corps were a little in rear of our division, throwing up breastworks and making preparations for an immediate attack, and that we might expect the enemy upon us at any moment. Involuntarily we looked to the open field in front, as though we expected to see the gray lines advancing. We listened for warning shots from the picket-line, but everything was quiet. The regiments had just been dismissed from drill, and were well scattered over their favorite blackberry ground.

They were quickly called in, and for a few moments there was a lively pulling down of shelter tents and rolling up of rubber blankets.

The Surgeon, donned his green sash and quickly placed himself in the line of non-combatants in a safe hollow in the rear.

All day and all night the troops waited, but no enemy came. On the 4th my company was detailed to relieve the company on picket. Capt. Smith had been detailed on a special duty of some kind, which required his absence for a day, and the Second Lieutenant was temporarily detached and was serving with another company. The duty of looking after the whole line fell upon me. A mile and a half in front I found the picket posts that I was to occupy. They extended along a thickly wooded, irregular hollow with an old cornfield in front and another in rear. The road leading from our camp to the picket-line was one of those blind, crooked ones, such as can only be found in the South. Where a big pine tree stood in the way, the road ran around it; swamp holes were left to take care of themselves. My "reserve" Serg't Scott and 10 men, were stationed on this road, at the junction of two roads, one of which led towards Norfolk, the other toward Weldon. To the right and left were numerous cross roads leading from the different plantations.

The men in groups of three were placed to the right and left of the reserve, about 200 yards apart, in such positions as would enable them to watch the roads and fields without being seen.

From the reserve one soldier was sent 100 yards in front, and another the same distance in the rear. We had no axes, but built a rude barricade of rails and brush across the road that it might annoy an enemy in the night.

Late in the afternoon I visited all the posts, and cautioned the men to keep

Fig. 4.1. "A heavy thunder shower came up, and the rain fell in torrents." Freeman S. Bowley, *A Boy Lieutenant*.

a sharp lookout, and to extinguish all fires before sundown. The usual instructions as to what they were to do in case of an attack were reiterated. Should I have occasion to visit them during the night, I would first signal by twice clapping my hands.

The Division Officer of the Day—a Major, radiant in a new uniform fresh from some sutler's stock—visited the posts and instructed them in the details of videt and outpost duty. Particularly did he charge them to make all mounted men dismount, before approaching to be recognized.

Said the Major, "Should Gen. Grant himself come out here, make him dismount before approaching within 10 yards."

Just after sundown we heard a shot in front; then several more in quick succession, and the videt came running down the road dodging behind the trees, closely pursued by a party of gray-coated cavalrymen, who were cracking away at him with revolvers. The men were promptly behind the little breastwork, and part of them sent a volley which caused the cavalry to wheel and scatter. As they did so, we saw one of them swaying in his saddle, one of his arms limp and broken; but he galloped off with the others. Every one of the firing party declared that they had aimed at that man.

The videt remained with the reserve until dark; then he was posted still farther to the front, behind a tall stump.

A heavy thunder shower came up, and the rain fell in torrents. The darkness was so intense that nothing could be seen—not even the shadows of the trees overhead. Grouped together behind our barricade, we stood for two long hours trying to shelter ourselves with rubber blankets, and eagerly listening for the warning musket-shot of the videts. Frequent blinding flashes of lightening would come, showing for a second everything around with a blue glare, only to make the darkness seem blacker than ever. At about 10 o'clock the rain ceased, and part of the men lay down to sleep. Their rest was of short duration. One of the pickets on the right, hearing a noise in the bushes, challenged and was answered by a shot. He instantly fired at the flash and his comrades fired with him. The crashing in the bushes increased, and the sound of retreating footsteps could be plainly heard.

The videt on the road in front, nervous from the first attack, and scared by the thunder and lightning, imagined that he saw something and fired and then rushed back on the reserve. To make our trouble worse, the cow, which had been brought along, became demoralized, and, breaking from her fastenings, rushed off through the woods, crashing and bellowing and making an awful noise. Any sound at such a time and place always seems close at hand, and that cow drew the fire of half the videts on the line thus completely revealing the position of our picket-line. With her vanished all our pleasant anticipations of fresh milk, also 10 yards of new rope. A few minutes later we heard the clatter of a horse's hoofs and the jingling of a saber, coming from the rear. The videt challenged sharply: "Who cum dar?"

"Division Officer of the Day," was the response.

"Halt, Division Ossifer ob de Day! Dismount! Advance and be recognized!" continued the sentinel.

There was a mudpuddle near there, and from the splashing we knew that the Major's horse must be in it.

"I am in the water," pleaded the Major; "you know who I am; never mind the dismounting; I want to see your officer in charge," and he started his horse.

"Halt! Dismount!" said the soldier, and his rifle clicked. There was a sudden checking of the horse and the officer commenced expostulating, "This is all unnecessary," when an emphatic "Dismount!" interrupted him. A flash of sheet lightening showed the Major dismounted and up to his knees in the puddle, while the black soldier stood with his musket at aim. In another second he would have fired.

"You obey orders well," said the crestfallen officer, "but my new trousers are ruined. Where is the officer of the picket?"

Having ascertained the cause of the firing, which was the object of his visit, he said, "I think you had better advance all your posts about a hundred yards, for the enemy must now know your exact location. Do it at once."

Then mounting his horse he rode off. The first duty of a soldier is implicit obedience to all orders from superiors, but I must confess that I had but little relish for this work. It was easy to say, "Advance the posts!" but to go stumbling around through the woods in a pitchy darkness and hunt up each separate post, running the risk of an ambush from the enemy known to be near, or being shot by mistake by your own men, bitten by moccasins and rattlesnakes, getting lost, scratched with briars, and drenched with wet underbrush, or mired in the swamp, was difficult and dangerous, and disagreeable in the extreme. For once I was tempted to disobey orders and risk the consequences. But I reflected the bad effect it would have on the company, as some had overheard the order, and I decided to make the attempt. Leaving Serg't Scott in charge of the reserve, I started out, pistol in hand, to grope the best way I could. It was past midnight before the work was accomplished, and I was wet through and nearly worn out. A dozen times I lost my way; only by an occasional flash of sheet lightning could I obtain my bearings. The men were alert and nervous, liable to shoot first and challenge afterwards.

In my wet clothes I lay down for a little rest. Before I could close my eyes, the vidette in the rear challenged, and the Division Officer of the Day rode up again.

He informed me that the troops had all been ordered to the left at Petersburg and were then on their way thither. He directed that my company be gathered in as quickly as possible and follow after. His directions were: "Follow this road to the second crossroad on the right; then follow that for a mile and turn to the left—that will take you to Prince George Courthouse; keep the Courthouse Road four or five miles, then take a crossroad to the left till you reach the Jerusalem Plank Road; that will take you to Petersburg. Hurry up; or the Johnnies may scoop all of you."

Then he galloped off without giving me a chance to inquire more minutely regarding the route I was to follow. There was no help for it. The division had left, and the sooner we followed after it the better our chances for life and liberty. It took nearly two hours to get all the men together, and the rain began to pour again. Cautioning them to keep together as well as possible, not to make any unnecessary noise, and on no account to fire at anything without orders, we started on the back track.

From wandering around so much we were all dizzy and confused. Every little while those in front would bump into a tree and their comrades following would jam into them, until the whole company was in a huddle. Then we would straighten out as best we could. Several times we wandered off the road, but after a little groping would find it. At last the trees were encountered so often, that I began to fear that we had lost the trail. Halting, I lit a match and, sheltering it with my rubber blanket, examined the ground. There was no sign of a road.

Thinking that we had wandered to the right of it, we turned to the left, but had not gone far when we sank to our knees in a swamp, and farther progress in the direction was stayed by a thick underbrush. So we turned back, but with no better success; the mire and brush seemed to be on every side. A dozen times we started, but after a short tramp would be halted by the underbrush. Knowing that we were completely bewildered and as liable to go wrong as right, I ordered a halt and waited for the clouds to break away, the rain having ceased falling. The clouds were breaking a little, when one of the men exclaimed: "Dere's one ob de regiment's cook-fires." We saw a flickering light, apparently a hundred yards off. Knowing that some of the companies had built their brush shelters over their fires to prevent showers extinguishing them, I thought it was possible that we might be in the vicinity of our division camp, and this light some smoldering ember of a campfire. With the light of our beacon, we started briskly towards it; but it appeared to recede as we approached. After going a short distance it seemed no nearer than before, and farther advance was stopped by our old enemies, the brush and mire. As we halted, the light rose several feet from the ground; for a second glowed a sickly blue, then vanished. We had been following the *Ignis fatuus*, or "will-o-the-wisp."[7]

A groan of superstitious horror ran through the ranks.

"Oh, de good Lordy hab masse. Dat am de Jack-o-lantern hisse'f. No good nebber come nobody arter chasing one ob dem lights!" ejaculated a terror-stricken negro.

A stampede seemed imminent. Knowing it would result in the loss of many men, I ordered the Sergeants to shoot anyone who attempted to run. "We are not going to have any Stonewall Jackson ghost business here," I said.

The mention of the "ghos'" started a laugh from some of them, and that laugh did more to restore their courage than all the arguments that any one could have advanced.

There was no alternative but to wait for the daylight. Our situation was serious. Before daylight the Union troops would be 10 miles away, and the roads leading towards them might be filled with the Confederate forces who defeated Gen. Wilson's command. Our greatest danger lay in encountering some of the roving regiments of the enemy's cavalry, who were always scouting in the rear of our army, and to whom my little band of 60 would be but a mouthful.

Death or capture would be the fate of most of us should we encounter one of these expeditions. I well knew that in case of capture, my white skin would not save me from being hung to one of the live-oak trees which abounded in this country. Even if we reached the regiment all right again, I dreaded the censure of the Colonel almost as much as an encounter with the enemy.

Two men were detailed to watch and the rest lay down and attempted to sleep. The woods were full of dismal noises. One of the great horned owls of Virginia perched on a branch above us and began his unearthly cry, "Who-o-who-o-o!" followed by a strangling sound and ending in a manic laugh that was fearful to hear. Dirt was thrown to drive him away, but it only made him snap his bill like a rattle. Whippoorwills, chuck-wills-widows, tree toads and locusts all seemed to combine to make a grand nocturnal concert.[8]

Slowly the hours passed till day light. A hearty breakfast was eaten, knapsacks snugly packed, and the arms carefully inspected and recapped. The road was found not 50 rods from where the division camp had been. No sound of artillery or musketry reached our ears, and we hoped the roads might yet be clear. With a Sergeant and two men ahead as skirmishers, and a like party in rear, we started. We reached the road that led to the Prince George Courthouse Road, and then stopped to deliberate. If the enemy were moving in that vicinity the broad Courthouse Road would be the one which they would occupy. A man climbed a tree, but could see nothing. The rain had soaked the ground so that no dust would arise from a marching column. I determined to keep farther off to the right and take the chances of finding another road that led to Petersburg. A march of a mile, and the men in advance gave a signal to halt. A clearing and a house were in view. While we were looking, an old negro with a hoe came out of the house. "If we only had that old man over here," I said, "we might find out something about our road." Then John Jackson, the butt of the company, whom the men had nicknamed, "Monkey," spoke up: "Reckon I kin dror him dis-a-way, sah."[9]

I knew that there was a signal code among the slaves and that John had been a slave man.[10]

"All right, Jack, you can try it," I said.

Jackson stepped a little to one side into a bunch of sassafras bushes. Then he gave a signal by cawing like a crow, "caw," "caw," "caw."

The old negro stopped.

"Caw," came from the bush. The old man took off his hat.

"Caw," "Caw," was repeated again. The old man scratched his head and dropped his hat, as if by accident, upon the ground. "He comin' right along, sah," said Jackson in a low tone. The old man walked slowly towards the bush, an occasional "caw" giving him the location. We could see that he was very lame—one foot dragged over the ground.

"Look at that, sir," said Serg't Scott; "that man has been hamstrung!"

The old man approached the clump of bushes where Jackson was, and the latter stepped out and asked, "Old man, is yo' *true?*"

"Yes, sah; 'deed I is," was the earnest response.

Jackson led him to where we were. He was much surprised, and informed us that we were in great danger, as scouting parties were around there almost daily. He knew nothing of any large bodies of troops, and as we felt able to stand off an equal number, our spirits rose. He advised us to keep well away from the Courthouse Road. With his stick he drew a rude map of the roads, showing the plantations and places to avoid. With a pencil and sheet of paper, I copied this map and jotted down the directions. When I thanked him, he said "Bress de Lord, I'se mighty glad to do sumfin foh de Linkum men. I cain' go wid ye, I'se got ter stay right yere; ya'rs ago, I runned away, an' w'en dey kotched me dey ham-strung me," showing the foot with the tendons severed just above the heel; "but bress de Lord, de great Day ob Jubilee's mighty clos' at han' an' I'se gwine ter die a free man, 'doe' I'se been a slave all my life!"[11]

Leaving the old man, we struck out at a lively rate. We found his roads exactly as described. By making detours, we avoided all houses. No one was seen and four miles from the rear line of the Petersburg defenses we met our cavalry patrol. They directed us the course to take. It was nearly noon when we reached the camp of the 30th U.S.C.T. Our arrival created quite an excitement. It was feared that we were lost. When I reported our night's adventures to the Colonel he said: "I am glad to see you back. You are very lucky to be here."[12]

We learned afterwards that a considerable cavalry force of the enemy had followed the line of march of our division. Some stragglers from the division, who fell out, and went to sleep by the roadside, were afterwards found by our cavalry scouts, with their heads split open by sabers. They had been surprised, captured, disarmed, and then murdered. Possibly our fate might have been a similar one, but for the assistance afforded by the old negro.

5

In the Petersburg Trenches

Just after sundown, a mortar battery of the enemy began to throw shells over among us. They dropped all around and exploded directly over us. If it was done with the intention of demoralizing the black soldiers, it was not a success, for the men crouched low, but showed not the least signs of wavering.

Our first experience in the Petersburg trenches occurred soon after our first arrival on the Petersburg line. For some reason the 30th U.S.C.T. was the only colored regiment which was placed in the front line, until after July 30. The first position which we occupied was in a hollow a little to the left of what was afterwards known as Fort Stedman. It was a dark night when we marched out to the front line, and, as quietly as possible, we relieved the white troops who were guarding the trenches. There was a constant flashing and popping of rifles on the picket line, only a short distance in front of us. The bullets buzzed over our heads, sometimes so closely that a person would dodge involuntarily. The troops whom we relieved cautioned us not to raise our heads above the breastworks. Finding a hole that seemed secure, I went to sleep, to be awakened in the morning by a shell bursting almost directly over me.

Looking cautiously over our breastwork, I found that our regiment was about 50 yards in rear of an earthwork, in which was the 6th Vt. L. A., a battery of six pieces. Our position was such that all the bullets and shells from the enemy aimed at the battery were almost sure to be caught by us. As our artillerymen were in front of us, we could not return the fire. Our location was a most unpleasant one.

The Vermonters had been with the Fourth Division all the way from the Wilderness, and if there was ever a man whom I envied, it was the Captain of that light battery. Whenever we of the infantry went into camp, we were thankful if a tree afforded us a shade, and we lay around in the dust or mud, as the case might be. Not so with the artillery officer. He had a wagon attached to his battery. When the battery camped for the night, a wall tent was pitched. Camp stools were brought out; a light portable table was spread; the servant baked biscuit in a skillet, cooked beans in a camp kettle and fried ham in a frying pan.

Our cooking utensils consisted of a very black coffee pot and a small frying pan. Our supplies were carried in our haversacks, and were always in a mussed-up condition. The supplies of the artillery officer, carried in a mess chest, were always abundant, fresh and nice, and of a much greater variety than we could ever hope for. I doubt if any of the generals fared better or were more comfortable. No wonder we envied him. But now the battery boys were up in the front line of trenches, and their wagon was somewhere back in the rear. We were all on the same footing, and it would not have been human if we had not chuckled a little at their discomfiture. Having a curiosity to see all that could be seen, I crawled over to the battery. The artillery Captain cautioned me not to look through or stand near the embrasure. Taking a cautious peep, I could see, 200 yards away, in the morning light, a red earth bank, about four feet high with abatis in front of it. This was the Confederate main line of rifle pits; their picket pits were 50 yards nearer to us in front of it.

The Union pickets were in scattered pits about the same distance in front of our line. This brought the pickets within 100 yards of each other, and from this close range they were shooting continually.

In the rear of the Confederate main line were a number of liveoak trees, and from the tops and branches of these trees the Confederate sharpshooters shot at any Yankee soldier who did not keep closely to his own breastwork. The artillerymen were greatly annoyed, so much so that the Captain of the battery loaded all six of his guns with canister, and fired the whole battery at once. There was a smashing of oaken branches, and some thought that they saw men fall to the ground. It stopped the sharpshooting for that day.[1]

The negroes showed their woolly heads above the parapet, but were soon glad to sit down and keep quiet, for no sooner did the Johnnies see their black faces, than they directed a most spiteful fire upon them.

The hot sun came up and fairly broiled us. If the piece of shelter tent which we spread overhead afforded a partial shade, it likewise kept off the light breeze that was blowing and made the heat more suffocating.

Just after sundown, a mortar battery of the enemy began to throw shells over among us. They dropped all around and exploded directly over us. If it was done with the intention of demoralizing the black soldiers, it was not a success, for the men crouched low, but showed not the least signs of wavering.

Darkness set in and there was an alarm. The pickets sent word back that the Johnnies "were getting ready to charge." Our artillery opened fire, and that of the enemy responded; the musketry broke out on the right and left, and the enemy's breastworks were a sheet of flame. Probably the alarm started from a working party placing abatis outside of their breastworks. During the night our regiment was moved a little to the left, and placed in an angle of the battery. This brought us in the front line and in better position for defense. We worked hard with spades nearly all night strengthening our position, for we knew that when daylight came we would be exposed to an enfilading fire, and it behooved us to get all the shelter possible. Our new position afforded us a fine view of the pickets and the enemy's line. Empty sacks were furnished us. These we filled with sand and clay and placed upon the parapet about three inches apart. The use of head logs was forbidden. The enemy's artillery was so close, that they could knock the logs off our breastworks, and thus render them a source of danger instead of protection.

That day I witnessed one of the famous truces between the pickets. All the soldiers in the Union picket pits were white men. The firing had been particularly sharp and spiteful. Towards noon the men on both sides were growing tired; a Confederate picket held up a piece of white paper over his little rifle pit and called out, "Oh, Yank!"

"Hello Johnny!" was answered back.

"Johnny" stood up in full view, holding up the piece of white paper.

"Let's stop firin' a little while; I want to cook my johnnycake."[2]

"All right, Johnny," was the response; "we want to cook some coffee too. We won't fire if you won't."

"All right, Yank; we 'uns'll tell you 'uns when we 'uns gwine ter fire."

On this agreement the pickets went to work and cooked their dinners. By mutual permission, canteens were filled from a spring that was located between the pits. The dinner was nearly over when an officer in the main line of the Confederate works yelled an order at his men.

"Hunt your holes, you Yanks. We 'uns gwine ter fire!" shouted the Johnny pickets, and the Yanks "hunted their holes" "right smart quick."

The first shots were high over, a fair warning that hostilities were resumed; the next ones were aimed to kill.

Afterwards, I saw the pickets meet in front of the Fifth Corps line and exchange newspapers for coffee and sugar. But no such courtesies were ever extended to the Ninth Corps men.[3] For three days we lay here, digging and strengthening the trenches, losing men each day by bullet and shell. Then we were relieved a night and sent to the rear to rest.

The "rest" was building forts and roads, making gabions (wicker cylinders filled with earth) for parapets, and cutting down hundreds of acres of splendid trees to give range for the artillery. Then we were back to the rifle pits in the front line. Our most disagreeable work was the placing of abatis outside of the breastworks. This was done after dark. Each man carried a tree to the outer line, went over outside the breastwork, laid down his abatis, and drove stakes across it to hold it in place. The Confederate pickets were not a hundred yards away and they would shoot at the working party.

It was ticklish work, this planting of the abatis under fire, and really required more nerve than to stand in line-of-battle. Our picket would shoot at the flashes of the Confederate rifles, to keep them down and protect the working party. If the fire was particularly annoying, the artillery would open sweeping the offending pits with canister. Then the enemy's artillery would reply, and all sought shelter who could seek it.

Such firing would sometimes extend for over a mile, and made as much noise as a great battle. Then for a time all became silent again and everything would be perfectly still.

Presently the whippoorwills would come out and sing, as if protesting bravely against this strange disturbance of their customary solitudes.

Near the Norfolk & Petersburg Railroad was an ice house. It was located on a little side hill about 50 yards outside of our breastworks. The door stood open on our side. To reach it, a man must run in full view of an angle of the enemy's line. Once inside of the ice house, the man was comparatively safe.

The men on that part of the line would take any chances to obtain a chunk of ice. The water in our canteens was warm and insipid, and after a few hours it grew stagnant and of disagreeable smell.

Some thirsty man would take his rubber blanket and announce his intention of going for ice. His comrades would divide themselves into parties, and when he started to run for the ice house they would fire a volley, then another, and another, "to keep the rebs down." But the "rebs" were not always to be kept down, and sometimes the ice man fell writhing in agony. But this would not deter others from making the attempt an hour later.

The cookery of the whole army during this campaign had been of the rudest character. The soldiers made their coffee in the little black tin cups that were carried strapped on the outside of their haversacks. When the coffee was boiled it was cooled by a little water from the canteen, and sweetened with brown sugar—that is, if the sugar tied in a rag, and carried in the haversack, had not been dissolved by rain or mixed with salt. For meat, the rule was four days' fresh beef and one day's salt pork for every five days' rations. The beef was blue, tough and poor of quality; and no wonder, for the steer was slaughtered, cut up and issued and sometimes cooked before the meat had time to properly cool.

Beans and rice were issued at times, but there was never a chance to properly cook them. The half-boiled beans killed as many men as were shot dead on the battlefield. The hardtack was always of good quality. I have heard many stale jokes of hardtack marked "B. C." and of hardtack that had been so long in the army that it could go out on the parade ground and drill in brigade evolutions. But I want to record my testimony that the hardtack which we received in the Army of the Potomac in the campaign of 1864 was sweet, clean and of most excellent quality. The soldiers cooked it in a dozen different ways; it was toasted, fried in salt pork, soaked in water and fried, boiled with salt pork or beef and made into a "scouse," pounded into crumbs and made a sort of soup, and any other way that the ingenuity of the soldier could devise. As stated before, the soldier cooked his coffee in his tin cup; the ramrod of his musket served as a toasting stick to cook the beef and pork. If he wished to fry his meat, half of an old canteen held on the end of a split stick was his only frying pan. No wonder that much sickness resulted, and that the hospitals were filled to overflowing. So alarming was the condition of the whole army that the Government assisted ably by the Sanitary and Christian Commissions, made great efforts to improve our fare.[4]

How the men were elated when the Commissionary issued to them rations of soft bread, potatoes and pickled onions.

One jubilant picket, holding up on a ramrod a fine loaf of bread, shouted to the videt on the other side, "Say, Johnny; how do you like the looks of that?"

"Bully," said the Confederate soldier, and sending a well-directed bullet, he knocked the loaf and ramrod into the dirt.

"Say, Yank," he called out, "how do you like that?"

Rations of whisky were issued to all soldiers while serving in the trenches. The whisky was drawn from the Commissionary in a camp kettle. Each man was given his ration by the Captain, and obliged to drink it then and there. It was found that some men would save up their whisky ration until they got a bottle full and then trade it for tobacco; others would save enough to make them drunk. So the order was issued: "Drink your whisky on the spot or let it alone entirely."

One hot day in July, when we were in the front line near the Norfolk Railroad, Lieut. Edgerton obtained permission to go to the rear to purchase "something good to eat." It was a risky matter to get back from the trenches, but Edgerton made the trip safely, and walked to a sutler's tent, three miles away, where he made his purchases.

From the Christian Commission's agent he obtained some corn starch, and returned loaded down with condensed milk, white sugar, cheese and self-raising flour. He promised us "slapjacks with white sugar on them," and corn starch pudding for supper.[5] This in addition to our regular fare, with the soft bread and some tea that we had obtained from the Commissionary, would make a meal good enough for Gen. Grant. In a square hole in the ground, which served as a kitchen, Lieut. Edgerton prepared his supper. The pudding was a grand success and was set aside to cool; the slapjacks were light and feathery, "just like the ones we used to have at home." How pleasant was the odor which came from them and how we applauded Edgerton's efforts. The last slapjack was browned; supper was ready.

Whish!—whish!—whish! "Shell! Look out, boys!"

We scattered. A deafening report, a cloud of smoke, and a cry of agony from Edgerton.

"O, Lieutenant, are you wounded?" I called.

"Wounded! Worse than that! See there!"

Edgerton pointed to the "cook hole," where lay our eagerly anticipated supper covered with dirt and a total wreck.

"That's a dirty rebel trick!" said Edgerton, almost crying.

I could have cried too, if it would have helped matters. Our supper that night had but one course—hardtack.

The Union breastworks on this part of the line were the strongest and best of any that we had seen. The top of the parapet was at least eight feet above the bottom of the trench or "traverse," as the passageway behind the earthwork was called. A transom, or bench of clay, was arranged for the men to stand upon when firing, and the top of the parapet was well supplied with sandbags. The traverse was wide enough for the men to march four abreast. Behind the traverse were long excavations about eight feet wide and from four to six feet deep. These were the "sleeping holes." Behind them were "cook holes," where the men made their coffee. All the earth taken from these excavations was thrown on the side towards the enemy, thus increasing the protection. All these places were connected with numerous little alleys and covered ways that ran in every direction. The construction of bomb proofs had not been carried out to any great extent at this time, but the constant dropping of mortar shells soon made them a necessity.

On the transom behind the parapet were a lot of forked stakes driven firmly in the ground. We soon learned that by resting a musket over the parapet and placing the small of the stock, just behind the trigger guard, in the forked stick, that the gun would be sighted just right to sweep the top of the enemy's works.

This was an arrangement for night shooting, and a very effective one it was. Behind us, the long, rifled, thirty-two pound siege guns kept up a constant fire day and night. The crack of those guns would almost lift a man off his feet, and the shrieking projectile would go hurtling through the air over our heads, with a "whir-r-r" that made our heads ache. We would sleep soundly with the artillery on both sides firing, but let the "pop!" "pop!" "pop!" of the picket rifles break out, and every man was up and in his place in an instant. As I watched nights, through a crevice in the sandbags, I could hear the town clock in Petersburg, striking the hours, and I set my watch with Petersburg time. The cars could be heard running back and forth, and sometimes we would hear the enemy relieving their troops who were in the trenches.

A little on our right a number of men had been shot. From the position of the men when shot, and the character of the wound, it was decided that a sharpshooter with a long-range rifle was located in the commanding position, and was picking off our men.

The 1st Mich. S. S. had two companies of Indians, and two of these men were selected to put a stop to the Confederate sharpshooter's work. These Indians worked their way down to the very front line of picket pits. They were provided with the long, heavy, eight-square barreled rifles with telescopic sights.[6] Nearly a mile away stood a high chimney. All day the Indians watched that chimney, and never fired a shot. The sun had gone down and the twilight was deepening, when one of the Indians fired. A man was seen to fall from the chimney. He had been located in the top of it, entirely hidden from view. In descending, he had incautiously exposed a portion of his body, and the Indian sharpshooter had instantly dropped him. The next day our artillery fire demolished the chimney. We were located on the extreme left of the Ninth Corps. Our left connected with the right of the Fifth Corps. On the Fifth Corps line everything was quiet. The pickets lay around in full sight of each other. The artillerymen sometimes had a duel, but the men in the trenches agreed not to shoot pickets and the arrangement was faithfully carried out by both sides. In sharp contrast was the condition of affairs on the Ninth Corps' line. There the sharpshooting, shelling and artillery duels were constantly going on, both day and night. The troops in these trenches had unlimited supplies of ammunition, and every man was obliged to expend one hundred rounds of ammunition each day. The men soon became expert marksmen, and would send a bullet through the three inch crevice between the sandbags every time.

The newsboys visited us in the trenches, selling New York, Philadelphia, Washington and Baltimore papers. The cry of "Here's your New York *Herald*,

Feladelfy *Inquirer*, Baltimo' *'Merican*, and Washington *Chronicle*—only ten cents a copy!" was heard daily, and the powder-stained, grimy soldier eagerly purchased a paper to read, while his musket, hot from firing, stood cooling against the parapet.[7] With all their danger, there was a fascination about the trenches, and generally the men preferred the front line to the duty in the rear.

6

The Crater

"There she goes!" shouted someone and we all looked toward the Confederate fort. From the earth there burst the red glare of flame, followed by the black smoke; with it came a terrible rumbling, that lengthened into a muffled roar. High into the air rose the cloud of smoke and dust, and with it great blocks of clay and many dark objects that might have been men or cannon. Back to earth the mess fell again, with another shock almost equal to the first.

During the month of July we heard frequent rumors of a mine that was being constructed somewhere on the line. On several occasions we had seen white soldiers, with their uniforms plastered with red clay of a peculiar shade, which certainly did not correspond with the sort we saw in the breastworks. That the unremitting firing kept up along the whole Ninth Corps line had a purpose, and that the purpose was to prevent the discovery of the mine, we could easily understand. The last week in July the 30th U.S.C.T. lay in the front line of breastworks to the west of the Norfolk Railroad. On the right of our regiment was a deep ravine, and when some of our officers would have made a social call down among the white troops stationed there, they were stopped and forbidden to pass. No explanations were given; only strict orders not to allow anyone to pass along that traverse. It was down in this ravine that the miners were working.

The earthworks at this point bulged forward, forming a sort of a horseshoe-shaped redoubt, which was only 130 yards from a Confederate fort of four guns, known as "Elliot's Salient." Half a mile in the Confederate rear of this fort was Cemetery Hill, so named from the cemetery, which we could plainly see.

Cemetery Hill was a gradual easy slope, with long, wide valleys on both sides. If the Union forces could once obtain possession of it, they could sweep the interior of the Confederate breastworks for more than a mile on each side. Near the cemetery an earthwork for a six-gun battery had been nearly completed, but no guns placed in position.

Lieut. Col. Henry Pleasants, 48th Pa., suggested the idea of running a tunnel from the Union line to underneath the Confederate fort, and blowing it up; the explosion to be followed by a grand assault. Col. Pleasants was a practical miner, and his regiment had been recruited from the mining regions of Pennsylvania, and were, nearly all of them, accustomed to underground work.[1]

Gen. Burnside, commanding the Ninth Corps, favored this plan, and Col. Pleasants was authorized to commence this mine. For some reason the Engineer officers at Army Headquarters did not sympathize with Col. Pleasants in his scheme, and he had the greatest difficulty in obtaining the necessary tools and instruments with which to conduct his operations. The tunnel was commenced June 25.[2]

Many difficulties were encountered, among them a sort of marl, which was so hard and tough that it had to be cut out with axes. On one part of the tunnel a streak of quicksand was encountered, which threatened to stop the whole work; and it became necessary to timber and brace up the tunnel on all sides.

As the workmen approached the Confederate line the danger increased. The jar of the earth that followed the discharge of the fieldpieces in the fort overhead was so severe, that the miners feared that it would cave in the whole tunnel and thus entomb them alive.

Ever alert and watchful, the Confederates suspected something of the sort, and sank deep shafts or counter-mines to discover what the Yankees were trying to do. So near did they come to discovering it that our men, when finishing their work, could hear the strokes of the pickaxes of the Confederate workmen.[3]

The tunnel was finished and ready for the powder July 23. Its exact length was 510.8 feet. Under the enemy's fort it branched to the right and left, and the galleries were 38 and 37 feet, respectively. Four cross-cuts were made in each gallery, and the bottoms and sides of the galleries were sheathed with poles to protect the powder from dampness. A charge of 8,000 pounds of powder was placed in the magazines, the fuse arranged, and the tunnel blocked and filled for some distance with the sandbags.[4] When it was found that all would be in readiness, Gen. Meade ordered the Second Corps and two divisions of the Cavalry Corps to the north side of the James River, to give the enemy the impression that an attempt was being made to break through the defenses of Richmond at that point. They arrived at Deep Bottom early on the morning of July 27, and a severe engagement ensued. Gen. Lee at once sent a large force of infantry and cavalry to check this movement. This was exactly what Gen. Meade desired and expected him to do. Every regiment that Gen. Lee detached from the Petersburg line would increase our chances of success when the mine should be exploded.[5]

On the afternoon of July 29, while we still lay in the trenches west of the railroad, our Colonel, Delevan Bates, called all the Captains and some of the First Lieutenants to the square hole that was occupied as regimental headquarters. When all were assembled, the Colonel addressed the officers:

"You have all heard rumors of a mine that is to be exploded; that mine is now ready. It will be blown up at 3 o'clock to-morrow morning. Gen. Burnside has directed that the Fourth Division lead the charge, which will be made as soon as possible after the explosion. This regiment will lead the division, and will be formed in double column closed in mass, behind our outer breastworks, opposite the place of explosion. As soon as the mine explodes the regiment will rush for the rebel works, and as soon as they are entered the regiment will execute right companies right into line wheel, left companies on right into line, and will go down the rebel works to the right as far as possible."[6]

"As Capt. Swift is sick, you, Capt. Proctor," addressing the young, handsome Captain of Co. F, "will command the first division." (Two companies constituted a "division," in regimental formations.) "You, Lieut. Sanders," he continued, "will take command of Co. A, in the absence of Capt. Swift. You will be assisted by Lieuts. Bowen and Plummer.[7] Your position will be a very important one. We will be supported by the other regiments of our brigade. The Second Brigade is to execute a similar movement to the left. The other three divisions of the Ninth Corps will follow us and rush for Cemetery Hill. It is hoped and expected that Petersburg will be captured. Company commanders will instruct the Lieutenants who are acting as file closers to shoot any man who leaves the line. Of course, if a man is wounded he can go to the rear if he is able to help himself. If he can't walk, let him lie on the ground until the stretcher-bearers come for him. I shall expect every officer to do his duty and set an example to his men. The information that I have given to you you will keep to yourselves. That is all, gentlemen." The officers retired; there were some sober-looking faces among them. The object of our drill at Second Swamp was explained. "We are to lead, and we will catch the butt end of it," said Capt. Smith; "we had better exchange our addresses of our folks at home, with each other." We did so, and I wrote on the fly leaf of my diary: "If anything happens to me, send word to Jesse D. Bowley, Worcester, Mass."

I ate my supper with my usual relish and the Captain jocularly remarked that the instructions which we had received had not affected my appetite. Extra ammunition and three days' rations were issued to the men. Each man now had

100 rounds of cartridges. "Wish dat dey'd gib us a chance to use dese cat'riges, or furnish a mewel to pack dem," growled one soldier as he stowed away the heavy brown-paper packages.

"Reckon yo'll git all de chance yo' wants, befo' de last bunch done used up," replied a comrade.

About 2 o'clock on the morning of the 30th, the Adjutant came around. "Pack up, and fall in immediately," was his order. The Captains roused the First Sergeants, who started around among the two-thirds of the men off duty—one-third were on duty, peering in the direction of the enemy through the crevices between the sandbags, and the packing up commenced. There was no need to caution silence; the men well knew that any unusual sound would draw a volley from the alert enemy. As all slept with their accouterments on and knapsacks packed nothing was to be done but to pull down the shelter tents and roll up the rubber blankets. The line was quickly formed in the traverse behind the works, and the men "counted twos" in whispers, and closed up towards the colors. Very little noise was made; yet the hum and stir had reached the ears of the vigilant Johnnies and the bullets whistled closely over our heads. Our pickets in the pits in front of us responded and the artillerymen, waking up, joined in. Soon there was noise enough for a first-class battle. We waited for half an hour for this storm to blow over, and most of the men fell asleep. The firing ceased; then we filed off to the rear as quietly as possible, until we reached a covered way leading to a sheltered place behind the railroad bank. Here the regiment was closed up, and we halted and rested till about 3.30 o'clock, when the men were aroused and we marched to the rear of the battery situated about 1,000 yards from the front of the Union works. All around us could be heard the shuffling tread of troops, but it was so dark that nothing could be seen. Down on the picket line the rifles were flashing, and overhead the bullets hummed with that peculiar droning sound of the nearly-spent bullet.

Our Major passed along the line. "There has been a change of orders," he said; "the three white divisions are to go in first; our division is to follow them."[8] The men were ordered to take off their knapsacks and rolls of rubber blankets and pile them into heaps. Two or three men were detailed to watch them.

The gray of early morning appeared, and the line of the enemy's fortifications could just be seen through the mist. Still there were no indications of an attack. The sky reddened and the day grew brighter and the sun began to show itself. Our Colonel took up a position overlooking the enemy's line, and many of the line officers gathered at a respectful distance from him and endeavored

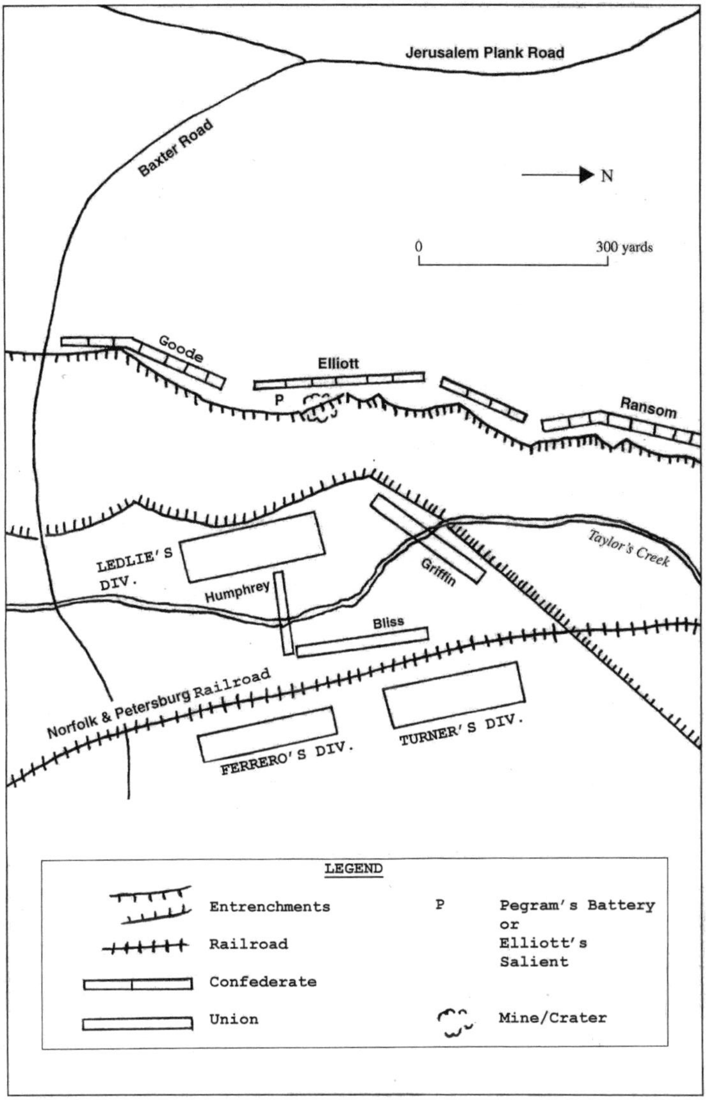

Map 2. "The Crater," immediately before the mine explo sion, July 30, 1864. (Adapted from maps in Kinard, *The Battle of the Crater*; Cav-anaugh, Marvel, *The Petersburg Campaign*.)

Confederate Forces
Elliott: Elliott's Brigade (S.C.) Brig. Gen. Stephen Elliott
Ransom: Ransom's Brigade (N.C.) Col. Lee M. McAfee
Union Forces
IX Corps
Ledlie: 1st Div. Brig. Gen. James H. Ledlie to lead the attack with the 1 Div., 2nd & 3rd Brigades, and 3rd Div., 3rd Brigade
Humphrey: 3rd Div., 2nd Brigade Col. William Humphrey
Griffin: 2nd Div., 2nd Brigade Brig. Gen. Simon G. Griffin
Bliss: 2nd Div., 1st Brigade Col. Zenas R. Bliss
Ferrero: 4th Div. Brig. Gen. Edward Ferrero
    1st Brigade Lt. Col. Joshua K. Sigfried (the 30th USCT was in Sigfried's brigade).
    2nd Brigade Col. Henry G. Thomas
X Corps (attached to 18th Corps)
Turner: 2nd Div. Brig. Gen. John W. Turner commanding 2nd Div., 1st, 2nd, & 3rd Brigades

to discern something down in the gloomy hollow which lay between us and the enemy. The reveille of camps in the rear began to sound. It was 4.30 o'clock, and the staff officers were galloping toward a clump of pine woods, when the flag of the Ninth Corps indicated the presence of its commander, Maj. Gen. Burnside.

In little groups we gathered and waited, wondering what was delaying the assault, when at twenty minutes to five the ground trembled beneath our feet.[9]

"There she goes!" shouted someone and we all looked toward the Confederate fort. From the earth there burst the red glare of flame, followed by the black smoke; with it came a terrible rumbling, that lengthened into a muffled roar. High into the air rose the cloud of smoke and dust, and with it great blocks of clay and many dark objects that might have been men or cannon. Back to earth the mess fell again, with another shock almost equal to the first. For a moment all was silent; it seemed as if both armies held their breath. The explosion seemed so close to the Union line that we almost feared that it was our line and not the enemy's that had been blown up.

Then there was a crash. Two hundred pieces of artillery along the whole Union line opened almost as one gun. Great clouds of dust marked the explosion of our shells, and we could see the abatis scattered and thrown in every direction. To us, it appeared as if the Confederate intrenchments were being plowed through and through. Of all the terrible cannonading of the late war, but few equaled and none exceeded that of this morning. The famous cannonade of July 3, 1863, at Gettysburg, perhaps numbered more pieces of artillery, but they were all light field guns. The artillery at Petersburg had a large proportion of heavy siege guns and mortars. In a moment more there were flashes from the embrasures of the Confederate batteries, and their guns were replying to ours. We eagerly listened for the yells of our assaulting column. Five, 10, 15 minutes passed, and every minute seemed an age. "Why don't they charge?" we asked. All of this time our artillery was keeping up its fire.[10]

Then we heard the yells of our charging column. Looking towards the scene of the explosion, we saw the Union soldiers going across the field to the Confederate works, in a scrambling, disorderly mass. As they reached the enemy's works, a sharp musketry fire greeted them. In a few minutes another division followed them, and were received by a much sharper fire. There was a sputtering fire that indicated the locality of our troops, and anxiously we waited to see the blue line rush up the slope of Cemetery Hill but after reaching the Confederate works our men disappeared from our sight.

Fifteen minutes later and a third division of white troops charged, and the conflict was much more stubborn and the musketry much heavier. While we watched, we saw a light battery making for the Confederate breastwork on Cemetery Hill. Some of the Union artillerymen trained their guns on them, but too late. The battery reached the breastwork and promptly opened fire on our charging columns. The artillery fire on our side was beginning to slacken. We could see the artillerymen dipping their sponges into buckets of water every time that they swabbed the gun, and the heat from the piece would turn the water into steam and raise little clouds around its muzzle. An Aid came running to our Colonel, and at once an order rang out and the regiment faced by the right flank, four abreast, and started down a coveredway leading to the front line. The coveredway was cut through the embankment of the railroad. When we were almost directly under the muzzles of the guns of one of our heavy batteries we were halted, and here we lay for half an hour, crouching low and holding on to our ears to avoid being deafened by those terrible guns. Then we moved forward again into a ravine. Here a line of stretcher-bearers passed us with their burdens of wounded. Some of the wounded were groaning piteously, but most of them made but little sound, only their pinched blue faces, betrayed their terrible sufferings. A few with comparatively slight wounds seemed to enjoy their situation. Probably the prospects of a furlough and an easy time in the hospitals were what they were hoping for. Curiously I watched my men, for I knew that this procession of wounded would unnerve them if anything would. One or two men, recruits who had only joined us a few days previously, were of an ashen hue, and their teeth were chattering; the "army ague" had attacked them. I knew what it was and sympathized with them, and in a few kind words endeavored to restore to them their confidence. But most of the men, I was pleased to see, were stolid and almost indifferent. They were munching hardtack or chewing tobacco, and whatever may have been their thoughts they made no outward sign. From the wounded, we learned that the troops engaged were the First, Second and Third Divisions of the Ninth Corps.

Following the wounded were about 50 prisoners on their way to the rear, under guard. Many of them were covered with dirt and showed signs of having been dug out of the clay, which was really the case. The sight of the black soldiers threw them into the greatest alarm, and some of them earnestly besought their white guards "not to let the niggers bayonet them." Among them were some wounded carried in pieces of shelter tent and rubber blankets. One of the wounded, a young man with a gaping, bleeding wound in the right breast, cried out to the men carrying him, "For God's sake, boys, don't let the niggers kill me! I can't live long; let me die in peace."

"Don't be skeered," said a black Corporal; "we don't kill wounded men."

"Here, take a drink of this," and he held his canteen, filled with cool water, to the lips of the dying man, and, wiping away the bloody froth, gave him all he wished; then carefully poured a little over the wound.

The other prisoners looked on in amazement, and one of them, with tears running down his cheeks, drew from his dirty cotton haversack two long plugs of Virginia tobacco and thrusting them into the hands of the black soldier, said, in a husky voice, "Here, boy, take these; it's all I've got to give ye, but 'fore God, if I had a million dollars here, you should have it all. He's my young brother, and I never looked for any kindness from any of yo 'uns."

This little act seemed to restore confidence among the prisoners, and one of them said to the Corporal, as they were hurried to the rear, "Good, boy, Sam, I hope that you don't catch it to-day!"[11]

The Confederate artillerymen were throwing shells into our ravine; we were about 50 yards out of range, and we watched the shells plow the ground and throw the dirt around. For some reason most of those shells failed to explode. Had they burst, as they struck the ground so near us, great damage might have been inflicted on us. Again we moved forward, and this time, for a short distance, we were exposed to the enemy's artillery fire. The men crouched low to avoid the showers of canister and bullets that were whistling overhead. The first man falls; a canister shot striking him squarely in the chest. His comrades lift him out of the path of the column following. When we passed him he was gasping his last. The distance that we were exposed to this fire was only a few yards; then we reached the shelter of our high breastworks in the horseshoe redoubt of the outer line. Here we were halted again. More wounded were being brought to the rear. Among them was a Captain from one of the white regiments, shot through the left arm between the elbow and wrist, and the right leg at the knee. A handkerchief was bound around the leg and tightly twisted with a bayonet to prevent bleeding, while a suspender and another bayonet did similar service for the arm. He was sitting on a stretcher, coolly smoking his pipe, wearing an unruffled countenance, as though war and wounds had never troubled him. "Go in, my bully black boys!" he exclaimed. "Go in and clean out those Johnnies over there; that's what the Government feeds you for!"

"Deed we'se gwine ter try it on an' do de best we kin," said one of the men.

The Colonel's servant came running up with a huge coffee pot full of hot coffee, and he filled Maj. Leake's [Leeke's] tin up, holding a quart, full to the brim.

"Here, Lieutenant," said the Major to me, "I've got more coffee than I want; I'll divide with you," and he gave me a generous share, which I accepted very gratefully.

"Better eat all that you can, a full belly makes a stiff back," said the Major merrily. I took the advice and ate quite a breakfast and drank all of my coffee, and felt much better for it. A staff officer passed us, hurrying to the front. "It's our turn now," said the Major.

It is proper to note here what had been done up to the time of the arrival of the Fourth Division at the outer line. When the mine was exploded, it overwhelmed all of the 18th and most of the 22d S. C. and Pegram's battery of light artillery, about 400 men in all. It caused the greatest consternation among the troops there, and they hastily abandoned their intrenchments for nearly 200 yards on each side of the explosion.[12]

On our side the men were massed behind the outer works, and ordered to lie down. Wearied and worn with hard duty, most of them fell asleep. When the mine exploded, it appeared to these men, awakening from their sleep, that the great volume of earth, then high in the air, was about to descend upon them, and a regular stampede took place. The formations of the regiments were broken, and when the men did get together again, their ranks were again broken by clambering over the high breastworks, no preparation having been made to facilitate the passage of the troops.

It was fully 15 minutes before the first rush was made, and then the men plunged into the "Crater," as the scene of explosion was afterwards called, in a disorganized, disorderly mass. A number of the Confederates were still alive, though partially buried, and our men dug them out.[13]

No officer seems to have been with the charging party to urge them forward to seize the crest on Cemetery Hill, and these precious moments were wasted. After a little time their officers urged them forward and they passed over the innermost rim of the Crater, and attempted to form a line outside, in an open field. The Confederates, who had retreated at first, hearing a second explosion, now ran back, and took position within 50 yards of the right of the Union line; a coveredway being selected as a rallying point. Thus, when our advance attempted to pass beyond the Crater, these Confederates, Ramseur's North Carolinians, paying no attention whatever to the terrible artillery and musketry fire that was sweeping the front line of their intrenchments, faced to the rear, and poured volley after volley into the rear and flank of our advancing party.[14]

At this short distance every shot from these men told, and the Union advance hastily fell back to the shelter of the Crater. Here was shown the wisdom of Gen. Burnside's original plan. With a strong force faced in line-of-battle to the right and left of each side of the Crater, such a flanking and rear fire would have been impossible, and a gateway would have been opened for a free passage of our troops to Cemetery Hill. It was not until the Second and Third Divisions of the Ninth Corps came up, and after sharp fighting and considerable loss, that the Confederates were driven out of these coveredways and the Union line extended to about 150 yards on each side of the Crater.

In the meantime a Confederate battery had occupied the partially finished earthwork on Cemetery Hill, and were throwing a plunging fire directly into the crowded mass in the Crater. Wright's Confederate battery, in the ravine on the right, were sweeping the Crater and intrenchments with canister.[15]

This was the position from 6 to 8 o'clock, when the Fourth Division was ordered to advance. An attempt was to be made by the Fourth Division to break the Confederate line and capture Cemetery Hill. The three white divisions had failed to accomplish it. In the three hours that had elapsed since the explosion, the enemy had placed artillery in position, and brought up reinforcements, and their troops had recovered from their panic. Surely the task assigned to the colored division was a most desperate one.

When the staff officer passed us, and Maj. Leake [Leeke] made the remark, "It's our turn now," Serg't Offer, of my company, heard him, and, taking off his cap raised his hand and signified that he had something to say to the men. Many of the colored men had a custom of braiding their hair into little pigtails, "plaiting" they called it, and then pulling out the "plaits" and making their wool stand out stiff all over, like an enormous wig.

Serg't Offer's hair was "plaited," and stood up stiff, like little spikes, all over his head. He could never forget that he had been a preacher on the Eastern Shore of Maryland, and he deemed this occasion a fitting one to offer some remarks.

Assuming his "Sunday voice," he began: "Now men, dis am gwine to be a gret fight; de gretest fight dat we seen yet; gret things is 'pending on dis fight; if we take Petersburg, mos' likely we'll take Richmond, and 'stroy Lee's army an' close de wah. Ebery man had orter liff up his soul in pra'ar for a strong heart. Oh, 'member de pore colored people ober dere in bondage. Oh, 'member dat Gineral Grant, an' Gineral Burnside, an' Gineral Meade, an' all de gret Ginerals is right ober yander a watchin' ye, an' 'member de white soldiers is a watchin' ye, an' 'member dat *I'se* a watchin' ye, an' any skulker am a gwine to get a prod ob dis yere bayonet; yo's alls heah me!"

The traverse behind the redoubt was filled with dismounted cavalrymen. The firing had died down; there was hardly a shot on either side.

Our Colonel's voice was heard: "Attention, battalion!" The men stood up. The arms were already loaded and capped.

"Fix bayonets!"

There was a sharp rattling of steel, and then the command rang out: "Trail arms! Forward, double quick—March!" and the regiment, in groups of fours, moved forward by the right flank over the outer breastwork.

When the regiment started, the Colonel commanding the dismounted cavalrymen waved his sword and they rose up in a body and opened fire.[16] This was to keep the enemy down as much as possible. All of our artillery again belched forth in full force. At the outer parapet a few sandbags had been placed for steps, but not enough for the purpose, and the ranks were much disordered before the open field was reached. The enemy were not to be kept down, as the fierce zip of the bullets about us abundantly testified. Co. H was the sixth in line, immediately on the left of the regimental colors. The appearance of our colors seemed to be a signal for the enemy's batteries on Cemetery Hill, and on our left, to open on us. We were not 10 yards away from the redoubt, when there came the rushing, hurtling sound of grapeshot in close proximity, and I heard a crashing sound almost at my side, like that made by a butcher when he strikes a piece of meat with his cleaver. Turning a little, I saw a great gap in the left of the company; a file of four men had been swept away from my very side. A yell to the men, and they sprang forward and closed the gap!

A Confederate battery on our right now opened and sent a charge of grape through the color guard, killing half of them. Down went the Stars and Stripes, the Color Sergeant spattering them with his blood and brains, a grapeshot having torn his head in pieces. A Corporal of the color guard, throwing down his musket, caught the colors up so quickly that they scarcely touched the ground. The color-lance was shattered by a grapeshot and the brave Corporal thrown down, but he clung fast to his colors and, rising, rushed ahead! The cry now was, "Forward, 30th! Forward, boys, forward!" To press forward was our only chance for safety. Half way across the field I glanced to the right toward the angle of the enemy's works, and I saw a row of brown hats rise over their parapet, and instantly a stream of fire ran down their line and a torrent of bullets came sweeping over us. But their aim was high and most of the bullets went over us. We reached the outer rim of the Crater, and there we passed and ran over a large number of Union dead, at least 50, and I could not help noticing that all these men had fallen on their faces with their hands extended forward; all had been killed while running forward.

We tumbled down into the Crater and were in comparative safety; but our warmest sympathies were enlisted for those following us, for we knew by the fearful rolling of the musketry, the roar of the cannon and the rushing of the grapeshot overhead, that they were exposed to a most furious fire.

In spite of the heat and roar of battle, I gazed curiously around and beheld a sight which I can never forget. The explosion had torn a chasm in the earth about 160 feet long, 60 feet wide, and in places 30 feet deep. Huge blocks of clay weighing tons were scattered around. Torn, blackened and crushed lay many dead Confederates, and mixed among them were many of our dead and wounded. On a stretcher lay Col. Gould, 59th Mass., mortally wounded. Brig-Gen. William F. Bartlett and his brigade were guarding the three sides of the Crater towards the enemy. Closely following the 30th U.S.C.T. was the rest of the brigade; viz., the 43rd, 39th and 27th U.S.C.T., in the order named. As we came crowding into the Crater, Gen. Bartlett and his staff officers made frantic efforts to keep us out.

Col. Bates immediately led the regiment to the right, where there was a traverse leading off among the Confederate intrenchments.[17]

As we passed down this traverse a sharp cry of pain and the exclamation, "Don't step on this wounded man!" arrested my attention. Two wounded Confederates were lying on the floor of the traverse; one, an old man with heavy beard, was trying to protect his wounded comrade, a smooth-faced boy, who was unable to help himself. The older man, badly wounded as he was, was cursing the negro troops most heartily. A little further on we found the trenches so filled with white troops that our passage was greatly impeded. At this point we climbed over the rebel breastworks towards the Union line and ran along just outside of the abatis. Here we were exposed to a pitiless musketry fire from the enemy in the angle of their works, and Wright's Confederate battery, No. 7, speeded up their fire to six discharges per minute to the gun. Never can I forget the dreadful flashings of those guns and the swish of the canister as it was hurled over our heads.

The brave Corporal who picked up the colors when the Sergeant was killed was shot dead, and a private seized them.

The right of Co. F. had become mixed with the left of Co. H, and Capt.

Woodward, commanding the former company, was trying to get the men into their proper places as we ran along. He was at my very elbow when he grasped his right arm with his left hand and began rolling up his sleeve. "I've got it!" he exclaimed, and a stream of blood ran down his wrist. "It's nothing," he added, giving the arm a vigorous squeeze, when out popped the bullet, which the Captain threw away. In a moment more the wound began to throb, and calling to his Lieutenant, he said, "Here, Dietrick [Detrich], you take command of the company; I'm growing faint; I'll go to the rear; I think there's a 30 days furlough waiting for me there!" and he started back for the Union line.[18]

Under a most galling fire we ran along outside of the abatis until our line lapped the Confederate line 100 yards or more. The 43rd U.S.C.T., going on a run, took a position to support us. Col. Bates, his hat on the point of his sword in his left hand, his pistol in his right, was seen gesticulating and pointing to the enemy's works. There was no need to cry, "By the left flank!" for the men saw him, and yelling wildly, faced to the left towards the breastworks where the enemy lay, and followed him.

These works were well protected with abatis and with wires strung along. Our artillery fire had displaced some of the abatis, and through these little gaps the men streamed. The air seemed alive with bullets, and so thick were they that it seemed a perfect rush and scream of lead.

To the top of the rebel works went the regiment, officers and men seeming to struggle which should be there first. As the line faced and dashed into the abatis, I had a good view of the faces of my men, and that view is indelibly photographed on my memory.

Their usually black faces were an ashy color; the eyes were set and glaring, the lips tightly drawn, showing the white teeth; the expression on every face was something terrible; it showed a determination to do or die. Over the top of the parapet we poured, and looking down we could see some of the enemy with muskets braced and ready to receive us on the bayonet's point. Right down among them we jumped, calling out, "Surrender! Surrender or die!" Fortunately for us most of them had emptied their guns before we made the final rush for their works. A few who had loaded guns fired and were almost instantly shot down or bayoneted, but most of them threw down their arms and begged for mercy.

The 43rd U.S.C.T. was close at our heels when we jumped down into the traverse. A Confederate Major calling on his men to "die but never surrender to niggers!" took refuge in a bombproof and defied us to do our worst. There was a volley and a dash, and the bombproof was quickly filled with blacks, and in its darkness ensued a hand-to-hand struggle such as seldom occurs even in war.

The conflict was of short duration and our defiant foes were ruthlessly bayoneted, but not until they had sold their lives dearly, and caused some of their assailants to bite the dust. A Confederate officer, rallying his men, sprang up from a coveredway not 30 feet away, calling out, "Rally, boys! Rally, and drive them back! They are nothing but niggers!"

A very howl of rage like the roar of wild beasts went up from the blacks. With a wild shriek and a cry of "Lord Jesus, save me; I'se only a pore nigger!" Serg't Offer went by me, his musket at a charge, dashing straight for the Confederate officer. The Sergeant's cap was off, and the "plaits" of his hair stood up like little horses, and his frenzied manner made him a grotesque and, at the same time, a most horrible-looking object. Closely following him were a dozen blacks. The officer saw his danger and called to the rebel soldiers near him to "Shoot that nigger down;" but the Confederate rifles were empty. The white men sprang to the assistance of their officer but they were too late. The black soldier drove his bayonet into the officer's breast, and bore him to the earth. The other blacks threw themselves upon the little group. I fired one shot from my pistol before the combatants mingled. Serg't Offer was struck and knocked down, and a powerful rebel soldier stood over him with uplifted musket, ready to dash out his brains. A musket, thrown harpoon fashion by my sailor Sergeant, Serg't Dudley, caught the uplifted rebel arm, and the man begged for quarter, which was granted.[19] All of that little group of Confederates were killed or captured. Some of their comrades, not 10 yards away, began firing at us, and we were glad to dodge back behind the bombproofs.

Our prisoners were at once started for the rear. Two hundred prisoners and a color had been captured by the First Brigade in this charge. But more than half of the 30th had gone down.

The officers made the greatest exertions to form their men again, for there was not a company that had anything like a line of battle, and the 43rd U.S.C.T. were as badly mixed up as we were.

The enemy's works on this part of the line were a perfect honeycomb of bombproofs, trenches, coveredways, sleeping-holes, and little alleys, running in every direction. A little knoll gave him an elevation of about 20 feet above the Crater. Bullets came through all the little alleyways and found victims in the most unexpected places. The right flank of the regiment was having a lively little fight with the enemy not a dozen yards away from them. The tops of the breastworks were continually being swept by grape and canister from the battery in the ravine in our front. Mortar shells came dropping down among us.

We heard the yells of a charging column on our left, and looking we saw the Second Brigade going in fine shape, over the line of the First Division over the bombproofs, out into the open field on our left and their front.

Instantly the batteries in Cemetery Hill and Wright's battery were turned on them, and a sharp infantry fire reached them from the ravine in their front. We could see the great gaps made in their line as the grape tore its way through. They reached a coveredway which ran diagonally across the ravine, jumped into it, and stayed there.

About 20 minutes after our charge, an officer from the staff of our division commander brought this order to Col. Bates: "The General commanding directs that you at once charge the battery in front of you!"

Without a moment's hesitation, Col. Bates commanded, "Forward, men!" and at once led the way to the open field himself. As he sprang out of the ditch he swung his sword from left to right to indicate the movement which he wished the line to execute. He was followed promptly by all the men of all the regiments in that immediate vicinity. But the men of the left wing of the regiment could not see him, and it was impossible to hear anything, and probably not more than 200 men went forward with him. This movement had been anticipated by the enemy, and they had crowded one of their numerous coveredways full of infantry on our front and right. Col. Bates had not taken 10 steps forward when this line rose up and at less than 50 yards range poured in a volley that almost annihilated the charging party. Col. Bates fell, shot through the head; our noble little Major, Robert Leake [James C. Leeke], fell, mortally wounded; other officers fell, and nearly all of the enlisted men went down. Those who survived jumped back into the trenches, bringing many of their wounded comrades with them. This movement threw our line into great confusion, but the officers did their best to hold the men up, and they pluckily faced the enemy and showed no signs of breaking.

Two men passed me carrying Col. Bates in a rubber blanket. He was lying face down, the blood running from his nose and mouth, a round, gory hole in the right cheek and another near the left ear, showing where the bullet had passed through his head. I remembered his order of the previous day, and it did not seem right to me, for two men to be taken from the line of battle to carry a dead man to the rear, for I considered that he had but a very short time to live. Then two men came bringing Maj. Leake [Leeke]. He was sitting up in the blanket, his coat open, and a bullet hole in his right breast. He smiled as he saw me.

"Are you hurt badly, Major?" I asked anxiously. "Very badly I fear; try and keep up the men." The bloody froth fell from his lips and a torrent of blood gushed from his mouth. He pressed my hand and his eyes spoke a sad farewell.[20]

A host of wounded enlisted men were making their way to the rear, groaning, swearing and praying, for the wounded negro must make some kind of a noise. I noticed, with great apprehension, that the men were growing nervous and timid. The great excitement of the charge had died away, and the scared faces all around me showed that the reaction had set in.

Col. H. G. Thomas, commanding the Second Brigade, had endeavored to advance his brigade just after our charging party were driven back. It was at this time that Lieut. Pennell, a young officer on Col. Thomas's staff, was killed.

Years afterwards, Col. Thomas wrote this concerning him: "With his sword uplifted in his right hand, the banner in his left, he sought to call out the men along the whole line of the parapet. In a moment a musketry fire was focused upon him, whirling him around several times before he fell."[21]

From the higher ground that I was on I saw him start out, and I knew that he was doomed.

The Second Brigade had hardly raised their heads when the cry broke out from our men. "The rebels are charging! Here they come!" Looking to the front I saw a splendid line of gray coming up the ravine on the run. Their left was nearly up to the bombproofs, and their right extended off into the smoke as far as we could see. They were coming, and coming with a rush. We all saw that they were going straight for the Second Brigade.

"Up, boys, up, and drive them back!" the officers shouted, and the men stood up bravely and opened an oblique fire on them.

We had the satisfaction of seeing their left break off and seek shelter in the cut-up ground. But the North Carolinians on our right and front were not idle, and pressed us hard. I have ever believed that we would have held them back had not the cry been raised, "The white troops are breaking! Close in to the left!" and we could see our whole line on the left going back. For a moment the men moved backwards to the left, firing as they retreated; then the enemy charged with a yell and poured a volley into their very faces. Instantly the whole body broke, went over the breastworks towards the Union line, or ran down the traverse towards the Crater.

For a second I was irresolute. Should I run back to the Union breastworks or stay on the field and try and hold the ground already gained? My father's words, "Stay with the line," came to me, and calling to all the men around me, "This way, boys, this way!" I ran down the traverse towards the Crater.

Fig. 6.1. Capt. William F. Bartlett, Company I, 20th Massachusetts Infantry. William F. Bartlett was appointed brigadier general of volunteers in June 1864. Dr. Kathleen Dietrick Collection, United States Army Military History Institute.

If the blacks were brave in their charge, they were demoralized and wholly unmanageable as a body in their defeat.[22]

When I started down the traverse, towards the Crater, a few men of the regiment followed me. About a hundred yards from the Crater a party of Confederates rose up from behind a bombproof, and fired into us. A number of the men fell, and among them was a Corporal carrying our regimental flag—the blue flag with the eagle, the coat of arms and the name of the regiment on it. As the Corporal fell he gave such a scream of agony that we all looked back. There 10 yards away from us lay our flag, and 10 yards beyond the flag was a crowd of Confederate soldiers rushing for it, loading their rifles as they advanced.

With me, was big Bob Bowen, of Co. H. Bob looked back. He saw the flag and the enemy almost on top of it. Quick as a flash he seized his musket by the bayonet and ran for the flag. As he ran, he threw the musket with all his giant strength and it went whirling and flying into the enemy, and as they ducked and dodged to avoid it, Bob grabbed the flag and sprang like a deer over the breastwork and ran for the Union line. This act was our salvation, for every Confederate rushed to the breastwork and fired at Bob, while we ran for the Crater.[23] Before we reached it, my foot struck a body and I fell headlong, and when I rose I saw that it was the body of the young Confederate whom I had seen lying there wounded; his life had been trampled out of him. Near him was the old man who had cursed us, gasping and nearly gone.

We were the last to reach the Crater by the way of the traverse, and the rifles of the Union soldiers were flashing in our faces when we jumped down in there. As I landed inside I turned for a second to look back and caught a glimpse of the Confederates bayoneting the wounded men who had just been shot down.[24]

Around the crest of the Crater a full line were loading and firing as fast as they could, and the men were dropping thick and fast, most of them shot through the head. Every man who was shot, rolled down the steep sides to the bottom, and in places they were piled up four and five deep.

Fugitives were still sweeping in from the ravine where the Second Brigade had charged. White and black, all shared in the panic, and came tumbling headlong down among us. Many pushed through towards our lines until probably not more than 700 men were left. Gen. Bartlett was standing up in the line of fire, calling wildly for the men to rally and hold their ground.

When I stopped near the traverse, down which my little party had come, the men who were with me turned and opened fire. They were terribly excited and shot wildly. Seeing this, a Captain of the 4th R. I., a veteran regiment, jumped in among them saying, "Shoot low, boys, shoot low" and taking a musket he aimed coolly and carefully before he fired.

"That's the way to shoot, boys; plug 'em on the belt every time," said the brave Captain, and his example steadied the men wonderfully. An officer, without hat, coat or belt, was wildly waving his sword and shrieking at the top of his voice: "Drive them back! You must drive them back! We'll all be killed if they capture us in here with the negroes!" But all the time he was yelling, he took good care to keep well down out of range. Some of the white soldiers called him to come up alongside of them, but he did not respond to their invitation. For a few moments it seemed as if the Confederates would carry everything with a rush, and as if we would be swept away. Our men fell so fast that there were gaps in the line and signs of wavering. From my little group three men fell at one time.

At this time, when the carnage was at its greatest height, a Sergeant carrying the colors of the 9th N. H. sprang to the top of the works and waving his tattered flag, called out, "Men of the 9th N. H., will you leave these old colors for the rebels? Rally, rally, rally on the old flag!"[25]

A little band clustered around him, and fought as only veterans can. Officers fought with muskets and revolvers; searched the cartridge boxes of the dead and wounded for ammunition; loaded rifles for their men; gave them other guns, when their own became hot and foul. So sharp and deadly was our fire that the enemy sought shelter.

But the artillery on Cemetery Hill were sweeping the crest of the Crater so that one side of our fort was absolutely untenable. In the little lull that followed, our men loaded a large number of muskets and placed them in readiness for instant use. An enfilading fire was coming through the traverse down which we had retreated. Gen. Bartlett ordered the colored troops to build a breastwork across it. They commenced by throwing in lumps of clay, but it was slow work. Some called out: "Put in the dead men," and the suggestion was instantly acted upon. There were plenty of dead, and the men piled them into the trench, officer and private, white and black, Union and Confederate, making a barricade of human flesh. Some of the working party were killed, and their comrades threw them in with the rest. This made a partial shelter, and enabled the working party to strengthen their breastwork.

The cries of the wounded, many of them pressed down under the dead, were piteous in the extreme. The day was fearfully hot; the wounded were calling for water, and the canteens were empty. A few of our troops held a ditch a few feet in front of the Crater, and were keeping up a brisk fire.[26]

Another movement was soon attempted by the enemy, but the musketry fire of the Union soldiers was so deadly that they hastily sought cover. The artillery kept up a constant fire, making the dirt fly around us all the time.

A mortar battery opened fire on us, and after a few trials succeeded in obtaining our range so well that they dropped their shells directly into the Crater. Looking up we could see them coming—a little black speck; then hear them "whish, whish, whish," then a deafening explosion, and the men would be stricken down. Many of the shells did not explode until they were buried in the earth, and did but little real damage, although the dead and wounded men were sometimes thrown high in the air. The few that burst directly over us cut the men down most cruelly.

The Major of a Maine regiment, a stout, portly man, was struck on the head by one of these shells, which exploded at that instant, and his head and neck were severed clean from the body. The headless trunk of the unfortunate man fell, sloping downward, and a perfect torrent of blood poured from it. It seemed to me that there were bucketfuls of it that flowed from that body. I never supposed that a human being could hold so much blood.

Many of our troops now attempted to make our lines, but to leave, they had to run up a sloping bank in full view of the enemy, who now surrounded us on three sides. Nearly every man who attempted it fell back, riddled with bullets.

At 11 o'clock a determined charge was made by the enemy, and for a moment the Union line wavered again, and seemed likely to give way. A young soldier, with a clear, strong voice raised the well-known song, "The Battle-cry of Freedom."

Amid the roar of musketry the singer sang, with a hundred voices joining in the chorus:

The Union forever,
Hurrah, boys, hurrah!
Down with the traitors,
And up with our Stars,
While we rally round the flag, boys,
We'll rally once again,
Shouting the Battle-cry of Freedom.

"Go on, go on; sing the rest of it!" the men shouted, and the singer sang the second verse and had just raised the chorus: "The Union for"—when he fell dead, killed instantly, with a bullet in the brain.

The enemy's charge was repulsed, but when the fire slackened the ammunition was running fearfully low. About this time, two men, each carrying all the cartridges he could manage in a piece of shelter tent, reached us.

Our thirst was now well-nigh intolerable, and the tongues of many protruded from their mouths. The dead were bloated to twice their natural size, and were already blackened and distorted. The blood had collected in small pools in every little cavity, and in places the clay was softened by it, and trodden to a mushy mortar. A sickening stench, such as can only be known on the battlefield, nearly choked us. Despair was depicted in the face of many a brave man, who, leaving the line of battle, sat down and seemed to resign all hope. In vain was the cry raised that all would be killed if captured with negro soldiers; the despairing men would not stand up.

The killing of a comrade by their very side would not rouse them in the least.[27] An effort was made to dig a covered way to the side towards the Union lines, but, with wornout men, it progressed but slowly. The rebels got the range of that hole and shot the bullets into it thick and fast; the white men refused to work in it, and a black soldier took the pick. The bullets struck all around him, but he kept at work until one bullet shaved a tuft of wool from his head, when he threw down the tool, saying "Ise gwine ter quit." No one else could be induced to work there. Once I felt the "burn" of a bullet on my cheek, and clapped my hand to my face, expecting to find blood, but the skin was not even broken.

Among our troops was a company of Indians, belonging to the 1st Mich. S. S. They did splendid work, crawling to the very top of the bank, and rising up, they would take a quick and fatal aim, then drop quickly down again. Some of them were mortally wounded, and, clustering together, covered their heads with their blouses, chanted a death song, and died—four of them in a group.[28]

Gen. Bartlett had his cork leg broken sometime during the shelling. Different stories have been told as to how it occurred, but my impression is that the leg was broken by the General's foot slipping while trying to stand upon the sloping side of the Crater.[29]

Of the men of my regiment who had rallied with me all but one, a Sergeant, lay dead or dying. As he stood at my elbow, loading and firing, I said to him, "Sergeant, things are looking very bad for us."

"Yes, Lieutenant," he answered, "dey is sho'ly lookin' powerful bad. I reckon, sah, we has to die right yere, sah!" And this was said not in a spirit of bravado, nor in a tone of regret, but as a matter of fact our duty had called us to this place, and it was part of that duty "to die right yere," and there was no thought of shirking the responsibility.

After the mortar shells began to fall among us, little firing was done by the white soldiers. From this time forth the fusillade was kept up mainly by the colored troops and officers handling muskets. My pistol was hot with firing; I had loaded muskets and searched the dead for cartridges until I was ready to drop from exhaustion. Between 1 and 2 o'clock in the afternoon our men in the ditch in front of the Crater, having expended all of their ammunition were quickly captured. Then the enemy planted their battleflags on the edge of the Crater, front and both flanks, not six feet away from our men. They quickly pulled them back, but we knew that they were there, just on the other side of the clay bank. Muskets with bayonets attached were pitched back and forth, harpoon style. In this last movement the Confederates exposed themselves most fear-

Fig. 6.2. "My pistol was hot with firing." Freeman S. Bowley, *A Boy Lieutenant.*

lessly, and had all our men stood up at that time the rebel loss would have been much more severe; but not more than 25 or 30 of our men were trying to make a defense, and some of these were calling for cartridges.

For a few moments the enemy rested, then I heard their officers' orders: "Every man get his gun loaded; give one spring and go right over; they are out of ammunition; they won't fight"; then "Forward, 41st!" And the Major who led the charge was the first to show himself. Gen. Bartlett had ordered a surrender when he heard the order to charge, but some of the negroes kept up a resistance and were shot down; among them was my brave Sergeant. As the Confederates came rushing into the Crater, calling to their comrades in their rear, "The Yanks have surrendered!" some of the foremost ones plunged their bayonets into the colored wounded. Instantly a lot of blacks, who had surrendered with the others, picked up the arms they had thrown down, and in the frenzy of despair dashed at the rebels, shot, bayoneted, clubbed their guns, and for a moment drove every thing before them. The rebel Major hastily ordered his men back, and called to the negroes that if they surrendered they should all be spared and treated as prisoners of war, but if they resisted, they would be killed. At his request some of the Union officers advised the men to lay down their arms, which they did slowly and reluctantly.

When the bayoneting commenced, a number of men, white and black, crowded into the hole that had been cut in the slope, and went wild with terror. When I heard the Confederate order to charge, I was standing well up to the edge of the Crater, pistol in my hand. A tall man in gray jumped up in front of me, his musket cocked and leveled. Both of us fired at the same instant. The flash of his musket burnt my face as I dodged my head; my antagonist fell forward into the Crater—dead.

A Union officer pulled me down. "Don't fire! We have surrendered!" he said. I dropped flat on my face to avoid the volley that I knew would come the instant that the enemy's line came over. It came, directed at the negroes, as already related. After the negroes had surrendered the second time, I raised up and looked around. A Confederate Sergeant, a tall, powerful man, said to me: "Lieutenant, as you have no furder use for them, I'd advise you to take off them thar 'quipments." As his musket was at full cock and his hand very, very nervous, the advice was taken, and unbuckling my sword belt, I let belt, sword and pistol fall upon the ground.

"This has been a fearful day, Sergeant," I said.

"Deed it has, sah," said the Sergeant. "You'uns has lost heaps of men," he continued, looking over the piles of dead. "Yes, Sergeant, we have lost heavily," I answered, "and your loss must have been heavy also,"

"Our loss is right severe, I reckon," he answered. The Confederate soldiers were hustling the prisoners to the rear. "Git to the ra'r, you Yanks—git,—you!" was heard on all sides. Then I realized that I was a prisoner in the hands of the enemy.

7

A Prisoner of War

Our captors proposed to make a grand spectacle of us for the benefit of the Petersburg citizens! I was in the third file of officers, and as the head of the column reached the streets of Petersburg we were assailed by a volley of abuse from men, women and children which exceeded anything of the kind that I ever heard. The women were particularly bitter.

Every regiment of the Ninth Corps was represented among the 700 men who had rallied at the Crater in the morning. Nearly all had been killed or wounded. A few made their escape to the Union lines, but more fell in attempting it. One hundred and thirty-six prisoners were captured in the Crater by the Confederates, and 485 dead bodies were taken from that terrible death-trap. The ground between the Crater and the Union lines was thickly strewn with the dead and wounded.[1]

The Sergeant to whom I had surrendered spoke to me, and told me that I must now go to the rear. He kindly directed me to go to the right, and not go across the open field, as "yo'uns people is a-shelling right smart."

I started for the rear towards the coveredway so kindly designated by the Sergeant, but found it full of troops—South Carolinians. A rebel Lieutenant grabbed my haversack, pulling it off, hit me with the flat of his saber, saying, "Git across that a-way you—Yank!" pointing to the open field across which our men were shelling. In my haversack were my commission, muster-roll, and letters. I attempted to expostulate with the Lieutenant, but his men drove me away at the point of the bayonet. There was no help for it, and I started out at a trot. Ahead of me, so near that I could have touched him, was a black soldier. A shell from the Union lines struck this man and knocked him at least a rod. My trot increased to a run, and my feet fairly flew until I jumped into a ditch filled with Confederate soldiers and Yankee prisoners.

Two young soldiers stopped me. "Here, you Yank, give me that watch. I want that watch!" said one catching hold of my watch chain and taking the watch.

I turned to them indignantly and said: "When we captured a lot of your men this morning we gave your wounded water and divided our hardtack with them."

"Reckon them rebels didn't hav nuthin' worth robbin'," said the one who had taken the watch; but his companion, a fine-looking young fellow, seemed ashamed, and gave me two Confederate bills, saying: "Here Yank, take this; perhaps it will help to buy you something to eat." He also called to one of the guards, and asked him to look out for me.

A dead negro was lying in the trench, and I opened his haversack, and took out a chunk of soft bread. I would have taken the whole haversack, but the guards drove me away.

A third line of battle was lying in a ditch across the ravine, and Confederate Gen. Mahone, riding a little sorrel horse, was close behind it.[2]

Utterly disheartened and despondent, and almost dead for thirst, I started back. My father's objection when I wished to apply for a commission now came to me in full force: "If you are captured, that will be the last of you." Was this to be the last of me? Would I be taken out and shot or hanged on my arrival at the Confederate rear? Could I not deny my regiment, and thus escape this fate? All my letters, papers, and diary were in my haversack, that had been taken away from me. These and other questions were rapidly passing in my mind as I walked by the side of my guard. Half a mile back we found a stream of running water, and we drank and drank. The water revived me.

Close by the brook, under the shade of some trees, were a number of wounded of both sides, among them Capt. William H. Seagrave, of my regiment. He was unconscious, and apparently mortally wounded. My guard was inclined to be sociable.[3]

"Reckon you Yanks is gitting mighty sick of fighting we'uns," he said.

"O, no," I replied, "we have only just begun to fight; there are plenty of men up North yet."

"We'uns have licked yo'uns every time this year," he said confidently.

"How about Spottsylvania [Spotsylvania], when the Second Corps ran over your breastworks?" I asked.

"Well, I reckon yo'uns did git a little the best of us that mornin,' but we'uns mor'n get even at Cold Harbor."[4]

To this I made no reply.

"Dog-goned if it don't look as if your officers jist sent their men in for we'uns to kill," continued the guard. "When our brigade charged you Yanks this mornin' derned if I didn't feel sorry for you-all. Yo'uns was jammed in that thick in them ditches that the men didn't have no chance to fight. 'Peared like down-right murder to me. I've been fightin' yo'uns over three years now, and I've seen a heap of fights, but I have never seen men handled wusser than you men this mornin.'"

"To what command do you belong?" I asked.

"De Sixty-one Virginny, Mahone's Brigade," was the answer.

"What regiments are in that brigade?" I asked, desirous of knowing what troops had charged us.

"De Six Virginny, de Twelve Virginny, de Sixteen Virginny, de Forty-one Virginny and de Sixty-one Virginny—all Virginny," answered the Confederate.[5]

"How do you like our Gen. Grant?" was my next question.

"He sho'ly is a hard 'un, but I reckon he's bout used up his army a-butting it agin 'Ole Marse Robert.' I'd think that your Gen. McClellan was a heaper sight better than Grant," said the rebel critic.

About this time he espied a little paste pin that I wore in my flannel shirt bosom. It was a cheap, showy little pin, worth perhaps $2.

"Say, Yank," he said, "I reckon that's a valerable pin you got thar?"

"It was given to me," I answered.

"Reckon I'll hev to have that pin, Yank."

"You wouldn't rob me of a keepsake, would you?" I asked.

"Mos' likely somebody else will git it if I don't. I'd like that mighty well as a soter keepsake to the day, you know." This was said in a sort of apologetic manner, and I knew that my guard, a good-natured, veteran soldier, would never use force to rob a prisoner, and, so far as he was concerned, that I was perfectly safe; but, as he had said, others might rob me if he didn't. He was carrying over his shoulder a roll of shelter tents. An idea struck me.

"See here," I said, "I'll trade with you. Give me those shelter-tents and I will give you the pin."

"An what will I do for a shelter tent?" he asked.

"You are going back to the trenches, are you not?" I asked. "There's lots of plunder up there—new rubber blankets and new shelter-tents, and haversacks with plenty of rations and coffee in them. When the Ninth Corps charged this morning they expected to be in Petersburg before night, and the men carried their knapsacks into the fight."

This was a lie out and out, but I considered everything was fair in war.

"Reckon a heap of them will be in Petersburg, too. But we'uns will be aguardin' them! All right, Yank, I'll trade; hyar's de tents; gimme de pin," and the exchange was made.

We soon encountered a reserve force, and among them were a lot of boys 15 or 16 years old. These youngsters began to plunder the prisoners, snatching hats from their heads and demanding canteens and haversacks. One of the boys grabbed my cap, but I snatched it back, and gave him a push that sent him over backwards. Another demanded my roll of shelter tents, but my guard interfered and notified them that, "Dis here gentleman is under special protection," and I was let alone.

A mile in the rear we joined a larger number of prisoners, who had been captured in the morning. Among them were a Captain and two Lieutenants of my own regiment. The Captain moved away, and seemed anxious to avoid me. I instantly divined that he intended denying his regiment and giving the name of another, so I gave him no sign of recognition. My veteran guard bade me good-by and returned to the trenches. I have often wondered if he found another shelter-tent that night.[6]

The guards were now separating the prisoners, putting the officers in a group by themselves. Our names and regiments were about to be taken. Should we of the colored troops deny our regiments and give the name of a white regiment? I thought of the black men who had rallied with me in the Crater, and who had died to the last man. Then I told my comrades that we were United States officers, and I believed that our Government would protect us (and the remembrance of that hearty, manly, clasp of President Lincoln's hand assisted me in my decision), and that I, for one, should face the music, and if I died, I should die without denying the brave fellows we had left behind in that trap of death.

One of my comrades, Lieut. Sanders, said: "I'm with you!"[7] When our names and rank were taken down, we said, "Thirtieth United States Colored Infantry!" and saw the words "negro officer" written opposite our names in the list. We were searched for knives and pistols. I had a small pocket knife, but it was not taken.

A woman dressed in homespun, with a blue sunbonnet on her head, came walking by with a tin pail on her arm, calling out, "Huckilberry dumplin's!" The Confederates bought of her and when I saw them eating I quickly realized that I too, was hungry. I remembered the Confederate money given to me by the rebel soldier, and I called to her: "This way with your dumplings, if you please, madam." She looked at me with suspicion. "Has you got any Confed'rit money?" she asked.

Fig. 7.1. Lt. Charles B. Sanders, Companies D and F, 30th U.S. Colored Infantry. RG98S-CWP Collection, United States Army Military History Institute.

"O, yes, Madam," I replied. "I've got some Confederate money."

"Reckon yo' mout as well lick out de pail," she said, and handed me the tin bucket. In it were two very small, doughy dumplings, with three or four huckleberries in each. A little milk, sweetened with sorghum, had been poured over them for a sauce. I made just two bites of each dumpling.[8]

"How much?" I asked, as I handed the pail back.

"Eight dollars!" was the response.

"What!" I gasped in astonishment.

"Eight dollars! Is yo' deaf?" was the tart reply.

I pulled out my money, two reddish Confederate bills. A glance showed that one bill was five, the other two dollars.

"Here's all I that have," I said, "I'd no idea that dumplings cost $4 apiece!"

"That money's old issue. I want the new issue money. I won't take it!" and the woman's voice rose shrill and angry.

"It's all I have, madam. You will have to take that or nothing," I said. The woman snatched the money.

"Yo' Yanks is all a miserable lyin' set of thieves, come down yere to steal we'uns niggers. If I was a man I'd git a gun and shoot ye dead; I'd git a sword and chop yer to pieces!"

The guards and prisoners were all laughing at me, but I managed to ask, "How many niggers do you own?" and got a snapping answer: "None of your derned business!"

One of the guards explained to me that there was a discount of 33 per cent, upon all Confederate money issued prior to 1863. The new issue was of a blue color, and had the words "Two years after a ratification of a treaty of peace between the Confederate States of America and the United States of America, the Confederate States will pay to bearer," etc., printed across the face of each bill.

A detail of guards came and took away all the negro prisoners who were able to work. The task of burying the dead was assigned to them. All the negroes had been stripped of everything but shirt and drawers. Blouse, cap, trousers, shoes and stockings had all been taken. We who were prisoners were soon moved to another position in a hollow. Near us was a battery of artillery, the pieces trained upon us.

Gen. William F. Bartlett was brought here and placed among us. I had met Gen. Bartlett in Worcester, Mass., during the previous Winter. He was then engaged in organizing the 57th Mass. On one occasion our Highland Cadet Company had been reviewed by him, and after the review I had been introduced. He recognized me now, spoke pleasantly, and complimented me on my behavior during the fighting in the Crater. A Confederate Lieutenant approached the General and said:

"Give me that sword-belt which you are wearing."

"The belt was presented to me," said Gen. Bartlett, "and Gen. Mahone told me that I could keep it."

"I want that belt," said the Lieutenant.

"And I decline to give it up without an order from Gen. Mahone," said Gen. Bartlett.

The Lieutenant went away. In a few minutes he returned. "The Captain of the Provost Guard says that I am to take that belt," he said.

"Ask the captain of the Provost Guard if he outranks Gen. Mahone?" replied Gen. Bartlett.

Again the Lieutenant retired, and again he returned for the third time. Accompanying him was the Captain of the Provost Guard. Going up to Gen. Bartlett, the Captain said with an oath:

"I've had enough of your Yankee impudence. I want that belt and I'm going to have it. Take it off, or I'll take it off by force!"

Gen. Bartlett took from under his vest a beautiful general officer's belt made of morocco leather. "Have any of you a pocket knife?" he asked. I handed him mine.

The Provost Captain quickly drew his sword. "If you cut that belt I'll split your head open!" he said.

"I do not intend to injure the belt, sir," said Gen. Bartlett, with dignity; "I only wish to place my initials upon it"; and he scratched upon the leather the letters "W. F. B." The other prisoners began to groan and hiss, but Gen. Bartlett raised his hand and said: "Oblige me gentlemen, by keeping quiet. Remember, we are prisoners now." The request was instantly complied with.

The sun went down, and darkness came creeping over us. Giving Gen. Bartlett one piece of my shelter tent, I spread out the other piece on the rough, stony ground, and Lieut. Sanders and myself lay down upon it. Around us were three lines of sentinels; next to us, who were officers, were about 150 wounded negroes; beyond the negroes were the captured white soldiers.

I lay down with a heavy heart. The smart of defeat, the uncertainty of my future, thoughts of home and of my sweetheart all were in my mind. The firing had all ceased; not even a picket shot could be heard. A light breeze blowing from the Union lines brought the sound of bugles, the artillery tattoo. How that bugle call sank into my heart as we lay there so heavily guarded. With it came one of the quaint sayings of the black soldiers: "Time 'nun to shake hands wid de debble when he stan'in de do'h."

I smiled as I recalled it, thought it good advice, and, putting my cap over my face to keep off the dew, went to sleep, and slept soundly. When I awoke the sun was shining brightly. Some of the wounded had died during the night, and a detail of white prisoners were digging a wide grave. The dead were buried there, their graves unmarked, their names unknown. With Sanders I divided the chunk of bread that I had taken from the haversack of the dead negro. Some of our enlisted men sent a cup of coffee and a couple of hardtack to Gen. Bartlett. But the greater portion of the Union prisoners had nothing to eat.

The order "Fall in, you Yanks!" was heard, and we commenced forming a sort of line.

"You Yanks is so mighty anxious to go inter Petersburg we'se gwine ter take you dere now," said the Provost Captain grimly.

A sorry looking horse, without saddle, was brought for Gen. Bartlett. Then four officers, viz., Col. E. G. Marshall, 14th N. Y. H. A.; Col. Stephen Weld,

Fig. 7.2. Capt. Elisha G. Marshall, 6th U.S. Infantry. Elisha G. Marshall was appointed colonel of the 14th New York Heavy Artillery in January 1864. Gil Barrett Collection, United States Army Military History Institute.

Fig. 7.3. Lt. Col. Stephen M. Weld, 56th Massachusetts Infantry. Roger D. Hunt Collection, United States Army Military History Institute.

56th Mass.; Col. Daniel White, 31st Mass., and Lieut. Col. Buffalo [Martin P. Buffum], 4th R. I.; then four wounded negroes; then four officers, and so on, alternating the whites and the blacks. Behind us came the enlisted men.[9]

Our captors proposed to make a grand spectacle of us for the benefit of the Petersburg citizens! I was in the third file of officers, and as the head of the column reached the streets of Petersburg we were assailed by a volley of abuse from men, women and children which exceeded anything of the kind that I ever heard. The women were particularly bitter. "Why didn't you kill all of the Yankee wretches?" they asked of our guards a dozen times along the route.[10]

The marks of union shells were discernible upon some of the houses in one part of the town, and we cheered mightily when we saw the work of our artillerymen. This set the guards in a great rage, and they threatened to shoot, and were advised to go up to the front and shoot the Yank that sent those shells over!

We paraded through all the principal streets of Petersburg, and were then taken to a little island near the cotton mills. No wonder the citizens had a poor opinion of the Yankees! We were indeed a hard-looking crowd. There was almost every nationality among the whites, and the negroes and Indians added variety of color. All of us were covered with red dust, our faces and hands were blackened by powder, our eyes were bloodshot, and many of us were bloody from wounds or the blood of comrades. Every union officer who had worn a hat had been robbed of it, and wore instead an old, dirty, greasy rebel slouch, with the cotton tassels hanging down behind. We gladly availed ourselves of the opportunity to get a good wash from the banks of the river. Bathing was prohibited. Crowds of people came to see us. We were hungry, and clamored for rations, and were told that the rations would come "after a little."

It was Sunday, and my thoughts went back to the quiet peaceful Sabbath of New England. At home, as I afterwards learned, my father and mother, as they were returning from church, saw upon a newspaper bulletin board in big letters the words:

"Great battle at Petersburg! Terrible slaughter of the Colored troops!"

The Monday morning papers of Worcester confirmed the story of the disaster, but gave no particulars. They waited impatiently for the New York papers. The train was late. At last it came, and they obtained a paper. There was the regiment; 30th U. S.; Col. D. Bates, mortally wounded; Maj. Robert Leake [Maj. James C. Leeke], mortally wounded; Capt. Woodward, slightly wounded; Capt. Quimby and Capt. Seagrave, missing; Lieut. Adams, severely wounded; Lieut. Edgerton, right arm amputated, and so on a long list. Fifteen out of 22 officers and over 200 enlisted men were lost, the paper said. Of Co. A only 18 now remained out of 66. My name was among the number reported "missing," but it was so hopelessly misspelled that even my own parents could not recognize it. Even the poor honor of having my name appear in the newspapers was denied me![11]

Then my parents waited for a letter. Eight days after the battle it came. It was from Capt. Smith, and it said:

"The last I saw of your son was when he was keeping up the men to the line. I think and hope that he is a prisoner. His body was not among the dead which were brought into our lines by flag of truce."

Then followed words of comfort kindly expressed, but they were little heeded by my anxious parents. For six weeks no tidings came to them, and hope had almost died out; but one day came the long-looked-for letter from me.

It was only a scrawl, written on a dirty piece of paper, which had been used on a tobacco package. This was what it said:

> Petersburg, Va., July 31, 1864.
> My dear Father and Mother:
> I was captured in the fighting yesterday. I am well and well treated. Don't worry about me. All's for the best. We start for Georgia tomorrow.
> Your loving Son.

8

A Journey into Captivity

After waiting an hour some box cars were brought up alongside of us. They had been used last for hauling cattle and had not been cleaned in the least. "Git in thar, you Yanks, and be lively about it!" was the order. After much wrangling the officer commanding the guards allowed a few men from each car to go under guard to some pines near-by and bring a few armfuls of pine branches. This made our condition a little more tolerable, but it was anything but pleasant.

Among the many deeds of heroism performed that day by the officers and men of the 30th U.S.C.T. I note the following:

Capt. Wm. H. Seagrave, of Co. K, in attempting to stay the rebel charge, had his leg shattered by a bullet. Unable to retreat, and refusing to surrender, he fought with sword and revolver, killing and wounding six of the enemy. He was finally knocked senseless by a blow upon the head from a musket-butt, after he had been shot and bayoneted in seven different places. Some of his faithful men attempted to rescue him, and were killed to the last man. After the charge was over, a rebel officer, who had seen Capt. Seagrave's gallant defense, sent two Yankee prisoners to carry him to the rear. Lieut. Van Alin, 43d Pa., was one of the men who carried the insensible Captain from the field. Capt. Seagrave was brutally treated while a prisoner, was exchanged after three months' imprisonment, and died at his home in Uxbridge, Mass., in October, 1865.

Capt. Arthur J. Smith, finding himself nearly surrounded by the enemy, emptied his revolver into a group of them, then threw the pistol into the face of one who was attacking him with the bayonet, leaped over the breastworks, and successfully made his escape.

Lieut. Sanders, who was commanding Co. A was on the extreme right of the line, and was making a gallant fight, when he found himself cut off, and was obliged to surrender.

This company went into fight with 66 men, and came out with 18; 48 were killed, wounded or missing, and none of the missing were ever heard from.[1]

Capt. D. E. Proctor tells the following story, which occurred after the successful charge of the regiment:

> There were quite a number of rebel dead near there, but I took no particular notice of any until a colored soldier said to me:
>
> "Captain, see that reb there; he ain't dead. Shall I kill him?"
>
> "O, no," I replied; "let the poor fellow live."
>
> Upon hearing this the Confederate rose up, and if any man ever pleaded for mercy and his life this poor fellow did. I sent him to the rear with the man who was anxious to kill him, had I even remotely suggested it.

When our men were driven back, Capt. Proctor leaped upon the top of the breastwork and gallantly endeavored to stay the tide of defeat. He says:

> In the brief time I stood there I saw the crest of the hill for which we had started, and which we were never to reach. I could see the enemy's lines to the right and left for a long distance, and the utter hopelessness of our situation. On our right and front the ground was literally covered with troops in gray; lines of battle behind other lines of battle, those lying down looking like a flock of dirty sheep. It was then that I saw our Capt. Seagrave sitting on a mound of earth, right under the Stars and Stripes of our regiment; he was badly wounded, and was pushing away a rebel bayonet with one hand and using his revolver with the other. One of the enemy raised a clubbed musket. I saw the blow fall upon the Captain's head, but I was powerless to assist him. I also saw bayonets plunged into colored men who had surrendered.
>
> Our dead and wounded lay under the pitiless rays of a July sun until the third day, when a flag of truce was arranged. During all this time, if a man moved an arm or a leg, plug would go a bullet into him or near him. It was impossible for any of us to assist our wounded in any way.
>
> The enemy even placed our colored wounded men upon their works and fired between their legs, well knowing that we would not return the fire without endangering the lives of our own men. The second day the stench from the battlefield was horrible, but nothing to that of the third day, when we went out under flag of truce to bury our dead and bring in our wounded. The dead men were so swollen that the belts would be nearly buried in the bodies, out of sight. White and black could only be distinguished by the hair. We dug a trench 300 feet long, and packed it closely with the bodies. During the truce both armies stood upon their

> works and called back and forth. Before the truce flag was hardly out of sight a shot was fired from the enemy, and in an instant not a man could be seen upon either side.

That great numbers of the colored men were murdered after they had surrendered there is little doubt. The whole civilized world was appalled and shocked at the massacre of negro soldiers at Fort Pillow, but at the battle of the mine nearly three times as many were butchered, yet the fact seems to have escaped general notice.

At Fort Pillow the losses among the colored soldiers were but little over 200. At the mine 801 men were reported missing from the Fourth Division, and there were but a few over 300 negro prisoners taken to the rear. A Confederate Sergeant, writing to a Southern newspaper, says:

> Of the 900 niggers who surrendered only about 300 ever lived to get back to our rear. During the charge Weiseger's [Weisiger's] Brigade killed with the bayonet everything which it met.[2]

In after years a Confederate veteran related the story of the battle. After describing the charge by Mahone's Brigade, Mr. Bernard says:

> A minute later I witnessed another deed which made my blood run cold. Just about the outer end of the ditch by which I had entered stood a negro soldier, a non-commissioned officer (I noticed distinctly his chevroash), begging for his life of two Confederate soldiers who stood by him, one of them striking the poor wretch with a steel ramrod, the other holding a gun in his hand, with which he seemed to be trying to get a shot at the negro. The man with the gun fired it at the negro, but did not seem to seriously injure him, as he only clapped his hand to his hip, where he appeared to have been shot, and continued to beg for his life. The man with the ramrod continued to strike the negro therewith, whilst the fellow with the gun deliberately reloaded it, and, placing its muzzle close against the stomach of the poor negro, fired, at which the latter fell, limp and lifeless, at the feet of the two Confederates. It was a brutal, horrible act, and those of us who witnessed it from our position in the trench, a few feet away, could but exclaim:
>
> "That is too bad! It is shocking!"
>
> Yet this, I have no doubt, from what I saw and afterwards heard, was but a sample of many other bloody tragedies during the first 10 minutes

Fig. 8.1. Capt. David E. Proctor, Company F, 30th U.S. Colored Infantry. RG98S-CWP Collection, United States Army Military History Institute.

Fig. 8.2. Pvt. William H. Seagrave, Company H, 25th Massachusetts Infantry. William H. Seagrave was appointed a captain in the 30th U.S. Colored Infantry in February 1864. RG98S-CWP Collection, United States Army Military History Institute.

> after our men got into the trench, many of whom seemed infuriated at the idea of having to fight negroes.
>
> Within 10 minutes the whole floor of the trench was strewn with the dead bodies of negroes, in some places in such numbers that it was difficult to make one's way along the trench without stepping upon them.[3]

From the 51st Pa. a detail of 20 men was made to carry ammunition to the soldiers in the Crater.[4] Of this detail but seven ever returned to their regiment; all the others were killed. It is doubtful if in any of the battles of the civil war as many men were slain on the same space of ground, or as much ammunition expended in the same time in the same space. During the truce for the burial of the dead, a soldier of the 51st Pa.—Hugh M. Lynch, of Wyalusing, Pa.—in a few minutes picked up bullets enough from between the lines to cast a toy mortar weighing 100 pounds. This he sent to his home in Pennsylvania as a relic of the battlefield. From the Crater alone 485 dead bodies were taken.[1]

The losses of the Ninth Corps on that day were 419 killed, 1,679 wounded, and 1,901 missing. Of these the Colored Division lost 176 killed, 688 wounded, 801 missing; total 1,665. As there were less than 400 colored prisoners the difference between that number and the missing gives the number of the wounded and disarmed who perished by the bayonet.

The losses of the 30th U.S.C.T. were, in killed, wounded, and missing, 11 officers and 216 enlisted men. Of these 78 were reported missing, and none of the enlisted men were ever heard from.

The heaviest loss of the companies were in Cos. A and F; viz. 48 out of 66 in the former, and 33 out of 58 in the latter.

The greatest regiment loss was sustained by the 23rd U.S.C.T., which lost, killed, 74; wounded, 115; missing, 121; total 310.

In after years the survivors of the 58th Mass. placed a little board upon the inner rim of the Crater, with the following inscription:

"This board marks the advanced position of the 58th Mass., July 30, 1864. Killed, 10; wounded, 33; prisoners, 91; total, 134; leaving 28 for duty. The colors also were lost."[5]

Some of the citizens who visited us at Petersburg on that Sunday were anxious to obtain greenbacks. One man in particular seemed so desirous that I asked him his terms. He said that he would pay $2 Confederate for $1 in green-

---

1 Extract from an address delivered before A. P. Hill Camp of Confederate Veterans at Petersburg, Va., June 24, 1890, by Hon. George S. Bernard, of Co. E, 12th Va., Mahone's Brigade. See report of Brig. Gen. William Mahone, C.S.A.

backs and inquired if I had any "Federal money." I told him that I had little money. As a matter of fact, I had about $40 in my pocketbook. As I showed no disposition to accept his offer, he told me, as if in confidence that he would give $25 Confederate for $10 greenbacks, as he desired to send the money to a relative of his, who was a prisoner in the North. I asked him where his relative was contained and he replied "Up North somewhere."

I was unable to see how the money could be sent with such a general direction, and concluded that the man wanted the greenbacks for himself. Taking out a new $5 note, I told him that I would sell it to him for $25 Confederate money.

He declined to give me so much, but I saw that he was anxious to obtain the note and so I held my price. Finally the man gave me $25 in Confederate money for my $5 bill.

Thinking that we might be searched, I placed three new $10 greenback notes in the cover of a pocket testament that I had, leaving about $5 in small bills in my pocket-book. With $25 Confederate in my pocket I began to look about for a chance to purchase something to eat. The promised rations had not come and I was very hungry. A woman with a basket on her arm came along and I asked her if she had anything to sell.

"Yes, sah, I'se got some pies to sell," was her reply.

Pies! If there was anything that the Yankee soldier delighted in, it was pies. Recollections of the warm, fragrant apple and mince pies, the golden pumpkin and tempting custard that my mother made at home, rose before me. My mouth fairly watered.

"What kind of pies have you, Madam?" I asked very politely.

"Sweet-tater custard," was the reply.[6]

Remembering the dumpling episode of the previous day, I inquired: "How much are they?"

"Five dollars a pie!" was the prompt response. Five dollars for a pie! And they were not much larger than an ordinary tea-saucer, and appeared very thin; but I was hungry, and there was no choice, so I parted with a $5 "Confed" bill, and took the pie.

I surveyed it somewhat dubiously. Its color was yellowish-brown with a tinge of green; its thickness would not exceed half an inch. I took a bite. The crust was about as thick as a silver dime, and of a leathery-like toughness, and fairly bitter with saleratus.[7] The filling, or "sweet-tater custard" part, was a little thin pat of boiled sweet potato mashed with the skin on.

My face must have expressed the astonishment that I felt for the pie-woman asked, with an air of one who expects a compliment, "I don't reckon you Yanks ever ate any pies like that one?"

"No, Madam," I answered truthfully; "I never did."

As I had anticipated, we were all stood up in line and searched again.

The Army of the Potomac had not been paid for four months, and very few of the officers had any amount of money. When my turn came I showed my pocket-book and testament saying: "This testament was given me by my mother." The officer looked at the pocket-book. The amount was too insignificant for him to trouble himself about. The testament he never looked at; greatly to my relief.

The long-looked-for-rations came to us after dark. Each man received three hardtack and a strip of bacon. This was the first mouthful that many of our enlisted men had eaten for over 48 hours.

Monday morning, August 1, 1864, we were loaded on the cars and started south. The officers were placed in passenger coaches and the enlisted men in box cars. Our train traveled very slowly. The track was in wretched condition and none of the box cars had any brakes on them. At no time did the speed exceed 12 miles per hour, and separate stops were always made for wood and water. The white engineer seemed to be the only railroad man on the train. We could not help contrasting the old ramshackle of a train with the finely equipped and efficiently-handled trains of the North. We congratulated ourselves on having comfortable cars to ride in, but, alas, at Burkeville Junction all our dreams were dispelled. We were ordered to disembark, and the passenger coaches were taken away. After waiting an hour some box cars were brought up alongside of us. They had been used last for hauling cattle and had not been cleaned in the least. "Git in thar, you Yanks, and be lively about it!" was the order. After much wrangling the officer commanding the guards allowed a few men from each car to go under guard to some pines near by and bring a few armfuls of pine branches. This made our condition a little more tolerable, but it was anything but pleasant.

From the first, I had made up my mind to escape if possible. At Petersburg I had decided, if the night was dark enough, to crawl into the water, and take the chances of floating down past the guards. But when darkness came on sentinels were posted near the water's edge and fires lighted, thus effectually blocking any plan to escape in that direction.

All night we jolted slowly along over the rough railroad track, with a guard in each car door and half a dozen on the car roof. I worked my way to a position near the door and pretended to go to sleep, but in reality, I was wide awake

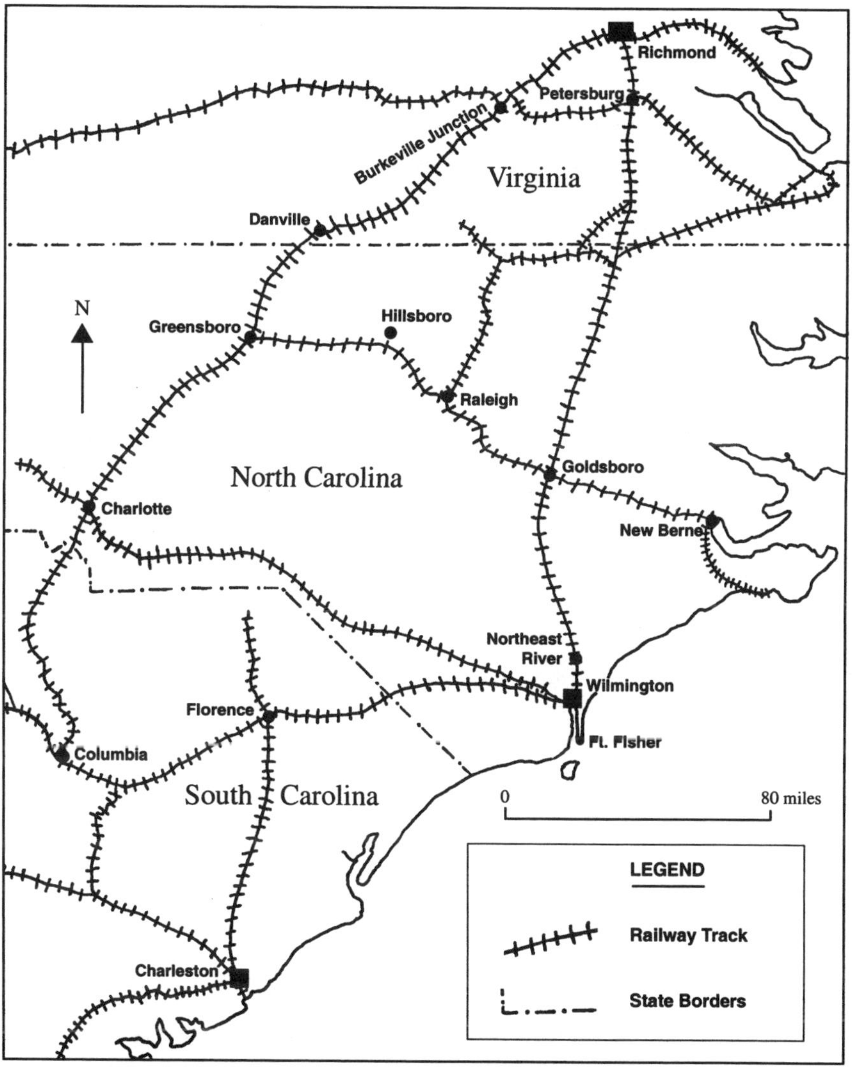

Map 3. Freeman S. Bowley travels South to imprisonment, August 1864, and North to freedom, February–March 1865. (Adapted from U.S. War Department, *Atlas to Accompany the Official Records*, Plates CXVII, CXXXVII, CXXXVIII.)

Journey south to prison: August 1864. Petersburg via Burkeville Junction, Danville prison, to the Richland Jail in Columbia, S.C.

Journey north to freedom: February–March 1865. Columbia, S.C., via Greensboro, Raleigh, Goldsboro to Northeast River, N.C. (Bowley is paroled near Northeast River on March 1, 1865.)

watching our guards. The sentinels were veteran soldiers, and I had my trouble for nothing, for not for a moment did they relax their vigilance. In the morning we entered Danville.

A crowd of citizens gathered around the depot. The sight of negroes among the prisoners excited them greatly. Cries of "Kill them! Hang the niggers!" resounded on all sides. Two officers were pointed out as being officers of colored regiments. The mob howled with fury and some one brought a rope. The two officers, Lieut. Shell [Shull], 28th U.S.C.T., and Lieut. Dowling [Downing], 31st U.S.C.T., were dragged from the car, and it seemed as though they were to be hanged then and there.[8]

One of our Union officers made a most eloquent appeal to our guards, veterans of Stonewall Jackson's Brigade. He had met them in battle before and had been exchanging reminiscences with them.

"Soldiers of Stonewall Jackson's Brigade," said the Union officer, "shall it be said of you that you stood idly by and saw prisoners captured in battle, murdered by citizens and shealts, who stayed at home, and never heard the sound of cannon nor smelt Yankee gunpowder? If you value your good name, save these men from the mob. If they are to die let them die like soldiers!"

This appeal roused the guards to a sense of their duty, and they rescued the two officers not a moment too soon.

My feelings were far from being pleasant ones. I had been pointed out as "That little Yankee cuss, who was an officer in a nigger regiment," and I knew not if my turn would come next.

But no one was hanged that day. Lieuts. Shell [Shull] and Dowling [Downing] were taken away under guard. Two days afterwards they returned to us. They were told to go among the other prisoners, and keep out of sight as much as possible.

We were marched through the streets of Danville. The town had a deserted look about it. Through the open doors of the stores we saw the empty shelves; the merchants had nothing to sell. In many streets the grass was literally "growing in the middle of the street."

We reached the tobacco warehouses where we were to be confined. Around the warehouses was a high plank fence with sentry boxes at frequent intervals. The enlisted men were sent off to another warehouse, while the officers were turned into the first floor of one of the warehouses near the gate. As we entered the door an almost overpowering stench assailed our nostrils; and such a stench. It was the smell of the hospital and of the battlefield combined; enough to take away the breath. Coming from the bright sunlight into the interior of the warehouse, which was darkened by low ceilings and heavily-barred windows, we were at first unable to distinguish anything clearly. A wild clamor of voices reached us.

"Fresh fish! Fresh fish!" "More Yanks!" "Don't steal the man's blanket!" "Don't put that louse on the man!" and other cries were all around us. As our eyes became more accustomed to the darkened room, we saw that we were surrounded on all sides by crowds of almost-naked, haggard, dirty, wild-looking men.[9]

"Where were you captured?" "What is our army doing?" "Is there any news of exchange?" were the questions asked by all. Were these wild, miserable looking creatures Union soldiers? We could hardly credit it. None of them wore anything but shirt and drawers, and many dispensed with the shirt. Why were they so filthy? We could not comprehend it.

They gathered around us, wildly anxious for news. One man told me that he belonged to the Third Division of the Sixth Corps, and had been captured at Monocacy but little more than a month ago; and now he was almost a skeleton.[10]

The prospects were dismal enough. It was evident that the stories of the horrors of Southern prisons, about which we had heard so much, had not been exaggerated. Indeed, half the truth had never been told. We soon found the cause of the terrible stench of that prison. Across one end of the building was an open sink, used by all the prisoners confined in the three stories of the warehouse—at least 1,500 men in all. The deadly fumes from this pestilential spot came directly into the prison, sweeping through and rising up into every part of the building. A sweltering, overpowering heat pervaded the prison and we were soon compelled to throw off our outer clothing and adopt the prevailing style of the other prisoners.

Rations of coarse cornbread and a little boiled meat were issued to us. The rats had been in the meal-tub, for there was unmistakable evidence of it in the bread. I threw down my portion in disgust, and the piece of filthy bread was instantly caught up and ravenously devoured by one of the old prisoners. We were thirsty, and asked for water; there was none! After much delay a few buckets were obtained and a party sent for water. Determined to gain all the information possible, I secured a bucket and went along with the detail. We were taken to the banks of the River Dan and told to fill our buckets.

The river was running rapidly and the water was thick and muddy—perfectly filthy. We had passed a running brook of clear water on the way, and I asked the Sergeant of the Guard if we could not obtain the clear water. My request was refused with an oath, and we were told that the muddy water of the river was much too good for us. This explained why the prisoners were so filthy. The men hardly had sufficient water to satisfy their thirst. To wash or bathe was an impossibility.

Gen. Bartlett had a long talk with the officer in command of the prison regarding the water, and the result was that the prisoners who were officers had permission to fill the water-buckets at the running brook; but this privilege was peremptorily denied to the enlisted men.

Details went for water twice each day. I made two trips, but the third time I was roughly ordered to stay in the prison, and warned not to attempt to go with the detail again. It was evident that I was a marked man, and no possible opportunity for escape was to be granted me.

The old prisoners cautioned the newcomers not to touch the window gratings or stand near the windows after dark. The guards would fire without challenging at any one who touched the window bars. The enlisted men on our floor were driven over to one side of the building, and a rope stretched along to separate them from the officers. Sentinels patrolled the space between with strict orders not to allow any conversation between the officers and men.

I scraped the acquaintance of one of the guards, a simple, good-natured country boy, and found that the guards inside the prison only had three cartridges each in their cartridge-boxes. This was done to avoid giving the prisoners any supply of ammunition should they overpower and seize the guards. The presence of the guards precluded the possibility of any tunneling or any other attempt to escape.

We soon found that there were other occupants of the prison than the prisoners. Almost before we were aware of it we were covered with vermin. "Skirmishing" was the order of the day, and places where the light streamed through a window were at a premium.

Fortunately for us we were not to remain long at Danville. On the evening of the third day orders came for us to be ready to leave early the next morning. There was but little packing up to do. At daylight we were turned out, and marched to the depot and loaded into box cars. All the colored prisoners and part of the white soldiers who were captured with us remained behind. Among the latter was the Captain of my regiment. He had given the name of a white regiment, and passed himself off as a Sergeant. He remained a prisoner at Danville, contracted disease there, and died.[11] Before his death he found a brother Mason in the person of a Confederate officer. To him he confided his name, rank, and regiment. The Confederate, true to his Masonic obligations, sent word of the Captain's death to his friends in the North, and also made a memorandum of it on the official records of the prison.

When we left Danville we were informed that our destination was Georgia. We traveled slowly, making long stops on sidetracks, waiting for the regular trains. While waiting at one of these sidetracks there seemed to be a favorable opportunity to make an escape. On the right side of the train, not 20 yards away, was a thick forest of pines. The guards were all outside. Looking cautiously out, I saw that there was only one guard on the top of our car, and he was lying on his back, apparently asleep. His rifle was across his knees and his hat over his face. The other guards on the adjoining cars were seated facing the left side of the train. If the guard on our car was really asleep, it would be possible to slip off into the brush unobserved. I took a second look. He was still asleep. The other guards were all right, too. I prepared to make the attempt, when—"click-click!" Well did I know that sound! Mr. Johnny Reb was only feinting sleep, watching sharply to get a chance to shoot a Yankee! Had he cocked that musket noiselessly he might have obtained that coveted shot, and perhaps I would not have been here to tell the story.

On the evening of the second day our train arrived at Columbia, S. C. Orders were received here to detain the officers at Columbia and send the enlisted men to Georgia. They waved us a farewell as we left the cars. Poor, brave, noble fellows! Most of them lie buried at Andersonville. Not more than one-fourth of them survived the imprisonment.[12]

We were now in the Capital City of South Carolina, the place where the first ordinance of secession was passed—the very cradle of treason.

9

The Richland Jail, Columbia, South Carolina

There were no sanitary arrangements whatever in the jail. A few wooden buckets were provided. The nights were hot and sultry, and the jail was fairly alive with gray backs, bedbugs and cockroaches. The horrors of that place from midnight till morning were something that may be imagined but not described.

It was dark when we marched through the streets of Columbia, S. C. We were to be confined in the County jail, known as "Richland Jail."[1]

The orders from the Confederate Government to place our party of Petersburg prisoners in a separate place of confinement caused much uneasiness among some of our number. We were the first large lot of officers who had been captured with colored troops. At Macon, Ga., was an officers' prison, where nearly 1,000 officers were confined.[2] The stopping of our party at Columbia brought to our minds the following fact.

When the organization of colored troops was begun by the United States Government the Confederate Congress promptly passed the following act:

> That every white person being a commissioned officer, or acting as such, who, during the war, shall command negroes or mulattoes in arms against the Confederate States, or who shall arm, train, or organize them for service, shall be deemed as inciting servile insurrection, and shall, if captured, be put to death or otherwise punished as a general court-martial may decide.[3]

The question arose among us: Would the Confederate authorities attempt to enforce this act of their Congress?

The jail was then situated alongside of the City Hall, and in the rear of the Confederate Treasury building. On our way to the jail citizens spoke with us pleasantly, inquiring to what command we belonged, and where we were captured. There was no abuse, loud talking, or boasting that "one Southerner could lick five Yankees"; neither did they inquire "What you'uns come down yere to fight we'uns foh?" So accustomed had we become to this sort of talk that we missed it, and considering the fact that the Mine explosion had destroyed the 18th and 22d S. C., we thought the citizens of Columbia very polite and considerate.

Our arrival at the jail was unexpected, and we were detained outside for an hour. A heavy shower came up, and we were well soaked before we were admitted to shelter. Then we were crowded into a room that had been occupied by other prisoners. We were wet, tired and hungry, and we soon quieted down and sat down upon the floor; so crowded were we that there was not room to lie down.

The room was in total darkness, and as the buzz of conversation ceased there came from the adjoining room the sound of some one walking in chains; "clink," "clank," "clink," it sounded as the man went back and forth. We knew that it must be a prisoner under death sentence.

Never did anything sound so horribly to me as the clanking of those chains. My heart went way down; the depression was worse than any attack of the "army ague" or the sight of the Danville rope.

A light rap on the wall brought the prisoner to a halt. In a few words we learned that he was Capt. Edward Harris [Shad/Shadrock Harris], 3d Tenn. Cav. (Union), captured while recruiting inside the Confederate lines, and that he was under death sentence. The guards interfered, and further conversation was stopped.[4]

The next day we were removed to the second floor of the jail. We found that our fellow prisoners, whose quarters we had occupied the night before, were a lot of naval officers who had been captured in the famous night attack on Fort Sumter, a year before. There were also some officers who had been captured at the assault of Fort Wagner.[5] The Chaplain of the 1st S.C.C.V. (afterwards known as the 33rd U.S.C.T.) was confined in the same room as the Fort Wagner officers.[6] The Chaplain had been captured inside of the Confederate lines while tapping a telegraph wire. Our numbers soon increased by the arrival of officers who had been captured in the Shenandoah Valley. There were 130 of us on that floor, and there was barely room to lie down at night. In the jail-yard were about 200 prisoners, soldiers and sailors, about equal numbers of each. At 7 o'clock in the morning and at 3 o'clock in the afternoon, we were allowed half an hour in the jail yard; but the remainder of the 24 hours we were confined to the second floor.

There were no sanitary arrangements whatever in the jail. A few wooden buckets were provided. The nights were hot and sultry, and the jail was fairly

Fig. 9.1. "My heart went down; the depression was worse than any attack of 'army ague.'" Freeman S. Bowley, *A Boy Lieutenant*.

alive with gray backs, bedbugs and cockroaches. The horrors of that place from midnight till morning were something that may be imagined but not described.

At first our rations were for breakfast, a piece of cornbread, three by four inches and an inch thick, and a very small, thin slice of bacon; for dinner, a slice of cornbread one half larger than the breakfast ration. That was all for 24 hours. This was far from satisfying our hunger. My supply of money soon went to buy things to eat. Each day two negro women, "Aunty" and "Rose," came with baskets to sell things to the prisoners. It was said that they were owned by the Captain of the post guard, who had charge of our jail. They offered for sale "snacks" at $5 each. A "snack" consisted of two round biscuits, a little piece of fried chicken and a roasted sweet potato. Roasted sweet potatoes sold two for $1; sweetened cornbread, a dollar for a good sized chunk; pies, $5 each. Sometimes we could prevail upon a good-natured guard to buy us a little piece of fresh beef or a loaf of white bread from the market under the City Hall, not 25 yards away from us. After the first week the supply of bacon was cut off and cowpeas substituted. They were small, rank and wormy, and were boiled in water with only a very little salt for seasoning. They were not very palatable, but hunger brought us down to considering "cowpea soup" a very necessary if not luxurious article of diet.

The cornmeal was sour and much of it had ground cob and all. As a result of such food much sickness resulted, and scurvy soon prevailed among us. I was one of the first attacked, and my flesh rapidly wasted away. My eyes were yellow, my skin dry and feverish, and sores broke out all over me. My feet were greatly swollen, and my teeth loosened, and their gums would bleed upon the slightest pressure. A doctor accompanied by a Hospital Steward visited the jail each day. His only prescription that ever was furnished was a little persimmon bark. I saw the other prisoners looking at me with sober faces; and I partly overheard their remarks concerning me, and I knew what they thought. I would never leave Dixie alive. My chum, Lieut. Sanders, assisted me all that he could, and endeavored to cheer me up; but with no other diet than sour cob-meat and musty, wormy cowpeas, recovery was an impossibility. Accidentally, I learned that raw sweet potatoes were an antidote for scurvy. I traded off my cap for $20 and I bought a peck of sweet potatoes. These I ate raw, and an immediate improvement was the result. My vest, trousers and all my little trinkets followed and the proceeds were invested in sweet potatoes.

I was recovering from scurvy when my stock of trade had run out. Fortunately for me at this time, I received $20 in Confederate money. It reached me through the courtesy of a Confederate officer who, during a flag of truce, had met my uncle, an officer on the United States ship *Wabash*, off Charleston. I had written several letters to my parents, asking them to send me a bill of exchange on London, and the hope of receiving money from home kept my spirits up. I gained as rapidly as I had lost, and with the coming back of health and strength came the ever increasing desire to escape. I was looked upon as one who had "escape on the brain," and was laughed at for my enthusiasm on the subject.

One dark night two officers, Lieut. Williams, 43d U.S.C.T., and Lieut. Pearce [Pierce], 31st Me., did escape. Across the windows of the jail were heavy wooden bars. Two of these were quietly sawed off, and one night as the sentinel stood in the doorway, out of the pouring rain, these two officers let themselves down by a blanket rope, within three feet of the guard, and successfully made their escape. It was a daring piece of work and required great strength, coolness and courage to accomplish it. Lieut. Williams, after weeks of hardship, reached the Union lines near Newbern, N. C. His comrade, Lieut. Pearce [Pierce], was drowned while attempting to cross a river.[7]

The success of these officers intensified my desire to make an attempt to escape. On one side of the jail were some high trees. A comrade and myself debated upon the chances of throwing a stick, attached to a line, into the tree, and then crossing over on the line and sliding down the tree. The presence of a guard directly under us was the most serious obstacle to our plans. After much trouble we obtained a cord, attached a stick of wood to it, and one dark night threw it into the branches. The stick hit the tree with a clattering noise, and the guard fired up through the window. We were expecting something of the kind and were out of range. We saved the cord, but did not care to make another attempt at that window.

On the opposite side of the jail, about 12 feet away, was a one-story building, in which our guards slept. The idea was suggested that we put a bridge out from our window to the roof of the guard building; then by creeping along its ridge-pole and down the roof to the eaves, we could drop off on to the ground. This would be a ticklish piece of business, with three sentinels within 20 yards and one relief of the guards asleep in the guard building. The only material available for a bridge were some bunk boards. These were lashed together firmly, and by doubling the boards and "breaking joints" we made a stiff bridge about 15 feet long. We arranged guy-ropes to keep it in position.

A Lieutenant on the 1st Mich. S. S. claimed the privilege of being the first to make the attempt. Capt. Diebler [Dibeler], an old veteran of the 45th Pa., was the second, and I was to have third chance. A rainy, stormy night seemed to offer a favorable opportunity to make the attempt. Two wooden bars were carefully cut off and noiselessly the bridge was placed out upon the roof. Not a sound was made, and underneath the sentinel called out; "Post number foh; one o'clock, an' all's well!"[8]

The rain slackened, and we waited a few moments for it to descend again. As we waited the clouds parted, and the half-moon shone out. The sentinel looked up to the moon, and his eye caught the dark shadow of the bridge. We saw him run to the guardhouse, and in a moment more we saw the crouching forms of the guards in the shadow of the guard building. We were discovered; our "cake was all dough," but we did not propose to lose those bunk boards. We started to pull in the bridge, and the Sergeant of the Guard shouted; "Stop! Gol dern yer, or I'll shoot ye dead!"

"In with her, boys!" said Capt. Diebler [Dibeler], and we pulled the bridge in over the lower bars, making a horrible screeching noise.

"Shoot boys, shoot!" ordered the Sergeant. "Load an' shoot jis as fas' as you kin!" and a volley came up through the window. The brick walls of the jail protected us, and, back out of the line of fire, every man of us was yelling at the top of his voice, giving orders to imaginary companies, regiments, and brigades. All of the guards outside were firing at the windows. The City Hall bell was clanging the alarm, and the steam whistles at the railroad shops sounding. We could hear the patter of feet as the citizens with their shotguns came running to the jail. Across the way was a pack of bloodhounds and bulldogs, used for hunting escaped prisoners. Every dog was howling his loudest and every other dog in Columbia joined in the chorus. The bullets were smashing through the window bars and going up through the floor above us, where a lot of citizen prisoners were confined. Their yells of terror were soon added to the din, much to our delight.

Capt. R. D. Senn, commanding the Columbia post guard, came rushing with all his men from his camp two miles away, arriving breathless and excited. Everything was now quiet in the jail. Most of the guards had exhausted their ammunition, and were calling loudly for more. Some of the citizens bombarded our windows with their shotguns.

Capt. Senn came up the stairway and pounded on the door, and called loudly for Capt. Dicey. Capt. Dicey, 1st Mich. S. S., was our senior Captain, and had been chosen to represent us in all communications with the Confederate authorities.[9]

Everybody was asleep apparently, and it took a long time to arouse them. Then it was fully 10 minutes before Capt. Dicey could be found and made to believe that Capt. Senn wished to see him at the jail door. When he arrived there Capt. Senn said:

"Capt. Dicey, I'se gwine ter come inter dis yere jail with my post gyard an' count yo'uns, an' I warn you's all that if ary man makes a move, dog-goned if I don't shoot him dead!"

"All right, Capt. Senn," responded Capt. Dicey; "come right in; no trouble in here; all quiet, I assure you."

The door was opened and the "post gyard" entered with cocked muskets, burning pitch-pine knots, and shaking hands. The "Yanks" were counted and by means of a hastily-constructed dummy there was found to be one in excess of the number required. The jail was searched for the bridge, but the bunk boards, replaced to their proper position, gave no information of its construction. Capt. Senn and his guard retired completely mystified.

The *Daily South Carolinian* the next day published a two-column article on the "Daring and desperate attempt to escape made by the Yankee prisoners confined in Richland Jail. Only for the promptness, bravery and efficiency of Capt. Senn and his gallant post guard, the city would have been given over to the Yankee ghouls and vandals to become the scene of murder, rapine, arson, and pillage!"

The Confederate authorities were urged to at once remove us to a more secure place of confinement. The daily papers of Columbia were two in number—the *Carolinian* and the *Guardian*. They afforded us much amusement, both on editorial and advertising pages. The *Guardian* had a blood-curdling editorial one day concerning the state of affairs near Atlanta. It depicted the Yankee army as made up of conscripts, substitutes, and bounty-jumpers, kept on short rations, and that they were terrified because of their broken line of communication, and were ready to go to pieces, while the Confederate army was "gathered like a crouching lion preparing to spring upon its prey!"[10]

Down in one corner of the paper was a two-line paragraph. It read: "An ugly rumor prevailed on the streets last night that Atlanta had fallen!"

The advertisements were nearly all relating to slaves. "Choleo lots of prime, long cotton negroes" were freely offered for sale. There were numerous advertisements regarding runaway slaves, and each advertisement had a comical little picture of a running darky with a stick and bundle over his shoulder.

Every Wednesday and Saturday morning there was a "public vendoo" or auction sale of these "prime, long cotton negroes" from the steps of the Courthouse, only a block away. From one of our windows we could watch the sale and we saw the darkies parceled out and sold "in lots to suit the purchaser." Every night at 9 o'clock the City Hall bell rang for five minutes. We could hear the slaves hurrying away on the run, for to be caught on the streets after 9 o'clock without a pass consigned them to the calaboose.

The negro calaboose was close to the jail and every morning the black culprits were taken out. If it was their first offense they were dismissed with a warning; if a second offense their hands were placed in stocks, and they were given from five to 39 lashes. The blows were laid on with a heavy black-snake whip. The men were stripped of their shirts and lashed upon the bare back. The women's hands were placed in the stocks the same as the men, their skirts pulled up over their shoulders, and the blows laid upon the bare legs and hips. These sights never failed to arouse our greatest indignation, and the shrill screams of some poor negro woman crying, "Oh-h-h, Lordy!" would start a fearful stream of maledictions from the profane ones of our number.[11]

Two negro prisoners, dressed in the neat blue sailor suits of our navy, were brought to the jail. A planter came and claimed them as his slaves. Their uniforms were taken from them and coarse negro clothes substituted. We saw them driven off, their arms tied together with cotton ropes, followed by two men on horseback with shotguns. The daily papers said that "they were turned over to their lawful master to be dealt with as he might think proper." In all probability they were taken outside of the city and murdered. In the meantime our condition in the jail was growing worse and worse.

The Confederates evidently considered Richland Jail as a sort of "catch-all" for all the hard-character prisoners in that part of the Confederacy.

A lot of men charged with "treason" to the Southern Confederacy were confined in the third story, the floor above us. We received additions to our numbers in the persons of some officers of Kentucky and Tennessee Union cavalry regiments. They were members of Gen. Kilpatrick's command, captured while on a scouting expedition.[12] The most intense bitterness existed between them and the Confederates. As masters of profanity our new prisoners excelled; and could easily have beaten the army teamster in the use of strange and original oaths. The utter fearlessness with which they would curse our guards and call down anathemas upon Jeff Davis and the Southern Confederacy was a revelation to us. Had one of our "Yanks" attempted it he would have been shot down; but the guards seemed to accept abuse from these new prisoners as a matter of course. Probably the fact that both parties were Southerners had something to do with the forbearance of the guards.

Two rooms on the first floor of the jail were occupied by conscripts and deserters. Among them were some men who had been hiding in caves for months to avoid conscription. They were brought to the jail with their hands tied behind them with cotton ropes. Among the deserters arrested was one who proved to be a woman. She had enlisted to follow her lover, but the privations and perils of a soldier's life soon dispelled the romance of love's dream; and she ignominiously deserted, leaving the lover to fight his country's battles without her cheering presence. She was arrested and brought to the jail. To avoid being sent back to the front she declared her sex. We saw her lying down on a blanket in the lower jail hallway, the guards not having courtesy enough to offer her a chair or stool for a seat. She was clad in a man's suit, with a long butternut coat; her face was coarse, freckled and sunburnt. There was no difference in her appearance than that of hundreds of the conscript boys who filled the rebel ranks. It would require a vivid imagination to make a heroine of her.[13]

In strong contrast to this deserter was a little woman who held a Captain's commission in the Confederate artillery. She had lost a leg by a shell wound while serving with the army defending Charleston. She came into the jail to "see the Yanks," leaning on her crutches. She was attired in the full uniform of a Confederate artillery Captain. Her short, curly hair was partly covered by a jaunty forage cap, and the snug, neatly fitting gray uniform showed a fine, plump figure. Her face was pretty, and the manners officer-like and dignified.

After chatting pleasantly with some of our officers for a few minutes, she bade us adieu. She declared her intention of returning to duty with her troops again.

Visitors "to see the Yankees" were an almost everyday occurrence, and the guards never failed to designate me as "That thar little Yankee cuss is an officer in a nigger regiment." I had never made any retort, until one day a woman made the remark, "He 'un had orter be hung for makin' the niggers fight we 'uns," when I turned and said, "Yes, madam; I am an officer of a nigger regiment and I am proud of it. The time will come when the blackest nigger who wears blue will be a better man than any rebel who ever wore gray!"

The woman flushed, furious with anger.

"If I had my way, I'd kill all you Yankees who came down here to fight we 'uns, and steal we 'uns niggers—niggers we brung up jes' like our own children—an' teach 'em to fight we 'uns," she said.

"I haven't the least doubt of it, Madam," I said, and my friends hustled me away, fearing that my tongue would get me into trouble.

A half dozen prisoners who had escaped from Andersonville were brought in. They were ragged and dirty, and from them we learned of the fearful death rate at Andersonville, and of the horrors of that place. One of their number was a strong, wiry-looking man, with sharp, black eyes and a square jaw. He said nothing to any one, but I saw him and the Kentucky officers exchange glances and I knew that they were acquainted. The Andersonville men were placed on the cars to be sent back to Georgia. In a day or two the papers had an account of how some Yankee prisoners had knocked down the guards, leaped from the running train and successfully made their escape. Then the Kentucky officer told me that the black-eyed man was one of Kilpatrick's most daring and desperate scouts. Had the Confederates known whom their prisoner was, he would have been hung at once.

In September the naval officers left us, a special exchange having been arranged for them. This exchange was arranged by Lieut. Com. Williams, the senior officer of the naval prisoners. He was paroled by the Confederates, to arrange the exchange. He gave his parole to proceed to Washington and endeavor to arrange an exchange of naval prisoners. Should he fail to effect the exchange, he promised to return and surrender himself a prisoner again. How anxiously the blue jackets awaited the result of his mission.[14]

One evening we heard them cheering, and we knew that Capt. Williams had succeeded. They went off gaily enough the next morning. Before they left they gave us everything that they could possibly part with. Thanks to their generosity, my wardrobe was somewhat replenished. Two of their number, Lieuts. Preston and Porter, were afterwards killed in the assault on Fort Fisher.[15]

The ugly rumor that prevailed on the streets that Atlanta had fallen, proved to be founded on fact. The newspapers frantically called upon the Confederate authorities to fortify Columbia.

Every man was ordered to report for military duty, and the wildest excitement prevailed in the city. The Senior Reserves, old men between 55 and 65 years, and the Junior Reserves, young boys from 14 to 16 years of age, were both called out.

The spectacle of grandfather and grandson both under arms was not an uncommon one. We watched the unwilling recruits come in, each man loaded down with cotton haversacks stuffed with corn bread and sweet potatoes, and over each man's shoulders a big roll of cotton bed quilts. If possible, our "Kaintuck" and Tennessee Union officers would yell at the conscripts and inform them that "Sherman's men would walk through them like eating pie!"[16]

One poor old "Senior Reserve" came into town on a little old two-wheeled cart drawn by a rat-tailed mule. His wife, in homespun and sun bonnet, was with him, driving the mule. They stopped directly in front of the jail. Both were smoking corncob pipes. The old man took his old smoothbore musket, four well-filled haversacks and a big roll of bed quilts off the wagon. They both took the pipes out of their mouths and kissed each other. Then the old woman drove off, crying, whipping the mule, smoking and expectorating right and left. Instead of being touched by this affecting scene, the Yanks roared with laughter, and some of them started the song:

Our Johnny has gone to live in a tent,
They've grafted him into the army;
He finally puckered up the courage and went,
When they grafted him into the army![17]

Some of the best men of our post guard were detached and sent to the front. So much was the home guards force reduced that the men guarding the jail were doing almost continuous duty, four hours on and four hours off.

Again the plan for escape was ignited, and this time a general break was planned. When not on duty the guards always piled their muskets in a corner of the guard-room and were generally lying down outside of the building in the shade. Under the stairway of the jail were a dozen or more large boxes filled with cartridges. We could see the marks "Millidgeville Arsenal, buck-and-ball cartridge" on the ends of them. A mile away was the Columbia Arsenal, where there were plenty of arms.[18] The only guards there were three men and a Corporal, and we even knew their names, and had a very poor opinion of their courage. Our plan was to jump the guards in the back yard and in the jail hall and those guarding the front entrance; then half a dozen men were to dash through the open window of the guard-house and secure the arms of the guards off duty. With these in our possession we could quickly drive away the guards on the side of the jail and release our enlisted men. This would augment our force to 350 men, and a dash would be made for the arsenal, where arms could be obtained for all. The telegraph wires ran past the jail and were to be cut as soon as the guards were driven off. With arms in our hands, we would capture the railroad shops and disable all the engines. By seizing every horse and mule in the city and country we could mount our entire party and then we would make an attempt to reach Sherman's army.

It was a most desperate and daring scheme, but we were desperate men. "Might as well die fighting, as starve like rats in a hole," said a big Lieutenant of the "Six Kaintuck, Union" and so we all thought. Three men, each with a half brick in a stocking for a slingshot, and with a keenly-sharpened case-knife, were detailed to "jump" each sentinel. The Tennessee officers were to dash through the open window into the guard-room and secure the guns. The time selected was to be in the afternoon when we went down into the yard. My part was to climb the telegraph pole and cut the wires. The plot was exposed by one of our own number. We had believed him to be a cavalry officer but probably he was a spy confined with us for the express purpose of obtaining such information. When we went down in the afternoon nerved to make the break, all the guards were under arms and drawn up on the opposite side of the street. Never again did the Confederates relax their vigilance so as to give us the least opportunity.

The weeks dragged slowly along. The cornmeal was worse; it was ground cob and all, very dirty and often sour. The cowpeas were "last year's crop," musty, with more bugs than peas. Exchange seemed farther off than ever, and the daily papers were denied us. One day I saw a Captain of an Ohio regiment trying to rid his clothing of the vermin that infested the jail. The man had been shot through the right arm, a fearful wound, and was wholly unable to move his right hand. He had pulled off his shirt, and with his left hand was awkwardly picking the graybacks from his garment.[19] As he caught each offending pest he laid it on a little flat rock by his side and with a smooth round pebble smashed it flat. It was comical and at the same time, a piteous sight. "Cap," I said, "that's mighty tough; I'll skirmish for you," and I completed his task for him. I washed his clothing for him, and with an old flat-iron, without any handle on it, pressed out the seams of his underwear and made it possible for him to live a little more comfortably. I cared for him for some time. He was very grateful. An exchange was to be made of wounded men, and my Ohio Captain was among those selected. He offered to carry any letter that I might write. Our letters that were sent via flag of truce were limited to six lines.

I had long desired to write a letter to a certain girl way up North.[20] I communicated the desire to the Captain, and he told me to write the letter and he would smuggle it through the lines. The letter was written—a long one. A bandage was wrapped around the Captain's wounded arm, then the letter was wrapped over the bandage, then another bandage wrapped over the letter, and the whole thing wet with cold water.

The letter went through the lines, and was received by my sweetheart. She still preserves it, a precious relic of those war-time days.

Cold weather was coming on and many of us were almost naked; we had no blankets, and were growing weaker every day. One day, the last of November, my name was called at the door. I rushed eagerly forward, hoping for a letter and the long expected remittance. Capt. Lewis and a Confederate Lieutenant-Colonel stood at the door. Capt. Senn said: "This is the officer."

The other officer surveyed me for a moment and then said: "Please step down into the guard-room." I followed and was taken to the office. Even now, after a lapse of 34 years, I can see the expressions of horror, dismay and sympathy that were expressed on the faces of my fellow prisoners. It was their unanimous belief that I had been taken out to receive the death penalty. Arriving at the office the Lieutenant-Colonel motioned me to take a seat; the others left the room. In a very pleasant manner the officer began: "You are, I believe, an officer in the United States Colored Troops?"

My heart sank at this question, but I answered, firmly, "Yes, sir; I am."

"Did you pass the examination before Gen. Casey's Board?"

"Yes, sir."

"Had you any military experience before your examination?"

"I had, sir."

"Well, Lieutenant," said the officer, "the matter stands like this: Your Government cares nothing for you men; your Generals refuse to exchange prisoners with us. Your men are dying fearfully at Andersonville, more than 200 daily. Even if an exchange was arranged, our Government would never release you, gentlemen who are officers in negro troops. Now, I don't have any such prejudice myself, but the Confederate Government does. I recognize an officer and a gentleman when I see him. What I want to say to you is this: I am organizing what is known as the 'Foreign Legion,' for service in the Confederate army."

"They are to guard bridges, depots and stores. They will not be sent to the front. After the war is over, they will be retained as part of the Regular Confederate army. Most of the men are recruited from your men who are prisoners. Some of the officers are Southern gentlemen, and some are to be taken from you gentlemen who are prisoners. Now, you are young, well educated, and, I should judge, a very efficient officer. Capt. Senn informs me that you are a very high-spirited one, and I admire your pluck. I will make you this offer: Upon your taking the oath of allegiance to the Confederate Government I will give you a Captain's commission in the Foreign Legion, a full uniform sword, belt and revolver, a servant to wait on you, and $600 in Confederate money. Now think over this matter seriously before you answer."

Remember reader, that this was an offer to a boy not 19 years of age, to one who was proscribed by reason of his being an officer in a black regiment, weak from hunger and disease, and with little prospect of anything but death before him. I thought the whole matter over in a moment. I thought of the armless Sergeant waving the bloodstained flag in the hall in Worcester; of the men who died by my side in the Petersburg Crater; of my soldier father, of my mother, whose only child I was; of the dear blue-eyed girl way up in Massachusetts, whose only brother was with the old Sixth Corps and I didn't need to think any more, and rising I said: "Colonel, I cannot accept your offer."

He was disposed to argue the matter, and said some things that were very offensive, when I replied hotly and told him: "That sooner than be a 'Galvanized Yank,' I will see you, your Foreign Legion and the whole Confederacy deeper in h______ than a pigeon could fly in a thousand years!"[21]

I was immediately sent back to the jail and when I told my story my fellow-prisoners gave me a regular ovation.

Among our enlisted men the Colonel found eight who were willing to enter his Foreign Legion and to take the oath of allegiance to the Southern Confederacy. These men deserted in a body the very first night. They were recaptured, brought back to Columbia, court-martialed and shot to death, all within a week.

Two Lieutenant-Colonels from the staff of Gen. Robert E. Lee visited our prison and made inquiries concerning our condition. They promised us an improvement in rations and we were notified that we would be allowed to receive boxes of clothing from our friends at home. But the rations did not improve and the boxes sent by our friends in the North were never received.

On election day an election was held in the jail. Previous to the election political clubs of "Wide-Awakes," "Know-Nothings," "Loco-Focos," etc. were formed and mock speeches made; "grand-parades" marched all around the second floor of the jail, running over every one who got in their way. The election resulted in 132 votes being cast. The result was: Lincoln, 124; McClellan, 8.[22]

The Union officers who had been prisoners at Macon, Ga., had been removed to Columbia and were camped outside of the city. This camp was afterwards known as "Camp Sorghum." They also held an election with the following result: Lincoln, 1,024; McClellan, 143.

The Columbia papers were much interested, and published the result.[23]

10

Camp Asylum, Columbia, South Carolina

A cold, sleety rain came on, and we spent a most miserable time, huddled together, with our little pieces of shelter tent, trying to keep off the wet. When morning came, and we attempted to cook a little hot mush to keep the life in our shivering bodies, we found it impossible to keep the fire burning.

Although newspapers were denied us, we still managed to obtain the news. Sometimes we received a paper from a friendly guard, and sometimes the officer of the guard would allow someone to read his paper for a few moments; but our chief source of information was Capt. Harris, the prisoner under death sentence. Capt. Harris was confined in the corner room of the first floor nearest the guard-house of the jail.

Although he was compelled to wear chains on his ankles, he really fared much better than any of us. The United States Government had placed a Confederate Major, a prominent South Carolinian, as hostage for Capt. Harris, and notified the Confederate Government that if Capt. Harris was executed the Confederate Major would be hung at once. Both men had wealthy friends, and an arrangement was made whereby Capt. Harris's friends furnished the Confederate Major with such articles and extras as he desired, and the Major's family, who resided in Columbia, supplied the wants of Capt. Harris. By these means Capt. Harris received good food and considerable Confederate money.

A newspaper was also supplied him, and it did not take long for the Yanks to devise means to borrow that newspaper. A hole was cut through the plank flooring and the ceiling below, and by wrapping the paper on a stick, we soon had possession of it. It was necessary to return the paper to the Captain, as he was obliged to give it back to the guard officer. This line of communication was discovered one day, and promptly suppressed. It seriously troubled the prison authorities, and they turned us all down into the back yard and searched the jail thoroughly.

Among other discoveries were some short-hand notes. One of our officers was a good short-hand writer, and to pass the time and also keep himself in practice he would jot down any story of conversation that he might hear. Capt.

Senn found a dozen or more sheets covered with these phonetic characters, and at once concluded that he had detected a conspiracy. He took the papers to the local authorities, and they were able to translate just enough to assure themselves that it was a veritable find, if the cipher could be solved. The whole affair was sent to the Secret Services Bureau at Richmond. We never heard the result of the Bureau's investigation.

The other Union officers who were confined at "Camp Sorghum" were escaping in great numbers, though most of them were soon recaptured.[1]

In a small brick house directly opposite the jail were a pack of bloodhounds and English bulldogs. These dogs had been trained to hunt runaway negroes, but were now being used to trail and run down escaped Yankee prisoners. Every morning we would see this pack of dogs, followed by four or five men on horseback, each man armed with a shotgun and two revolvers, start out in search of escaped Yankees.

Lieut. Edward B. Parker, Co. B, 11th Vt., was brought into our jail, badly bitten by these dogs. He was sent to the hospital and died Oct. 8, 1864, from the effects of the wounds.[2]

On the morning of Dec. 12, 1864, all the prisoners at "Camp Sorghum" were transferred to the yard of the insane asylum. They passed in front of the jail, and a most curious and comical sight they presented. They had all sorts of uniforms, and their bundles and baggage were of the greatest variety. The same day, just after we had received our dinner allowance of cowpeas and cornbread, we were ordered to pack up. A heavy guard was waiting outside for us. We noticed that the new guards were altogether a different set of men from those who composed the post guard. There was something about them that indicated the veteran soldier. They handled their arms with ease, and moved with a celerity and precision that denoted previous experience. We soon learned that they were the 2d S. C. Reserves, composed of men who had been wounded and disabled at the front. Their position corresponded to that of the Veteran Reserve Corps of the Union army.[3]

Bidding the post guard "good-by," and cautioning them never to get too near to "Mr. Sherman and his company," we left the jail. As we marched away we saw the pale, anxious face of Capt. Harris watching us through the prison bars. He waved us a sad farewell. A march of a mile brought us to the yard of the insane asylum. A heavy gate of plank had been placed in one of the brick walls, and opposite the gate was a 12-pound brass fieldpiece. The gates were swung open and we were driven in. A chorus of yells and shouts of "fresh fish!" greeted us. We were not "fresh fish" by any means, but we were questioned as eagerly as if we were recent captives. Some of our party found comrades from their own regiments.

The grounds where we were confined were about four acres in extent. On three sides were high brick walls, and on the fourth side next to the asylum building, was a high plank stockade. Sentry-boxes were placed at the tops of the walls all around, about 35 feet apart. Four pieces of artillery were ready to sweep the interior in case of revolt. Forty feet from the wall, on the inside, was the "dead line," a single furrow turned up with the plow. To step on or over this dead line was to be shot without challenge. Two or three rough board houses were in process of construction, and we were promised lumber to make shelter for all. In one corner of the yard was a two-story frame house, some building connected to the asylum. In another corner of the lot were six water troughs filled with good, clear water. Three of these were to be used for cooking and three for washing. It did not take us long to make a survey of this place and come to the conclusion that "we were in a mighty tight box." The chances for escape or revolt were most decidedly poor.

Our arrival had swelled the number of prisoners there to about 1,300, all officers. We were directed to form ourselves into messes of 36 men; three messes made a squad. Our destination was "Mess One, Squad Seven."

A cold, raw wind was sweeping over the country, and our thin, ragged clothing furnished us but little protection. We were chilled to the very bone when the sun went down. With the setting of the sun the wind died away and the cold, sharp, white frost came down upon us. Sanders and I, wrapped in my pieces of shelter tent, lay down close together, trying to keep each other warm, for we had neither shelter, blankets or fires. As we lay there shivering we heard the band playing "Dixie" and "Bonnie Blue Flag," in honor of President Jeff Davis, who had arrived that day, and was stopping at the Congaree Hotel.[4]

The cold was intense, and to prevent freezing to death we got up and ran around to restore our warmth. We stamped around until we were exhausted and then lay down to shiver again, and in that way passed a long, miserable night. When daylight and sunrise came the other prisoners commenced cooking their breakfasts, making mush and corncakes. Some baked sweet potatoes and a few had loaves of white bread and pieces of fresh beef. In one corner of the prison was a sutler's tent, and those who had money could purchase bread, beef and potatoes. We of the Richland jail crowd made anxious inquiries about our rations, and were informed that the rations had been issued to the camp on the previous day, and that there would be no more rations issued for four days. This prospect was most discouraging.

We urged our case to the commanding officer of the prison, and, after a long delay, he promised to send a team to the jail to bring our supplies, which had been left behind. We waited until noon, and no rations appeared. Then I started in to "rustle," and managed to borrow a pint of cornmeal. This I cooked into mush in my quart tin cup and divided with my two comrades. No rations came that day, and we went supperless to bed, if lying shivering on the frozen ground could be called going to bed.

The next morning we were ravenous, but there were no rations. The other prisoners pitied us, but they had nothing to spare. I picked up and ate some sweet potato skins that had been thrown into a slop-hole. The loaves of fresh, white bread looked most tantalizing at the sutler's, but we had no money. I attempted to trade some of my military buttons for a loaf, and was jeered at by the sutler. I turned away, almost ready to break down with weakness and hunger and smarting under the insult.

A cheery voice addressed me: "What's the matter, Lieutenant? You look down at the mouth!"

A short, stout man with a Captain's straps, had accosted me. There was something about him that indicated the "old prisoner." In a few words I explained the situation.

"That's rough," he said. "Where are you from?"

When I told him that my parents resided in Worcester he was much interested. Did I know certain parties that he named? Fortunately, I was well acquainted with them.

"I think," he said, "that I can help you a little. Take this and when it's gone come to me, and I'll put you in the way of getting some more," and he placed a Confederate bill in my hands and walked off into the crowd. I grasped the bill closely; $5 would buy me a loaf of bread; $10 would make me happy! I looked at the bill and nearly fainted! One hundred dollars!

I read it over and over again. There was no mistake; the words were there, the "Confederate Government promises to pay Bearer, One Hundred Dollars," etc.

It did not take me long to purchase three loaves of bread and some sweet potatoes and take them to my chums. I did not explain to them the extent of my good fortune, but merely informed them that I had "made a raise."

The officer who so kindly assisted me in my hour of need was Capt. Wm. W. Wilson, 104th N.Y. He was one of the Gettysburg prisoners. Our long delayed rations, consisting of meal and sorghum, were finally brought to us, and the question arose, how should we save them? One of my mates solved the

Fig. 10.1. Col. Warren Shedd, 30th Illinois Infantry. Roger D. Hunt Collection, United States Army Military History Institute.

problem by cutting off part of his drawers leg and making a meal sack of it. Our share of the sorghum molasses, was entrusted to the care of a friend who had a canteen. My quart tin cup and the two side plates of an old canteen were the only utensils that three of us possessed, and we soon found that the tin cup was sufficiently large enough to cook all the meal that we could afford to use at one time. A cold, sleety rain came on, and we spent a most miserable time, huddled together, with our little pieces of shelter tent, trying to keep off the wet. When morning came, and we attempted to cook a little hot mush to keep the life in our shivering bodies, we found it impossible to keep the fire burning.

The driving rain would put out the fire as often as we lighted it. The wood was green pine, and gave out much smoke, but no heat. After several failures, two of us held a piece of shelter tent over the fire, and the third man stirred the mush. It was the most discouraging cooking that I ever attempted. For a few days lumber came in quite rapidly, and five or six rough homes were erected. We also received the frame for our squad building. Then the issue of lumber stopped. My two mates and myself succeeded in obtaining permission to sleep on the ground floor of the house belonging to another squad. This was such an improvement over lying out in the frost and rain, that we considered ourselves very fortunate.

A regular government was established inside the prison. Col. Warren Shedd, 30th Ill., the senior officer among the prisoners, was the commanding officer inside of the prison; Lieut. Col. Thorp, 1st N. Y. Dragoons, was our Chief Com-

Left: Fig. 10.2. Col. Thomas J. Thorp, 19th New York Cavalry. Roger D. Hunt Collection, United States Army Military History Institute.

Above: Fig. 10.3. Col. Daniel White, 31st Maine Infantry. RG98S-CWP Collection, United States Army Military History Institute.

missary; Adj't A. O. Abbott, 1st N. Y. Dragoons, was the Inside Adjutant. All orders to the prisoners were sent through Col. Shedd. The rations were delivered in bulk to Lieut. Col. Thorp, and all letters were received and delivered by Adj't Abbott.[5]

Every squad had its Chief and its Commissary. Col. Daniel White, 31st Me., was Chief of Squad Seven. Each mess likewise had its Chief, who acted as Chief and Commissary. Capt. Dicey, 1st Mich. S. S was the senior officer of our mess.[6]

The rations of meal and sorghum were hauled inside the stockade and placed on the ground. Then Lieut. Col. Thorp would order the sacks of meal placed in 13 piles, one pile for each squad. The amount of sorghum for each squad was easily estimated and fairly divided. Sometimes there was a little rice and a little salt. This extra food would be divided down by a tin cupful all around; then a smaller cup, and I have seen a tablespoon used to equalize the ration.

The wood was piled into 13 piles and some officer would turn his back and the Commissary would ask: "Who shall have this pile?" The officer would name the squad, and its Chief would immediately take possession of it. This distribution would continue until all the piles were gone. The Squad Commissaries would now have their rations carried to their particular part of the camp and the cry would be raised, "Mess Commissaries, come get your meal and sorghum!" The rations would then be redivided, and a third part would be given to each mess.

The Mess Commissaries would then divide among the 36 men. Generally three or four men formed a little mess. Sanders, representing our mess, would say: "I draw for three men." The meal would be divided with a pint tin cup; the tin must be filled and then scraped off exactly level. The ration was supposed to be a pint of meal per day to each man, but it seldom held out. Four and a half and four pints for the five days was about average. The rice and salt were in such meager quantities that generally only half the mess received any. The remainder waited for the next issue.

There were regular cliques and factions among the prisoners; generally a man associated with the comrades who were captured in the same battle. The oldest prisoners were from Gen. Milroy's command, captured near Winchester in June 1863. They were generally known as "Milroy's Thieves," though what they had ever done to merit this appellation I never knew. "The Gettysburg prisoners" were a large body, but they were subdivided into different corps organizations. The First Corps men kept by themselves, and were not on very good terms with the Eleventh Corps men. Most of these latter were Germans, and many fights occurred between the "Eleventh Corps Datel" and the "First Corps Irish." The Germans were fond of singing in their mother tongue, and the First Corps boys would exasperate them by singing, "Say, dutchy, will you fight mit Sigel?"[7]

Another song that was particularly offensive to the Germans was one known as the "Virginia Lowlands." The particular verse at which they took umbrage was the one referring to the rout of the Eleventh Corps at Chancellorsville.[8] The words were as follows:

Joe Hooker made a movement
Not many months ago;

And when he made it, boys,
He didn't make it slow!
The rebels they soon found it out,
And flanked him on the right,
And that's the reason why, my boys,
We're bumming here to-night
In the South Car'lina Lowlands, low.

Any remarks about the "flying Half Moon," or "I fights mit Sigel and runs mit Howard," would bring out a volley of German expletives.[9]

The aristocracy of all the prisoners were the Regulars. They held aloof from the common volunteers, and formed a little coterie of their own. Some of "Streight's Raiders" who escaped from Libby through the famous tunnel, only to be recaptured, divided with the Regulars in exclusiveness. They were not all members of Col. Streight's command, but the name covered them.[10] The "Chickamauga Gang," a lot of officers captured in that battle, claimed the distinction of being the greatest travelers. After their capture they were sent south; then north to Richmond to be confined in Libby; then to Danville; then to Macon, Ga.; then to Savannah; thence to Charleston to be placed under fire; from there to "Camp Sorghum," Columbia; then to "Camp Asylum."[11]

The "Plymouth Pilgrims" was the name bestowed upon the officers captured at Plymouth, N. C. It included all the officers of the 16th Conn., two companies of the 2d Mass. H. A. and all of the 101st and 103d Pa. and 85th N. Y. When these officers were captured they were allowed to retain all of their clothing and blankets.[12] They brought their valises with them. Consequently, they were the best supplied and most comfortable of any of the prisoners.

A lot of officers of colored troops were among the "Olustee" prisoners, so called from the unfortunate battle of that name. Among them was Maj. Archibald Bogle, 35th U.S.C.T. The Confederates, thinking to humiliate him, placed him with the enlisted men, in the prison pen at Andersonville. The Major immediately set about organizing an outbreak. Under his directions tunnels were run so as to undermine the stockade. Detachments were told off to charge and seize the rebel artillery, and gunmen selected to man the guns. A heavy force sufficient to overrun the guards was to beat down the infantry and obtain their muskets. The tunnels were built but the plot was exposed by some renegade. Before the Confederates could strengthen the stockade a heavy shower came up, and part of the undermined stockade fell down. The rebels got the biggest scare of their lives, and concluded that Maj. Bogle's "humiliation" had better be completed in some other place. He was taken out of Andersonville and placed with the other officers at Macon.[13]

"Wilderness," "Wilson and Kautz's Raiders," "Cold Harbor Heavies" (officers of the heavy artillery captured at Cold Harbor), "Second Corps Men," from the Petersburg night attack of June 22, "Big Shanty's," "Resacs," "Hunter's Drewry's Bluffs," "Monocacy's Hundred Dayzers"—a long "Hundred days" it was too, for many of them,—"Atlantas," and "Stoneman's Raiders," were only a few of the names of clans who held fast together for mutual benefit and protection.[14]

A most unfortunate set were the "Stoneman Raiders." Starting out from the Union lines with the intention of liberating the Union prisoners at Andersonville, a series of misfortunes overtook them, which resulted in their getting into prison themselves. They generally attributed their capture to mules. Many of their horses gave out and most of them were mounted on mules captured in the country. There came a critical moment when it was necessary for them to charge and cut their way through the enemy's ranks. The mules started all right, but when they were nearly upon the enemy's line the sight of the glistening bayonets was too much for the long-eared steeds and every mule came to a dead stop. Most of their riders were pitched off and ignominiously captured.[15]

For a person to place his thumb on his ear, move his fingers back and forth at the same time saying, "waw-hee-waw-hee-e!" in the presence of a "Stoneman Raider," was to take a chance of a thrashing or being thrown into the slop-hole. The "Raiders" would fight, even if their mules wouldn't. An officer of the 1st Ill., L. A., who had been captured near Atlanta, July 23, 1864, was one of the characters of the prison. He had been struck over the head with a musket butt at the time of his capture, and thus rendered insane. Ordinarily he was quiet enough, but on dark and stormy nights his affected brain took his mind back to the battlefield, and in clear, stentorian voice he would be heard giving orders to his battery. He would yell all the orders of the light battery drill, and the crazy people over in the asylum, would take up his cries and scream their loudest. Then some one of the Yanks would cry out, "Pack up! All Exchanged!" and that was the signal for a general uproar. Every man in the camp would yell something. We would hear the drums beat and our guards would turn out and double guard the sentry-boxes and man the artillery. They threatened to open fire on us if the noise was ever repeated, but after a few quiet nights the uproar would break out again. Some of the prisoners, fearing that the artillery might be opened on the camp, dug trenches in the earth.

Fig. 10.4. "Saying 'waw-hee-waw-hee-e!' in the presence of a 'Stoneman Raider' was to take a chance of a thrashing." *National Tribune*, July 27, 1899.

The Confederate Adjutant was gravely informed that "the Yanks were hollerin' to keep warm." An increase of wood supply was suggested as a remedy to prevent further alarms. But the reply to this suggestion was that they would "warm us up in a way that would give us something to yell about," if the disturbances did not cease.

My purchases of bread and sweet potatoes were shared with my two comrades, consequently my $100 did not last very long. The prices of the Confederate sutler at Camp Asylum were nearly double those charged in the city markets. Capt. Wilson did not forget his promise to assist me when the $100 were gone. He introduced me to the officer who acted as agent for a speculator, who was supplying the Union officers with Confederate money. This speculator's name was Potter. He was a professional blockade runner. To the Union officers he pretended to be a Union man, and to the Confederates he was a bitter rebel.

This is the way that he loaned the money: A bill of exchange was drawn up in triplicate on some well-known bank in the North. In my case the bill was addressed to my father, payable at the Mechanic's Bank of Worcester. This was signed by the officer who obtained the money, giving his name, rank, and regiment. On the back of this note was an indorsement that read like this: "This money was loaned me while a prisoner of war at Columbia, S. C., at my urgent request and when I was in great need. I consider it a debt of honor and request that it be promptly paid." Also, "The omission of United States Revenue stamps is not done for the purpose of defrauding the United States Government, but because it is impossible to procure them."

Two and one-half dollars Confederate money were generally paid for each dollar greenback order drawn in this way.

Thanks to Capt. Wilson's influence, my paper was considered "gilt-edged," and I obtained three for one. These notes were sent through the lines, no one knew how, and in most cases promptly paid.

My father paid $300 for me, the cost of my Winter's board at Columbia.

Probably this money that I obtained saved my life, and the lives of my two comrades. With money in my pocket, I was enabled to purchase a pair of coarse brogan shoes for $100, and an old six-quart tin pail for $20. The pail was leaking badly, and had to have nine plugs put in it every time we cooked mush. It was on account of this defect that I was enabled to purchase it so cheaply. For $10 we obtained at least two quarts of coarse, dirty salt, and it was a great luxury to us.

The purchase of bread and sweet potatoes increased our fare so much that I borrowed a sieve, made from an old tin plate with holes punched in it, and preceded to sift our meal. This brought out a remonstrance from one of our colleagues, for after the cob and dirt was screened from the meal, its quantity was reduced at least one-third. But I insisted, and had my way. Taking the screenings from the meal, I browned them in a frying-pan, and with the addition of some brown, burnt sweet potato parings I made coffee.

The coffee was considered a great success, and was immediately adopted by all members of our squad who could afford it. It was black and hot, and in those particulars at least it resembled the well beloved coffee that Uncle Sam furnished to his soldiers.

The increase in our food supply enabled us to sometimes borrow a skillet and bake a pone. How we watched and waited for the first corn pone that we made to bake. I nearly got into a fight with one of my mates because I sprinkled a little salt over the slice of pone that I was eating. He insisted that corn pone was good enough plain, without the extras, and that sprinkling salt over it was an extravagance and a waste.[16]

I retorted by saying that I wanted the salt and that I was going to have it while it lasted; that I had "made the raise" that purchased all these things, and if he didn't like it he might leave the mess. He had tried to raise money and had failed, and I had the advantage of him.

When I purchased my new shoes I was in great need of a pair of stockings. The Confederate Sergeant who superintended the roll-call of our squad gave me a pair of homespun ones. He was a plain, honest man, a most devout Methodist, and gave me the stockings because, as he gravely informed me, his Bible taught him "to love his enemies."

Perhaps, also, my smooth face and boyish appearance might have had something to do with it.

It must not be thought that because the prisoners were hungry, ragged and cold that they were a dejected lot of men sitting down despondently and bemoaning their fate. Nearly all of these officers were old, veteran soldiers. Many of them had entered the service at the very outbreak of the war. All were tried and well-seasoned veterans. They accepted their unlucky condition as part of the fortunes of war; it was all in the three years. To despond and give up hope in that place was to die, and none knew it better than they.

They sang, danced, made speeches, played chess, checkers and fox and geese. Poker games, faro banks, and chuck-a-luck boards and other gambling games were in full blast.[17]

The rebel Adjutant came in one evening and took a hand in a poker game, and was speedily relieved of all his money. The next night he came in again and tackled the faro bank, with no better success. The Yanks relieved him of over $1,700 in the two evenings.

Some of the prisoners carved beautiful pipes of brier-wood; others mended shoes and did good business.

Every 10 days the whole lot of prisoners were formed in line of four ranks and counted. By "flanking" and sliding down to the left, the number was made to appear larger, and the Confederates generally found a surplus of prisoners. Some of the old prisoners had their names in two or three squads and managed to draw rations from all of them.

A change of prison commanders was made in January, and an old Frenchman, ranking as Major, assumed command of us. He made us a speech in which he stated that the Federals had held him a prisoner at Fort Delaware for 11 months, and that he sympathized with us, as he "knew how it was himself." He promised us tents with straw in them, and our expectations rose quite high. But, alas, for the expectations. Our old Major got drunk and quarrelled with the Surgeon and was relieved from duty.

Probably the real reason of his disgrace was the fact that he would not be a willing tool for Gen. Winder, who never neglected an opportunity to oppress and humiliate the prisoners.[18]

Many letters were received at "Camp Asylum," and I was one of the fortunate recipients. Among my letters, was one from the blue-eyed Massachusetts girl, in answer to the one which I had written to her and sent through the lines on the wounded arm of the Ohio officer. It was a long letter, four pages, and I could never account for it coming through the lines only on the theory that the examining officer had a sweetheart of his own, and that a "fellow feeling makes me wondrous kind." To me, that letter was a treasure. It was read and re-read, committed to memory, and carried until it was worn to shreds. A small bill of English exchange for my father was also received. This exchange, being the same as gold, could have been sold in Columbia for $36 Confederate for each dollar in gold. The Quartermaster of the prison, Capt. Richardson, allowed me 13 for 1, about one-third of the prevailing rates.

Newspapers had been denied us, and we were wildly anxious for news. Various efforts were made to bribe the guards to bring in the paper, but none succeeded. An idea occurred to me, that if I could make it known to one of the colored laborers who came inside the stockade each day, to unload the sutler's wagon, that I was an officer in a colored regiment a paper might be obtained. The idea was communicated to several of my messmates, who readily promised their assistance. When the sutler's wagon came in, we were all gathered around, and the attention of three guards was taken up by my companions, who kept them close to the wagons. The negro that I selected for the trial was a big, powerful black fellow. At the corner of the tent, out of sight of the guard, I stopped directly in front of him, so that he was obliged to stop.

"Git outer de way, dar; dosn' you see I'se totin' dose sweet 'taters," he exclaimed angrily, but I pressed close to him and in a whisper, that only he could hear, I asked, "Boy, are you true?" The negro cast a swift glance around, and then answered in a whisper, "Deed I is, sah!"

"I'm an officer in a colored regiment. I've got a whole company of black soldiers back in the Yankee army," I said in a low tone.

"I'd like mighty well to be one ob dem, sah," was the response of the man as he passed into the tent with his load. When he came out, I asked, "Can you get me a newspaper?"

"Deed, an' I'll try, sah," was the whispered answer. When he brought the next sack of potatoes, I asked: "Do you know anyone who can read? We want the news. Do you understand?"

"Yes, sah, I unnerstan's. I know a yaller barber dat kin read. I git him to git de paper. Yo' stan's right yere tomorrer w'en we comes in; hab yo' cote open a leetle, so" and the black man illustrated his meaning and hurried on.

The next day I was waiting anxiously. The sutler's wagon had stopped, and as one of the negroes lifted a sack of potatoes from it, the sack burst and its contents were spilled among the Yankee prisoners. There was a mad scramble for the potatoes, the guards trying to save them from the prisoners. At this moment, my man came around the tent and ran squarely against me.

"Git outer di way yere! Wha foh' you a clutterin' up de way!" he said roughly, but at the same time something was quickly thrust into the breast of my coat, which I instantly buttoned up.

I stepped quietly from the crowd and went to the place where our squad were gathered. "I've got a paper!" I said, and they all gathered around. On the first page was a dispatch about Gen. Hardee's army being safe in Charleston. We turned the pages over and eagerly read an editorial entitled "The Situation." Then we learned that Sherman had marched to the sea and captured Savannah; that the rebel General Hood had been defeated at Nashville, and obliged to retreat with the loss of more than half his army and all of his artillery; that the Union forces had been repulsed in their first attack on Fort Fisher, but that another attempt would soon be made to capture it. One page contained a graphic account of Sheridan's victory over Early at Fisher's Hill in the Shenandoah Valley.[19]

The article was copied from the *New York Herald*, and the editor of the Columbia paper cautioned his readers to make great allowance for "Yankee bluster and bragadocio."[20] But it was good enough for us.

We knew that our armies were not idle, that the great and important victories had been won, and that "the beginning of the end" was at hand. The news spread like wildfire. A thousand excited men gathered around and told the news to each other. Then an officer in a clear voice read aloud and all within hearing of his voice listened in breathless silence.

When the capture of Savannah was announced, the Western men went wild with enthusiasm, and when the story of Sheridan's brilliant victory was told, the men of the Sixth, Eighth, and Nineteenth Corps were frantic with their demonstrations of joy. As soon as the paper was exhausted by one reader, another took it up and read it to another group. Then they cheered; cheered for Grant, for Sherman, for Thomas, for "Little Phil," for the Union and the old flag, and for "everybody up in God's country." Then they groaned; groaned for Jeff Davis, for Hood, for Early, for the whole Southern Confederacy inclusive.

Our Confederate guards were much exercised as to what the Yanks were about until some of them saw one of our men reading the paper. Then they sent in a guard with an officer, who demanded that the paper be at once given up. He threatened to stop all rations unless the paper was at once delivered to him. No one in the prison could be found who knew anything about that paper or any other paper, and after an unsuccessful search, the rebel officer retired.

Under the inspiration of the glorious news, Adj't S. M. Byers, 50th [5th] Iowa, composed the words of the song: "Sherman's March to the Sea." The music was arranged by Lieut. W. O. Rockwell, 134th N.Y., and was sung as a quartette from the steps of the hospital.[21] The singers were encored until they could sing no longer.

About the middle of January some pieces of old canvas were issued to the prisoners, there being no prospect of ever obtaining lumber to finish the houses that had been promised us. Our mess of 36 men obtained the "fly" of an old hospital tent. By digging out a cellar in the ground we all succeeded in getting under cover.

From the fact that a number of our mess were officers of colored troops, our domicile was nicknamed "The Crow's Nest," and the name inscribed in charcoal on its outside.[22] As soon as the tents were up everybody set about building fireplaces and chimneys. The bricks were made by patting the tough coarse red soil into brick-shaped lumps. Our first chimney, built with great labor, fell the first night under a heavy rain. The next one was made of sticks and mud, and was more successful. Every tent had its slop hole, into which was thrown the dirty water of the mess. The tents were pitched without regard to line or position, and the slop holes were dug on the same principle. The result was that walking about the camp after dark became a risky exercise. Every night some unlucky fellow would walk into a slop hole, and his imprecations and the shouts and yells of derision of those around him, who did not fall into the pit, would waken the whole camp.

No sooner were the tents in position than a tunnel was started from one.

This tent was located as near as possible to the dead line. Under the pretense of making a sketch of the camp, an officer succeeded in getting outside and locating a fine spot for a tunnel. The tent from which the tunnel started was about 10 feet from the dead line; the dead line was 40 feet from the brick wall; 30 feet from the wall on the outside, was a deep ditch or gully made by the rain. This gully turned off and ran back away from the wall; a better location for the tunnel could hardly have been selected. The distance, about 80 feet, was quite an obstacle, but the hard, tough clay was very favorable for such work. A shaft about four feet deep square was sunk for about 10 feet, then the tunnel was started towards the wall. As the ground was sloping, it was estimated that this would give from six to four feet of earth overhead and pass under the brick wall.

Great care had to be taken in disposing of the dirt, and here was where the utility of the slop holes came in. By dumping the dirt into a slop hole all traces of it was at once covered up. During the day some cross boards were placed in the tunnel shaft and clay four feet deep packed into it, and a fire built on top of the clay. The confederates suspected something of the sort, and visited this tent frequently, but nothing but a hard, fire-blackened, earthen floor was to be seen. They sank ramrods into the earth, but failed to reach the tunnel. Every night men worked in it until it was out under the wall, nearly out to the gully. Only a dark night was needed to "crack" it, and it was hoped that it would enable many prisoners to escape. Only reliable, well-known prisoners were in the secret. It was stipulated that when the time came, those in the secret should have the privilege of taking one friend. Every arrangement was made to get the men out quietly and successfully. Every man had his number, decided by lot, and was sworn to abide by it. There was to be no "flanking," crowding or confusion.

I was among the chosen ones, and my number placed me well in the front. Anxiously we waited for a dark, stormy night, but none suitable for our project came.

One morning a Confederate officer and guards came inside. The officer carried a long steel rod, and with his guard proceeded directly to the tunnel tent. He endeavored to sink the rod down through the fireplace, but the earth was packed so solid that he could not accomplish it; then he went out over the dead line, but the six feet of clay crust over the tunnel held our secret.

We began to hope that his efforts would result in failure. At the brick wall he again began sounding, and on the second trial the steel rod went down about four feet and then slid down for three feet more. We were discovered! The officer sent outside for spades and crowbars, and soon opened up a hole large enough to reveal the extent of our operations. The Confederates were greatly elated and we were correspondingly depressed.

That afternoon the following order was posted in the camp hospital and at various places about the camp:

> ASYLUM PRISON.
> COLUMBIA, S. C., Feb. 4, 1865.
> GENERAL ORDER NO.—
> Prisoners of war will take notice that I am directed by Gen. Winder, commanding prisoners of war, in case any more tunneling takes place in the prison, he will remove all barracks and tents so that it will be the fault of the prisoners themselves, if they have no covering from the weather. They will further take notice, that if any injury is done any fellow prisoner suspected of giving information, I shall use force for force, and the guilty parties will be punished.
> E. Griswold.
> Major commanding C.S. Military Prison.[23]

But in spite of the order, two tunnels were immediately started one each in houses numbers 1 and 2.

An occasional paper was received from the faithful negro, and by that means we learned of the capture of Fort Fisher by the Union forces. This was the occasion for another celebration, and the Confederates searched every guard and negro who entered the stockade. My faithful negro attempted to hide the paper in the toe of his shoe. He was detected, taken out, and given 100 lashes on the bare back. Stiff and sore from the terrible beating, he was sent back to work. As he passed among us he said: "Dey may kill dis nigger, but dey can't make him hate de Yankees." Brave fellow; I hope that he lived to enjoy the freedom that he so earnestly desired.

Gen. Winder died very suddenly. Another celebration was held, and we burned up all our pine wood in a torchlight procession, celebrating his demise.

Two officers died in the prison hospital. The authorities refused to allow them to be buried in the public burying-ground. A request that some of the officers might attend the bodies to the place of interment was peremptorily refused. A prominent Southern clergyman preached to us one Sabbath. His discourse was strictly a theological one, and was listened to with respect. The fact that this same clergyman had prayed in the pulpit at the beginning of the war, "that yellow fever and pestilence might sweep the Yankee invading horde off the face of the earth," was remembered by some and quoted against him. I do not think that his sermon produced any moral benefit among his hearers.

The health of my companion, Lieut. Sanders, began to fail, and I realized that unless something was done for him he would not survive his imprisonment. After much trouble, I succeeded in obtaining an order admitting him to the hospital. His condition here was an improvement over our crowded, damp, stifling tent. My money was again exhausted, and I was unable to obtain any more. Every day I looked for a letter containing a remittance, but none came.

Many of our old veteran guards had been sent off to the front, and their places taken by the South Carolina Cadets. These young men were insufferably conceited, very insulting and overbearing. We frequently told them, "Boys, the men at the front don't talk that way," in answer to their boastings. They had an idea that if they were only in front of Sherman that they could stop his whole army. They had the choice offered them of remaining in Columbia, and guarding the prisoners, or going to the front, and they eagerly chose the latter. They ran against a line of Sherman's "Bummers" near Branchville, almost the first morning of their arrival at the front. Sherman's men seeing that they were boys, called out to them to go back. The cadets answered with a volley and charged the Yankee line. There was a single volley from the "Bummers," and most of the cadets were laid low. Of the whole company not a dozen escaped. There was mourning in Columbia when the news came back that this band of high-spirited boys had almost been annihilated.[24] Among the particulars of the capture of Fort Fisher, that reached us, was the news of the death of Lieuts. Preston and Porter, of the United States Navy, both killed in the assault on the fort. These two officers were among our lot of naval officers in Richland Jail, and were well known and liked by all of us. Even the Columbia papers spoke kindly of them and regretted that such a sad fate should have fallen to such brilliant young men.

11

The Confederacy in Retreat

All was quiet until 4 o'clock in the afternoon, when "bang!" "bang!" "bang!" a whole battery broke out, not more than three or four miles away. Sherman had come. How we cheered. Our cheering was brought to a sudden close by the appearance of guards, who hustled us out in a lively manner. A number of prisoners had dug holes and stowed themselves away, but nearly all were discovered and dug out, covered with clay. Their recapture was made a source of great amusement for the guards.

Although the Confederates deprived us of the newspapers, we were able to read the signs of the times with tolerable correctness. From the Asylum yard, a view of the railroad leading north could be had, and the unusual activity, loaded trains moving north, running day and night, assured us that Sherman was fast approaching Columbia. We often saw bands of cattle and horses being driven away to some place secure from Sherman's foragers.

We watched eagerly for the arrival of troops to oppose his advance, and one night there was great cheering and yelling at the depot. We counted the cars, and estimated that there were about 4,000 men—a very correct guess as we afterwards learned. Our guards were increased, and every night they lighted large fires all around the stockade to detect any attempt to escape.

They brought us in a clipping from a paper, stating that Confederate Commissioner Halet [Hatch] had had an interview with the Federal authorities at City Point, Va., and that the articles for a general exchange had been agreed upon, and that an exchange of prisoners would certainly take place soon.[1] Some of our "Fresh Fish" took considerable stock in this rumor, but the old prisoners refused to believe it, and prophesied a move of prisoners in the near future. The exchange rumor, they said, was given out to discourage any attempt to escape. On the morning of February 14, 1865, the first six squads, 648 prisoners, were sent off on the cars. Our guards told us that these men were to be sent to Richmond for exchange. It occurred to us that if they were to be exchanged, that they would have been paroled in Columbia, and their 400 guards retained with the Confederate forces guarding that city. We did not think that the rebels would detail troops for a guard if an exchange was really intended.[2]

The party left us in the forenoon; in the afternoon the rain began to pour in torrents. As soon as they vacated their houses a rush was made to secure them by those of us who were to remain behind. My men captured house No. 2, and we congratulated ourselves that we would have shelter from the driving storm.

We were all snugly stowed away, talking of the probability of being recaptured by Sherman, and enjoying the unwonted luxury of a good fire in the fireplace, when the door of our house was burst open and a dozen guards entered. Every guard had all his things with him in marching order, and every man of them carried a blazing stick of pitch pine.

"Git out of yere, you Yanks, right quick, now! Hurry up, gol dum ye!" were their orders.

We tumbled out, and so excited were the guards, that they would hardly allow us to pick up our things, but fairly drove us away at the point of the bayonet. Giving Sanders one piece of my shelter tent, and wrapping the other around me, and carrying a little pack of meal in the old tin pail, all the baggage three of us possessed, we plunged out into the mud and driving rain. The guards were "rounding up" the prisoners from all around, and we were soon driven into a sort of a line. The prison gates swung open and we passed out and more guards with torches surrounded us. Through the mud and water, sometimes more than knee deep, we were hurried to the depot, where a train was waiting for us. A few were placed in the carts, and then ordered out again. For two long hours we stood in that fearful storm, drenched through and chilled to the bone. The torches of our guards burned out and barrels of tar were lighted. The rebels were in a panic about something. Their officers were rushing around, and we heard fragments of conversation,—"Wires down," "Kilpatrick's cavalry," "Yankees have cut the road,"—and we were soon in as great a state of excitement as they were.[3]

"About face," was the order, and we were rushed back to Camp Asylum. The gates had been left open, and we all rushed in before the guards had time to get around to their sentry boxes. For 10 minutes there were no guards on three sides of the camp. I could have escaped by scaling the wall, aided by a piece of scantling, and several did so escape; but the storm was so terrible, and I was so cold and weak, that I feared that I would perish if I attempted it.

Our fires were soon rebuilt, and we passed the remainder of the night steaming and drying ourselves. From all over the camp the cry of "Pack up! All exchanged!" would be raised every few minutes, making sleep an impossibility. The guards fired several shots through the houses as a hint for us to keep quiet, but nothing could quiet that gang, when once the cry of "Pack up! All exchanged!" was raised.

The next day was clear and pleasant, and as we lay sunning ourselves in the warm sunshine, some of the prisoners said that they could hear cannonading. They were ridiculed by their companions; but about 1 o'clock in the afternoon the dull "boom!" "boom!" of distant artillery could be distinctly heard. It produced a buzz of excitement. There were a few reports and then it ceased.

"Nothing but the advance guard shelling some crossroad; they'll go into camp and we won't hear any more of them," said some one.

"Sherman's men don't go into camp at this time of day," insisted the Western men; "You'll hear from 'Uncle Billy' before sundown."

All was quiet until 4 o'clock in the afternoon, when "bang!" "bang!" "bang!" a whole battery broke out, not more than three or four miles away. Sherman had come. How we cheered. Our cheering was brought to a sudden close by the appearance of guards, who hustled us out in a lively manner. A number of prisoners had dug holes and stowed themselves away, but nearly all were discovered and dug out, covered with clay. Their recapture was made a source of great amusement for the guards.

A large number of officers did escape by hiding between the ceiling and flooring of the hospital. The ceiling overhead was pine boards and the space between it and the flooring above would allow a thin man to squeeze in. A board was cut out, and after all were hidden who could hide, the board was replaced and the cracks stuffed with corn bread. These men remained in this position from the forenoon of the 15th until the afternoon of the 17th.[4]

We who could not hide away were marched to the depot, where a train of box cars awaited us. We were given rations of three hardtack and a small strip of bacon, the first meat issued to us for five and one-half months. It was dark when we left Columbia. The train was heavy and the engine was barely able to pull it. Fourteen miles north of Columbia, near Winsboro, our engine ran off the track.

The trainmen were not able to replace it, and finally managed to turn the locomotive over on its side. We lay there, wishing that there might be some means of getting word to Sherman of the predicament which the train was in. When daylight came there was a thick fog, making it impossible to see more than a few yards. Our guards were excited and nervous, ready to shoot on the slightest provocation. There were at least 500 guards around the 700 prisoners.

The rebels were so demoralized that had a dozen of Kilpatrick's dashing cavalrymen dashed in on them with a whoop and a hurrah, the whole force of guards would have stampeded. It was noon before the negro laborers finished a temporary track around the wrecked engine and our train proceeded on its journey. In the afternoon the guards on the top of the cars amused themselves by shooting at any Yankee who showed himself at the car door. As two guards were stationed in each car door, they narrowly escaped being shot by their own men. Their officers soon put a stop to their amusement.

The next morning we arrived at Charlotte, N. C. In the back corner of the car that I was in, some of us had worked nearly all night with a saw made from an old case knife, cutting a hole through the bottom of the car. When we stopped at Charlotte, an officer, a Captain in a Western regiment, attempted to escape through this hole. As he slipped his leg through the hole, a guard on the outside fired at him, shattering the knee. The wounded man was pulled out cursed and abused for attempting to escape. He was taken to the hospital in Charlotte and his leg amputated. What finally became of him we never knew. We were turned into a camp in a lot of scruboaks, where we found the six squads who had preceded us.[5] It was a cold, cheerless place; the snow lay on the ground in places, and we had no tents, blankets or shelter of any kind.

With my two pieces of shelter tent, my mates and I erected a covering, and by driving down sticks at the ends and weaving them with pine branches we endeavored to make ourselves a little more comfortable. Leaves were gathered for a bed, and the three of us cuddled in together and endeavored to keep each other warm; but the wind searched every part of our tent; and we lay shivering, with chattering teeth, through the long dreary night. To make it worse, our rations gave out, none were issued, and nothing could be purchased. The next day, made desperate by the cold and hunger, I informed my comrades that I intended to make an attempt to escape, even if I got shot in the attempt. Our guards were old men, the Senior North Carolina Reserves. Many of our officers bribed the guards to let them escape, but I had nothing to offer. But an opportunity presented itself to slip by the guards, and I improved it. A number of the prisoners were allowed outside the guard line, under guard, to cut wood and pine branches for their brush shanties. I watched one party go out, and seeing that the sentinel was a stupid looking old chap, I took my pieces of shelter tent over my shoulder and marching directly up to the man I said, "I am going out after brush, along with that detail yonder," pushed by him and started as if to follow the working party. The old man said nothing, and I kept going, though for a moment it was with a nervous dread that he might send a bullet after me.

I followed in the direction of the detail for a short distance, then turned into a little gully. In 10 minutes I was a mile away from the camp. At last I had escaped! After almost seven months' endeavor I had passed the guards. My spirits rose with the prospect, and I struck out at a lively rate, following a course that would screen me from observation as much as possible. My hunger was forgotten, and in my excitement my strength seemed to come back to me. I decided that I would swing well around the town of Charlotte, find a plantation, obtain food from the negroes, and, if possible, reach Sherman's army.[6]

As soon as I was a safe distance from camp I would hide in the brush, and wait for darkness before attempting to cross the open fields. "Halt, thar! You Yank, cum hyar. We want you, Yank!" My air castles came to an abrupt ending. There, behind a clump of bushes not 10 yards away, was a rebel Sergeant and half a dozen men. Their cocked muskets covered me. Escape was impossible.

"I was looking for you boys," I said with a faint attempt at a smile.

"I reckon you have found us, Yank," said the Sergeant with a grin. My captors were much elated over their success; they had already captured and sent back several escapes.

"How did you get out, Yank?" asked the Sergeant.

"Bribed the guard," I answered boldly.

The Sergeant looked over my ragged, dirty wardrobe, and remarked: "That yer rebel must a-b'en mighty keen for a bribe!"

Seeing that the guards had their haversacks with them, I asked for something to eat. They gave me some cornbread and sweet potatoes, which were very acceptable to me. The Sergeant ordered one of his men to take me back to the camp, and cautioned the man to be extremely careful and not let the Yankee get away from him. My guard was an old man, and as soon as we were out of hearing, he began to tell me about his troubles.

"Say, Yank," he said, "dis yere's a rich man's wah, an' a pore man's fight. South Car'leena war mighty keen fer a fight, but North Car'leena, she done furnish mos' all the men to git killed. I've had two sons killed—one at Newbern an' one at Gettysburg, an' now de conscript officer had done tuk me away from my cabin an' my ol' woman, and made me sarve as a geard, to watch out for yo'uns!"

I sympathized with the old man so warmly that he gave me nearly all the rations that he had in his haversack. I proposed that he should let me escape, but he dare not risk it; but told me that the first time that he was on guard he would let me slip out, if I managed it quietly. He advised me not to try to escape, as he had heard that the prisoners would certainly be paroled in a day or two. His further advice was that if I did make another attempt to escape to strike out for the mountains of western North Carolina. There were plenty of Union men in those mountains, he said, who would assist me.[7] He earnestly warned me not to try to reach Sherman. Wheeler's rebel cavalry were scouring the country all around Sherman, and should I fall into their hands, my chances for life would be very uncertain.[8] They were moving rapidly, and did not like to be encumbered with prisoners.

My reappearance in camp caused some excitement among my messmates, and they were inclined to laugh at me, but I boasted that I had obtained a good meal, which was more than any of them could say.

Exchange rumors still continued plentiful, and on the 19th of February, orders were given to begin making out the rolls.

On the 21st 600 prisoners including my squad, having signed the parole, were loaded into cars and started North. We were informed that we were to be sent through the lines at Wilmington.

The morning of the 22d found us at Greensboro. After a long wait we were started on the road towards Raleigh. The guards were taken off; only an officer, Sergeant and half a dozen men accompanied us. Our hopes ran high. Soon we would see the old flag, and be back in "God's country," and then after a leave of absence we would "go back to the regiment." In all the time of my imprisonment I have no recollection of ever hearing a prisoner wish for home; it was always, "If I was only back with the old regiment." The idea of leaving their colors while the war lasted never seemed to occur to any of them.

Our train made slow progress, and it was nearly sundown when we reached Raleigh. As we waited and wondered why we didn't go ahead, a body of troops came down the track and surrounded our train.

"They are putting us under guard!" was the cry, and our fond hopes fell to zero. "Git out of dese yere kyars, you Yanks—git out! Right smart, now!" It was the old cry, that we were so familiar with. We got out of the train. The railroad embankment formed a triangle, and in its center we were placed. The guards were posted on the top of the embankment, close to the railroad track.

A Confederate officer came in among us and informed us that Gen. Terry's forces had captured Wilmington that morning, and that the advance of our army had broken up all arrangements for an exchange.[9] The officer seemed to be as much disappointed about it as we were. While we rejoiced at the success of the Union arms, we could not help wishing that they had postponed their advance for a day or two. But there was no help for it; the old familiar figure of the sentinel with the loaded musket was on all sides, and there was no alternative but to obey orders. It was considered that placing us under guard again was the same as relieving us of our parole, and many of our officers announced their intention to escape if possible. Part of our guards were cadets from the Hillsboro Military Academy, some of them not more than 14 years of age.[10] I soon made my acquaintance of one little fellow, and by telling him that I, too, had been a cadet I was soon on excellent terms with him. I expressed a desire to go uptown, and, after a little persuasion, he agreed to let me pass his beat after dark. I waited until it was fairly dark, and then made my presence known to my friend. He arranged with the cadet on one side of him to walk away while he walked the beat in the opposite direction. This brought the two sentinels back to back and uncovered the guard-line the length of two beats. I promptly took advantage of it, and slipped over the railroad embankment, and in a few minutes was well up town.

There were no street lamps, and everything seemed to be in darkness. After a little I found a cabin, which I judged to be negro quarters, and I determined to apply for assistance. The light was shining through the chinks of the cabin, but I was unable to see its occupants; but from the voices I was sure that they were negroes. I knocked on the door. There was a sudden silence. The knock was repeated.

"Who dar?" came from the inside.

"A friend. Open the door."

"What yo' wants?" was the cautious query.

"You open this door quick," was the response.

"Reckon dat's a white man," said a woman's voice on the inside.

An old negro opened the door cautiously, and I at once pushed myself inside. An old colored woman—his wife evidently—was baking a pone in a skillet by the fireplace. Both of them were greatly alarmed at my appearance.

"I'm a Yankee officer, uncle," I said, "and I belong to a colored regiment in the United States army, and I want you people to help me."

"G'way fum yere, man; g'way fum yere!" said the old woman earnestly. "If de Provost cotches yo'in dis cabin, we're bofe dead niggers! G'way fum yere, now, I tole yo'!"

The old man joined her in asking me to leave. Both were too much frightened to assist me in the least. In vain did I tell them that the Yankees had captured Wilmington and would soon be in Raleigh. They would have nothing to do with me. The old man threatened to go for the Provost Guard, and I at once ordered him to sit down and keep quiet or it would be the worse for him. Accustomed to submission all his lifetime, he obeyed. Then I demanded some supper and told them that I would not go until I had something to eat. They protested that they had nothing, and I proposed to wait until the pone was baked, and then take that.

This proposition did not suit them at all, and the old woman brought out some hoecake, a sweet potato, and a little cold bacon.[11] I ate it all, and inquired about the roads leading in various directions from Raleigh. But very little information was obtained, and my unwilling host constantly urged my departure.

Probably he feared for the ash-pone as much as the approach of the Provost Guard.[12] Telling him not to say anything about my visit, I took my departure. Outside everything was so dark that I decided to take the chances of passing through the city and finding some negro quarters whose occupants were more enthusiastic for the Union cause. As I crossed one of the principal streets, a door opened, letting out a flood of light, and an officer, with saber and revolver, followed by several guards, stepped out. The light was thrown directly upon me, and the quick eye of the officer saw me, and instantly knew that I was an escaped prisoner.

"Hullo, there, Yank. What are you doing here?" His voice was pleasant, but I heard the "click, click" of his pistol, and knew that he had me covered.

"Taking a stroll about the town," I replied, walking up to him.

"Rather a dark night for strolling, ain't it?" he asked, good humoredly.

I remarked that I had other engagements during the daytime, and this answer seemed to amuse him greatly. He ordered me to come inside. The room was a bar-room, and an old man was behind the bar.

"I wasn't lookin' fer any of yo'uns," said the Provost officer. "My men run guard from the camp, and I have to hunt them up."

I told him that I hoped that he wouldn't give himself any unnecessary trouble about me; that I could find my way back to the prisoners' camp at the railroad again. He replied that he feared that I might miss the way, the night was so dark, and then he invited me to come to the bar and have a drink. I was brought up strictly on temperance principles, but this was the only instance that a Confederate had ever tendered me any courtesy, and I determined to accept the proffered hospitality.

"What'll you have?" asked the bar-keeper, as we braced up against the bar.

"What have you got?" was the query.

"Got some right peart old applejack," said the old man.[13]

"Applejack it is, then," I said, and the barkeeper set out some tumblers and a stone jug. Now, I had no more idea of what "applejack" really was than a child.

"Help yourself, Lieutenant," said the Provost officer, politely passing me the jug. I poured out nearly half a tumblerful, and I saw the officer and his companions exchange glances, and I realized that I had made a mistake; and was sure of it a moment after, when I saw my companion take less than half the quantity that I did. With a polite bow the officer raised his glass and drank it off. I did the same, and for a wonder the liquor did not strangle me. It was smooth and oily, and I felt warm as soon as I swallowed it.

"I think," said the officer, "that I will be obliged to send you back to your camp at once."

He directed a Sergeant to go with me to the camp, and before I reached there I understood why he wished to return me to the camp so promptly. The applejack was taking effect, and I was staggering, and in a highly exhilarated condition. My mess-mates took me in charge, and made me go to sleep. The next morning, I awoke thirsty, but otherwise none the worse for my big drink of applejack.

12

Paroled and Home in Worcester, Massachusetts

It was 3 o'clock in the morning when my train reached Worcester, and I walked to my home, and when I neared the house my parents heard and knew my footsteps on the sidewalk. When I reached the gate my father was at the door, and took me in his arms. Then, with my parents on each side of me, we sat and talked until the 7 o'clock whistles began to blow. Then my mother remembered that breakfast was needed.

"I'll stir up a johnny-cake," she said; "it will bake quickly, and you used to like it so much."

On the day after my escape, in Raleigh, a lot of our enlisted men, over 3,000 in number, were brought to our camp and placed on the opposite side of the railroad embankment. They were the old Andersonville prisoners who had passed the "Winter at Florence." I went over among them. The sight can be but faintly described. There were 3,000 men, all reduced to mere skeletons; many were so emaciated that the bones had worn through the skin at the elbows and hips.[1]

Their hair was long and filled with vermin, and they were as black as pitch-pine smoke could make them. None of them had more than two garments, and hardly any shoes. Many wore only a pair of old drawers, and a few were absolutely naked, save a portion of an old meal sack or a part of an old rotten army blanket.

The feet of all were fearfully swollen with scurvy. Many had lost toes, and two men, whose feet had dropped off, and whose ankle bones were protruding from the rotting flesh, were lying on the ground.

When I went over a lively fight was in progress over a lot of old beef bones. The skeleton-like appearances of the fighters made the whole scene horribly grotesque. Those who had secured a bone were charring it in a fire, gnawing off the burnt bone, and then charring it again.

To the credit of the citizens of Raleigh it should be said that as soon as the pitiable condition of these men became known to them they brought all the food and old clothing that they had to spare to relieve the sufferings of these wretched prisoners.

Many of the citizens were accompanied by their dogs, and every dog that came in among these men was captured, killed, cut up, cooked, and eaten before the owner was aware of his loss. I saw one prisoner, a demented man, who had secured the head of a dog. This head he had thrust into the fire and singed off the hair, and smoked and blackened the flesh. The man was seated on the ground, tearing with his teeth the flesh from the dog's head. The blood trickled down and smeared the man's dirty face, and as he glanced around with a maniacal glare, fearful that some one would rob him of his horrid feast, it made the most revolting, horrible sight that my eyes ever looked upon.

Yet these men had resisted every effort of the Confederates to shake their allegiance to the old flag, and cheerfully accepted a horrible death than turn traitors to their country and live under the stigma of being "a galvanized Yankee."

More enlisted men were to arrive, and the officers were loaded on flat cars and taken to a place called "Camp Holmes," about five miles north of Raleigh. Here we obtained shelter in a lot of old log huts. Our rations were so poor that threats of a revolt were openly made. Our guards were very inefficient, being composed of very old men and the Hillsboro Cadets.

The Confederate authorities were greatly alarmed, and did all in their power to pacify us. Over and over again they assured us that we would certainly be exchanged in a day or two. In the meantime we were nearly famished, and loudly demanded more rations. On the afternoon of Feb. 26, 1865, we were placed on the train and sent to Goldsboro. At this place a number of us were confined to the Courthouse. Again I slipped past the guard, and was well out of town when a Confederate soldier stopped me. This time I was taken before the post commandant, Col. Poole, 14th N. C. H. A. He treated me in a very surly manner, and when I left him I remarked that he "might meet me again some day."[2]

I obtained a loan of $10 in Confederate money, and purchased some roasted sweet potatoes at $2 each.

On Feb. 27 the work of making out the rolls for paroling was again commenced, and on the following day we signed the following parole:

> We, the undersigned prisoners of war, do give our parole of honor that we will not take up arms again nor serve as military police or constabulary force in any fort, garrison, or field troops, nor guards of prisoners, depots, or stores, nor discharge any duty usually performed by soldiers, until exchanged under the provision of the cartel entered into July 22, 1862.[3]

That night we were loaded into and on the outside of box-cars, and started for Wilmington. I was one who preferred the rain outside to the horrible crowding inside. I passed a wet, cold, dreary night of it, but the thoughts that I should soon see the old flag kept me up. On the morning of March 1, 1865, we arrived at the Confederate front, near Northeast River, 10 miles from Wilmington. The morning was cold and drizzly. Our guards came around and demanded: "How many dead Yanks in this kyar? You Yanks throw out your dead yere!" A number of shallow graves near the track show where a lot of our enlisted men had died the previous day, almost within sight of the old flag. Anxiously we waited—still in our box-cars—for the special train of Col. Hatch, the Confederate Commissioner, to appear. At last he came. A special engine and one coach bearing Col. Hatch and staff took the lead, and our train slowly followed.[4]

In a few moments those of us who were outside caught sight of a group of blue-coated cavalrymen, who conspicuously displayed a large white flag of truce. How we cheered and yelled. Arriving at the point of exchange, every sound was hushed, and many a brave man was white and trembling.

The Confederate Officer of the Guard gave his last order:

"You Yanks git off, on dis yere side," pointing to the exchange officers.

A facetious rebel private added:

"Any Yank what gits off on this side will be shot."

"And he ought to be," quickly responded one of the prisoners.

By my side, on the outside of the car, was a young Captain, one of the "Gettysburg gang." He had escaped through the famous Libby tunnel, and had been recaptured within sight of the Union pickets. Several other attempts to escape had likewise been unsuccessful. His face was deathly pale, and, unconsciously, his thoughts found expression in words.

He kept repeating to himself, utterly unaware that he was speaking aloud: "I'll die before I'll go back! They shall never take me back alive!" And I felt just as he did.

I was about to climb down from the car, when an officer, who was on the outside, called to me: "O, Lieutenant, won't you help me to take this man down?" pointing to one of our enlisted men whom he had wrapped up in a blanket. The man was a mere skeleton, and was crying bitterly and saying: "I can't get down alone, and nobody will help me. Don't let them take me back!"

The officer said to me:

"This is one of my men; he belongs to one of the best families in Ohio. He has a lovely wife and two beautiful children and a fine home. Look at him now!"

I helped the man down. He could not have weighed more than 70 pounds.

Sanders, my mate, joined me, and we passed through a line of Confederate officers, then through a line of Union officers; each of us being counted by four different officials. Then we passed a file of Union cavalrymen standing at "present arms."

Cheering, yelling, singing and perfectly happy, we started down the road pointed out to us. A walk of a half mile and we met the infantry pickets. They were colored soldiers. The one on post was the blackest negro I ever saw wearing the blue. An officer of our prison squad, who had been extremely bitter against colored soldiers, rushed up to the black soldier, and, grasping him by both hands, shook them again and again. With tears running down his cheeks, he exclaimed:

"God bless you Sam, old boy; it does my heart good to see you! God bless you again! You are a—sight whiter man than those sons of chivalry over there!"

Seeing some of us laughing at him, he added:

"Don't say a word. I'll take it all back, and pay for the oysters and champagne as soon as we reach 'God's country.'" And he did.

The Sergeant of the picket at the reserve post paraded his guard and saluted us with "shoulder arms."

Many compliments were passed upon the soldierly bearing of his command. Going on at a trot the main Union lines were soon reached. The leading ones began cheering frantically, and their hats went high in the air. Passing over a little knoll a glorious scene burst upon our view. The clouds had just parted, and the sun shone out brightly, and there, under the green trees, were the long lines of the blue and "Old Glory" was waving. Bright arms and equipments were flashing in the sunlight, and strains of martial music were wafted to us.

Never did crusader of old experience greater feelings of ecstasy and thankfulness at the first sight of the Holy City than we did at the sight of our glorious old flag. Approaching nearer we found the Second Division, Tenth Corps, drawn up in line at the left of the road to receive us. On the right of the line was the veteran 6th Conn.; the brigade band was playing patriotic airs, and over the road was a beautiful evergreen arch, the center of which bore the words: "Welcome Brothers!"

How noble, strong and manly those brave boys in blue looked! How clean their clothing seemed; how neatly their equipments fitted them, and how bright their arms were! There were no streaks of tobacco juice running from the corners of their mouths; no long, lanky hair; no tallow faces; no shoes with wooden soles.

Fig. 12.1. "A walk of a half mile and we met the infantry pickets." Freeman S. Bowley, *A Boy Lieutenant*.

As we passed under the arch, and approached the flag of our country, every head was bared and reverently bowed, and every eye was streaming with tears. Many paused and kissed the banner which they loved so well. With the tears running down my dirty cheeks, but feeling so happy as to be utterly oblivious to the fact that the soldiers were making irreverent remarks concerning my personal appearance, I passed along the front of the division. The cause of the soldiers' merriment was a patch on my trousers, made from a meal bag, and the words "C. S. Sub. Dep't. Tax in Kind" in large black letters showed with startling distinctness.[5]

As I turned to look for Sanders a strong pair of arms caught me up and hugged me hard. A bearded lip kissed me squarely on the mouth, and Capt. Smith's voice was saying:

"God bless you, old fellow; you are the boy I'm looking for. Your mother will be glad to know of this!"

It was my old Captain with a Major's straps on his shoulders. Sanders came up and was warmly greeted.

"You boys must come over to the regiment for dinner," he said, "and I'll send you to Wilmington on a river steamer."

Of course, we accepted his invitation. Then I felt another grip of the hand, and saw a black, smiling face.

"How yo' do, Lieutenant. Mighty glad to see yo,' sah!"

"No more so than I am to see you, Dickson," said I. "And you are a Sergeant now, eh?" (I glanced at the chevrons on his sleeves.)

"Promoted for bravery, too," said the Major.

"Yes, sah; I'se wearing de stripes," said Dickson proudly; "but dere's mighty few ob de ol' boys lef' in H now; mos' all new men."

"We'll go through the company street as we go to headquarters," said the Major.

Dickson ran along ahead and as we neared the shelter-tents, we heard him shouting:

"Turn out, H, turn out! De little Lieutenant hab come! Now, den, three cheers for de little Lieutenant. Hurrah! Hurrah!! Hurrah!!!" Every man of them cheered. Such crowding around, such handshaking, such greetings!

"Why, Carter, I thought I saw you killed at Petersburg," I said.

It was Evans, the wag of the company, who answered my wondering remark:

"Grapeshot hit Carter in de head, sah," he explained gravely. "Spile de grapeshot!"

Carter grinned and raised his cap, and showed a large white scar where the shot had grazed his left temple.

"Cotched a ball in dis leg at Hatsboro's Run, sah, annudder in de shoulder at Fort Harrison, an' a flesher in de wris'," said Carter, showing a bandaged wrist, "at de 'Sugar Loaf' (Fort Fisher) t'oder day, but I don't reckon I'se gwine ter git killed in dis wah!"

In fact, the man had been hit four times; but he came home all right with the regiment.

In answer to anxious inquiries about comrades long missing, I could only tell of the fate of those who had died by my side in the Crater at Petersburg.[6]

I looked around among the men for old familiar faces. Serg'ts Scott and Dudley were there. Brave Bob Bowen, who saved the regimental flag at the Crater was wearing a Corporal's chevrons and carrying the flag which he had so gallantly rescued.

Big Joe Wright and John Jackson, nicknamed "Monkey," were among the familiar faces, but many, very many, were missing.

The Major fairly pulled me away from the soldiers and took me to headquarters. Here the officers came to greet me, and what a greeting it was! But many were missing. While I had been a prisoner three officers had fallen while in command of my company. Col. Bates, whom I thought was dead, had recovered, and was now commanding the brigade. He was wearing the star of Brigadier-General, given for "gallant and meritorious conduct on the battlefield at Petersburg, July 30, 1864."

Maj. Leake [Leeke] was dead. My chum and most intimate friend, Lieut. William [Thomas J.] Wood, of Co. C, had been killed by grapeshot at Hatcher's Run, while commanding my company. Lieut. Edgerton had lost his right arm. The list was a long one; scarcely an officer had escaped from wounds or severe sickness.[7]

A servant announced that dinner was ready. The Major apologized for the scantiness of the larder, but to us who had been prisoners, the dinner was perfection itself. To be sure it was only boiled salt pork and sweet potatoes, biscuit made from "self-raising flour," hardtack and coffee, with condensed milk for the coffee. How good the coffee tasted!

Dr. Peebles [Peables], our Surgeon, watched us closely and said: "Boys, you must have had a very light breakfast?"[8]

"Didn't have any breakfast, Doctor."

"No? Well, no wonder you are hungry. What did you have for supper last night?"

"Didn't have any supper, Doctor."

"What? No supper? Well, what did you have for dinner yesterday?"

"Didn't have any dinner, Doctor."

"My God, is it possible!" said the Doctor. "Tell me, when did you have anything to eat?"

I replied that I had two sweet potatoes yesterday morning and Sanders said that he had obtained about a pint of mush at the same time.

"And you men have had nothing else to eat over 30 hours!" exclaimed the Doctor in amazement.

The other officers were interested; they began to realize what prison life meant. The Doctor warned us to be very careful not to over eat, and we promised to obey but Sanders and I both cast longing glances at the hardtack and meat, when the servant cleared the table.

Before we left on the steamer, the men of Co. H. would have clothed me in new clean clothes from their scanty stock, and pressed me to take all the money they had.

I could only say: "Thank you, boys; but in three days I'll be up in 'God's country,' where I can get anything that I want. You will need your clothes more than I shall, but I thank you all, just the same."

God bless their brave and generous hearts, every one of them wherever they are!

Nearly the whole company escorted me down to the river bank where the hospital steamer lay. Stretched across the river was a pontoon bridge, the pontoon boats being rough pine scows. With great pride the men called my attention to the bridge. "Dat yere's de rebil pontoon-bridge, Lieutenant," they said; "de rebels tried to 'stroy it, but de ole 30th, she was on de skirmish-line, an' de rebs jes' natchelly has to leab dat bridge!"

"An' de rebs dat we was fightin' was Hoke's Division; same troops we fit at de Crater, an' Fort Fisher, an' w'en I seed dem North Carolina flags, 'peared like I was strong as a lion, an' I couldn't ram de catridges fast 'nuff!" said another.[9]

"And the rebels knew us, too," said Serg't Scott; "and they didn't care about having us get too close to them!"

Bidding our comrades good-by, and telling them that we would be back with them in six weeks, Sanders and myself boarded the hospital steamer, and after two hours' trip the steamer landed us at Wilmington. As we stepped onto the wharf, a Christian Commission agent gave each of us a cupful of milk punch, saying: "Here, boys, drink that; it'll do you good." And it did revive us, and was the very thing we needed. Almost the first man whom I noticed on the wharf was my own Sergeant, John H. Offer. He was on recruiting service, and was arrayed in all the glory of a new uniform, dress coat, with shining brass scales on the shoulders. Around his portly form was a gorgeous, red worsted sash, and he wore the straight brass-hilted sword of the non-commissioned officer. He saw me and came to "attention" and saluted me in the grandest manner. Around him were a number of black soldiers, whose new uniforms and generally awkward appearance betrayed the raw recruit. It was plain from the respect with which they regarded Serg't Offer that they considered him a very important personage. I requested the Sergeant to show us the headquarters of Gen. Bates.

Turning to his squad of men, the Sergeant remarked impressively, "Men, I'se about to perceed wid dese ossifers to de headquarters of General Bates. You, Isaac, I 'pints yo' lance Corpril endurin' my absence, an yo' will be 'beyed and 'spected 'cordingly."

Leaving "lance Corpril" Isaac in charge of the men, the Sergeant attended us to the headquarters of Gen. Bates, which were located in one of the deserted mansions of the city. We received a hearty welcome. That evening the battle of the Mine was fought over again, and we exchanged reminiscences until a late hour.

Offers of clothing and money were freely made by Gen. Bates and his staff, but we declined them. We hoped to be in Annapolis in two days, and we knew that a new suit would be ruined on the transport steamer. The next morning, March 2, 1865, we went on board the steamer *Euterpe*, and started for home. Arriving at the bar, opposite Fort Fisher, the pilot decided that the water was too low, and we were obliged to wait 24 hours. It seemed the longest 24 hours that we had ever waited. We crossed the bar the next day at noon. Before we were fairly out to sea, Old Neptune began to assert his claim and nearly everyone was seasick. The steamer was fairly crammed with the paroled officers, and many were unable to get below. I escaped the seasickness and was glad to remain on deck away from the seasick crowd. Sanders obtained a place in the cabin, but when night came on, I sought shelter in one of the ship's boats and was soon fast asleep.

Towards morning I was awakened by the cold. A north west wind was blowing, and I was chilled through and through. Realizing that I would freeze to death if I remained in the boat, I turned out and sought the engine room. A draft of hot air was coming up through the iron grating, and I sank down upon it. The engineer came around and said roughly, "You can't stay in here," then taking a second glance at me said, "I guess you can get warm, and stay here during my watch," and he gave me an old coat to put around me. I fell asleep, and a delicious feeling of warmth and comfort came over me. When I awoke the sun was shining brightly, and I was conscious that I was covered up warmly. I heard someone saying in a low tone: "Poor little fellow! Why, he's nothing but a boy; but I guess he has seen some mighty hard times and suffered more than any of us."

Then I found that I was wrapped up in a big soldier's overcoat, and the engineer was talking with a soldier of the 6th Conn. This veteran soldier had taken off his overcoat to cover me over, as I lay asleep. He was going home on a furlough of 30 days, granted him for "conspicuous bravery" at the assault on Fort Fisher. Verily, "the bravest are the tenderest."

On the afternoon of March 4 we arrived at Annapolis. It was Sunday; the churches were just out as we passed through the streets. The ladies and gentlemen looked at us smilingly and curiously. A newspaper correspondent took our names and regiments. The clothing dealers of Annapolis opened their stores and offered us everything we desired. We could pay for our things when we received our money, they said.

Engaging the services of a colored man, by the promise of a dollar, I soon obtained from the clothing dealer an entire new stock of clothing, which my servant carried for me to a bathroom. Here, the darky scrubbed me vigorously, and a barber was brought in, who cut my hair and shampooed me. Arrayed in a new uniform, everything on me clean and new, I could hardly recognize my own self, but kept talking and asking questions, half afraid that it might after all be only a dream, and that I would awaken, as I had so many times before, and find myself in prison.

From my old uniform coat, I took the worn and weather-beaten shoulder-straps; the two pieces of rebel shelter-tent and a little wooden spoon, my only feeding utensil for seven long months, were saved as mementoes of those prison days.

What shouting and laughter and grievings there were among the paroled officers as they met each other after passing through the hands of the barber and clothier.

Old friends failed to recognize each other and some of our most unkempt and hardest looking prisoners now appeared as handsome, stylish officers, veritable dandies. A few celebrated their release by going on a spree, and one of our most popular officers, the Major of an Iowa cavalry regiment, died from the effects of too much champagne. The next morning there was a mournful procession through the streets of Annapolis.

A boat containing our enlisted men had arrived a few hours after our steamer. On board of it were a number of dead and dying prisoners; 34 pine coffins, loaded in ambulances, were on their way to the Soldiers' Cemetery. An escort, with the band playing the dead march, preceded them through the streets. It seemed hard that those men must die when almost within sight of their homes.

Fig. 12.2. "Then the old soldier broke down, and sobbed like a child." Freeman S. Bowley, *A Boy Lieutenant*.

At home in Worcester, the morning after my arrival in Annapolis, my father and mother were seated at the breakfast table. For more than three months they had not heard a word from me. The last news had been unfavorable, and their hearts were almost breaking with anxiety.

My father was looking over the morning paper, when he frightened mother by jumping up and almost upsetting the table. Swinging the paper around his head he gave the regular charging yell of the soldiers.

"Hurrah! Mother, hurrah!" he shouted. "Our boy is alive! He reached Annapolis yesterday. O, my God, I thank thee!"

Then the old soldier broke down, and sobbed like a child. That forenoon a telegram assured my parents that I was well, and would be at home in a few days.

At Annapolis the Paymaster paid all of the paroled officers two months' pay, and in five days a leave of absence for 30 days was granted me. In those days there were no Grand Union Depots in the city of Philadelphia, and passengers were transported in horse cars from the Baltimore Depot to the New York Depot. I was feeling far from well. The reaction had set in, and at Annapolis only the prompt assistance of a skilful physician had saved me from severe sickness. A loss of appetite had followed the ravenous hunger of the first few days of my return to liberty, and I arrived in Philadelphia feeling weak and faint.

As I entered the horse car my bronzed face and weary, tired appearance attracted general notice. An old gentlemen, whose very appearance was an evidence of wealth and the highest respectability, spoke to me.

"My young friend," he said, "you are looking very tired. Have you been ill!"

"I have been a prisoner for seven months, sir," I answered, "and I am not very strong."

At the word "prisoner" every one in the car was greatly interested. The old gentleman questioned me, and in a few words I told him where I was captured, where I had been confined, and when I had been released. The old man was extremely sympathetic. Drawing a card from his pocket, he said, "Here is my card. If you wish you can come to my house and remain to-night. I will call a carriage and take you there. You can call a policeman or any one you like to identify me. I am well known here. After a good night's rest I will send you on your journey."

I thanked him kindly, but told him that I was anxious to reach my home as soon as possible; that I knew my parents were anxiously awaiting me. In the next car was a beautiful young lady of about 20. She wore the Quaker bonnet and dress, and a lovelier, more modest, ladylike face never looked out from under a drab bonnet. She came and took the vacant seat by my side.

"Friend," she said, laying her little hand on my arm, "thee surely needs some refreshment. I will go with thee to the depot, and will procure something for thee."

I thanked her, but told her that I feared it would be too much trouble for her.

"It will be a pleasure to do a little for a soldier who has sacrificed so much. Surely thou will grant me that favor."

She was so irresistibly charming that it was impossible to decline her kind offer. The old gentleman nodded approvingly. When the depot was reached my fair conductress escorted me to my train, and saying, "Remain here, I will be back presently," disappeared in the direction of the "Soldiers' Refreshment Rooms."[10]

In a few moments she returned with a bowl of steaming soup and cup of tea. I did not think that I could eat anything, but I would have choked myself sooner than have refused the refreshment so kindly offered. To my surprise, after the first few mouthfuls, my appetite seemed to return, and I relished the soup, and ate it all.

My fair entertainer watched me interestedly, and smiled approvingly. I gave her my name in return; but she only said, "Thee can remember me as a Philadelphia girl," and wishing me a safe journey, bade me farewell. Even now, after long years have passed, the vision of that lovely, saint-like face comes before me. If the wish and prayer of a grateful soldier boy have been fulfilled every earthly blessing and happiness has been hers all her life long.

It was 3 o'clock in the morning when my train reached Worcester, and I walked to my home, and when I neared the house my parents heard and knew my footsteps on the sidewalk. When I reached the gate my father was at the door, and took me in his arms. Then, with my parents on each side of me, we sat and talked until the 7 o'clock whistles began to blow. Then my mother remembered that breakfast was needed.

"I'll stir up a johnny-cake," she said; "it will bake quickly, and you used to like it so much."

"Never mind, mother," said I; "I've had cornmeal enough to last me the rest of my life."

As I related the story of the battle my father listened with flashing eyes, his soldier experience enabling him to appreciate every point and comprehend exactly how every movement had been executed.

When I told of the fall of the bearer of the regimental flag, and how Bob Bowen had dashed in and rescued the colors from the very clutches of the enemy, the old soldier could hardly contain himself. With clenched hands and set teeth he sprang to his feet as though he would charge the enemy then and there.

My mother objected to my telling any more war stories.

"If you don't stop talking about charging and fighting," she said, "the first thing that we will know father will be off down to the recruiting office and enlist for another three years; then I'll go and enlist for a nurse, and Uncle Sam will have the whole family."

Soon after breakfast a neighbor came in to inquire for me, and in a very short time the news of my return had spread, and I was besieged with callers. Among them was a careworn, motherly looking lady, and my heart sank when I saw her. Her son, a former schoolmate of mine, had enlisted in the 57th Mass., and had been captured at the battle of the mine. I had seen him at Petersburg the day after our capture. When we met the Andersonville prisoners at Raleigh I inquired after my friend and was told that he had died at Andersonville. He was a Sergeant when captured, and soon after his commission as Second Lieutenant arrived at his regiment. But the poor boy never lived to see or wear the coveted shoulder-straps.

As gently as I could, I told his mother the sad news, and I could hold out no hope that there might be a mistake and that he would yet return. She listened with a white face and trembling lips and then went away crying softly. To me the mother's grief seemed worse than the slaughter of the battlefield.

The days passed quickly. Of course, I visited the blue-eyed girl who had written me such a sympathetic letter while I was a prisoner, and she seemed to have grown prettier than ever.[11] Another visit that was greatly enjoyed was to my old cadet friends at the Highland Academy. Attired in a new uniform, with a broad-rimmed regulation army hat, which was ornamented with gold cord and tassels with silver Tenth Corps badge, and a large "30" on its front, I arrived at the Academy just before the drill hour.

My appearance made a sensation. The report had gone around that I was dead, and my cadet friends welcomed me as one from the grave. How the cadets seemed to envy me my practical army experience, and to some of the officers who had formerly patronized me I was very dignified, and managed to impress upon them the great difference between a real soldier and officer of the army and a school-boy cadet official.

Before my leave of absence expired the news of the capture of Richmond and the surrender of Lee's army had reached us. From Maj. Smith came a long letter, telling how in North Carolina the regiment had done great service. It was desired to capture a certain bridge over the Neuse River, that it might enable Gen. Sherman's army to promptly obtain supplies from Gen. Schofield's army, who were marching to join them. The Confederates made desperate attempts to burn this bridge, but "the old 30th, she was on de skirmish line," and the rebels were driven away. In this action—Cox's Bridge N. C., March, 1865, the 30th had their last man killed in battle. "Hurry up," wrote the Major, "and get back to the regiment, so as to be in it at the death."[12]

13

With the Regiment in North Carolina

The men became restless and uneasy. The hard work and tiresome drills in the hot, dirty sand was such a contrast to the stirring, exciting scenes of actual campaigning that discontent began to creep in among them. To counteract this feeling furloughs were granted to many of the most deserving men, and the officers busied themselves in obtaining for the men, their back bounty, which, in many cases, was long over due. But, in spite of all this, the restless spirit of the negro soldier manifested itself. Every chicken-roost and watermelon patch for miles around was raided, and everything stolen that could be carried off.

On April 12 I reported at Camp Parole, Annapolis, Md.[1] On the night of April 14 we heard the long roll beating in the camp of the soldiers who formed camp guard, and soon after some cavalry went by on the run. In a little while we heard the infantry going off on the double-quick. At that time there were several commands of Confederate cavalry who had not yet surrendered, and we thought it probable that they might be trying to make a desperate attempt to do some further damage before surrendering.

"It will be time enough for us to turn out when we hear the infantry firing," we said, and went to sleep again. In the morning we learned the dreadful news of the assassination of President Lincoln. No passes were allowed to any one, and all trains were stopped. The troops that we had heard moving the night before had extended a continuous guard line from the Chesapeake Bay to Annapolis Junction; a distance of over 30 miles. This was done before daylight. A number of persons living in that vicinity, known to be Southern sympathizers, were arrested while returning to their homes. Their horses were tired, muddy and jaded. They gave as an excuse that they had been attending some country party. But that the conspiracy to assassinate prominent Union leaders was well spread and general there can be no real doubt.

When the great funeral services of President Lincoln took place at Washington, April 19, 1865, it was my privilege to form one of the escort, and to stand directly opposite the funeral car as it stood in front of the White House. How I remembered President Lincoln's hearty clasp of the hand the previous year, and his kindly greeting then!

On May 1 orders were issued declaring all paroled prisoners exchanged and directing them to report at once to their regiments. My orders directed me to report to the Headquarters of the Lieutenant-General, Washington, for an order for transportation, the location of my regiment not being known to the authorities at Annapolis. As I entered the building at Washington where Gen. Grant had established his Headquarters I met him coming out of the door. He was smoking the inevitable cigar, and wore citizens' clothing. I took a good look at him, knowing that, without his uniform, he could not exact any salute or reprimand me for my impertinence. Remembering my reception by the Regular officer a year previous, I entered the office with some little trepidation. An Orderly inquired my business, and then immediately took me to a desk where a Colonel was seated. I saluted, produced my orders, and stood waiting. The Colonel politely asked me to be seated. He then inquired in what corps my regiment was serving, and immediately sent a clerk to look the matter up. In less than two minutes the clerk had found the location of the regiment, and had filled out a blank order. The Colonel signed it, and passed it to me with a pleasant word. Had I been wearing a General's stars, instead of being only a little "line officer in a nigger regiment," I could not have been treated with greater courtesy.

When the colored troops were driven out of the rebel intrenchments at the right of the Crater, July 30, 1864, they were so completely routed and broken that not even a company organization remained. Mixed with the other regiments of the brigade most of the 30th U.S.C.T. ran across the open field, between the Union and Confederate lines, and jumped down behind the Union breastworks among the white troops. In crossing this field they were subjected to a terrible crossfire, and some fell. Seventy-eight of the regiment were reported as missing. None of these men were ever heard from. They were, without doubt, all shot down after they had surrendered, or ruthlessly bayoneted while lying wounded.[2]

All that day the men remained in the front line, and when darkness came they were transferred to the very same breastworks that they had quitted the night before the battle. The regimental line was only half as long as it had been before the fight, and there were sad stories to tell of comrades dead or missing.

For six weeks they remained in this position, only leaving the breastworks for a short time to take part in the movement at Chaffin's farm, Sept. 30, 1864, and at the assault and capture of Fort Harrison.[3]

Although under fire in both of these engagements, the regiment had no direct encounter with the enemy. During the month of August, 1864, the Fourth Division of the Ninth Corps was broken up, and some of the troops, among them the 30th U.S.C.T. became the Third Division.[4] In October Gen. Grant ordered a flanking movement to the left, and on Oct. 27, 1864, the regiment, with the other troops of the Ninth and Second Corps, took part in the battle of Hatcher's Run. Col. Delevan Bates had been brevetted Brigadier-General "for gallant and meritorious service at the Petersburg Mine, July 30, 1864," and had been given command of the brigade.[5]

Capt. Arthur J. Smith had been promoted to Major, and at the fight at Hatcher's Run was commanding the regiment. In advancing in line-of-battle the regiment came suddenly upon a Confederate battery which opened upon them with canister. Lieut. William [Thomas J.] Wood, who was commanding Co. H, was struck in the neck by a canister shot and mortally wounded. In this battle an incident occurred, and brave Bob Bowen again distinguished himself. I will tell the story as after my return to the regiment I heard it told by one of the black veterans to a recruit. The recruit had noticed that all of his officers took great notice of Bowen, and always spoke to him when they answered his salute. Said the recruit:

"Wha' foh all de ossifers allers talk to Bob Bowen jes like he one ob de white men?"

"Boy," said the veteran impressively, "dey has a right to talk 'spectfully to Bob Bowen."

"How a right?" queried the recruit.

"Sit down dar on dat gun blanket, and I tole yo' about it," said the old soldier.

The recruit seated himself and the veteran, first borrowing a chew of tobacco from his listener, began:

"'Spec' yo's heered how Bob Bowen saved de blue rig'mental flag at de Mine battle, an' how he was made a Corpril and given de flag to carry?"

"Yes," said the recruit, "I heered 'bout dat."

"Berry, well den, jes' listen, an' I tell yo' 'bout de charge dis brigade made at Hatcher's Run. De Color-Sergeant was sick, and Bob he was actin' Sergeant, carrying the Stars an' Stripes. W'en de brigade advance in line-of-battle, day run plum agin a rebil battery; fus ting dey knew it wos bang! bang! bang! and knocks ober 'bout 40 men right outen de line.

"A shot kill Lieut. Woods; he was wid Co. H. When de Lieutenant fall ober, Serg't Scott he say, 'Steady, men, steady; doan' forgit your good name'; but de line wavered an' dar was some 'fusion, but Bob Bowen he jes' steps right out and hol's up de flag, an' he voice roar out like a bull; 'Dis flag stays yere! Doan' ye dar to leave yoore flag!'

"Umph! Boy, we'n I yere dat my heart swell right up, an' I 'low I gwine ter stay jes' as long as Bob Bowen does; but dis 's not de story I 'tending ter tell yo' 'bout.

"Dey move de brigade 'way fum dere an' come to a cl'arin' 'bout two hun'nerd yards across it; on de oder side was de Johnnies, an' dey had a light breast-work.

"I didn't right like de' 'pearance ob tings myself, but de Major he rides up behin' de colors an' he say, 'Bob!'

"Bob say, 'Yes, Major?'

"Major say, 'Yo' see dat tall stump oberyander, in de rebil line?'

"Bob say, 'Yes, Major!'

"Major say, 'De brigade am gwine ter charge dat rebil line; w'en yo' gets de word, yo' go straight for dat stump; yo' understan'?'

"Bob say, 'Yes, Major!'

"We's all's was lyin' down mighty flat, but in a minnit we heerd de Major 'peared like yo' could a heerd him a mile—"'Tention, Battalion! De men all stand up—'Forrard—guide center'—Bob he walk right out in front wid de colors—'double quick!'—de men all toss de rifles on de right shoulder—'March!'—an' 'way go Bob, not six paces, boy, but more dan 40 paces, ahead, holdin' de colors up high an' runnin' straight for de stump! An' de 30th seen him, boy, an' dey all yell like one man, an' dey goes after Bob! An' de odder rig'ments, dey seen, de ole 30th a-chargin,' an' dey yell an' charge too. De Johnnies didn't wait for us; dem rebils had a heap ob sense—dey got out ob dere.

"Bimeby de Major he cum round, an' he say: 'Whar was yo' goin,' Bob?'

"Bob say: 'Straight for de stump, Major!'

"An' w'en de regiment was down at Fort Fisher, an' Hoke's Division ob rebils cum out to charge us, Gineral Bates he rid along de line an' he say, 'Here's my ole 30th; yo's de boys foh me. Yo've licked dem troops ober yander befo,' an' yo' kin do it agin'; an' he say, 'Here's brave Bob Bowen, de right man in de right place.' Now does yo' unnerstan' why de white ossifers all speak to Bob? It's kase he's a man!"[6]

In December, 1864, the Twenty-fifth Corps was organized, and the 30th U.S.C.T. was assigned to Gen. C. J. Paine's First Division. This corps was composed entirely of colored troops. The square was chosen as a corps badge. Its significance was that all the colored troops desired was an equal chance—a "square deal," in soldier language.[7]

Gen. Paine's Division, to which the regiment was attached, was detached in December and sent on the first Fort Fisher expedition. Two terrible storms were encountered, and the transport on which the regiment was embarked sprang a leak, and came near foundering. Many of the men were fearfully seasick. Among the worst cases of seasickness was that of big Joe Wright, who was badly frightened, and who prayed most loudly and earnestly. The storm subsided, and the troops were successfully landed near Fort Fisher. Joe's courage returned with the firm land under his feet, and he was swearing and stuttering most vigorously over the loss of his haversack, when Serg't Offer rebuked him with, "Joseph, yo' shouldn't be a-cussin' dat-a-way; yo'd better be 'gaged in pra'r."

"P-p-pra'r be—!" stuttered Joe. "I-I-I-I'm a-a-ashore now!"

The first Fort Fisher expedition was a most miserable failure, and the troops were re-embarked in their transports.

A second expedition was sent out in January, and for the second time the 30th U.S.C.T. were landed on the sandy peninsula near the fort.

The division of colored troops was assigned the duty of protecting the rear line against the attack of a force which was expected from Wilmington. This line was attacked by Hoke's Division of veterans, and the brunt of the attack was borne by the 30th U.S.C.T. In this engagement the Captain who was commanding Co. H was severely wounded and a number of men killed and wounded. The direct assault upon the fort was made by Curtis's Brigade of white troops. But these white troops were preceded by details of colored soldiers with axes, who chopped away the heavy, palisade of logs, which surrounded the fort.[8]

Lieut. Schwartz commanded the detachment from the 30th U.S.C.T. Gallantly leading his men, they waded through a swamp up to their waists, reached the palisade, and under a severe fire of musketry, chopped down the palisade and afforded a passage for the white troops.

After the Union troops had gained partial possession of the fort the regiment was detached from the defense of the rear line and sent to the fort. They arrived a few minutes after its surrender.

A terrible explosion of the magazine of the fort occurred soon after its capture. By this explosion a number of the regiment perished. When Gen. Terry captured Wilmington the regiment was among the first to enter the city. They followed the rebel rear guard so closely that the latter were unable to destroy a fine pontoon bridge over the Northeast River, and the bridge was saved for the Union army.[9]

In the march to Goldsboro the regiment took a prominent part, and distinguished itself by driving the rebel skirmishers away from Cox's Bridge, thereby saving the bridge for the army of Gen. Sherman, and enabling him to at once obtain many much needed supplies. In this skirmish, March 23, 1865, the 30th U.S.C.T. had their last man killed in battle.

While on the march to Raleigh the news of Lee's surrender was received, and the troops went wild with delight. The surrender of Gen. Joseph E. Johnston and his army soon followed. At Raleigh all the regiments of the Colored Division were reviewed by Gen. Sherman, who complimented them highly on their excellent drill and fine military appearance. A few weeks of provost duty at Raleigh, and the brigade were marched back to Goldsboro, where they were placed in camp about a mile from the city. In May an order was issued assigning the command to the First Brigade, Third Division, Tenth Corps.[10]

The route designated in my orders, and for which I was furnished transportation by the Quartermaster's Department, was by steamer from Washington, down the Potomac River to Fortress Monroe, thence to Norfolk; from there through the Dismal Swamp Canal to Albemarle Sound; thence by steamer to Newbern, and from Newbern to Goldsboro by railroad.[11]

The trip through the Dismal Swamp Canal was made in a flat-bottomed, stern-wheeled steamer, the class known as "wheelbarrow boats." Arriving at the south end of the canal, the steamer, which was a poor sea boat, was delayed 48 hours by a heavy gale. At Roanoke Island another tedious delay occurred.

Hotel accommodations were limited, and 13 of us were packed into the attic chamber of the little shanty which was called a "hotel." The bill of fare was hot saleratus biscuit, sweet potatoes, fried bacon, and fried mullets, the last being a fat, greasy fish very abundant in the vicinity.[12] A number of wrecks were scattered on the beach. When Gen. Burnside captured Roanoke Island these vessels had been destroyed by the Confederates to prevent their falling into the hands of the Yankees. The mouth of the Neuse River was also obstructed by sunken vessels, but the obstructions had proved no obstacle to the Yankee tars.

From Newbern to Goldsboro the trains were operated by the United States Military Railroad authorities, and the amount of service that they succeeded in obtaining out of each locomotive was something astonishing.

When I arrived at Goldsboro I found Maj. Smith in command of the regiment, and he at once ordered me to take command of my own company, the Captain being absent, wounded.

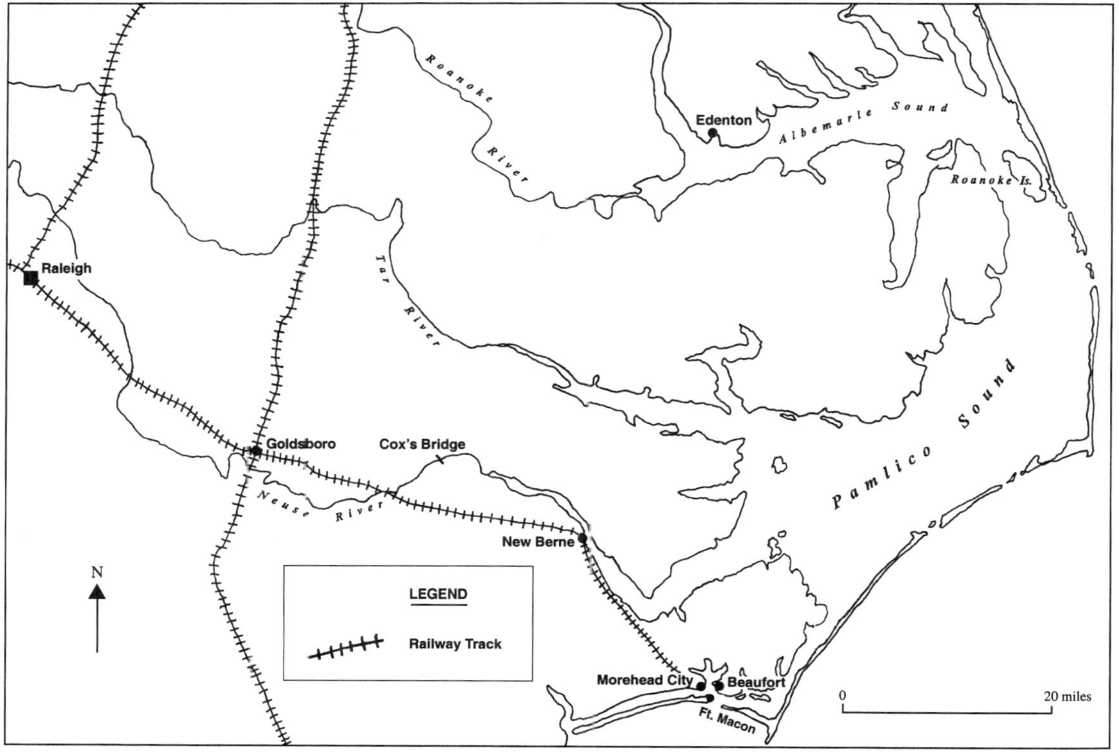

Service in the vicinity of: Goldsboro, Morehead City, Beaufort, Edenton, and Roanoke Is.

Map 4. Freeman S. Bowley's service in North Carolina, May–December 1865. (Adapted from U. S. War Department, *Atlas to Accompany the Official Records*, Plates CXVII, CXXX–VII, CXXXVIII,)

My reception by the men of Co. H was a most cordial one. The officer who had charge of the company was a Lieutenant, recently appointed. He had neither the tact nor the experience to command colored men, and as a result the company was making a very poor showing.[13]

Many recruits had been obtained since the capture of Wilmington, and the active campaign had allowed but little chance for drilling. The old soldiers were particularly disgusted with the awkwardness and the stupidity of the recruits, forgetting that there had been a time when they too, were raw and awkward. Great things in the way of drills had been promised the recruits by the veterans "when de little Lieutenant come back," and I found my reputation as a drill-master at stake. On my first drill I called all the old soldiers to the front and put them through the manual, and found they still remembered my former instructions.

Then I divided the recruits into little squads, and, selecting the best-drilled non-commissioned officers and men, set them at work on the squads, watching all of them closely in the meantime. The old men were extremely anxious to please me and to bring the company up to its former high standard. It was noticeable that the recruits who had been slaves were a very different class from our old Baltimore and Maryland men.[14]

"'Pears like dese yer Norf Car'leena mokes is de dumbest niggers alive. Dey's reg'lar Guineas!" said a disgusted Corporal to me one day. It must be admitted that great patience had to be exercised with them. It was a new experience to me to be addressed, as I frequently was, as "Massa" or "Boss."

Some of the new men were downright ugly. One of them answered me back saucily on drill. In less than five minutes he was tightly "bucked and gagged," the "gag" used being the bayonet of his own gun.[15] He was kept in that uncomfortable position until he was well humbled. The men would have thrashed him soundly afterwards if they had not been warned to leave him alone.

In a day or two after my return to the regiment I was ordered on "fatigue duty" with a detail of 200 men. Sherman's great army had been encamped all around Goldsboro, and the plains were covered with the filth and debris of old camps. Hot weather was coming on, and it was necessary to destroy all decaying substances, to prevent the spread of diseases.

The terrible visitation of the yellow fever was feared, and every precaution was taken to prevent it.[16] Everything that could be burned was destroyed that way, and the rest buried. My men were all working busily, and sought the shade of an attractive-looking house, surrounded by a fine garden. Upon the piazza was a middle-aged man in a gray suit. His face seemed familiar to me, but I could not recall where I had seen it.

"Good morning, sah; won't yo' come up hyah in de shade?" he said.

Then I recognized him. It was Col. Poole, formerly of the 14th N.C.H.A., the officer who had abused me so heartily at Goldsboro little more than two months before.[17]

"This is Col. Poole?" I said.

"Yes, sah; but I don't remember evah having the pleasure of meeting yo' befo,' sah. Fact is, sah, I meet so many of yo' Northern gentlemen recently that I don't quite remember yo' all."

"But I remember you perfectly, Colonel," I said. "I was among those Yankee prisoners confined in the Courthouse over there during the last week of February. I escaped, and one of your men arrested me and took me to your office. You told me that if you had your way none of us would ever be sent back alive. I told you that we might meet again. Do you remember that?"

The Colonel flushed. It was plain that he remembered the incident, and he did not relish the situation.

"I am a paroled prisoner, sah," he said, with an attempt at dignity.

"And it's a good thing for you that you are, sir," I answered angrily; "for if you were free to defend yourself you would have a chance to show your courage, and prove whether you are a soldier or only a contemptible coward who bullies unarmed men!"

As I spoke some of the men entered the front gate. They had come to fill their canteens with water, and had heard every word of the conversation.

"Take yo' niggers off my premises, sah, or I'll set my dawg on them," said Col. Poole angrily, and as he whistled a big brute of a dog came out.

The dog growled and started towards the soldiers, but he never reached them. A shot from my pistol stopped him, and he turned over, yelping, in mortal agony. The Colonel sprang up as though he would have assaulted me, and instantly two of the black soldiers, powerful men, bounded up the steps and seized him roughly, forced him backwards, and would have choked him to death had they not been ordered to release him.

"Jes' say de word, Lieutenant, an' dis ol' Secesh goes down in de ole well ober yander. We'll put him under 30 feet of groun' in no time! Bury him so deep dat he'll nebber hear de toot of Gabriel's horn!"

"Release him, boys," I said and addressing the Colonel as he arose, pale and breathless: "You see, sir, that that temper of yours is liable to get you into trouble. You want to understand distinctly that the 'nigger-driving' days are over, and that it won't do for you to set your dog on any one wearing the United States uniform. If you want to be protected as a paroled prisoner, conduct yourself like a gentleman. Good day, sir!"

The men were so extremely anxious to retaliate on the Confederate officer that I moved them away to another locality, fearing that they would do him or his property some mischief.

The regiment did not remain long at Goldsboro. Their services were needed near the coast, and they were sent by railroad to Morehead City, the terminus of the railroad, in Beaufort Harbor, N. C. Fort Macon, situated at the mouth of the harbor, was a desirable post, as was the village of Beaufort; but the 30th U.S.C.T. were not fortunate enough to secure either place.[18]

The regiment was encamped in a hot, dusty plain outside the town limits. One flank of the regiment rested in a graveyard; the other flank of the regiment reached a swamp. Heavy details were made for fatigue duty, and many ships and steamers loaded with supplies for the army had their cargoes transferred to the cars by the working parties of black soldiers. All of the arms and public property that had been surrendered by the rebel army commanded by Gen. Joseph E. Johnston came down on the trains to Morehead City, and were unloaded by our men.

There were car-loads of muskets thrown together loosely in piles, many of them loaded and capped. Sometimes some of them went off, and that no one was killed by the careless handling was simply a piece of good luck.

The men became restless and uneasy. The hard work and tiresome drills in the hot, dirty sand was such a contrast to the stirring, exciting scenes of actual campaigning that discontent began to creep in among them. To counteract this feeling furloughs were granted to many of the most deserving men, and the officers busied themselves in obtaining for the men, their back bounty, which, in many cases, was long over due. But, in spite of all this, the restless spirit of the negro soldier manifested itself. Every chicken-roost and watermelon patch for miles around was raided, and everything stolen that could be carried off. Midnight roll-calls were sometimes made, and very severe punishment meted out to those who were caught outside of the camp limits without permission.

A drum and fife corps were organized; our old original drummers and buglers having nearly disappeared. A new and better location was chosen for the camp and "A" tents were issued to take the place of the shelter-tents. Teams were furnished to haul lumber for tent floors, and pine boughs to make shades for the tents. But some men disappeared and for the first time the word "deserter" appeared on the rolls of the regiment. An incident occurred on the Fourth of July that showed the temper of the men. The colored people living in the village of Beaufort were extremely desirous of celebrating the Fourth of July by a parade, music and speeches. It was the first National celebration in which they could take part as freemen, and they decided to parade in honor of their recently acquired freedom. There were many old veteran Confederates in Beaufort, and the idea of a "nigger procession" was so distasteful to them, that they notified the leading colored men that the parade would not be allowed.

The colored men appealed to Gen. Bates, who was commanding the District, and he told them to go ahead with their parade, and ordered Co. F, Capt. Proctor commanding, to proceed to Beaufort and act as escort for the colored procession. This exasperated the rebel element greatly, and threats were made to attack the soldiers, procession and all concerned. These rumors were so numerous that it was deemed best to have the men remain in camp on the Fourth of July.[19] This Fourth being the first one after the war, the Honorable Secretary of War directed that a National salute should be fired at noon from every National fort, and a similar order was issued to all warships of the navy. But very few of the officers, and none of the men, were aware of this order. Precisely at noon the guns of Fort Macon thundered forth, and at the same time three or four gunboats in the harbor began their salute. As the sound of the guns came over the water, the men sprang to their feet and listened intently. A dozen discharges followed in quick succession, and as they listened, the drummer of the guard, who had been sent to beat the dinner call, commenced sounding the long roll. When the men heard the r-r-r-r-r-r of the long roll there was a general yell and rush for their guns and accouterments.

The Sergeants were yelling "Fall in!" and the companies were in line in a few seconds. In sharp, nervous tones the men were counting off: "One!" "Two!" "One!" "Two!" "De Johnnies hab jumped de Co. F boys!" was the general exclamation. Some of the recruits who did not understand the meaning of the long roll were kicked into their places by the impatient Sergeants, and cursed most heartily for their stupidity. Officers came running to their companies, buckling on swords and revolvers as they ran. The camp was a scene of lively excitement.

When the mistake was discovered, there was a general expression of disappointment among the men that the alarm had been a false one. "Jess like to gib dem yar johnnies one more warmin'; reckon dey needs it!" they said.

Nearly all of the officers commanding companies were carrying on their official returns a much greater number of knapsacks, haversacks and canteens than they could possibly account for. These articles had been lost and thrown away by the men during the active campaigning, and the company commanders were responsible for them. To be sure, they could charge them on the pay-roll against the men, but it was manifestly unfair to deduct the price of a knapsack from the small pay of a soldier who had thrown it off, that he might be free to do his best in a charge or the forward rush of a skirmish-line. The "military" way was to have an inspection of wornout articles by an officer appointed for that purpose, and on his order the condemned articles could be destroyed, and the officer who was responsible for them allowed to drop them from his report. Accordingly the company commanders gathered together as many as possible old knapsacks, haversacks, canteens, wornout shelter-tents and other "camp" and garrison equipage. At their request the Division Inspector came to inspect and condemn these articles. They were piled at the end of the company street, and the Captain of the first company who wished to be relieved of something like the following, 15 knapsacks, 12 haversacks, 9 canteens, 14 shelter-tents, 20 great-coat straps, would have his blanks already prepared and would count the articles off in the presence of the Inspector.

The Inspector would say: "All right Captain; these articles are inspected and condemned. Have them destroyed immediately."

"Yes, sir," the Captain would say. "Please be kind enough to step into my tent and have a little refreshment while you are signing the inspection reports." Calling a Sergeant the Captain would say: "Sergeant, take those articles away and destroy them."

While the Inspector was signing the reports and partaking of the refreshment, which was in a bottle, the Sergeant would carry the articles over to the next company, and the officers there would fix up the proper number to equalize their reports. Then the Inspector would go through the same performance, including "refreshment," and the articles would be passed along to another man. Before half the companies were inspected, the Inspector was in such a genial condition that he was willing to take their word for anything, and before the inspection was completed he would have condemned any amount of anything had it been requested.

But, as the inspection was only a "matter of form" anyway, it could hardly be called cheating; certainly it was not fair to make officers and men pay for a lot of old rubbish that had been lost on the battlefields. We were longing for a change and we got it. In comparison with our new station, Morehead City was a bustling town. In October the regiment was ordered to Roanoke Island, and on this flat, sandy, swampy island we passed some very disagreeable weeks.[20]

There were a number of forts on the island, armed with heavy old-fashioned cast iron smooth-bore cannon, and it was to remove these and their stores of ammunition that the regiment was sent to Roanoke. It was necessary to take a complete inventory of all these cannon, count all the piles of round shot, stands of grape and canister, and barrels of powder. Three captains were detailed for this purpose, and in the performance of their duty the following incident occurred.

On entering the magazine at Fort Parke, they took off their shoes and put on carpet slippers. A "magazine lantern" was provided to hold the candle which furnished the light. The barrels of powder were piled three tiers high with wooden chocks between each barrel to allow for free circulation of air. As one of the officers raised the lantern to take a survey, it fell apart and the lighted candle fell out on top of the upper tier of powder barrels. For a second it rested, then slid off to the middle tier, and slipped through the bottom tier to the ground, still burning. One of the officers started to run; the second one nearly fainted, and the third man reached down and extinguished the candle with his hand. The nerves of all of them were badly shaken, though probably there was no actual danger. Still, the sensation of standing in a powder magazine and watching a lighted candle fall through three tiers of powder barrels would be overpowering enough to unnerve the strongest.

A friendly rivalry existed between the different companies as to which could present the finest military appearance. Arms and accouterments were polished and cleaned and particular attention was paid to the packing of knapsacks. By general consent it was acknowledged that the distinction of "finest company" lay between Co. E and Co. H. There was to be a knapsack inspection, and the men of those companies were exerting themselves to carry off the honor. I was somewhat anxious myself, and went over each man's outfit and saw that nothing was neglected. An idea occurred to me. Calling a Sergeant, I had him take a trusty man, and take off all the canteen straps. These straps were a wide, white cotton web, which soon became soiled. Taking a mess kettle and some soap, the Sergeant and his comrade went outside the camp, out of sight, and washed and dried all the canteen straps, and then secretly brought them back to camp. The time for inspection arrived, and the various companies, in dress coats, with shining brass shoulder scales, white gloves, polished shoes and bright muskets, assembled for inspection. As we marched to the color-line I noticed with delight that our clean, white canteen straps, placed in the center of the wide, black haversack strap, were showing off Co. H to great advantage, and that not another company had made any attempt in that direction. The men saw it too, and could hardly keep down their delight. When the Lieutenant-Colonel, who was inspecting the regiment, appeared in front of the company, every man was standing motionless as a statue. At the command "Inspection, arms!" the rammers rang in the musket barrels. In vain did the inspecting officer endeavor to find a dirty musket barrel which would soil his white glove. Everything was clean and bright; knapsacks packed exactly according to regulations, every button shining and in its place. After the inspection of the whole regiment, the Lieutenant-Colonel returned to Co. H, and in a few words of praise regarding their excellent appearance, informed us that he had been directed to send his best company for special duty to the town of Edenton, and as Co. H had made the best showing, they would be detached for that purpose, and would leave on the steamer the next day.

This was a great surprise to all, and my brother officers congratulated me on my success. In the company street most of the talk was "De ole 30th, she de boss rig'ment; but her boss company am de H company!" We were packed up and ready to leave when the steamer should arrive. It was the 25th day of October, and a total eclipse of the sun occurred. Some of the black soldiers thought that the great Judgment Day had come, and prayed most lustily.

We found the town of Edenton a beautiful village, located at the head of Albemarle Sound and near the mouth of the Chowan River.[21] A large, deserted mansion was taken possession of as headquarters, and the men were quartered in the comfortable cabins that had formerly been used as "quarters" for a large force of house servants.

Produce of all kinds were very cheap, and we had no trouble in arranging an exchange of coffee, sugar, salt pork, and hardtack for an abundance of sweet potatoes, milk, and oysters. Fish were plentiful and easily caught, and the fare provided for the men was superior to anything that they had experienced while in the army. Our principal duty was the regular drills and inspections. We met many of our former antagonists—members of Hoke's old division. The company drills were held in a little park near the camp, and were generally watched by an interested group of Confederate veterans.

These old soldiers appreciated every movement which was well executed, and frequently applauded when difficult portions of the drill were executed with precision. How the black soldiers glowed and swelled with pride at the privilege of "showing off" before their late adversaries.[22]

Strict orders were received from Department Headquarters to strip any person of any buttons, braid, or any insignia of rank of the late Confederate army.

Acting under these instructions, several persons were relieved of "C.S.A." buttons and the gold braid from their coat sleeves. This provoked considerable resentment, and threats were made against the black officers and the "little Yankee Lieutenant" commanding them.[23]

A lot of drugged whisky was given to the men one night, but only one man drank any, and he was made so sick that the others took warning and threw the liquor away. The white man who gave the whisky to the soldiers was promptly arrested. Some of his friends endeavored to rescue him, and fired two shots at the soldiers. They were at once arrested, and, attempting to resist, were severely pricked with bayonets, and emphatically informed that they would get worse unless they submitted quietly. A heavy fine was exacted from each of them.

Assistance was granted to the local authorities in arresting several men who had been guilty of numerous crimes, and the prisoners were forwarded to Newbern under military guard.

The Autumn passed away pleasantly. One day a steamer came to the wharf, and we received orders to at once embark in her and proceed to Roanoke Island. The regiment was to be mustered out.[24]

Arriving at Roanoke Island, we found that our brother officers had completed their muster-out rolls. It was quite a task to make out the muster-roll of a company. The name of every man that had ever been borne upon the rolls of the company must be shown, and his complete military history given. All of his accounts of pay and bounty received and due must be shown. When the rolls were completed the company was paraded and formally mustered out of the service by a Mustering Officer, who signed the rolls and the discharge paper of every man. But though they were mustered out, the men were not to be released from service until they could be taken to Baltimore and paid off and discharged.

The night before the muster-out one of my men—George Uncles—died. He had been sick for a long time, but had struggled to keep up and reach home alive. This was the last death in the regiment.[25] He had been an active, wiry little fellow, always ready to do his duty. In the Wilderness he had thrown away his knapsack, that he might keep up with the column. The afternoon before his death he sent for me. I tried to speak a few words to comfort him, but he cut me short, saying:

"I knows what yo' means, Lieutenant. It's mighty kind of yo' to talk dat-away, but Ise mos' gon,' an' I wants yo' to tell my mudder w'en yo' sees her in Balimo' dat I allers don' bes' I could. I nebber straggled, I 'beyed the ossifers, an' in de fight I stay right wid de ole 30th."

He had been a good, faithful soldier and I assured him that everything should be done as he wished. That night he died, and his last words were, "I know de little Lieutenant will tell my mudder."

I ordered a coffin made for him; the company went to the grave, a volley was fired in his honor, and with my own hands I prepared and placed the headboard over his grave. On the board I carved his name, company, regiment, and date of death, and as an epitaph I added: "He Always Stayed with the Line."

Some delay was experienced in obtaining transportation, and it was a week before a steamer came to take us away. Our route was through the Dismal Swamp Canal. It was the morning of the fourth day after leaving Roanoke that, loaded in open barges, and towed by a little wheezy tug, we approached Norfolk. A large man-of-war was lying in the stream, and the strong current carried our barge almost alongside of the big warship.

Our men were cold, dirty and huddled together, and the bluejackets at once began to guy them most unmercifully. An Irish sailor asked: "An' is the rest of yez regiment down South a'pickin' cotton?"

Quick as a flash Bob Bowen pulled the cases from the colors and held them up. The flags were tattered, torn, bullet-riddled, stained with blood and powder; the color-lances bore bullet-marks, and their brass ornaments had been shot out of shape. Shaking the colors, Bob called out:

"Sixteen hundred men have followed dem colors, an' we'se alls dat's leff. Dem colors was at Fort Fisher, an' de line didn't break an' run back!"

This last sentence was a center-shot, for at the assault on Fort Fisher the naval assaulting force had been broken and forced back to the beach.[26] For a moment the sailors gazed at the war-worn flags, then they cheered long and loud. Again the ready wit of Bob Bowen had shown itself at the right time and place.

We arrived at Baltimore at daylight Sunday morning. It was cold, and the snow-flakes were falling. A few sleepy, shivering policemen were the only persons visible. For weeks the men had been anticipating the pleasure of marching through the streets of Baltimore. "W'en de ole 30th march up Baltimo' street past de monument, den yo' see de style!" had been their talk, and it was a bitter disappointment to them that they could not parade before the admiring eyes of their friends. The regiment was marched to Fort Federal Hill and quartered in the barracks there. Some of the men were given passes, and before noon a good share of the colored population of Baltimore began to flock into camp.

Serg't Scott came to my room, and with him was a good-looking, middle-aged mulatto woman and a bright, pretty yellow girl of 16. The Sergeant's face

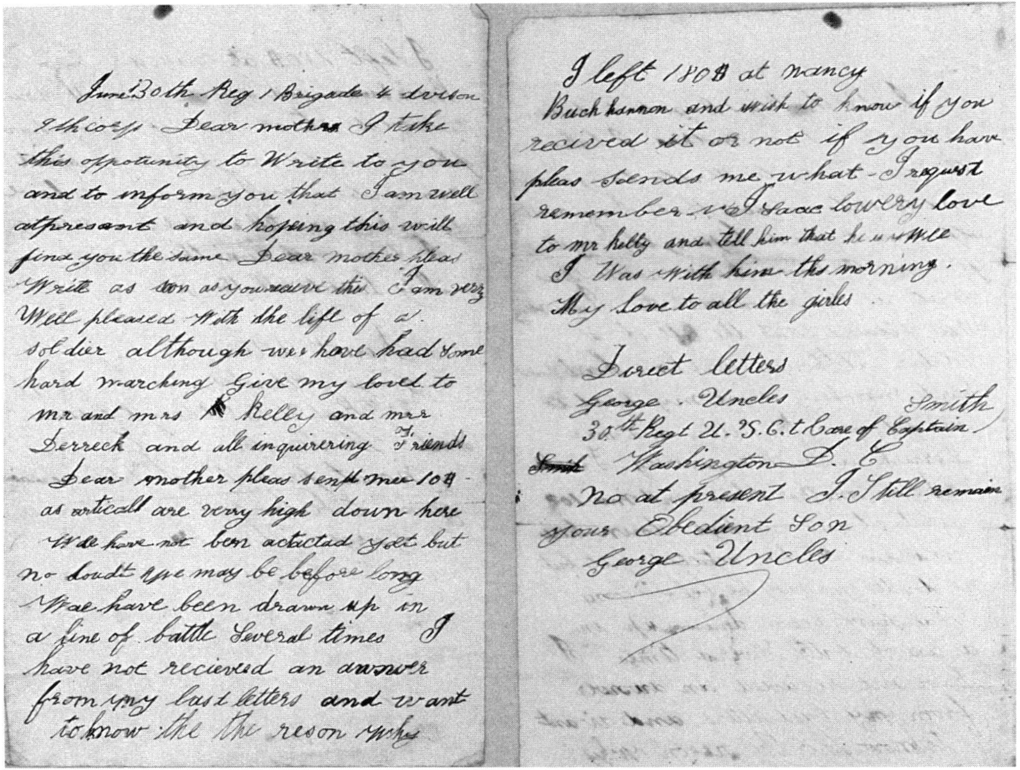

June 30th Reg 1 Brigade 4 dvison
9th corps Dear mother I take
this opportunity to Write to you
and to inform you that I am well
atpresant and hoping this will
find you the same Dear mother pleas
Write as son as you recive this I am very
Well pleased With the life of a
soldier although wee have had some
hard marching Give my lovel to
mr and mrs Kelley and mrs
Derreck and all inquiering friends
Dear mother pleas send mee 10$
as articall are very high down here
Wee have not been acticted yet but
no doubt we may be before long
Wee have been drawn up in
a line of battle Several times I
have not recieved an answer
from my last letters and want
to know the the reson why

I left 180$ at nancy
Buchhannon and wish to know if you
recived it or not if you have
pleas sends me what I request
remember me to Isaac lowery love
to mr kelly and tell him that he is well
I Was with him this morning.
My love to all the girles

Direct letters
George Uncles
30th Regt U.S.C.t Care of Captain Smith
Washington D. C
No at present I Still remain
yours Obedient Son
George Uncles

Fig. 13.1. Pvt. George Uncles's letter to his mother. Pension Application, Civil War Pension File, George Uncles, 30th U.S. Colored Infantry, Record Group 15, National Archives.

was very sober, and my heart sank when I saw them, for I knew instinctively who they were.

"Lieutenant," said the Sergeant, saluting, "here is the mother and sister of Geo. Uncles," and he turned and walked away. I knew at once that the mother and sister were ignorant of the sad news that awaited them.

"W'at my George been doin,' sah?" asked the mother. "Been cuttin' up some shine an' got put in de geerd-house, I reckon!" and she laughed pleasantly. Then, seeing my sober face, she asked wildly: "Is he sick? Is he dead?"

As I quietly as I could [I] informed her of the death of her son. I praised his soldier-like qualities, and faithfully delivered his last message. She listened quietly, said, "Thank you, sah," and then both of them went away crying.[27]

It was three days before the Paymaster came to us. Then the men received their pay and bounty and an honorable discharge. On the muster-out roll of my company were the names of 160 men, and there were just 60 present. The others had died or been disabled. The Government allowed the men to retain their rifles upon the payment of a small sum, and most of them chose to do so.

On Dec. 22, 1865, the time of parting came.[28] Every man of Co. H came to me, shook me by the hand, giving me every kind wish, and receiving mine in return. Then Serg't Scott formed the company, and the men "counted twos" for the last time.

"Present—Arms!" It was the last salute of the men to their officers.

At the word of command they faced to the right in four ranks, tossed their rifles to the "right-shoulder-shift," and with the old swinging, veteran step marched out through the gates of Fort Federal Hill. As they reached the crowded streets of Baltimore the ranks dissolved in the moving tide of civil life, never more to be reunited, and the glorious old 30th was only a memory.

Appendix

Extract from "A Dark Night On Picket"

Slowly the hours passed till daylight. A hearty breakfast was eaten, knapsacks and blankets snugly packed, and the arms carefully inspected and recapped. The road was found not fifty rods distant, near where the Division-camp had been. A Sergeant and two men were sent a short distance ahead, as skirmishers, and a like party followed in rear. No sound of artillery or musketry reached our ears, and we hoped that the roads might yet be clear.

Prince George Court-house was passed without an alarm, and our spirits were rising, when the skirmishers ahead stopped and gave the signal to halt. The Sergeant came back, and made report: "Cap'n, some debbiltry gwine on ober yander. I done heerd de driber's lash and Black peoples holler." With the Sergeant I cautiously advanced, and, peering through a clump of bushes, saw, two hundred yards distant, a log-and-splint house, situated in the middle of a corn-field.

Suspended from an oak-tree, by their thumbs, were two Black Men, stripped; and the blue clothing lying near them showed that they were soldiers. Two stalwart men in Rebel gray were standing by them, each with a black snake-whip in hand. Three other Rebels were seated on the ground, while another stood by their horses, which were hitched a short distance off. Their carbines hung to the saddles, but all had revolvers and sabres buckled on. In the door-way of the house stood a dirty-looking female, with a snuff-stick in her mouth, and some tallow-faced children around her. Three large, ferocious, yellow dogs lay near the horses.

Alternately the men with whips would measure the lash across the back of the Negro nearest them, to mark the place where the blow should fall; then giving the whip a full, round swing over their heads, would bring it down on their victim. We could hear the lash whiz and crack as it struck, and see the blood follow the stroke. One Negro never flinched nor moaned. His comrade yelled, cried, and begged piteously. The Rebels, woman, children, and dogs were closely watching the proceedings, and seemed greatly edified by the spectacle—the woman in particular.

My plans were quickly made. A breeze blowing toward us prevented the dogs scenting or hearing us. A squad was stationed near the road, and another squad started by a circuitous route to reach the road on the other side of the house, to prevent the Rebels escaping in that direction. With the remainder I crept quietly toward the house, through the corn. The rustling sound of the corn prevented any noise that we made being heard, and we reached safely within five rods of the house without alarming our foes. They were sitting down, backs toward us, watching the whipping. The man at the horses was unloosing a saddle-girth. One Negro was crying; the other was defiant. We heard him say: "Kill me, if ye dare; the cullud soldiers will come back, and dey will find me, and will settle wid you 'uns. Do your wust; my speerit shall haunt ye all!" Giving the signal, we started for them, and before the Rebels could draw their revolvers from the holsters, they were struck with musket-barrels, half stunned, and lay with glistening bayonets pricking their breasts. The orders had been not to fire, except in the last extremity, and they were faithfully obeyed. Our prisoners were disarmed and securely pinioned, before they fairly knew what had happened to them. The Negroes who had been whipped were quickly released. When the rush was made, the dogs flew at the men so fiercely that it was with difficulty that they were subdued, and not till they were dead did they cease fighting.

The woman set up a yelling, but was quickly awed into silence. Clad in a dirty cotton dress, hair uncombed, face unwashed, feet bare, a snuff-stick in her mouth, and the snuff-juice running down her chin, she presented a picture for "hirelings" to gaze upon. Before I was aware of their intentions, the soldiers had triced up the two Rebels who had done the whipping, and were asking permission to do unto them as they had done unto others. Permission was granted, and thirty-nine lashes were well laid on their bare backs. On the persons of the other prisoners were found the shoes and underclothing of the two Negroes they had captured. These articles were restored to their rightful owners. Our prisoners seemed to expect no mercy, and were surprised when orders were given them to fall in and prepare to march. A serious proposition was made by some of the Blacks to hang them then and there, and it took all of my authority to prevent it. By telling them that six prisoners, with their horses, arms, and equipments, would be something to boast of and show the other companies and that I would shoot the first man who dared disobey my orders, their mutinous spirits were quelled.

Again we started, with our skirmishers out, marching with that long swinging gait so well known to old soldiers. The Negroes we had released explained their capture as we marched along. They had been tired and sleepy, and sat down to rest. Falling asleep, they did not wake till daylight. On the road they were surprised by the Rebel scouts, and easily captured. I think that this lesson cured them of straggling.

Before noon the Union pickets were found, and we were directed to the camp of the Division, and marched straight to regimental head-quarters. A frown was on the brow of the Colonel when I made my appearance; but it disappeared when I told him the story of our night's adventures and showed him the prisoners. And when I gave him an ivory-handled, silver-mounted Colt's revolver that I had taken from one of the Rebs, his grim features relaxed into a smile; and he sent his servant after a canteen of fine old Bourbon, telling me that after such a night I must be nearly used up, and that something stimulating was necessary to revive me.

(Capt. Freeman S. Bowley, "A Dark Night On Picket.")

Notes

Introduction

1. *National Tribune*, April 20, 1899.

2. [Freeman S. Bowley], "A Story by a School-Boy—with a Moral"; Bowley, "The Battle of the Mine," 319–27, "A Dark Night On Picket," 31–37, "The Crater," "Life in Prison," "The Petersburg Mine," "Seven Months in Confederate Prisons," "A Boy Lieutenant in a Black Regiment," *A Boy Lieutenant*. In 1997 the 1906 edition of *A Boy Lieutenant* was reprinted by Sergeant Kirkland's Press; see Bowley, *A Boy Lieutenant*, rev. ed., Seagrave, ed.; Freeman S. Bowley to Secretary of War, July 11, 1891, Maj. Gen. Nelson A. Miles, October 10, 1895, Hon. David S. Lamont, October 10, 1895, Letters Received, B-561 1864, ser. 360, CTD, RG 94, NA.

3. McPherson, *For Cause and Comrades*, 6, 13, 25–26, 76, 78, 134–40; Jimerson, *The Private Civil War*, 24–25; Mitchell, *Civil War Soldiers*, 17–18, *The Vacant Chair*, 4–5, 10–18; John Bently, "Wrongs of Passage: Bastardization, Symbolic Politics and Military Cultures," in Dixon, Auton, *War, Society and Culture*, 63, 67; Rotundo, "Boy Culture: Middle-Class Boyhood in Nineteenth-Century America," in Carnes, Griffen, *Meanings for Manhood*, 15–16, 31–36; "Learning about Manhood: Gender Ideals and the Middle-Class Family in Nineteenth Century America," in Mangan, Walvin, *Manliness and Morality*, 35–51; Wyatt-Brown, *Yankee Saints and Southern Sinners*, 9–10, 185–87, 189–93, *Honor and Violence in the Old South*, 24–39, *The Shaping of Southern Culture*, xii–xv, 303; Linderman, *Embattled Courage*, 7, 11–16, 32, 277; Ayers, *Vengeance and Justice*, 19–26. For discussion of how codes of honor shape concepts of rank, social status, and manhood see Cox, *A Proper Sense of Honor*, 32, 38–41, 66; Nye, *Masculinity and Male Codes of Honor in Modern France*, 8–13; Taylor, *Sources of the Self*, 20; Harris, "Honor, Emasculation, and Empowerment," in May, Strikwerda, and Hopkins, *Rethinking Masculinity*, 275–88. For comment on the relationship between the meaning of personal sacrifice and concepts of manhood, citizenship, nationhood, and a soldier's feeling of self worth see Damousi, *The Labour of Loss*, 4, 26–27, 57, 63–65; Luckins, *The Gates of Memory*, 57–67; Gabriel, *To Serve with Honor*, 155–60. Shortly before Bowley saw combat the U.S. government promulgated the Lieber Code, which laid out the rules of honorable warfare. Meron, *Bloody Constraint*, 12–14. For a discussion of the rules of honorable warfare and the use of black troops see Wilson, "In the Shadow of John Brown: The Military Service of Colonels Thomas Higginson, James Montgomery and Robert Shaw in the Department of the South," in Smith, *Black Soldiers in Blue*, 306–35. In her study of Northern and Southern efforts at reunion, Nina Silber argues that Southerners and Northerners had different codes of manhood during the antebellum period. Whereas the Southern white men's code of manhood sought community endorsement for a code of chivalry, violence, and deferential respect for women, North-

ern men focused on the cultivation of dignity, self-improvement, and self-control in an institutional context. These contrasting versions of manhood had merged into a new, virile form of patriotism by the time of the 1898 Spanish-American war. Silber, *The Romance of Reunion*, 8, 195–96. For discussion of the link between masculinity and developing concepts of nationalism see Nagel, "Masculinity and Nationalism," 242–69. Kristin L. Hoganson argues that the fear of the rapid socio-political changes occurring at the end of the nineteenth century reinforced the popular notions that the Civil War had developed the mettle of the men who were fighting in it. In this climate the veteran was idealized as a model citizen and determined efforts were made to hold on to fading military virtues. Hoganson believes the development of a manly jingoistic culture towards the end of the nineteenth century was a primary causal factor in the Spanish-American and Philippine-American Wars. Hoganson, *Fighting for American Manhood*, 9–14, 28, 117, 144, 201; O'Leary, *To Die For*. For comment on the crisis in manhood at the end of the nineteenth century that resulted in assertions of manly militarism, imperialism, and a focus on the strenuous life see Kimmel, *Manhood in America*, 77–78, 111–12, 184–88.

For a discussion on the way African Americans were written out of Civil War history and Civil War commemorations see: Blight, "Quarrel Forgotten or a Revolution Remembered?" in Blight, Simpson, *Union and Emancipation*, 151–79, especially 151–52, 166, 170–71; Blight, *Race and Reunion*, 2–5; Savage, "The Politics of Memory: Black Emancipation and the Civil War Monument," in Gillis, *Commemorations*, 113–15, 143; Savage, *Standing Soldiers, Kneeling Slaves*, 18–20, Chapters 5, 6; Shaffer, *After the Glory*, 7–8, 169–93. Recent research by William Blair has shown that black community commemorations were not silenced. In the South black communities struggled to hold their own commemorations and memorials. Blair, *Cities of the Dead*, 23–48.

4. *National Tribune*, April 20, 1899.

5. Ibid.

6. Ibid., April 20, 27, 1899.

7. Ibid., May 4, 1899; Mitchell, *The Vacant Chair*, 12–13.

8. Mitchell, *Civil War Soldiers*, 17–18, *The Vacant Chair*, 4–6, 8–11, 13–18, 166; McPherson, *For Cause and Comrades*, 6, 13, 24–27, 31, 134–37.

9. *National Tribune*, April 27, 1899.

10. Ibid.

11. Ibid.

12. Mitchell, *Civil War Soldiers*, 56–57, 69–75, *The Vacant Chair*, 43–46, 54.

13. *National Tribune*, April 20, 27, 1899.

14. Ibid., April 27, 1899.

15. Ibid., May 4, 1899.

16. Ibid., May 11, 1899.

17. Ibid., May 4, 1899.

18. Ibid.

19. Ibid.

20. Wilson, *Campfires of Freedom*, 29–31.

21. *National Tribune*, May 11, June 29, 1899.

22. Ibid., May 11, 25, 1899.

23. Ibid., April 27, August 24, 1899; Like Bowley, Thomas Wentworth Higginson, colonel of the 33rd United States Colored Infantry, wrote a serialized account of his service with black troops. However, unlike Bowley's, Higginson's account was based on journal records and was published in the *Atlantic Monthly* during the war and the early postwar period, 1864–1867. The *Atlantic Monthly* articles formed the main body of a book published in 1869. See Higginson, *Army Life in a Black Regiment*, with introduction and notes by Robert D. Madison, xvii–xix; Looby, ed., *The Complete Civil War Journal and Selected Letters of Thomas Wentworth Higginson*, 20–25.

24. Linderman, *Embattled Courage*, 7, 8, 10, 23, 31, 166–67; McPherson, *For Cause and Comrades*, 36, 77–81; *National Tribune*, April 27, May 11, 25, 1899.

25. *National Tribune*, May 11, June 8, 1899.

26. Ibid., June 6, 22, 29, July 6, 13, 1899; Bowley, "The Battle of the Mine," 319–27, "The Crater," "The Petersburg Mine"; Freeman S. Bowley to Secretary of War, July 11, 1891, Maj. Gen. Nelson A. Miles, October 10, 1895, Hon. David S. Lamont, October 10, 1895, Letters Received, B-561 1864, ser. 360, CTD, RG 94, NA.

27. *National Tribune*, June 22, 1899.

28. Ibid., June 29, 1899.

29. Ibid.

30. Ibid.

31. Ibid.

32. Ibid.

33. Ibid., July 13, 1899.

34. Ibid., June 29, July 6, 1899; Freeman S. Bowley to Secretary of War, July 11, 1891, Maj. Gen. Nelson A. Miles, October 10, 1895, Hon. David S. Lamont, October 10, 1895, Letters Received, B-561 1864, ser. 360, CTD, RG 94, NA.

35. *National Tribune*, June 29, July 6, 13, 1899.

36. Ibid., July 6, 1899.

37. Ibid.; Cox, *A Proper Sense of Honor*, 62–63.

38. *National Tribune*, August 3, 1899.

39. Ibid., July 20, 1899.

40. Ibid., July 13, 20, 27, August 17, 1899.

41. Ibid., August 17, 24, 1865.

42. Ibid., August 31, September 7, 1899.

43. Ibid., August 31, 1899.

44. Ibid., September 7, 1899. Uncles was a faithful son who was concerned about the welfare of his mother. See George Uncles to Mother [undated 1864], June 1, [1864], April 9, May 11, August 22, 1865, Pension Application, Civil War Pension File, George Uncles, 30th USCI, RG 15, NA.

45. Ibid. For comments on the bonds that developed between soldiers see McPherson, *For Cause and Comrades*, 82–89; Linderman, *Embattled Courage*, 234–36.

46. For comment on the link between reputation, respect, and honor in the military see Cox, *A Proper Sense of Honor*, 38–41; *National Tribune*, May 4, 1899.

47. For comment on the cultural activities of soldiers in the 30th USCI see the chaplaincy report of Chauncey E. Bristol, 30th USCI, for May 1864. Chaplain Bristol believed that the soldiers' strong religious beliefs and fervent singing helped to make them Christian soldiers. Chaplain C. E. Bristol to Brig. Gen. L. Thomas, May 31, 1864, B-657 1864, Letters Received, ser. 360, CTD, RG 94, NA; Wilson, *Campfires of Freedom*, 12–15, 210–12.

48. Chaplain Bristol observed that the soldiers in the 30th USCI "gather about their camp fires even after hard marching and with their characteristic éclat sing the songs of Zion, as well as the popular National melodies." Chaplain C. E. Bristol to Brig. Gen. L. Thomas, May 31, 1864, B-657 1864, Letters Received, ser. 360, CTD, RG 94, NA; *National Tribune*, April 27, May 11, 1899.

49. Chaplain Chauncey E. Bristol reported that it was "a rich treat" for him "to pass along the lines after 'taps' and hear prayers ascending from many little shelter tents." Chaplain C. E. Bristol to Brig. Gen. L. Thomas, May 31, 1864, B-657 1864, Letters Received, ser. 360, CTD, RG 94, NA; Lt. George H. Walcott, 30th USCI, believed the soldiers of his regiment were profoundly religious and morally superior to white soldiers. Tyler, *Memorials*, 50; *National Tribune*, May 11, June 22, 1899.

50. For a discussion of military communities in black regiments and the way black soldiers used their cultural activities and traditions to ease their transition into army life and freedom see Wilson, *Campfires of Freedom*.

51. *National Tribune*, August 31, 1899.

52. Ibid.

53. Ibid., May 4, 1899.

54. Ibid., May 18, 1899.

55. Ibid.

56. Ibid., May 11, 1899.

57. Ibid., May 18, 1899.

58. Ibid., April 27, 1899.

59. Ibid., May 4, 1899.

60. Ibid., May 18, 1899.

61. Ibid.

62. Ibid., June 15, 1899.

63. Blight, *Race and Reunion*, 211, 216–17, 221–31, 240–43.

64. *National Tribune*, September 7, 1899.

65. For discussion of the Civil War as a revolutionary conflict and a war of black liberation see: Berlin, "Who Freed the Slaves? Emancipation and Its Meaning," in Blight, Simpson, *Union and Emancipation*, 105–21; Berlin et al., *Slaves No More*, 3–75, especially 3–6, 8–10, 74–75.

Thelen, "Memory and American History," 1119, 1125–26; Joyner, "Forget Hell: The Civil War in Southern Memory," in Grant, Parish, *Legacy of Disunion*, 26; Donald, "A Generation of Defeat," in Fraser, Moore, *From the Old South to the New*, 16; Linderman, *Embattled Courage*, 267–69; Burke, "History as Social Memory," in Butler, *Memory*, 98–100; 275–80; Blight, "Quarrel Forgotten or a Revolution Remembered?" in Blight, Simpson, *Union and Emancipation*, 151–79, especially 151–52, 166, 170–71; Blight, *Race and Reunion*, 2–5; Kammen, *Mystic Cords of Memory*, 6, *In the Past Lane*, 204–05, 210; O'Leary, "'Blood Brotherhood': The Racialization of Patriotism, 1865–1918," in Bodnar, ed., *Bonds of Affection*, 53–81; Savage, "The Politics of Memory: Black Emancipation and the Civil War Monument," in Gillis, *Commemorations*, 113–15, 143; Savage, *Standing Soldiers, Kneeling Slaves*, 18–20, Chapters 5, 6; Shaffer, *After the Glory*, 7–8, 169–93.

66. For comment on autobiography and memoirs as literary forms for ordering personal experience and revealing subjective truth see Popkin, *History, Historians, and Autobiography*, 68–71; Vernon, *Arms and the Self*, 12–15, 17–21, 29–32; Rose, *Victorian America and the Civil War*, 248, 250, 252; Smith, Watson, *Reading Autobiography*, 15–24, 58–71, 198; Fabian, *The Unvarnished Truth*, 2–7; Zinsser, *Inventing the Truth*, 6. Literary historian Kathleen Diffley argues that popular narratives helped the American people renegotiate their citizenship during the Civil War and Reconstruction period. Diffley, *Where My Heart Is Turning Ever*, 11. Michael Kammen argues that history created from the collective memory is the essential element from which individuals and nations construct their identity. Kammen, *Mystic Cords of Memory*, 10; Grant, "The Charter of Its Birthright: The Civil War and American Nationalism," in Grant, Parish, *Legacy of Disunion*, 197–98; Blight, *Race and Reunion*, 15–18, 217–21, 316–19, *Beyond the Battlefield*, 93–119.

John R. Neff claims that the obstacles to reconciliation between the North and South have been underestimated in the current debate on memory and the Civil War. He argues that the North generated its own mythology, "the Cause Victorious," which celebrated the triumph of Northern ideals. Neff, *Honoring the Civil War Dead*, 5–9.

67. Bowley, "The Battle of the Mine," 319–27, "A Dark Night On Picket," 31–37, "The Crater," "Life in Prison," "The Petersburg Mine," "Seven Months in Confederate Prisons," "A Boy Lieutenant in a Black Regiment," *A Boy Lieutenant*; Freeman S. Bowley to Secretary of War, July 11, 1891, Maj. Gen. Nelson A. Miles, October 10, 1895, Hon. David S. Lamont, October 10, 1895, Letters Received, B-561 1864, ser. 360, CTD, RG 94, NA.

For comment on the construction of historical memory see Blight, *Beyond the Battlefield*, 192, 278, "Quarrel Forgotten or a Revolution Remembered?" in Blight, Simpson, *Union and Emancipation*, 151–52. Bowley was not alone in endeavoring to set the record straight and claim his personal place in the national memory. For Civil War veterans the memory of the war was a contested landscape. For example, Ellem "The Fall of Fort Fisher: Contested Memories of the Civil War," 198–233; Levin, "'On That Day You Commanded the Full Measure of Your Fame,'" 18–39; Reardon, *Pickett's Charge*. For comment on military service as a rite of passage to manhood see Mitchell, *The Vacant Chair*, 4–18.

68. McPherson, *For Cause and Comrades*, 118, see also 117–30; Wiley, *The Life of*

Billy Yank, 115; Berlin, "Who Freed the Slaves? Emancipation and Its Meaning," in Blight, Simpson, *Union and Emancipation*, 112–15.

69. *National Tribune*, April 27, May 11, 25, 1899.

70. Ibid., June 1, 1899; Bowley, "A Dark Night On Picket," 35–37; Mitchell, *The Vacant Chair*, 72–75, 82–101. The incident involving black soldiers whipping captured rebel soldiers is described in the Appendix of *Honor in Command*.

71. *National Tribune*, July 20, August 3, 1899.

72. Fabian, *The Unvarnished Truth*, 119–20. Ann Fabian has written a perceptive analysis of the racism embedded in the Civil War prisoner of war narratives. See Fabian, *The Unvarnished Truth*, 117–57; Blight, *Race and Reunion*, 219, 221–28, 235–36, 287–88, *Beyond the Battlefield*, 163–64; Aaron, *The Unwritten War*, xvii; *National Tribune*, June 1, August 3, 10, 1899.

73. Blight, *Race and Reunion*, 236–51.

74. *National Tribune*, June 15, 22, 29, July 13, 1899.

75. Freeman S. Bowley to Secretary of War, July 11, 1891, Maj. Gen. Nelson A. Miles, October 10, 1895, Hon. David S. Lamont, October 10, 1895, Letters Received, B-561 1864, ser. 360, CTD, RG 94, NA; Glatthaar, *Forged in Battle*.

76. *National Tribune*, June 15, 1899.

77. Ibid., July 13, August 17, 1899. The belief that combat ennobled men's character and made them more honorable was strongly held by many veterans like Bowley in the last decades of the nineteenth century. It contributed significantly to sectional reconciliation. Blight, *Race and Reunion*, 189–90, 200–201, 208–10.

78. Blight, *Race and Reunion*, 199; For comment on generosity being a key virtue in an honor code see Taylor, *Sources of the Self*, 153–55; Bowley, "A Dark Night On Picket," 35–37; *National Tribune*, June 1, 1899; Freeman S. Bowley to Secretary of War, July 11, 1891, Maj. Gen. Nelson A. Miles, October 10, 1895, Hon. David S. Lamont, October 10, 1895, Letters Received, B-561 1864, ser. 360, CTD, RG 94, NA; Lt. Col. H. A. Oakam to Maj. C. W. Foster, August 16, 1865, Letters Sent, 30th USCI, Regimental Books & Papers USCT, RG 94, NA.

79. Gallagher, "A Contested Historical Landscape."

Chapter 1. A Commission in a Black Regiment

1. Books that discuss the role of white officers in black Civil War regiments include: Berlin et al., *Freedom: A Documentary History of Emancipation, 1861–1867, Series II, The Black Military Experience* (hereafter cited as Berlin et al., *The Black Military Experience*); Cornish, *The Sable Arm*; Glatthaar, *Forged in Battle*; Quarles, *The Negro in the Civil War*; Smith, *Black Soldiers in Blue*; Trudeau, *Like Men of War*; Westwood, *Black Troops, White Commanders and Freedmen*; Wilson, *Campfires of Freedom*.

Joseph T. Glatthaar's representative sample of 386 officers indicated that 147 were born after 1840. (Date of birth not available: 16.) Glatthaar, *Forged in Battle*, 265.

2. Berlin et al., *The Black Military Experience*, 2–14; Ross, *Tabular Analysis of the Records of the U.S. Colored Troops*, 1.

3. The Fort Pillow, Tennessee, massacre occurred on April 12, 1864, when Brig.

Gen. Nathan Bedford Forrest forced the surrender of the Union fort. After the surrender scores of black troops were massacred. The Fort Pillow massacre galvanized the black soldiers' resistance to the rebel cause. However, Bowley's claim that 90 percent of the black soldiers enlisted in the last year of the war and that "a greater portion" of them enlisted after the Fort Pillow massacre is an exaggeration. Only one-third of USCT regiments were organized after March 1864. Ross, *Tabular Analysis of the Records of the U.S. Colored Troops*, 19–27; Glatthaar, *Forged in Battle*, 156–58; Cimprich, "The Fort Pillow Massacre: Assessing the Evidence," in Smith, *Black Soldiers in Blue*, 150–68.

4. Glatthaar argues that black troops had fewer casualties because they had fewer combat opportunities. Those that did experience combat suffered a higher casualty rate than white soldiers. Glatthaar, *Forged in Battle,* 160; Berlin et al., *The Black Military Experience*, 633.

5. Bowley is quoting from the May 1, 1863, joint resolution of the Confederate Congress. U.S. War Department, *The War of the Rebellion,* 2nd ser., 5: 940–41 (hereafter cited as *OR*); Smith, *Black Soldiers in Blue*, 45.

6. *Worcester Daily Spy*, February 1, 2, 22, 1864.

7. The Highland Military Academy was established in 1856 in Worcester, Mass. Military training featured prominently in the school curriculum. Freeman S. Bowley appears to have been at the school for only twenty-six weeks. *Catalogue of the Highland School,* 5–8; Shaw, "The Highland Military Academy," 118–28; Freeman S. Bowley to Hon. E. M. Stanton, March 14, 1864, Letters Received, B-561 1864, ser. 360, CTD, RG 94, NA.

8. Plunkett received a Medal of Honor for his bravery at Fredericksburg. *OR*, 1st ser., 21: 327–28, 1124; O'Reilly, *The Fredericksburg Campaign*, 340; *Worcester Daily Spy*, February 2, 1864; *Aegis and Transcript*, February 6, 1864; Marvin, *History of Worcester in the War of Rebellion*, 233–36.

Bowley's motives for joining the Union Army were shared by another young officer in his regiment, Lt. George H. Walcott. Walcott, a deeply religious soldier, had a strong sense of patriotic duty. Tyler, *Memorials*, 29.

9. Freeman's father, Jesse D. Bowley, enlisted in the 46th Mass. Vols. at Agawam, Mass., for nine months' service on September 24, 1862. On January 16, 1863, he was detailed to the ambulance corps. When his regiment was mustered out of service in July 1863, Jesse was recorded as being sick at home in Agawam, Mass. Service record of Pvt. Jesse D. Bowley, 46th Mass. Vols., Carded Records, Volunteer Organizations: Civil War, ser. 519, RG 94, NA. (Hereafter records from this depository of the National Archives will be cited as Carded Records, Volunteer Organizations: Civil War.)

For comments on bounties, pay, and the political appointment of officers see *Worcester Daily Spy*, February 4, 1864; Boatner, *Civil War Dictionary*, 624; Wiley, *The Life of Billy Yank*, 24–26; McPherson, *Ordeal by Fire*, 165, 269–73; Swart, "The Military Examination Board in the Civil War," 227–45.

10. The Bureau of Colored Troops' charter established a system of officer examination boards. The board Bowley came before was Maj. Gen. Silas Casey's board. Berlin

et al., *The Black Military Experience*, 5, 10, 14, 76, 113, 339; *OR*, 3rd ser., 3: 215–16. For a discussion of the operation of the officer examination boards for United States Colored Troops see Wilson, "Thomas Webster and the 'Free Military School for Applicants for Commands of Colored Troops,'" 101–22. Bowley informed Stanton that he attended the Highland Military Academy and that he had "a good thorough knowledge of the School of the Company, Skirmishing, and the Bayonet Exercise." He assured Stanton that he was "eighteen years of age, stout and healthy." Although he was "perhaps young," he believed he was "fully competent to fill the position of Lieutenant." Freeman S. Bowley to Hon. E. M. Stanton, March 14, 1864, Letters Received, B-561 1864, ser. 360, CTD, RG 94, NA.

11. The congressman was probably antislavery Massachusetts Senator Henry Wilson. Henry Wilson had sons at the Highland Military Academy. After the war Bowley sought the support of Henry Wilson in his unsuccessful attempt to secure a commission in the regular army. See *Catalogue of the Highland School*, "References"; Shaw, "The Highland Military Academy," 121; F. S. Bowley to Hon. H. Wilson, July 27, 1866, B-2051 1866, 6 June, 1867 B-1337 1867, Commission Branch, RG 94, NA. In circumstances similar to those of Freeman Bowley, Pvt. George H. Walcott, 22nd Mass. Infantry, was entertained by Senator Wilson's family while he was in Washington, D.C., and through Wilson he gained a recommendation to come before Casey's board. George H. Walcott successfully passed the board's examination and was commissioned 1st lieutenant in Co. E, 30th USCI. Lt. Walcott was stricken with disease in June 1864 and died on July 10, 1864. Senator Wilson wrote the Introduction to the *Memorials of Lieut. George H. Walcott*, compiled by C. H. Tyler to commemorate George Walcott's life. Tyler, *Memorials*, 12, 37, 39.

12. Maj. Gen. Christopher Columbus Augur commanded the 22nd Army Corps, Department of Washington, from October 13, 1863, to June 7, 1865. Warner, *Generals in Blue*, 12.

13. Kautz, *The Company Clerk*.

14. Bowley came before the Washington board on April 4, 1864. "List of Persons Who Have Passed Examining Boards 1863–65," vol. 1, 130–31, ser. 382, CTD, RG 94, NA.

Chapter 2. Joining the 30th United States Colored Infantry in the Field

1. Flora Ella Pepper became Bowley's wife. Flora's brother, Bennett H. Pepper, was in the 62nd N.Y. Vols. before he was mustered in as a sergeant in the 37th Mass. Vols. in September 1862. He served with this regiment until he was mustered out in June 1865. Service record of Sgt. Bennett H. Pepper, 37th Mass. Vols., Carded Records, Volunteer Organizations: Civil War; Civil War Pension File, Freeman S. Bowley, 30th USCI, RG 15, NA.

2. The 30th USCI was first organized at Camp Stanton, Md., in early to late February 1864, to serve three years. U.S. Adjutant General's Office, *Official Register*, 8: 201.

3. Prejudice directed against black troops was manifest in all ranks in the Union Army. Glatthaar, *Forged in Battle*, 197–99.

4. Elmer Ephraim Ellsworth was famous for organizing the Chicago Zouaves and employing them to present drill displays. On May 24, 1861, he was killed by the proprietor of Marshall House Tavern, Alexandria, Va., for tearing down a Confederate flag that hung from the roof of the tavern. His death contributed significantly to a great outpouring of patriotism. Boatner, *Civil War Dictionary*, 261–62. Bowley is referring to Christ Church. George Washington was on the vestry of Christ Church, Alexandria. "City of Alexandria, tourism and history, themes from the past, George Washington," http://ci.alexandria.va.us/, accessed June 16, 2004.

5. Hardtack was a hard biscuit made out of plain flour and water. It generally came in the form of a square about half an inch thick and three inches square. Lyman, *Civil War Wordbook*, 29.

Bowley was mustered in on May 4, 1864, when he joined his regiment at Manassas Junction. Individual Muster-in Roll, service record of Freeman S. Bowley, 30th USCI, Carded Records, Volunteer Organizations: Civil War. Delevan Bates was appointed colonel of the 30th USCI on March 22, 1864; Boatner, *Civil War Dictionary*, 50; U.S. Adjutant General's Office, *Official Register*, 8: 201.

6. Capt. Arthur J. Smith and 2nd Lt. Silas W. Edgerton were both in Co. H., 30th USCI. U.S. Adjutant General's Office, *Official Register*, 8: 201.

7. The Ninth Corps was under the command of Maj. Gen. Ambrose E. Burnside. The 4th Division of the Ninth Corps was commanded by Brig. Gen. Edward Ferrero and consisted of two brigades of black troops. The 1st Brigade (27th, 30th, 39th, 43rd USCI) was commanded by Col. Joshua K. Sigfried, and the 2nd Brigade (30th Conn. [Cld], 19th, 23rd, USCI) was under the command of Col. Henry G. Thomas. *OR*, 1st ser., 36 (1): 114; Trudeau, *Bloody Roads South*, 343; Matter, *If It Takes All Summer*, 359.

8. "The Colored Volunteer" was probably a variation of "Give Us a Flag," written by an anonymous member of Co. A of the 54th Mass. Vols. The song was written shortly before this elite black regiment left Massachusetts for South Carolina. Many versions of the song exist. The lines that Bowley is alluding to form part of the third verse. "Give Us a Flag" was often sung to a tune borrowed from Billy Holmes's "Hoist Up the Flag," which was published by Sep Winner. "That's What's the Matter, Boys" is probably Stephen Foster's "That's What's the Matter," which was performed by minstrel companies. Wayne D. Shirley, Music Specialist, Music Division, Library of Congress; Silber, *Songs of the Civil War*, 274–75, 293–95; Heaps and Heaps, *The Singing Sixties*, 302.

9. The soldiers may have been alluding to President Davis's order to Confederate commanders, issued in December 1862. *OR*, 2nd ser., 5: 797.

10. See service records of George N. Scott, Thomas Worrell, John Dudley, John Offer, Thomas Festus, 30th USCI, Carded Records, Volunteer Organizations: Civil War.

11. The badge of the Sixth Corps was the St. Andrews cross. Boatner, *Civil War Dictionary*, 191.

12. Wiley, *The Life of Billy Yank*, 147; Ward et al., *The Civil War*, 296.

13. Ague is a malarial type fever that induces cold and hot sweating and quaking fits. "Army ague" is the trembling fear caused by the approach of battle. Gove, *Webster's Third New International Dictionary*, 44.

14. "Brogans" were coarse army shoes that were usually laced and ankle high. Lyman, *Civil War Wordbook*, 29.

15. The brigade commander Bowley is referring to is Col. Joshua K. Sigfried. Matter, *If It Takes All Summer*, 259.

16. Bowley describes the fires raging in the vicinity of the lines of Hancock's 2nd Corps. The Ninth Corps had been called up to help Hancock's corps resist a fierce counterattack. Trudeau, *Bloody Roads South*, 61, 109; McPherson, *Ordeal by Fire*, 415; Ward et al., *The Civil War*, 290.

17. "Will you, will you Fight for the Union?" is loosely based on Daniel Decatur Emmett's "The Black Brigade." It was significantly altered when sung by the men of the 30th USCI. Library of Congress, "American Singing: Nineteenth-Century Song Sheets."

18. "Joe Johnsing" probably refers to Confederate Gen. Joseph Eggelston Johnston. Boatner, *Civil War Dictionary*, 441.

19. Union casualties at the Battle of the Wilderness included: killed and wounded, 14,283; captured, 3,383; total, 17,666. Confederate "minimum" casualties included: killed and wounded, 8,949; captured, 1,881; total, 10,830. Trudeau, *Bloody Roads South*, 119.

20. The 19th Ind. formed part of the 1st Brigade of the 4th Division of the Fifth Army Corps. The brigade performed with distinction at the Battle of Antietam and then became known as the Iron Brigade. See Boatner, *Civil War Dictionary*, 427–28.

21. Trudeau, *Bloody Roads South*, 131.

22. The 37th Mass. Vols. was on duty in New York between July 30, 1863, and October 17, 1863. Dyer, *Compendium*, 2: 1262.

23. The Old Vermont Brigade (1st Vt. H. A., 2nd, 3rd, 4th, 5th and 6th Vt. Vols.) was in the 2nd Brigade of the 2nd Division of the Sixth Army Corps. Boatner, *Civil War Dictionary*, 352, 869–70.

24. Bowley is referring to Benjamin Emory, Capt. Arthur J. Smith's servant. Seagrave, *A Boy Lieutenant*, 98.

25. Trudeau, *Bloody Roads South*, 129. McPherson, *Ordeal by Fire*, 319–23, 414; Ward et al., *The Civil War*, 289.

26. Bowley probably heard the gunfire from the initial assault on Confederate lines near Spotsylvania on May 8, 1864. Trudeau, *Bloody Roads South*, 133–42; McPherson, *Ordeal by Fire*, 416–18. A videt is a mounted sentry. Lyman, *Civil War Wordbook*, 177.

27. A rod is a measure of length equal to 16.5 feet. Simpson, Weiner, *The Oxford English Dictionary*, xiv: 28.

28. McPherson, *Ordeal by Fire*, 414.

Chapter 3. On the March

1. Trudeau, *Bloody Roads South*, 198–99.

2. Bowley may be describing the death of 22-year-old Pvt. Daniel Johnson, Co. H., who is listed as having died of "cramps" at the "Petersburg front" July 1, 1864. Register of Deaths Co. H, Descriptive Roll of Co. H., 30th USCI, Regimental Books and Papers USCT, RG 94, NA.

3. For discussion of the call response pattern in songs see Levine, *Black Culture and Black Consciousness*, 33, 209–211; Owens, *This Species of Property*, 171.

4. Bowley is referring to the 2nd Ohio Cav., not the 3rd Ohio Cav. The 3rd N.J. Cav. was attached to the Ninth Corps and assigned to patrol the northern bank of the Rapidan River. They wore an elaborate Hussar uniform that had a yellow trim. Matter, *If It Takes All Summer*, 20; Dyer, *Compendium*, 2: 1354, 1475; Stryker, *Record of Officers and Men of New Jersey in the Civil* War, II: 1321.

5. The Zouave uniforms were patterned on the elite French North African troops' uniforms. The uniform generally consisted of baggy red pants with white leggings and short blue jackets. The 140th and 146th N.Y. Vols. were Zouave regiments. Trudeau, *Bloody Roads South*, 8, 53, 56.

6. The wedge of the "A" tent consisted of a piece of canvas stretched over a horizontal bar and staked to the ground on either side, with extensions for closing front and rear. Wiley, *The Life of Billy Yank*, 56.

7. Grant, *Personal Memoirs*, 2: 449.

8. Bowley has mistaken Perry Gibson for Perry J. Gibbs. He was "killed in action in front of Petersburg Va." on July 30, 1864. See service record of Perry J. Gibbs, 30th USCI, Carded Records, Volunteer Organizations: Civil War.

9. Officers often called upon racial stereotypes to explain the black soldiers' poor health. In reality the high rate of sickness in black regiments was a combination of many factors, including poor diet and inferior medical services. Berlin et al., *The Black Military Experience*, 633–36.

10. Maj. Gen. James E. B. (Jeb) Stuart commanded the Cavalry Corps of the Army of Northern Virginia. Boatner, *Civil War Dictionary*, 812–13.

11. The Potomac Home Brigade consisted of the 1st, 2nd, and 3rd Md. Infantry (Potomac Home Brigade). Aman, *Personnel of the Civil War*, 2: 114–15; Dyer, *Compendium*, 2: 1229, 1232–34.

12. The Henry Repeating Rifle was the first rifle with a magazine used in large numbers during the Civil War. It had a tubular magazine under the barrel that held 15 copper cartridges. This magazine, plus one round in the barrel, gave a total of 16 rounds, hence "Henry 16-shooter." Boatner, *Civil War Dictionary*, 397.

13. Tyler, *Memorials*, 81.

14. In the summer of 1864 the governors of a number of Northwestern states proposed the employment of state militia for the short term of 100 days. These troops were to be used to relieve veteran troops from guard and garrison duty.

15. Bluejackets were naval enlisted men. Dupuy et al., *A Dictionary of Military Terms*, 31.

16. "The Girl I Left Behind Me" was one of the most popular sentimental farewell ballads sung by both Union and Confederate soldiers during the Civil War. Based on an old Irish air, the song told of the parting of sweethearts mixed with emotions of pride and sorrow. Heaps and Heaps, *The Singing Sixties*, 97, 133.

17. File closers kept the formation of the unit in order by closing files. This prevented gaps from appearing in the lines as the unit moved forward. Lyman, *Civil War Wordbook*, 67.

18. Bowley is referring to the 60th Ohio Infantry. Reid, *Ohio in the War*, 2: 361; Dyer, *Compendium*, 2: 1525.

19. Manufactured in the Springfield Armory, Mass., the Enfield rifle was the most common rifle used in the war. It weighed nine pounds with bayonet attached and fired a bullet similar to the minie accurately to 800 yards. The "Springfield" rifle muskets were officially designated United States Rifle Musket Models 1861, 1863 (Types 1 and 2). The models were basically the same weapon, with only minor changes. Boatner, *Civil War Dictionary*, 266, 790.

20. "Just Before the Battle, Mother" was written by George F. Root. It was sung in both armies but appears to have been more popular with Southern soldiers. This very popular song lent itself to parody. Commager, *The Blue and the Gray*, 576–77.

21. Bowley is probably referring to Capt. Joseph Backus, 1st Conn. Cav., who was reported killed in action near Old Church Tavern, Va., on June 10, 1864. U.S. Adjutant General's Office, *Official Register*, 1: 258.

22. Whitelaw Reid was the war correspondent for the *Cincinnati Gazette.* It is unlikely that Bowley met Reid because in June 1864 Reid was writing his war dispatches from "Newspaper Row" in Washington. Whitelaw Reid did not join the *New York Tribune* until 1868. Boatner, *Civil War Dictionary*, 690; Reader's Digest, *The Reader's Digest Family Encyclopaedia of American History*, 936–937; Smart, *A Radical View*, 1: 6–8.

Chapter 4. Picket Duty at Petersburg, Virginia

1. The reaction of black soldiers to "Ole Stonewall's ghos'" may be at least partly attributed to the former slaves' beliefs in ghosts and the supernatural. Gen. Stonewall Jackson's military triumphs made him a legendary figure among Union troops. During the battle of Chancellorsville Jackson was mortally wounded by firing from his own men, who mistook his reconnaissance party as Union cavalry. See service record of Joseph H. Wright, George N. Scott, 30th USCI, Carded Records, Volunteer Organizations: Civil War. Joyner, *Down by the Riverside*, 150–53; Boatner, *Civil War Dictionary*, 432–33; McPherson, *Ordeal by Fire*, 239–48, 317–23, *Battle Cry of Freedom*, 464–71, 638–46.

2. An abatis is an obstacle made from trees that are felled towards the enemy. Boatner, *Civil War Dictionary*, 1.

3. Bowley is referring to Maj. Gen. William Mahone's attack on Union lines late in the afternoon of June 22, 1864. Trudeau, *The Last Citadel*, 71–79.

4. On June 22, 1864, Gens. James Wilson and August Kautz led their cavalry division on an ill-fated raid to destroy the Southside and Danville Railways. See Boatner, *Civil War Dictionary*, 931–32; Trudeau, *The Last Citadel*, 59, 68– 69, 87–90.

5. Embrasures were openings built into a wall or a parapet. Guns were fired through the embrasures at a minimum exposure to the gunners. Gabions were round wicker or metal baskets several feet high with open ends. They were filled with dirt and used to strengthen fieldworks. Boatner, *Civil War Dictionary*, 320; Dupuy et al., *A Dictionary of Military Terms*, 81; Faust, *Historical Times Illustrated Encyclopaedia*, 295.

6. Boatner, *Civil War Dictionary*, 931–32; Trudeau, *The Last Citadel*, 59, 68–69, 87–90.

7. Bowley is referring to *Ignis fatuus*, or will-o'-the-wisp, or jack-o-lantern, which is a phosphorescent light seen in swamps and marshes. Gove, *Webster's Third New International Dictionary*, 1: 1125.

8. Whippoorwills are nocturnal birds distinguished by their distinctive "whippoo-will" call. Folk tradition depicted the whippoorwill as a bird of ill omen and death. Chuck-will's-widow is the largest of the American goatsuckers. These long-winged, crepuscular or nocturnal birds are larger than the whippoorwills. They have short, wide bills, mottled plumage, and feed on insects they catch in flight. Gove, *Webster's Third New International Dictionary*, 404, 972; Mathews, *A Dictionary of Americanisms*, 323, 1854.

9. John Jackson was a former slave of Daniel Scholl, Frederick County, Md. Service record of John Jackson, 30th USCI, Carded Records, Volunteer Organizations: Civil War.

10. Slaves secretly communicated with each other using codes often hidden in songs. Levine, *Black Culture and Black Consciousness*, 53–54; Webber, *Deep Like the Rivers*, 196.

11. For comment on former slaves acting as guides for the Union Army see Jimerson, *The Private Civil War*, 78, 80–81; Wiley, *The Life of Billy Yank*, 116. For reference to owners maiming slaves to prevent them from running away see Miller, Smith, *Dictionary of Afro-American Slavery*, 604.

12. Bowley's version of his return journey to camp is very different from an earlier one he produced in 1870. In the 1870 version he rescued a group of black soldiers who were being whipped by rebel soldiers. Bowley allowed his soldiers to whip the rebels before he took them back to Union lines as prisoners of war. See Appendix, *Honor in Command*; Bowley, "A Dark Night On Picket," 36–37.

Chapter 5. In the Petersburg Trenches

1. Liveoak (live-oak) is an American evergreen, hard-wooded tree (*Quercus virens*), grown in the southern states of North America. The name is also applied to some other species in the Pacific states. Simpson, Weiner, *The Oxford English Dictionary*, viii: 1052.

2. Johnnycake is made by mixing cornmeal with salt, milk, or water and either baked in a pan or dropped by spoonfuls on a hot griddle. It can also be cornmeal bread made with water or milk and leavened with or without shortening and eggs. Gove, *Webster's Third New International Dictionary*, 1218.

3. Jimerson, *The Private Civil War*, 170–71; Wiley, *The Life of Johnny Reb*, 318–21, *The Life of Billy Yank*, 353, 355.

4. For comment on the diet of Billy Yank and black troops see Wiley, *The Life of Billy Yank*, 237–45; Berlin et al., *The Black Military Experience*, 635. Established in 1861 to save lives and souls, the Christian Commission set up a network of delegates to distribute Christian literature and relief supplies in Union Army camps. The Sanitary Commission was a voluntary organization that was established to improve medical and hygienic conditions in the Union Army. It was staffed largely by women. Paludan, *A People's Contest*, 351–55; McPherson, *Battle Cry of Freedom*, 480–82; Frederickson, *The Inner Civil War*, Chapter 7.

5. Slapjacks were prepared by frying corn cakes in a mixture of pork fat, corn meal, and salt. Robertson, *Soldiers Blue & Gray*, 68.

6. One hundred and fifty Indian troops served in the 1st Mich. Sharpshooters. The Indian troops were armed with new Sharps NM 1859 breechloaders in 1863. These rifles enabled them to fire 10 shots a minute without changing position. Hauptman, *Between Two Fires*, 125–44, especially 126–27, 130–31, 133–44.

7. Bowley is referring to the *New York Herald*, *Philadelphia Inquirer*, *Baltimore American*, and the *Washington Chronicle*. Trudeau, *The Last Citadel*, 202–204; Wilson, *Campfires of Freedom*, 74–80.

Chapter 6. The Crater

1. Col. Henry Pleasant was a mining engineer before the war, and many of his men were coal miners from Schuykill County, Pennsylvania. Cavanaugh, Marvel, *The Petersburg Campaign*, 4–5; McPherson, *Battle Cry of Freedom*, 758–59, *Ordeal by Fire*, 427–28.; Lykes, *Campaign for Petersburg*, 24–25.

2. Lykes, *Campaign for Petersburg*, 5, 24–27; McPherson, *Battle Cry of Freedom*, 758–59; Trudeau, *The Last Citadel*, 103–104; Cavanaugh, Marvel, *The Battle of the Crater*, 5–6.

3. Lykes, *Campaign for Petersburg* 28; Cavanaugh, Marvel, *The Battle of the Crater*, 10–11.

4. McPherson, *Battle Cry of Freedom*, 759; Lykes, *Campaign for Petersburg*, 28–29; Boatner, *Civil War Dictionary*, 647–48.

5. McPherson, *Battle Cry of Freedom*, 759; Marvel, *Burnside*, 395.

6. Trudeau, *The Last Citadel*, 106; Berlin et al., *The Black Military Experience*, 521–22; Cornish, *The Sable Arm*, 272–78; Quarles, *The Negro in the Civil War*, 300–305; U. S. Congress, *Report of the Joint Committee on the Conduct of the War on the attack on Petersburg, on the 30th day of July 1864*; *OR*, 1st ser., 40 (1): 246–48.

7. Capt. Charles N. Swift had been on sick leave since July 14, 1864. See service record of Capt. Charles N. Swift, 30th USCI, Carded Records, Volunteer Organiza-

tions: Civil War. The other officers Bowley refers to are Capt. David E. Proctor, 1st Lt. Charles B. Sanders, 1st Lt. James E. Bowen, and 1st Lt. Alonzo Plummer. U.S. Adjutant General's Office, *Official Register*, 8: 201.

8. This change in the attack plan occurred because Meade lacked confidence in the inexperienced black troops and Grant, fearing heavy casualties, did not want to be accused of using black troops recklessly. Cavanaugh, Marvel, *The Battle of the Crater*, 16–23; McPherson, *Battle Cry of Freedom*, 759; Marvel, *Burnside*, 393–95; Trudeau, *The Last Citadel*, 107.

9. The explosion was set to occur at 3:30 a.m. However, because of problems with the fuse, it did not take place until 4:40 a.m. Lykes, *Campaign For Petersburg*, 30.

10. Trudeau, *The Last Citadel*, 109

11. "Sam" was an abbreviation for "Sambo."

12. Trudeau, *The Last Citadel*, 109; Boatner, *Civil War Dictionary*, 648.

13. Cavanaugh, Marvel, *The Battle of the Crater*, 41–42.

14. Poor leadership created confusion at the Union front. When the attack began the general selected to lead it, Brig. Gen. James H. Ledlie, retired to a bombproof hospital to have a drinking session. Cavanaugh, Marvel, *The Battle of the Crater*, 3, 21–23, 41–42; Marvel, "And Fire Shall Devour Them," 125, *Burnside*, 399–405.

15. Cavanaugh, Marvel, *The Battle of the Crater*, 23, 146, 148; Trudeau, *The Last Citadel*, 111.

16. Bowley is referring to Lt. Col. Walther C. Newberry, who was commanding the 24th N.Y. (Dismounted Cavalry). Cavanaugh, Marvel, *The Battle of the Crater*, 51, 123.

17. Col. Jacob Parker Gould, 59th Mass. Vols., died in a Philadelphia hospital on August 21, 1864, from the wounds he received at the Crater. See service record of Col. J. Parker Gould, 59th Mass. Vols., Carded Records, Volunteer Organizations: Civil War.

18. Service record of Capt. George T. Woodward, 30th USCI, Carded Records, Volunteer Organizations: Civil War; the lieutenant Capt. Woodward called upon was 2nd Lt. Lewis W. Detrich. U.S. Adjutant General's Office, *Official Register*, 8: 201.

19. Marvel, "And Fire Shall Devour Them," 128; Service record of John Dudley, 30th USCI, Carded Records, Volunteer Organizations: Civil War.

20. Although Col. Delevan Bates was severely wounded in the face, he made a full recovery and returned to active duty. For his heroism on the field of battle he was awarded the rank of Brevet Brigadier General and the Medal of Honor. Maj. James C. Leeke died in the hospital on August 15, 1864. Service records of Col. Delevan Bates, Maj. James C. Leeke, 30th USCI, Carded Records, Volunteer Organizations: Civil War; U.S. Adjutant General's Office, *Official Register*, 8: 201; Cavanaugh, Marvel, *The Battle of the Crater*, 132

21. Col. Henry G. Thomas, 19th USCI, is referring to 2nd Lt. Christopher Pennell, 19th USCI. U.S. Adjutant General's Office, *Official Register,* 8: 190; Thomas, "The Colored Troops at Petersburg," in Johnson, Buel, *Battles and Leaders of the Civil War*, 4: 565; *OR*, 1st ser., 80 (1): 598–99.

22. Cavanaugh, Marvel, *The Battle of the Crater*, 58–59, 87–89.

23. After the battle controversy raged over who had saved the flag of the 30th USCI. Brig. Gen. Adelbert Ames to Maj. William Russell, 31 July 1864, Lt. Col. H. A. Oakman to Capt. George A. Hicks, 4 August 1864, Miscellaneous Records, 30th USCI, Regimental Books and Papers USCT, RG 94, NA.

24. Cavanaugh, Marvel, *The Battle of the Crater*, 56, 96, 105–106; Marvel, "And Fire Shall Devour Them," 127–28, 132.

25. Marvel, "And Fire Shall Devour Them," 118–40.

26. Cavanaugh, Marvel, *The Battle of the Crater*, 95.

27. Marvel, "And Fire Shall Devour Them," 132.

28. Hauptman, *Between Two Fires*, 143–44, 153–57.

29. Brig. Gen. William Francis Bartlett commanded the 1st Brigade of the 1st Division of the Ninth Corps. Bartlett's brigade was the second brigade involved in the Union attack. When the attack failed, Bartlett rallied the remnants of the Union force in the Crater. In contrast to Bowley's account, Matthew Spear, a Massachusetts soldier, reported that Gen. Bartlett's cork leg was smashed when a Confederate shell dislodged a large boulder, which crashed into it. Trudeau, *The Last Citadel*, 110, 123–24, 490.

Chapter 7. A Prisoner of War

1. Cavanaugh and Marvel give the casualties for the Ninth Corps as being 473 killed and mortally wounded, 1,646 wounded, and 1,356 missing, giving a total of 3,475. Brig. Gen. Ferrero's black division suffered by far the highest casualty rate. Ferrero lost 209 killed and mortally wounded, 697 wounded, and 421 missing, giving a total of 1,327 casualties. Cavanaugh, Marvel, *The Battle of the Crater*, 128; *OR*, 1st ser., 40 (1): 246–50.

2. Brig. Gen. William Mahone was ordered by Lee to rush two brigades to Blandford cemetery to check the federal advance. Cavanaugh, Marvel, *The Battle of the Crater*, 53–56, 125–26.

3. Capt. William H. Seagrave was hospitalized, imprisoned, and paroled in October 1864. He died of his wounds in November 1865. See service record of William H. Seagrave, 30th USCI, Carded Records, Volunteer Organizations: Civil War.

4. Bowley is referring to Hancock's 2nd Corps May 12, 1864, attack against the "mule shoe" salient at the Battle of Spotsylvania. McPherson, *Ordeal by Fire*, 418–19; Matter, *If It Takes All Summer*, Chapters 13–16; at Cold Harbor on June 3, 1864, Grant ordered 50,000 federal troops to attack three miles of strongly entrenched Confederate lines. The attacks were repulsed with heavy casualties. McPherson, *Battle Cry of Freedom*, 734–36.

5. Brig. Gen. William Mahone sent his old brigade (6th, 12th, 16th, 41st, 61st Va. Vols.), under the command of Col. David A. Weisiger, to stop the Union advance. Trudeau, *The Last Citadel*, 117, 499; Cavanaugh, Marvel, *The Battle of the Crater*, 125–26.

6. Bowley is referring to Capt. Franklin B. Quimby, Co. F., 30th USCI. The two lieutenants Bowley is referring to are 1st Lt. Charles B. Sanders and 1st Lt. Samuel B.

Smith, 30th USCI. See service record of Franklin B. Quimby, 30th USCI, Carded Records, Volunteer Organizations: Civil War; Abbott, *Prison Life in the South*, 367; U.S. Adjutant General's Office, *Official Register*, 8: 201; List of Commissioned Officers, Descriptive Book, 30th USCI, Regimental Books and Papers USCT, RG 94, NA.

7. Lt. Charles B. Sanders' military career had some similarity to that of his close friend, Freeman Bowley. A mechanic from Lowell, Mass., Sanders joined the 13th N.H. Vols. as an 18-year-old on August 11, 1862. Discharged from that regiment on February 24, 1864, with the rank of corporal, he was mustered into the 30th USCI on March 3, 1864, with the rank of lieutenant. He was captured along with Bowley at the Crater on July 30, 1864. He served in the same prisons as Bowley until they were both paroled at N. E. Ferry, N.C., March 1, 1865. Like Bowley he returned to the 30th USCI after a period of recuperation. However, chronic attacks of diarrhea forced him to resign early in July 1865. Service record of Charles B. Sanders, 30th USCI, Carded Records, Volunteer Organizations: Civil War; Lt. C. B. Sanders to Adj. Gen. USA, July 2, 1865, S-96 1864, Letters Received, ser. 360, CTD, RG 94, NA.

8. A homespun garment was one that was spun or wrought at home. Therefore, it was generally coarse, plain, and homely. Sorghum is a grass, varieties of which include millet and a type of sugarcane. Bowley is probably referring to sorghum molasses syrup being used as a sauce to cover his dumplings. Huckleberry dumplings were masses of boiled or baked dough enclosing berries from the huckleberry shrub. Huckleberry is a low-level shrub that produces dark blue to black edible berries. Fowler and Fowler, *The Concise Oxford Dictionary*, 373, 571, 579, 1201; Mathews, *A Dictionary of Americanisms*, 821–22, 846–47, 1597; Gove, *Webster's Third New International Dictionary*, 701, 1083, 1098.

9. Bowley has confused Lt. Col. Buffalo for Lt. Col. Martin P. Buffum. See service record of Col. Elisha G. Marshall, 4th N.Y. Heavy Artillery, Col. Stephen Minot Weld Jr., 56th Mass. Vols., Col. Daniel White, 31st Maine Vols., Lt. Col. Martin P. Buffum, 4th R. I. Vols., Carded Records, Volunteer Organizations: Civil War; Boatner, *Civil War Dictionary*, 513, 900, 913.

10. Cavanaugh, Marvel, *The Battle of the Crater*, 128.

11. The newspaper report contained inaccuracies. The losses of the 30th USCI were significantly exaggerated. Service record of Delevan Bates, James C. Leeke, George T. Woodard, Franklin B. Quimby, William H. Seagrave, John Q. Adams, and Silas W. Edgerton, 30th USCI, Carded Records, Volunteer Organizations: Civil War; Descriptive Book, 30th USCI, Regimental Books and Papers USCT, RG 94, NA.

Chapter 8. A Journey into Captivity

1. The casualties of Co. A, 30th USCI, were 5 enlisted men killed, 0 enlisted men wounded, and 4 enlisted men missing in action. Descriptive Book, 30th USCI, Regimental Books and Papers USCT, RG 94, NA.

2. Bryce Suderow supports Bowley's claim that the massacre of black troops at the Crater was worse than the massacre at Fort Pillow. Suderow, "The Battle of the Crater," 224, 219–24; Levin, "'On That Day You Commanded the Full Measure of Your Fame,'"

23–24; Glatthaar, *Forged in Battle*, 156–57; Trudeau, *Like Men of War*, 168–69; Cimprich, "The Fort Pillow Massacre: Assessing the Evidence," in Smith, *Black Soldiers in Blue*, 150–68; Trudeau, *The Last Citadel*, 117, 498. Col. David Weisiger's brigade consisted of the 6th, 12th, 16th, 41st, and 61st Va. Vols. Cavanaugh, Marvel, *The Battle of the Crater*, 125–26.

3. Bernard, "The Battle of the Crater," 11–15.

4. Cavanaugh, Marvel, *The Battle of the Crater*, 94.

5. Bowley appears to have significantly exaggerated Union losses. *OR*, 1st ser., 40 (1): 247–48; Regimental Descriptive Book, 30th USCI, Regimental Books and Papers USCT, RG 94, NA.

6. "Sweet-tater custard" is sweet potato custard. Mathews, *A Dictionary of Americanisms*, 1591.

7. Originally saleratus was a name used for potassium bicarbonate. Later it was used to refer to sodium bicarbonate, or "baking soda." Mathews, *A Dictionary of Americanisms*, 1447.

8. Bowley is referring to Lt. Jacob T. Shull, 28th USCI, and Lt. Henry A. Downing, 31st USCI. See U.S. Adjutant General's Office, *Official Register*, 8: 199, 202.

9. Prisoners who were recent arrivals were called "fresh fish." Speer, *Portals to Hell*, 315.

10. Brig. Gen. James Brewton Rickett's force suffered heavy losses at Monocacy, Md., on July 9, 1864. Boatner, *Civil War Dictionary*, 560–61, 699–70, 887; McPherson, *Ordeal by Fire*, 428–29; Warner, *Generals in Blue*, 403–4, 535–36.

11. Bowley is referring to Capt. Franklin B. Quimby, 30th USCI. Affidavit of John P. Pette, September 1, 1865, in Q-6 1864, Letters Received, ser. 360. See service record of Franklin B. Quimby, 30th USCI, Carded Records, Volunteer Organizations: Civil War.

12. The largest Confederate prison, Andersonville, Ga., suffered from overcrowding and a high death rate. Of the 45,000 men imprisoned there, 13,000 died. The prison held only enlisted men. McPherson, *Battle Cry of Freedom*, 796; Speer, *Portals to Hell*, 261; Marvel, *Andersonville: The Last Depot*.

Chapter 9. The Richland Jail, Columbia, South Carolina

1. A few weeks after Bowley's arrival, the Richland Jail was holding 132 officers, 99 privates, 27 Confederate deserters, and some political prisoners and common criminals. On the first floor naval officers were held along with deserters and conscripts; on the second floor, army officers; and on the third floor, criminals and runaway slaves. Weld, *War Diary*, 364; Speer, *Portals to Hell*, 270.

2. Speer, *Portals to Hell*, 266–68; Hesseltine, *Civil War Prisons,* 159–61.

3. Bowley is quoting from the Joint Resolution of the Confederate Congress. Glatthaar, *Forged in Battle*, 201; Smith, *Black Soldiers in Blue*, 45; *OR*, 2nd ser., 5: 940–41.

4. Bowley is referring to Capt. Shad Harris, 3rd Tenn. Cav. (Union). Harris, a deserter from the Confederate Army, was condemned to death, but this sentence was

commuted to imprisonment by President Davis. Captain Harris was held in irons and subject to close confinement. In retaliation the federal authorities placed Capt. Frank Battle, 12th Tenn. Vols., in irons and close confinement. See *OR*, 2nd ser., 6: 416, 7: 16–17, 1175, 1229, 1263–64, 8: 6, 159, 208, 225; Service record of Shad [Shadrock] Harris, 3rd Tenn. Cav., Carded Records, Volunteer Organizations: Civil War.

5. Failed attacks on Fort Wagner, S.C., took place on the July 10 and 18, 1863. The naval night attack on Fort Sumter on September 8, 1863, failed with the loss of 125 men. Boatner, *Civil War Dictionary*, 300–301.

6. Bowley is referring to Chaplain James H. Fowler, 33rd USCI. U.S. Adjutant General's Office, *Official Register*, 8: 204.

7. Bowley is referring to the escape of 1st Lt. George W. Williams, 43rd USCI, and 2nd Lt. William B. Pierce, 31st Maine Infantry. Williams made his way to the South Carolina coast, where he was picked up by a U.S. gunboat. After he was rescued, Williams reported that Pierce might have drowned. Service record of George W. Williams, 31st Maine Infantry, Carded Records, Volunteer Organizations: Civil War; U.S. Adjutant General's Office, *Official Register*, 1: 58, 8: 216; Weld, *War Diary*, 377; Sherman, *Battle of the Crater*, 29–30.

8. The captain Bowley is referring to is Capt. John B. Dibeler, 45th Pa. Vols. U.S. Adjutant General's Office, *Official Register*, 3: 847.

9. The senior captain Bowley is referring to is Capt. Elmer C. Dicey, 1st Mich. Sharp Shooters. U.S. Department of the Interior, National Park Service, "Civil War Soldiers and Sailors System."

10. Local newspapers sensationalized the numerous escape attempts and criticized Capt. Senn's "indulgent" attitude toward federal prisoners. This newspaper coverage contributed to the public demand for prisoners to be housed in a more secure location. These demands, together with increases in prisoner numbers, resulted in prisoners being moved to Camp Sorghum, located two miles from Columbia. Prison escapes did not abate until the prisoners were finally moved to an even more secure location, Camp Asylum, located in South Carolina State Hospital, Columbia. *Tri-Weekly South Carolinian*, September 27, 1864; Speer, *Portals to Hell*, 270–72. Prisoners were able to purchase copies of the local papers; Weld, *War Diary*, 374–75. Capt. R. D. Senn commanded the Company Post Guard, Columbia, South Carolina. Speer, *Portals to Hell*, 270.

11. Weld, *War Diary*, 364.

12. Brig. Gen. Hugh Judson Kilpatrick made an ill-fated raid on Gen. Hood's lines of communication south of Atlanta during August 18–22, 1864. Kilpatrick's force consisted of soldiers from the 2nd, 3rd, and 5th Kentucky Cavalry. See Warner, *Generals in Blue*, 266–67; Boatner, *Civil War Dictionary*, 459–62; Dyer, *Compendium*, 1: 717.

13. Weld, *War Diary*, 390; Leonard, *All the Daring of the Soldier*, 239–40, 250–52, 271.

14. Weld, *War Diary*, 367; Hamersly, *The Records of Living Officers*, 114; Soley, *The Sailor Boys*, 265–269.

15. Lt. Samuel W. Preston and Lt. Benjamin H. Porter were killed during the assault

on Fort Fisher on January 15, 1865. Soley, *The Sailor Boys*, 268–69; Selfridge, "The Navy at Fort Fisher," Thomas, "The Colored Troops at Petersburg," in Johnson, Buel, *Battles and Leaders*, 4: 563–67, 655–62; Weld, *War Diary*, note 364.

16. "Kaintuck" refers to Kentucky.

17. The song the prisoners were singing was Henry Clay Work's humorous song satirizing the poor, reluctant draftee, "Our Jimmy Has Gone for to Live in a Tent." Heaps and Heaps, *The Singing Sixties*, 101–102.

18. A common load used by Confederate soldiers using cal. .69 muskets was three buckshot placed behind a regular-sized musket ball. Boatner, *Civil War Dictionary*, 94.

19. "Graybacks" was a name for body lice. Speer, *Portals to Hell*, 316.

20. Bowley wrote to his sweetheart, Flora E. Pepper.

21. "Galvanized Yankees" was the term originally used to refer to federal prisoners who enlisted in the Confederate Army. However, the term was also used to refer to U. S. volunteers who were recruited from the ranks of rebel soldiers in federal prisons. Confederate authorities authorized special recruiting officers to visit prisons in South Carolina and Georgia and recruit Union prisoners in early 1864. Marvel, *Andersonville: The Last Depot*, 223, 300, note 27; Boatner, *Civil War Dictionary*, 322; Weld, *War Diary*, 383.

22. Weld, *War Diary*, 385.

23. Hesseltine, *Civil War Prisons,* 163–66; Abbott, *Prison Life in the South*, 138–41.

Chapter 10. Camp Asylum, Columbia, South Carolina

1. Speer, *Portals to Hell*, 270–72.

2. Glazier, *The Capture,* 194–95; U.S. Adjutant General's Office, *Official Register*, 1: 94–95.

3. Bowley is referring to soldiers from the South Carolina State Reserves and Williams' Battalion (South Carolina) State Reserves. *OR*, 1st ser., 44: 876, 2nd ser., 7: 886; Speer, *Portals to Hell*, 271; Boatner, *Civil War Dictionary*, 870.

4. "Dixie," composed by Daniel D. Emmett in 1859, became the anthem of the South. "The Bonnie Blue Flag," a Confederate song that was first sung in the theaters of New Orleans and Richmond in 1861, is attributed to comedian Harry Macarthy. It became the most popular song in the South next to "Dixie." President Davis arrived in Columbia on October 5, 1864. Heaps and Heaps, *The Singing Sixties*, 45–50, 54–56; Commager, *The Blue and the Gray*, 563–54; Boatner, *Civil War Dictionary*, 73, 149, 242; *Tri-Weekly South Carolinian*, October 6, 1864.

5. Allen Abbott published a book about his prison camp experiences. Abbott, *Prison Life in the South*, 151, 367; Fabian, *The Unvarnished Truth*, 117–18, 120, 124, 139; U.S. Adjutant General's Office, *Official Register*, 2: 347; Service record of Allen O. Abbott, 19th N.Y. Cav., Warren Shedd, 30th Ill. Vols., Thomas J. Thorp, 19th N.Y. Cav., William C. Wilson, 104th N. Y. Vols., Carded Records, Volunteer Organizations: Civil War.

6. The prisoners' government of Camp Sorghum was similar to that which existed in the Richland Jail. Weld, *War Diary*, 361–62.

7. "Milroy's Thieves" were captured when Lt. Gen. Richard S. Ewell defeated Maj. Gen. Robert Huston Milroy at Winchester, June 13–15, 1863. Because of the large number of soldiers of German extraction, the Eleventh Corps became known as "the German Corps." The Eleventh Corps was organized in September 1862 from Maj. Gen. Franz Sigel's First Corps, Army of Virginia. The phrase "I fights mit Sigel," is taken from the title of a popular song and poem. It became the slogan for the German soldiers. Satirical versions of "I fights mit Sigel" were used to ridicule soldiers of German descent. The "First Corps Irish" are from the Irish Brigade from the 1st Div., Second Corps. See Warner, *Generals in Blue*, 326; Boatner, *Civil War Dictionary*, 193–94, 427, 761, 937; Dyer, *Compendium*, 1: 349–50, 827–28; Burton, *Melting Pot Soldiers*, 111, 184.

8. "Virginia Lowlands" is probably a parody of "Seven Days Fight from June 26th to July 4th 1862," by James Smith, Co. H., published by Johnson, Song Publisher, Philadelphia, n.d. The tune is from "In the Louisiana Lowlands." Library of Congress, "American Singing: Nineteenth-Century Song Sheets."

The rout of the Eleventh ("Dutch") Corps, under the command of Maj. Gen. Oliver O. Howard, at Chancellorsville, May 2, 1863, reinforced negative opinions about the combat capabilities of German American soldiers. McPherson, *Battle Cry of Freedom*, 638–45.

9. A half-moon house was an outhouse or privy. Cassidy, *Dictionary of American Regional English*, 878.

10. "Regulars" were officers who were part of the United States' permanent standing army; On February 9, 1864, 108 prisoners led by Col. Abel D. Streight used the "Great Yankee Tunnel" to break out of Libby Prison, Richmond. Speer, *Portals to Hell*, 232–33.

11. The "Chickamauga Gang" was composed of soldiers captured at Chickamauga, Tennessee, September 19–20, 1863. McPherson, *Ordeal by Fire*, 335–38.

12. The "Plymouth Pilgrims" were captured at Plymouth, N.C., April 17–20, 1864. Boatner, *Civil War Dictionary*, 656. "Pilgrims" is an ironical reference to the Puritan Pilgrims who established a colony at Plymouth, Mass., in 1620.

13. At Olustee, Fla., February 20, 1864, Gen. Truman Seymour's force was defeated by a Confederate force led by Gen. Joseph Finegan. Adams, *On the Altar of Freedom*, 108–109; Trudeau, *Like Men of War*, 129–55; U.S. Adjutant General's Office, *Official Register*, 8: 207. Bogle arrived suffering severely from wounds, which the Confederate medical staff refused to treat because he commanded black troops. Sherman's advance, not repeated escape attempts, forced Confederate authorities to move Bogle and other Columbia prisoners to Macon. Marvel, *Andersonville: The Last Depot*, 33, 41–42, 221–22.

14. Some groups, or "clans," of prisoners took their names from the battle in which they were captured. These included "Wilderness" (Wilderness, Va., May 5–7, 1864); "Cold Harbor Heavies" (Cold Harbor, Va., May 31–June 12, 1864; the Union heavy

artillery regiments involved in the battle of Cold Harbor included 1st Maine H. A., 1st Mass. H. A., 7th, 8th, 14th, and 15th N.Y. H. A., and the 1st Vt. H. A.); "Big Shanty's" (Big Shanty, Ga., June 6–9, 1864); "Resacs" (Battle of Resaca, Ga., May 13–16, 1864); "Hunter's Drewry's Bluffs" (Drewry's Bluff, Va., May 16, 1864); "Monocacy's Hundred Dayzers" (Monocacy, Md., July 9, 1864; these prisoners were state militia men who were offered for service for 100 days. See note 14, Chapter 3); "Atlantas" (Atlanta, Ga., July 20–Sept. 8, 1864); the "Wilson and Kautz's Raiders" took part in the ill-fated cavalry raid by Gen. James H. Wilson and Brig. Gen. August V. Kautz, June 22–July 1, 1864, on the Weldon and Lynchburg Railroad, Va.; the "Second Corps Men" were captured when Gen. David Birney launched an ill-fated attack on Petersburg's southern defenses on June 22, 1864; the "Stoneman Raiders" were captured in July 1864 when Sherman sent Gens. Stoneman and McCook on an ill-fated raid into Georgia and Alabama. Dyer, *Compendium*, 1: 705–706, 708, 715, 736, 943, 946; Trudeau, *The Last Citadel*, 68–69, 68–80, 87–90; Boatner, *Civil War Dictionary*, 801–2.

15. During Stoneman's raid, Gen. McCook's men took the best mules captured from the Confederate forces as remounts. Starr, *The Union Cavalry in the Civil War*, 2: 471.

16. A pone is cornbread that has been baked and then shaped into large, oval cakes by hand. A loaf or patty of cornbread is also called a pone. Mathews, *A Dictionary of Americanisms*, 1280–81; Gove, *Webster's Third New International Dictionary*, 2133.

17. "Fox and geese" is a board game played using pegs or checkers. Faro banks was a popular gambling game played with cards. During the game a permanent banker dealt the cards from a dealing box. Chuck-a-luck was a banking, gambling game played with players betting on the fall of dice. Robertson, *Soldiers Blue & Gray*, 89, 95; Wiley, *The Life of Billy Yank*, 50; Gove, *Webster's Third New International Dictionary*, 900; Speer, *Portals to Hell*, 315; Mathews, *A Dictionary of Americanisms*, 323.

18. Bowley is referring to Maj. Elias Griswold, who succeeded Lt. Col. R. S. Means in command of Confederate prisons in Columbia. Griswold was eventually removed from his position because of his inefficiency and for allowing prisoners to escape during their movement from Columbia to Charlotte, N.C. Bowley's unfounded criticism of Brig. Gen. John Henry Winder, the Confederate Provost Marshal General, reflects a view of Winder strongly held by Union prisoners of war. *OR*, 2nd ser., 8: 450, 461–62; Speer, *Portals to Hell*, 272; Abbott, *Prison Life in the South*, 168–69; Marvel, *Andersonville: The Last Depot*, ix–xi, 12–13, 34–35, 87; Boatner, *Civil War Dictionary*, 940–41; Wakelyn, *Biographical Dictionary of the Confederacy*, 422–23.

19. Unable to stop Gen. Sherman's advance, Lt. Gen. William Joseph Hardee, the commander of the Department of South Carolina, Georgia, and Florida, evacuated Savannah on December 18, 1864, and Charleston in January 1865.

Bowley is referring to the defeat of Lt. Gen. John B. Hood at Nashville, Tenn., December 15–16, 1864; the failure of the first assault on Fort Fisher, N.C., December 7–27, 1864; preparations for the successful second attack on Fort Fisher, December 15–16, 1864; and Maj. Gen. Philip H. Sheridan's defeat of Gen. Early at Fisher's Hill, Va., September 22, 1864. Boatner, *Civil War Dictionary*, 280–81, 292–93, 374, 579–82.

20. *New York Herald*, September 24, 1864.

21. Samuel Byers was adjutant in the 5th Iowa Infantry, not 50th Iowa Infantry. He wrote a book about his prison experiences, *What I Saw in Dixie*. The text of "Sherman's March to the Sea" is found in Roach, *The Prisoner of War*, 174–75; U.S. Department of the Interior, National Park Service, "Civil War Soldiers and Sailors System."

22. "Crow's nest" may allude to "Jim Crow," a popular term for African Americans in the nineteenth century. Jim Crow was depicted as a fun loving, childlike character. This description may have originated from the title of a popular minstrel song first performed in the 1830s. Hurwitz, *An Encyclopedic Dictionary of American History*, 364. The entrance to an army post is known as a "crow's nest." Dickson, *War Slang*, 8.

23. Abbott, *Prison Life in the South*, 171–72.

24. The phrase "Sherman's 'Bummers'" refers to Sherman's foragers, who were active during his March to the Sea and his campaign in the Carolinas. The deterioration of the war situation forced Confederate authorities to employ cadets from the Arsenal Academy, Columbia, S.C., to guard the prisoners at Camps Sorghum and Asylum. There is no record of Arsenal cadets suffering heavy casualties in the fighting that occurred in the vicinity of Branchville in February 1865. However, they were active in the defense of Columbia, and in December 1864 they defended Confederate lines near Pococtaligo, S.C. Lyman, *Civil War Wordbook*, 151; Boatner, *Civil War Dictionary*, 105; *OR*, 1st ser., 44: 443–48, 47 (1): 19–24, 2nd ser., 8: 451–52; Conrad, *The Young Lions*, 38, 45, 112, 118–24, 131.

Chapter 11. The Confederacy in Retreat

1. Bowley is probably referring to Capt. W. H. Hatch, the assistant to the Confederate Commissioner for Prisoner Exchange, Col. Robert Ould. *OR*, 1st ser., 24 (1): 231, 2nd ser., 8: 92.

2. *OR*, 2nd ser., 8: 449–57.

3. Brig. Gen. Hugh J. Kilpatrick commanded Sherman's cavalry division during his March to the Sea. Warner, *Generals in Blue*, 266–67.

4. *OR*, 2nd ser., 8: 453; Byers, *What I Saw in Dixie*, 78–81.

5. Scrub oak is a stunted variety of oak that often overgrows relatively barren, rocky land. Mathews, *A Dictionary of Americanisms*, 121, 1480.

6. Officers who escaped from Columbia were often assisted by "friendly Negroes." Abbott, *Prison Life in the South*, 207–18; Hadley, *Seven Months a Prisoner*, 118–19; Roach, *The Prisoner of War*, 155–59.

7. In the mountain regions of western North Carolina, networks of pro-Union Southerners helped escaped Union prisoners of war flee the Confederacy. Many of these escapees came from Camp Sorghum, Columbia, S.C. Crawford, "The Dynamics of Mountain Unionism: Federal Volunteers of Ashe County, North Carolina," and Inscoe, "Moving Through Deserter Country," in Noe, Wilson, *The Civil War in Appalachia*, 55–77, 160–65.

8. Maj. Gen. Joseph Wheeler's Cavalry Corps covered Gen. Joseph E. Johnston's retreat through South Carolina. Boatner, *Civil War Dictionary*, 371, 910.

9. Wilmington, N.C., fell to Maj. Gen. Alfred H. Terry on February 22, 1865. Dyer, *Compendium*, 1: 824; Warner, *Generals in Blue*, 497–98.

10. Hadley, *Seven Months a Prisoner*, 87.

11. Hoecake is a large, flat cake of bread made from mixing salt and water with corn meal. Mathews, *A Dictionary of Americanisms*, 813.

12. Ash-pone is a pone (a loaf or patty) of cornbread baked on an open fireplace in a container covered or surrounded with ashes. The provost guard are soldiers who are appointed to do police and guard duties. Provost guard duty often involved guarding prisoners. Mathews, *A Dictionary of Americanisms*, 46, 1322; Dupuy et al., *A Dictionary of Military Terms*, 177.

13. Applejack or applejohn is an alcoholic drink made from apples. Mathews, *A Dictionary of Americanisms*, 38.

Chapter 12. Paroled and Home in Worcester, Massachusetts

1. Sherman's advance forced Confederate authorities to move the Andersonville prisoners to Florence, S.C., in September 1864 and then in February 1865 to Raleigh, N.C. Speer, *Portals to Hell*, 265, 281.

2. The commander of the Confederate post at Goldsboro, N.C., was Col. Stephen D. Poole, Co. H., 1st N.C. Artillery (10th State Troops). Compiled Service Record of Col. Stephen D. Poole, 1st N.C. Artillery (10th State Troops), Records of Confederate Soldiers Who Served in Organizations from the State of North Carolina, RG 109, NA. Microfilm M270, roll 57.

3. The parole agreement that Bowley refers to was negotiated between Maj. Gen. J. A. Dix and Maj. Gen. D. H. Hill in July 1862. A parolee was a prisoner of war who was released on the understanding that he would not wage war until he was exchanged. The names of parole prisoners were placed on parole lists and each side kept a copy of these lists. In addition, soldiers signed a parole pledge, which was similar to the pledge signed by Bowley. Paroled soldiers generally carried their copy of the pledge with them. By November 1864 the South became so burdened with prisoners of war that it began sending paroled prisoners to the North without a man-to-man exchange. *OR*, 2nd ser., 4: 265–68, 5: 431; Boatner, *Civil War Dictionary*, 270–71, 619–20; Speer, *Portals to Hell*, Chapter 5.

4. Lt. Col. W. H. Hatch was the Confederate assistant agent for exchange at Northeast River, N.C., in mid-February 1865. *OR*, 2nd ser., 8: 449–50.

5. "C.S. Sub. Dep't. Tax in kind" refers to "Confederate States Subsistence Department Tax in kind." The Confederate Subsistence Department was responsible for the subsistence of all prisoners of war. See report of Brig. Gen. J. H. Winder on military prison at Florence, S.C. *OR*, 2nd ser., 8: 137–39.

6. Carter claims he was wounded at Fort Harrison, Va., September 29–30, 1864; Hatcher's Run, Va., October 27–28, 1864; Fort Fisher action near Sugar Loaf Battery, N.C., January 19, 1865. Service record of James H. Carter, 30th USCI, Carded Records, Volunteer Organizations: Civil War; Dyer, *Compendium*, 1: 823, 954, 956.

7. Only five officers of the 30th USCI died in service. Of these only Maj. James C.

Leeke was a member of Co. H. Lt. Thomas J. Wood, Co. C, died on November 1, 1864, of wounds received in action at Petersburg, Va. Service record of James C. Leeke, 30th USCI, Carded Records, Volunteer Organizations: Civil War; U.S. Adjutant General's Office, *Official Register*, 8: 201.

8. Bowley is referring to Surgeon Andrew M. Peables, 30th USCI. U.S. Adjutant General's Office, *Official Register*, 8: 201.

9. Maj. Gen. Robert F. Hoke's division included Brig. Gen. Thomas L. Clingman's North Carolina's Brigade. Clingman's brigade fought at the Crater and the second attack on Fort Fisher. Howe, *The Petersburg Campaign*, 144; Boatner, *Civil War Dictionary*, 293–94, 404–405.

10. Soldiers' Refreshment Rooms were established by charitable organizations, principally the Sanitary Commission. They were run mainly by women. Paludan, *A People's Contest*, 353–55; *OR*, 1st ser., 38 (1): 182.

11. Bowley is referring to Flora Ella Pepper, his future wife. Civil War Pension File, Freeman S. Bowley, 30th USCI, RG 15, NA.

12. Pvt. Obediah Foster, 30th USCI, was killed on the picket line at Cox's Bridge, Neuse River, N.C., March 24, 1864. Regimental Descriptive Book, 30th USCI, Regimental Books and Papers USCT, RG 94, NA; Dyer, *Compendium*, 1: 825, 2: 1728.

Chapter 13. With the Regiment in North Carolina

1. When excess numbers of Union soldiers were paroled from the eastern camps they were sent to Camp Parole in Annapolis, Md. The prisoners stayed there until documentation was complete officially exchanging them. Speer, *Portals to Hell*, 104.

2. The 30th USCI lost 54 missing in action and 22 killed or mortally wounded. Regimental Descriptive Book, 30th USCI, Regimental Books and Papers USCT, RG 94, NA. For discussion of the rout and massacre of black troops at the Crater see Cavanaugh, Marvel, *The Battle of the Crater*, 88–89, 91; Suderow, "The Battle of the Crater," 222–24.

3. The 30th USCI was not directly involved in the engagements at Chaffin's Farm and Fort Harrison in September 1864. Record of Events, Co. H, 30th USCI, Compiled Records Showing Service of Military Units in Volunteer Union Organizations, RG 94, NA. Microfilm M594, roll 208. (Hereafter cited as Record of Events, Co. H, 30th USCI); Dyer, *Compendium*, 2: 1728.

4. Dyer, *Compendium*, 2: 1728.

5. Boatner, *Civil War Dictionary*, 384–85; Trudeau, *Like Men of War*, 300–304. Service record of Delevan Bates, 30th USCI, Carded Records, Volunteer Organizations: Civil War.

6. The 30th USCI took part in the first and second expeditions against Fort Fisher. Hoke's Division was involved in resisting the two federal assaults. Boatner, *Civil War Dictionary*, 292–94; Trudeau, *Like Men of War*, 358–64; Dyer, *Compendium*, 2: 1728.

7. Composed entirely of black troops, the 25th Corps was created on December 3,

1865. The badge of the corps was a diamond (lozenge) on a square. Dyer, *Compendium*, 1: 403–404; Boatner, *Civil War Dictionary*, 201.

8. General Terry employed Paine's 3rd Division to prevent Hoke's army from breaking through federal lines. While resisting this attack, Capt. George A. Herbert, Co. H, 30th USCI, was wounded. The attack on Fort Fisher Bowley is referring to was led by Col. N. Martin Curtis, 3d N.Y. Vols. *OR*, 1st ser., 46 (1): 398; List of Commissioned Officers, Regimental Descriptive Book, 30th USCI, Regimental Books and Papers USCT, RG 94, NA; Selfridge, "The Navy at Fort Fisher," in Johnson, Buel, *Battles and Leaders*, 4: 661; Trudeau, *Like Men of War*, 358–64.

9. Two members of the 30th USCI were killed by the explosion of the Fort Fisher magazine. Descriptive rolls, Cos. A–K, Regimental Descriptive Book, 30th USCI, Regimental Books and Papers USCT, RG 94, NA; Trudeau, *Like Men of War*, 362–65.

10. Gen. Joseph E. Johnston surrendered to Gen. William T. Sherman at Bennett's House, Durham Station, N.C., on April 26, 1865. Dyer, *Compendium*, 1: 826, 965. Gen. Sherman reviewed the 3rd Division of the 10th Army Corps on April 19, 1865. Barrett, *The Civil War in North Carolina*, 344; Record of Events, Co. H, 30th USCI; Dyer, *Compendium*, 1: 362.

11. The Dismal Swamp Canal was opened in 1828. It connected the Pasquotank River in North Carolina with the Elizabeth River in Virginia. Carbone, *The Civil War in Coastal North Carolina*, xxi; Cecelski, *The Waterman's Song*, 32, 106.

12. A saleratus biscuit is one made from sodium bicarbonate, or baking soda. Mathews, *A Dictionary of Americanisms*, 1447.

13. Bowley reported for duty in his regiment on May 8, 1865. The inexperienced officer Bowley is referring to is 2nd Lt. Henry R. Dunbam. Regimental Descriptive Book, 30th USCI, Special Order No. 16, H.Q. 30th USCI, 1 June 1865, Order Book Co. H, 30th USCI, Regimental Books and Papers USCT, RG 94, NA.

14. In March 1865, Lt. Henry B. Howell, 30th USCI, recruited former slaves in the vicinity of Wilmington, N.C. See Regimental Descriptive Roll, Descriptive Book, 30th USCI, Regimental Books and Papers USCT, RG 94, NA.

15. Bucking and gagging was a common form of punishment used in the Union Army. It involved having a piece of wood or a bayonet placed in the mouth and a string tied behind the ears to keep it in position. The offender was then seated on the ground with his knees drawn up. A stick of wood was run through the legs, and his arms were placed under the stick on either side of the knees. His hands were then tied in front. Robertson, *Soldiers Blue & Gray*, 133.

16. In the summer and fall of 1864 a serious epidemic of yellow fever occurred in the Beaufort and New Bern area. There was considerable fear of future outbreaks occurring in the summer and spring of 1865. Barrett, *The Civil War in North Carolina*, 225; Browning, Smith, *Letters from a North Carolina Unionist*, xxi, 228–33, 235, 240–41; Farnham, King, "'The March of the Destroyer,'" 435–83.

17. The hostility Col. Poole displayed to black troops was commonplace in North Carolina. See Alexander, *North Carolina Faces the Freedmen*, 9–10.

18. The movements for the 30th USCI were Goldsboro (May 1–June 4, 1865) and Morehead City (June 4–Sept. 20, 1865). See Record of Events, Co. H, 30th USCI; Dyer, *Compendium*, 2: 1728.

19. William Blair argues that during Reconstruction African Americans adopted a new civic calendar. In the South, Independence Day became a black holiday for over a decade. Blair, *Cities of the Dead*, 23–48.

Beaufort was a center of black political activity before and during the Civil War. During Reconstruction it remained a focal point for black political organization. Cecelski, *The Waterman's Song*, 177, 190–91.

The Beaufort 4th of July celebrations were held under the auspices of the Salmond P. Chase Equal Rights League. Although black soldiers were confined to barracks, one soldier, A. H. Galloway, delivered a speech at the celebrations claiming equal rights for the freedmen. African American residents of Beaufort also held pro-Union national day celebrations on July 4, 1863. Alexander, *North Carolina Faces the Freedmen*, 16; Browning, Smith, *Letters from a North Carolina Unionist*, xx, 135–36.

20. The 30th USCI arrived at Roanoke Island on October 26, 1865. The movement of the 30th USCI to Roanoke Island may have been partly a response to fears of racial conflict. Fearful of racial tension in the cities and towns of North Carolina, Gen. Thomas H. Ruger, commander of the Department of North Carolina, wrote to President Andrew Johnson and Gen. George C. Meade requesting that black troops be removed from populated areas of tension to forts and depots on the more remote coastlands. Record of Events, Co. H, 30th USCI; Alexander, *North Carolina Faces the Freedmen*, 9, 12.

21. Co. H served on detached duty in Edenton, N.C., from October 27, 1865, until December 7, 1865. See Morning Report Book, Co. H, 30th USCI, and Special Order No. 8, H.Q. 30th USCI, 18 Oct. 1865, Order Book Co. H, 30th USCI, Regimental Books and Papers USCT, RG 94, NA.

22. Alexander, *North Carolina Faces the Freedmen*, 10–11.

23. Ibid., 137; Evans, *Ballots and Fence Rails*, 63.

24. On December 7, 1865, Co. H left Edenton for Roanoke Island, where it joined the rest of the regiment. See Morning Report Book, Co. H, 30th USCI, Dec. 1865, Regimental Books and Papers USCT, RG 94, NA; U.S. Adjutant General's Office, *Official Register*, 8: 201.

25. Pvt. George Uncles, a free farmer, enlisted in the 30th USCI at Baltimore as a 20–year-old on March 10, 1864. He died of disease shortly before his regiment's departure for Baltimore, Md., in mid-December 1865. Service record of George Uncles, 30th USCI, Carded Records, Volunteer Organizations: Civil War.

26. Selfridge, "The Navy at Fort Fisher," in Johnson, Buel, *Battles and Leaders*, 4: 659–60; Ellem, "The Fall of Fort Fisher: Contested Memories of the Civil War," 207–8.

27. George Uncles was a devoted son who wrote to his mother asking after her welfare and informing her of his military experiences. See George Uncles to Mother,

[undated 1864], June 1, [1864], April 9, May 11, August 22, 1865, Pension Application, Civil War Pension File, George Uncles, 30th USCI, RG 15, NA.

28. The men of the 30th USCI arrived in Baltimore on December 17, 1865. They were paid on December 20 and finally mustered out of service on Friday, December 22. Morning Report Book, Co. H, 30th USCI, Dec. 1865, Regimental Books and Papers USCT, RG 94, NA; U.S. Adjutant General's Office, *Official Register*, 8: 201.

Bibliography

Primary Sources

ARCHIVES: MANUSCRIPTS AND PHOTOGRAPHS

National Archives, Washington, D.C.

Record Group 15. Records of the Veterans Administration: Civil War and Later Pension Files

Record Group 94. Adjutant General's Office

Compiled Records Showing Service of Military Units in Volunteer Union Organizations, RG 94, NA. Microfilm M594, roll 208.

Regimental Books and Papers USCT and U.S. Volunteer Organizations

Records of Divisions of the Adjutant General's Office: Colored Troops Division

Series 360. Letters Received 1863–88 and Later

Series 370. Applications for Appointments 1863–65

Series 382. List of Persons Who Have Passed Examining Boards 1863–65

Records of the Record and Pension Office

Series 519. Carded Records, Volunteer Organizations: Civil War

Record Group 109. Records of Confederate Soldiers Who Served during the Civil War

Compiled Military Service Records for Confederate Army Volunteers, NA. Microfilm M270, roll 57.

United States Army Military History Institute, Carlisle Barracks, Pennsylvania

Special Collections Branch: American Civil War Photograph Collections

PUBLISHED SOURCES: BOOKS AND ARTICLES

Abbott, Allen O. *Prison Life in the South: Richmond, Macon, Savannah, Charleston, Columbia, Charlotte, Raleigh, Goldsborough, and Andersonville during the Years 1864 and 1865*. New York: Harper and Brothers, 1866.

Adams, Virginia M., ed. *On the Altar of Freedom: A Black Soldier's Civil War Letters from the Front.* Amherst: University of Massachusetts Press, 1991.

Berlin, Ira, ed., Joseph Reidy and Leslie S. Rowland, asst. eds. *Freedom: A Documentary History of Emancipation, 1861–1867.* Series 2, *The Black Military Experience.* New York: Cambridge University Press, 1982.

Bernard, George S. "The Battle of the Crater." *Southern Historical Society Papers*, 28 (January–December 1890): 11–15.

Bowley, F. S. *A Boy Lieutenant*. Philadelphia: Henry Altemus, 1906. Rev. ed. Seagrave, Pia S., ed. *A Boy Lieutenant: Memoirs of Freeman S. Bowley 30th United States Colored Troops Officer*. Fredericksburg, Pa.: Sergeant Kirkland's Press, 1997.

———. "A Story by a School-Boy—with a Moral." *Springfield Daily Union*, March 20, 1869.

———. "The Battle of the Mine." *Overland Monthly Devoted to the Development of the Country*, 4 (1870): 319–27.

———. "A Dark Night on Picket." *Overland Monthly Devoted to the Development of the Country*, 5 (1870): 31–37.

———. "The Crater." *National Tribune*, November 6, 1884.

———. "Life in Prison." *National Tribune*, September 12, 1885.

———. "The Petersburg Mine." *The California Commandery of the Loyal Legion of the United States*, November 6, 1889.

———. "Seven Months in Confederate Prisons." *The California Commandery of the Loyal Legion of the United States*, May 2, 1890.

———. "A Boy Lieutenant in a Black Regiment." *National Tribune*, 1899: April 20, 27, May 4, 11, 18, 25, June 1, 8, 15, 22, 29, July 6, 13, 20, 27, August 3, 10, 17, 24, 31, September 7.

Byers, S.M.H. *What I Saw in Dixie: Sixteen Months in Rebel Prisons*. New York: Robbins and Poore, 1868.

Commager, Henry Steele, ed. *The Blue and the Gray: The Story of the Civil War as Told by Participants*. New York: Bobbs-Merrill, 1950.

Glazier, William W. *The Capture, the Prison Pen, and the Escape, Giving an Account of Prison Life in the South*. Albany, N.Y.: J. Munsell, 1866.

Grant, Ulysses S. *Personal Memoirs of U. S. Grant*. 2 vols. New York: Charles L. Webster, 1885–86.

Hadley, John V. *Seven Months a Prisoner, by "An Indiana Soldier."* Indianapolis: Meikel, 1868.

Hamersly, Lewis R. *The Records of Living Officers of the U.S. Navy and Marine Corps; with a History of Naval Operations during the Rebellion of 1861–5, and a List of the Ships and Officers Participating in the Great Battles*. Philadelphia: J. B. Lippincott, 1870.

Higginson, Thomas W. *Army Life in a Black Regiment*. New York: Houghton Mifflin, 1870. Repr. with intro. and notes by Robert D. Madison. New York: Penguin, 1997.

Highland School. *Catalogue of the Highland School*. Worcester, Mass.: July 18, 1863.

Johnson, Robert U., and Clarence C. Buel, eds. *Battles and Leaders of the Civil War*. 4 vols. New York: Century, 1887–88.

Kautz, August V. *The Company Clerk: Showing how and when to make out all the returns, reports, rolls, and other papers, and what to do with them. How to keep all the books, records, and accounts required in the administration of a company, troop, or battery in the army of the United States*. Philadelphia: J. B. Lippincott, 1863.

Looby, Christopher, ed. *The Complete Civil War Journal and Selected Letters of Thomas Wentworth Higginson*. Chicago: University of Chicago Press, 2000.

Marvin, Abijah P. *History of Worcester in the War of Rebellion*. Worcester, Mass.: published by the author, 1870.

Reid, Whitelaw. *Ohio in the War: Her Statesmen, Her Generals, and Soldiers.* Vol. 2, *The History of Her Regiments, and Other Organisations*. New York: Moore, Wilstach, and Baldwin, 1868.

Roach, Alva C. *The Prisoner of War, and How Treated.* Indianapolis: Railroad City Publishing House, 1865.

Sherman, Summer U. *Battle of the Crater and Experiences of Prison Life*. Providence: Rhode Island Soldiers and Sailors Historical Society, 1898.

Soley, James Russell. *The Sailor Boys of '61*. Boston: Estes and Lauriat, 1888.

Stevens, Michael E., ed. *As If It Were Glory: Robert K. Beecham's Civil War from the Iron Brigade to the Black Regiments*. Madison, Wis.: Madison House Publishers, 1998.

Stryker, William S. *Record of Officers and Men of New Jersey in the Civil War, 1861–1865*. 2 vols. Trenton: New Jersey Legislature, 1876.

Thomas, Henry G. "The Colored Troops at Petersburg." *Century Magazine*, 12 (September 1887): 777–82. In Johnson and Buel, eds., *Battles and Leaders of the Civil War*, 4.

Tyler, C. H. *Memorials of Lieut. George H. Walcott, Late of the 30th U.S. Colored Troops*. Boston: Massachusetts Sabbath-School Society, 1865.

Weld, Stephen Minot. *War Diary and Letters of Stephen Minot Weld, 1861–1865*. 2nd ed. Boston: Massachusetts Historical Society, 1979.

FEDERAL GOVERNMENT PUBLICATIONS

U.S. Adjutant General's Office. *Official Register of the Volunteer Force of the United States Army for the Years 1861–65*. 8 parts. Washington, D.C., 1865–67.

U.S. Congress. *Report of the Joint Committee on the Conduct of the War on the attack on Petersburg, on the 30th day of July 1864*. Washington, D.C., 1865.

U.S. War Department. *Atlas to Accompany the Official Records of the Union and Confederate Armies*. Washington, D.C.: Government Printing Office, 1891–95.

———. *The War of the Rebellion: A Compilation of the Official Records of the Union and Confederate Armies*. 128 vols. Washington, D.C.: Government Printing Office, 1880–1901

NEWSPAPERS

Aegis and Transcript 1864
National Tribune 1899
New York Herald 1864
New York Tribune 1864
Springfield Daily Union 1869
Tri-Weekly South Carolinian 1864
Worcester Daily Spy 1864

Secondary Sources

BOOKS AND ARTICLES

Aaron, Daniel. *The Unwritten Civil War: American Writers and the Civil War*. New York: Knopf, 1973.

Alexander, Roberta S. *North Carolina Faces the Freedmen: Race Relations During Presidential Reconstruction, 1865–67*. Durham, N.C.: Duke University Press, 1985.

Aman, William F., ed. *Personnel of the Civil War*. 2 vols. New York: Thomas Yoseff, 1961.

Ayers, Edward L. *Vengeance and Justice: Crime and Punishment in the 19th Century South*. New York: Oxford University Press, 1984.

Barrett, John G. *The Civil War in North Carolina*. Chapel Hill: University of North Carolina Press, 1963.

Berlin, Ira, Barbara J. Fields, Steven F. Miller, Joseph P. Reidy, and Leslie S. R. Rowland. *Slaves No More: Three Essays on Emancipation and the Civil War*. New York: Cambridge University Press, 1992.

Blair, William A. *Cities of the Dead: Contesting the Memory of the Civil War in the South, 1865–1914*. Chapel Hill: University Press of North Carolina, 2004.

Blight, David W. *Race and Reunion: The Civil War in American Memory*. Cambridge, Mass.: Harvard University Press, 2001.

———. *Beyond the Battlefield: Race Memory and the American*. Amherst: University of Massachusetts Press, 2002.

Blight, David W., and Brooks D. Simpson, eds. *Union and Emancipation: Essays on Politics and Race in the Civil War Era*. Kent, Ohio: Kent State University Press, 1997.

Boatner, Mark M. *The Civil War Dictionary*. New York: David McKay, 1959.

Bodnar, John, ed. *Bonds of Affection: Americans Define Their Patriotism*. Princeton, N.J.: Princeton University Press, 1996.

Browning, Judkin, and Michael Thomas Smith, eds. *Letters from a North Carolina Unionist: John A. Hedrick to Benjamin S. Hedrick 1862–1865*. Raleigh: North Carolina Division of Archives and History, 2001.

Burton, William L. *Melting Pot Soldiers: The Union's Ethnic Regiments*. New York: Fordham University Press, 1998.

Butler, Thomas. *Memory: History, Culture and the Mind*. New York: Basil Blackwell, 1989.

Carbone, John S. *The Civil War in Coastal North Carolina*. Raleigh: North Carolina Division of Archives and History, 2001.

Carnes, Mark C., and Clyde Griffen, eds. *Meanings for Manhood: Constructions of Masculinity in Victorian America*. Chicago: University of Chicago Press, 1990.

Cassidy, Frederick G., ed. *Dictionary of American Regional English*. Cambridge, Mass., and London: Belknap Press, 1991.

Castel, Albert. "The Fort Pillow Massacre: A Fresh Examination of the Evidence." *Civil War History,* 4 (March 1958): 37–50.

Cavanaugh, Michael A., and William Marvel. *The Petersburg Campaign: The Battle of the Crater "The Horror Pit," June 25–August 6, 1864*. Lynchburg, Va.: H. E. Howard, 1989.

Cecelski, David S. *The Waterman's Song: Slavery and Freedom in Maritime North Carolina*. Chapel Hill: University of North Carolina Press, 2001.

Cimprich, John, and Robert C. Mainfort, Jr. "Fort Pillow Revisited: New Evidence about an Old Controversy." *Civil War History*, 28 (December 1982): 293–306.

Conrad, James L. *The Young Lions: Confederate Cadets at War.* Mechanicsburg, Pa.: Stackpole Books, 1997.

Cornish, Dudly T. *The Sable Arm: Negro Troops in the Union Army, 1861–1865*. New York: W. W. Norton, 1956.

Cox, Caroline. *A Proper Sense of Honor: Service and Sacrifice in George Washington's Army*. Chapel Hill: University of North Carolina Press, 2004.

Damousi, Joy. *The Labour of Loss: Mourning, Memory, and Wartime Bereavement in Australia*. Melbourne: Cambridge University Press, 1999.

Dickson, Paul. *War Slang: Fighting Words and Phrases of Americans from the Civil War to the Gulf War*. New York: Pocket Books, 1994.

Diffley, Katherine Kathleen. *Where My Heart Is Turning Ever: Civil War Stories and Constitutional Reform, 1861–1876*. Athens: University of Georgia Press, 1992.

Dixon, Chris, and Luke Auton, eds. *War, Society, and Culture: Approaches and Issues, Selected Papers from the November 2001 Symposium Organised by the Research Group for War, Society and Culture*. Newcastle, Australia: Research Group for War, Society, and Culture, University of New South Wales, 2002.

Dupuy, Trevor N., Curt Johnson, and Grace P. Hayes, eds. *A Dictionary of Military Terms: A Guide to the Language of Warfare and Military Institutions*. New York: H. W. Wilson, 1986.

Dyer, Frederick H. *A Compendium for the War of Rebellion*. 2 vols. Des Moines: Dyer Publishing, 1908.

Ellem, Warren. "The Fall of Fort Fisher: Contested Memories of the Civil War." *The North Carolina Historical Review*, 79 (April 2002): 198–233.

Evans, W. McKee. *Ballots and Fence Rails: Reconstruction on the Lower Cape Fear*. Chapel Hill: University of North Carolina Press, 1966.

Fabian, Ann. *The Unvarnished Truth: Personal Narratives in Nineteenth-Century America*. Berkeley, Los Angeles: University of California Press, 2000.

Farnham, Thomas J., and Francis P. King. "'The March of the Destroyer': The New Bern Yellow Fever Epidemic of 1864." *The North Carolina Historical Review*, 73 (October 1996): 435–83.

Faust, Patricia L., ed. *Historical Times Illustrated Encyclopaedia of the Civil War*. New York: Harper and Row, 1986.

Fowler, H. W., and F. G. Fowler, eds. *The Concise Oxford Dictionary of Current English*. Oxford: Clarendon Press, 1960.

Fraser, Walter J., and Winfred B. Moore, Jr., eds. *From the Old South to the New: Essays on the Traditional South*. Westport, Conn.: Greenwood, 1981.

Frederickson, George M. *The Inner Civil War: Northern Intellectuals and the Crisis of the Union*. New York: Harper and Row, 1965.

Gabriel, Richard A. *To Serve with Honor: A Treatise on Military Ethics and the Way of the Soldier*. Westport, Conn.: Greenwood, 1982.

Gillis, John R. *Commemorations: The Politics of National Identity*. Princeton, N.J.: Princeton University Press, 1994.

Glatthaar, Joseph T. *Forged in Battle: The Civil War Alliance of Black Soldiers and White Officers*. New York: Macmillan, 1990.

Gove, Philip B., ed. *Webster's Third New International Dictionary of the English Language*. Springfield, Mass.: G. & C. Merriam, 1976.

Grant, Susan-Mary, and Peter J. Parish, eds. *Legacy of Disunion: The Enduring Significance of the American Civil War*. Baton Rouge: Louisiana State University Press, 2003.

Hargrove, Hondon B. *Black Union Soldiers in the Civil War*. Jefferson, N.C.: McFarland, 1988.

Hauptman, Laurence M. *Between Two Fires: American Indians in the Civil War*. New York: The Free Press, 1995.

Hayes, Grace P., ed. *A Dictionary of Military Terms: A Guide to the Language of Warfare and Military Institutions*. New York: H. W. Wilson, 1986.

Heaps, Willard A., and Porter W. Heaps. *The Singing Sixties: The Spirit of Civil War Days Drawn from the Music of the Times*. Norman: University of Oklahoma Press, 1960.

Hesseltine, William B. *Civil War Prisons: A Study in War Psychology*. Columbus: Ohio State University Press, 1930.

Hoganson, Kristin L. *Fighting for American Manhood: How Gender Politics Provoked the Spanish-American and Philippine-American Wars*. New Haven, Conn.: Yale University Press, 1998.

Houghton, Walter E. *The Victorian Frame of Mind*. New Haven, Conn.: Yale University Press, 1957.

Howe, Thomas J. *The Petersburg Campaign: Wasted Valor June 15–18, 1864*. Lynchburg, Va.: H. E. Howard, 2nd ed., 1988.

Hurwitz, Howard L., ed. *An Encyclopedic Dictionary of American History*. New York: Washington Square Press, 1974.

Jimerson, Randal C. *The Private Civil War: Popular Thought during the Sectional Conflict*. Baton Rouge: Louisiana State University Press, 1994.

Jordan, J. L. "Was There a Massacre at Fort Pillow?" *Tennessee Historical Quarterly*, 6 (June 1974): 99–133.

Joyner, Charles. *Down by the Riverside: A South Carolina Slave Community*. Urbana: University of Illinois Press, 1984.

Kammen, Michael. *In the Past Lane: Historical Perspectives on American Culture*. New York: Oxford University Press, 1997.

———. *Mystic Cords of Memory: The Transformation of Tradition in American Culture*. New York: Alfred A. Knopf, 1991.

Kimmel, Michael. *Manhood in America: A Cultural History*. New York: The Free Press, 1996.

Kinard, Jeff. *The Battle of the Crater*. Abilene, Texas.: McWhiney Foundation Press, 1998.

Leonard, Elizabeth D. *All the Daring of the Soldier: Women of the Civil War Armies*. New York: Penguin Books, 2001.

Levin, Kevin M. "'On That Day You Commanded the Full Measure of Your Fame': Remembering the Battle of the Crater, 1864–1903." *Southern Historian*, 25 (Spring 2004): 18–39.

Levine, Lawrence W. *Black Culture and Black Consciousness: Afro-American Folk Thought from Slavery to Freedom*. New York: Oxford University Press, 1977.

Linderman, Gerald F. *Embattled Courage: The Experience of Combat in the American Civil War*. New York: The Free Press, 1987.

Luckins, Tanja. *The Gates of Memory: Australian People's Experiences and Memories of Loss and the Great War*. Freemantle, Australia: Curtin University Books, 2004.

Lykes, Richard W. *Campaign for Petersburg*. Washington, D.C.: National Park Service, 1970.

Lyman, Darryl. *Civil War Wordbook including Sayings, Phrases, and Slang*. Conshohocken, Pa.: Combined Books, 1994.

Mangan, J. A., and James Walvin, eds. *Manliness and Morality: Middle-Class Masculinity in Britain and America 1800–1940*. Manchester: Manchester University Press, 1987.

Marvel, William. *Burnside*. Chapel Hill: University of North Carolina Press, 1991.

———. "And Fire Shall Devour Them: The 9th New Hampshire Infantry at the Crater." *Civil War Regiments. A Journal of the American Civil War*, 2 (1992): 118–40.

———. *Andersonville: The Last Depot*. Chapel Hill: University of North Carolina Press, 1994.

Mathews, Mitford M. *A Dictionary of Americanisms on Historical Principles*. Chicago: Chicago University Press, 1951.

Matter, William D. *If It Takes All Summer: The Battle of Spotsylvania*. Chapel Hill: University of North Carolina Press, 1988.

May, Larry, Robert Strikwerda, and Patrick D. Hopkins, eds. *Rethinking Masculinity: Philosophical Explorations in Light of Feminism*. 2nd ed. Lanham, Md.: Rowman & Littlefield, 1996.

McPherson, James M. *Ordeal by Fire: The Civil War and Reconstruction*. New York: Alfred A. Knopf, 1982.

———. *Battle Cry of Freedom: The Civil War Era*. New York: Oxford University Press, 1988.

———. *For Cause and Comrades: Why Men Fought in the Civil War*. New York: Oxford University Press, 1997.

Meron, Theodor. *Bloody Constraint: War and Chivalry in Shakespeare*. New York: Oxford University Press, 1998.

Miller, Randall M., and John David Smith, eds. *Dictionary of Afro-American Slavery*. Westport, Conn.: Praeger, 1997.

Mitchell, Reid. *Civil War Soldiers. Their Expectations and Their Experiences*. New York: Viking, 1988.

———. *The Vacant Chair: The Northern Soldier Leaves Home*. New York: Oxford University Press, 1993.

Munden, Kenneth W., and Henry P. Beers. *Guide to Federal Archives Relating to the Civil War*. Washington, D.C.: National Archives Publication, 1962.

Nagel, Joane. "Masculinity and Nationalism: Gender and Sexuality in the Making of Nations." *Ethnic and Racial Studies*, 21 (March 1998): 242–69.

Neff, John R. *Honoring the Civil War Dead: Commemoration and the Problem of Reconciliation*. Lawrence: University Press of Kansas, 2005.

Noe, Shannon Kenneth W., and Shannon H. Wilson, eds. *The Civil War. in Appalachia: Collected Essays*. Knoxville: University of Tennessee Press, 1997.

Nye, Robert A. *Masculinity and Male Codes of Honor in Modern France*. New York: Oxford University Press, 1993.

O'Leary, Cecilia Elizabeth. *To Die For: The Paradox of American Patriotism*. Princeton, N.J.: Princeton University Press, 2000.

O'Reilly, Francis Augustin. *The Fredericksburg Campaign: Winter War on the Rappahannock*. Baton Rouge: Louisiana State University Press, 2003.

Owens, Leslie H. *This Species of Property: Slave Life and Culture in the Old South*. New York: Oxford University Press, 1976.

Paludan, Phillip Shaw. *A People's Contest: The Union and Civil War 1861–1865*. Lawrence: University Press of Kansas, 1996.

Pleasants, Henry Jr., and George H. Straley. *Inferno at Petersburg*. Philadelphia, New York: Chilton, 1961.

Popkin, Jeremy D. *History, Historians, and Autobiography*. Chicago: University of Chicago Press, 2005.

Quarles, Benjamin. *The Negro in the Civil War*. Boston: Little Brown, 1953.

The Reader's Digest Family Encyclopaedia of American History. New York: Reader's Digest Association, 1976.

Reardon, Carol. *Pickett's Charge in History and Memory*. Chapel Hill: University of North Carolina Press, 1997.

Robertson, James I. *Soldiers Blue & Gray*. New York: Warner Books, 1991.

Rolph, G. V., and N. Clark. *The Civil War Soldier*. Washington, D.C.: Historical Impressions, 1961.

Rose, Anne C. *Victorian America and the Civil War*. New York: Cambridge University Press, 1992.

Ross, Joseph B. *Tabular Analysis of the Records of the U.S. Colored Troops and Their Predecessor Units in the National Archives of the United States*. Washington, D.C.: National Archives and Records Service, 1973.

Savage, Kirk. *Standing Soldiers, Kneeling Slaves*. Princeton, N.J.: Princeton University Press, 1997.

Shaffer, Donald R. *After the Glory: The Struggles of Black Civil War Veterans*. Lawrence: University Press of Kansas, 2004.

Shaw, Robert K. "The Highland Military Academy." *The Worcester Historical Society Publications*, 1 (April 1930): 118–28.

Silber, Irwin. *Songs of the Civil War*. New York: Columbia University Press, 1960.

Silber, Nina. *The Romance of Reunion: Northerners and the South, 1886–1900*. Chapel Hill: University of North Carolina Press, 1993.

Simpson, J. A., and E. S. Weiner, eds. *The Oxford English Dictionary*. Oxford: Oxford University Press, 1989.

Smart, James A., ed. *A Radical View: The "Agate" Despatches of Whitelaw Reid*. 2 vols. Memphis: Memphis State University Press, 1976.

Smith, John David, ed. *Black Soldiers in Blue: African American Troops in the Civil War Era*. Chapel Hill: University of North Carolina Press, 2002.

Smith, Sidonie, and Julia Watson, eds. *Reading Autobiography: A Guide for Interpreting Life Narratives*. Minneapolis: University of Minnesota Press, 2001.

Speer, Lonnie R. *Portals to Hell: Military Prisons of the Civil War.* Mechanicsburg, Pa.: Stackpole Books, 1997.

Starr, Stephen Z. *The Union Cavalry in the Civil War*. 2 vols. Baton Rouge: Louisiana State University Press, 1985.

Suderow, Bryce A. "The Battle of the Crater: The Civil War's Worst Massacre." *Civil War History*, 43 (September 1997): 219–24.

Swart, Stanley L. "The Military Examination Board in the Civil War." *Civil War History*, 16 (September 1970): 227–45.

Taylor, Charles. *Sources of the Self: The Making of the Modern Identity*. Cambridge, Mass.: Harvard University Press, 1989.

Thelen, David. "Memory and American History." *Journal of American History*, 75 (March 1989): 1117–29.

Trudeau, Noah A. *Bloody Roads South: The Wilderness to Cold Harbour, May–June 1864*. Boston: Little Brown, 1989.

———. *The Last Citadel: Petersburg, Virginia, June 1864–April 1865*. Baton Rouge: Louisiana State University Press, 1991.

———. *Like Men of War: Black Troops in the Civil War, 1862–1865*. Boston: Little, Brown, 1998.

Vernon, Alex, ed. *Arms and the Self: War, the Military, and Autobiographical Writing*. Kent, Ohio: Kent State University Press, 2005.

Wakelyn, Jon L. *Biographical Dictionary of the Confederacy*. Westport, Conn.: Greenwood, 1977.

Ward, G. C., R. Burns, and K. Burns. *The Civil War: An Illustrated History*. New York: Alfred A. Knopf, 1990.

Warner, Ezra J. *Generals in Blue: Lives of the Union Commanders*. Baton Rouge: Louisiana State University Press, 1964.

Webber, Thomas L. *Deep like the Rivers: Education in the Slave Quarter Community, 1831–1865*. New York: W. W. Norton, 1978.

Westwood, Howard C. *Black Troops, White Commanders, and Freedmen during the Civil War*. Carbondale, Edwardsville: Southern Illinois University Press, 1992.

Wiley, Bell I. *The Life of Billy Yank: The Common Soldier of the Union*. Baton Rouge: Louisiana State University Press, 1978.

———. *The Life of Johnny Reb: The Common Soldier of the Confederacy*. Baton Rouge: Louisiana State University Press, 1982.

Wilson, Keith P. "Thomas Webster and the 'Free Military School for Applicants for Commands of Colored Troops.'" *Civil War History*, 29 (Spring 1981): 101–22.

———. *Campfires of Freedom: The Camp Life of Black Soldiers during the Civil War*. Kent, Ohio: Kent State University Press, 2002.

Wyatt-Brown, Bertram. *Yankee Saints and Southern Sinners*. Baton Rouge: Louisiana State University Press, 1985.

———. *Honor and Violence in the Old South*. New York: Oxford University Press, 1986.

———. *The Shaping of Southern Culture: Honor, Grace, and War, 1760s–1890s*. Chapel Hill: University of North Carolina Press, 2001.

Zinsser, William, ed. *Inventing the Truth: The Art and Craft of Memoir*. New York: Houghton Mifflin, 1998.

WEB SITES

"City of Alexandria, tourism and history, themes from the past, George Washington." <http://ci.alexandria.va.us/>, accessed June 16, 2004.

Gallagher, Gary W. "A Contested Historical Landscape: Understanding and Interpreting the Civil War." Keynote address, Library of Congress Civil War Symposium, November 12, 2002, at <http://www.loc.gov/about/books/symposium/day1.html>, accessed June 14, 2004.

Library of Congress. "American Singing: Nineteenth-Century Song Sheets." American Memory: Historical Collection for the National Digital Library. <http://memory.loc.gov/ammem/amsshtml/amsshome.html>, accessed June 17, 2004.

U.S. Department of the Interior, National Park Service. "Civil War Soldiers and Sailors System." <http://www.itd.nps.gov/cwss/soldiers.htm>, accessed June 16, 2004.

Index

Page numbers in italics refer to illustrations

Keith P. Wilson is a senior lecturer in history at Monash University in Victoria, Australia. He is the author of *Campfires of Freedom: The Camp Life of Black Soldiers during the Civil War* and a number of scholarly articles on the role of African American troops in the Civil War.